The Library Assistant V3, 1901-1903: The Official Organ Of The Library Assistants' Association

Library Assistants' Association

In the interest of creating a more extensive selection of rare historical book reprints, we have chosen to reproduce this title even though it may possibly have occasional imperfections such as missing and blurred pages, missing text, poor pictures, markings, dark backgrounds and other reproduction issues beyond our control. Because this work is culturally important, we have made it available as a part of our commitment to protecting, preserving and promoting the world's literature. Thank you for your understanding.

The Library Assistant:

THE OFFICIAL ORGAN

OF THE

LIBRARY ASSISTANTS' ASSOCIATION.

VOLUME III.

1901-1903

LONDON:
THE LIBRARY ASSISTANTS' ASSOCIATION.

1903.

General Index to Vol. III.

Aberdeen 74, 208
Accrington, N.W.Br. Meeting at 14
American Libraries 127
Ancient and Modern Writing Materials, P. Evans Lewin on 189, 210
Anderson, J. P., Retirement of. *Photo.* 7
Annfield Plain, Adoption of Acts... 296
Appointments ... 27, 40, 52, 63, 76, 104, 128, 136, 146, 156, 172, 192, 204, 215, 236, 252, 278, 289, 300.
Australia, Legislature Debates 23
,, Library Statistics... 36
Axon, W. E., Exhibition of Specimens of Printing, &c. to N.W. Branch 32
Battersea ... 53, 62, 102, 163
Belfast, Carnegie Gift ... 170
Bermondsey, Opening of Branch 102
Birkdale, Blundell Gift ... 138
Birmingham, Memorial to Ruskin 88
Bishop Stortford 296
Blackburn, Delivery Stations 203
Blackley Library, N.W. Br., Meeting at... 272
Bodleian Library, Tercentenary Celebration of 170
Bowness, Carnegie Gift ... 9
Bookbinding and the Care of Books — Book by D. Cockerell 36
Book Lovers' Library, Note on 171
Books, Rare 38
Books, Stamping *v.* Defacing 38
Bow, Plans of Library ... 38
Bradford 9
Brentford, Course of Lectures 62
Brierley Hill, Carnegie Gift 154, 279
Brighouse, Application to Carnegie refused 170
Brighton, Opening of Museum 192
British Museum ... ~ 250, 296
Bromwich, West 171

Brown, J. W., Farewell Supper to 106
Buckley, Carnegie Gift ... 88
Bury, Opening of Public Library 27
Camberwell, Mutilated Newspaper 88
Carnegie Gifts, Letter from T. Greenwood 125
Carnegie, A., Note of Interview with ... ...
Carnegie Gifts ... 163, 127, 135, 139, 227, 289, 296.
Chennell, Frank E., on the Woes of a Librarian ... 56
Chorley, N.W. Branch Meeting at 285
Classification, Some Systems of, P. Evans Lewin on ... 140
Cockermouth, Waugh Gift to 154
Colonial Appointments ... 62
Correspondence ... 11, 90, 110, 134, 155, 202, 214, 225, 231, 276
Corwen, Ella F., Note of Paper by 218
Cotgreave, A. Photo of ... 40
Croydon Central Library, L.A.A. Meeting at ... 29
Daily Press & Public Libraries 172, 193, 200
Dalkeith, Carnegie Gift ... 9
Dickens, J. D., Note of Paper by 205
Dover, Carnegie Gift 227
Dunfermline, Carnegie's Birthplace 297
Durie, John, the Librarian's Apostle, P. Evans Lewin on 150
Dyer, B. L., on War and the Library—Stray Notes ... 97
Early Printed Books at British Museum, Guide to ... 36
East Ham, Carnegie Gift ... 163
Eastbourne 154
Edmonton 74
Educational Basis of the Free Library Movement, F. W. Haworth on 242
Edwards, Edward, by T.

Greenwood, notice of ... 111	Ipswich, Opening of Reference
Edwards, Edward, Unveiling	Library 36
of Monument of 75	James, Miss M. S. R., Obituary 284
Enfield 170	Keighley... 10
Exeter 163, 227, 234	Kershaw, S. W. 88
Festiniog, Closing of Branches 36	Kimberley ... 36, 139, 227
Finsbury, Adoption of Acts ... 26	King's Heath and Moselcy ... 228
,, Deletion of Betting News 138	Kingston, New Building ... 125
Foskett, Edward, Obituary ... 11	,, Opening of Library ... 250
,, ,, "An Apprecia-	Library Aids 127
tion,"—*photo* 24	,, Architecture 88
Fulham, Deletion of Betting	"Library Assistant," The,
News 9	Review of Work 1
,, Feret and Fisher	L.A.A., Award of Prizes ... 138
Donations to 74	,, Bohemian Concert ... 232
Germany : Soldiers' Libraries 154	,, Change of Editor ... 138
,, Konigsberg Public	,, Committee Proceedings 238
Library 208	,, Excursion 149
Gladstone Memorial Library 163	,, Excursion to Brighton 138
Glasgow... 127	,, Library Catalogue of,
,, Gift of Jeffery Collection 163	*Supplement*
,, Table of Issues 194	,, Library, Donations to 12, 28,
Glazier, T. W., on Anticipated	39, 51, 52, 64, 75, 92, 103,
Developments of Library	127, 156, 164, 179, 195, 203,
Practice 221	214, 228, 234, 247, 280, 290,
Gordon, P. D., Presentation to 166	293, 299.
Greenwich, Adoption of Acts 102	,, New Members ... 12, 23, 40,
,, Carnegie Gift ... 125	51, 64, 76, 92, 104, 128,
Greenwood, T., Note of Inter-	136, 148, 156, 163, 179,
view 9	195, 198, 209, 227, 236, 300
,, on Fiction Question ... 200	,, Programme of Meetings
,, Notice of Article on ... 75	—1902-3 118
Greenwood's Library Year	,, ,, —1903-4 294
Book, 1901: Gift to N.W.	,, Resignation of G. E.
Branch 29	Roebuck 73
Grinling, Address to L.A.A. ... 78	,, Resignation of J. Rad-
Guildhall, Inaugural Meeting at 16	cliffe 208
Guppy, H., Donation to L.A.A.	,, River Trip 5
Library 293	,, Social Gathering ... 77
Hackney 9, 62, 297	,, Summer Programme ... 133
Hammersmith 228	,, Seventh Annual Meeting 129
Hanson, Obituary 28	,, Eighth ,, ,, ... 273
Harris, W. J., on "How to	,, Seventh ,, Report 114
Popularise a Public Lib-	,, Eighth ,, ,, 261
rary" 49	,, Fourth ,, Dinner 43
Harwich 297	,, Fifth ,, ,, 182
Haworth, F. W. B., on "The	Library Association :
Educational Basis of the	,, 1901 Annual Meeting ... 8
Free Library Movement " 242	,, Appointment of Hon. Sec. 87
,, on Manchester Jubilee	,, Classes, The ... 68, 149
Celebrations 239	,, Examinations: Editorial 95
Hereford, Bequest of £1,000... 10	,, Examination ... 95, 187, 197,
Heywood 299	234, 275
Hull, ... 10, 279	,, Programme of Meetings 186
Ilford 102, 127	,, Summer School, Award
Ilkeston, Carnegie Gift ... 10	of Prizes 47

iii.

Entry	Page
Library Association, Summer School, N.W. Branch	278
Library Association Record, The, Notice of	37
Library Basements, Suggestions for	241
Library Economy, Book on, by J. W. Clark	37
Library Journals, Comments on	73
Library of the Future, The, E. A. Savage on	30
Library Practice, Anticipated Developments of, by T. W. Glazier	221
"Library World," The	10, 37, 102
Lambeth, Unveiling of Alfred the Great Tablet	37
Leadhills, Donation to Miners' Library	10
Leeds	27, 125
Lewin, P. Evans, on Ancient and Modern Writing Materials,	189, 210
John Durie, the Librarians' Apostle	150
Libraries and Museums	286
Some Systems of Classification	
Titles of Honour in Catalogues	69
"Liberty Review"	102
Librarians, Honours for	87
Librarian, The Young. C. Welch on	19
Librarians' Salaries	297
Limerick, Carnegie Gift	170
Literature for the Blind, G. E. Roebuck on	253
London County Council, Members' Library	75
London Library	154
London School of Economics, L.A.A. Meeting at	167
McAlister, J. Y. W., Offer of Prize	62
McKnight, Edward	127
Manchester, Athenæum Library, N.W. Branch Meeting at	54
Manchester, Chetham's Library, N.W. Branch Meeting at	218
Manchester, Gift of Greenwood Collection	279
,, Jubilee Celebrations	239
Manchester, N.W. Br. Meetings at	15, 42, 132, 198, 205, 238
Marylebone, "Punch" Cartoon	165
Mattocks, S. G., Obituary	104
Mold	10
Montrose, Adoption of Acts	63
Mould, R.W., on "Our Work"	80
Mullen, B., Note of Paper by	158
Neath, Fire at	203
New York Library, Collection of Menu Cards	298
Newcombe, C. F., An Appreciation of Edward Foskett	26
Newington Public Library, L.A.A. Meeting at	66
,, Gift by T. A. Gilbert	38
Normanton, Carnegie Gift	171
Northfleet, Adoption of Acts	298
Oldham, Free Lectures	63
,, N.W. Branch Meetings at	80, 231
Omagh, Carnegie Gift	88
Our Work, by R. W. Mould	80
Peddie, R. A., on Past, Present and Future of Public Libraries	107
Peel Park, Salford, N.W. Br. Meeting at	158
Pendlebury, Opening of Library	171
People's Palace, Closing of Library	38
Petrarch, H. G. Sureties on	277
Plaistow	193, 251
Poplar, L.A.A. Meeting at	94
Printing for Librarians, W. B. Thorne on	160
Public Libraries and Children	159
Public Libraries Act, 1901, Notice of Error in	10
Public Library, How to Popularise a, Wm. J. Harris on	49
Rawtenstall	299
Rees, Evan G., Note of Paper by	88
,, ,, ,, Elected Member of L.A. Education Committee	166
Roberts, H. D., on the Technichal Training of Library Assistants	175
Roebuck, G. E., Literature for the Blind	253
Russell, Sir Edward, on Carnegie Gifts	163
Russia, Novel Reading in	38

Rylands Library, Purchase of Crawford Collection	10	Sunderland, Carnegie Gift	280
St. Annes-on-Sea, Carnegie Gift	280	Sureties, H. G., on "Petrarch"	277
		Sydenham, Lower 163,	297
St. Bride Institute 38,	200	Sydney, N.S.W.	113
St. George's Library, Hanover Square, L.A.A. Meeting at	229	Taunton	280
		Technical Training of Library Assistants, The, H. D. Roberts on	
St. Giles, Holborn, L.A.A. Meeting at	107	Thorne, W. B., on Printing for Librarians	160
St. Pancras, Adoption of Acts	63	,, on John Southward	147
Salaries, President of L.A. on 34,	297	,, Appointed Editor of L.A.	138
Savage, E. A., on The Library of the Future		Tilbury, Carnegie Gift	280
		Tipton, Deletion of Betting News	113
Scunthorpe, Foundation Stone Laid	298	Titles of Honour in Catalogues, P. Evans Lewin on	69
Shakespeare Memorial Library	298	Tottenham	209
Shoreditch 10,	237	Views and Memoranda of Public Libraries	63
Society of Public Librarians, Meetings of ... 35, 51, 63, 209, 228, 240.		Wakefield 209,	299
		Wandsworth 63,	125
Soper, H. Tapley, elected Hon. Member	154	War and the Library—Stray Notes by B. L. Dyer	97
Southend 103,	299	Warrington, N.W. Branch Meeting at	181
Southward, John, Obituary	147		
Southwark 75, 88,	171	Welch, C., on the Young Librarian	19
Steeple Claydon, Erection of Library 103,	193	Westminster	290
Stepney ... 55, 203,	227	West Ham, L.A.A. Meeting at	41
,, Library for the Blind 39,	75	,, ,, ,, ,,	218
,, Opening of Limehouse Library	71	Windsor, Enlarging of Library	39
		Wilson, W. R., Honours conferred upon	279
,, Staffs of Mile End and Limehouse	27	Woes of a Librarian, The, F. E. Chennell on	56
,, Visit to Oxford	113		
,, Visit to Toynbee Hall	188	Wood, R. B., Elected Member of L.A. Education Committee	166
Stoke Newington... 11, 26, 75, 234, 246, 280.			
Stornoway, Carnegie Gift	155	,, on Bookbinding	230
Stratford-on-Avon, Carnegie Gift	113	Wood Green	88
		Woolwich ... 27, 33, 77, 155,	209
Study Circle ... 4, 18, 35, 47, 61, 72, 89, 101, 109, 135, 150, 158, 166, 184, 199, 207, 220, 232, 246, 251		Wolverhampton, Conference 136,	139
		,, Opening of Library	75

The Library Assistant.

The Official Organ of the Library Assistants' Association.

No. 46. OCTOBER, 1901. Published Monthly

OURSELVES.

With this number the third volume of the *Library Assistant* is commenced, and we may be permitted, without undue egotism, to review the work which has been accomplished during the four years of its existence.

The first number of the *Library Assistant* was published in January, 1898, and was the outcome of the deliberations of a band of enthusiasts, whose progressive views led them to believe that the time was ripe for the establishment of an organ representative of the views and interests of Library Assistants. Nothing daunted by the opposition they met with, and the obstacles they had to overcome, these men set to work to carry out their ideas with the result mentioned above. Sanguine of its ultimate success as were many of its promoters, few, if any, expected that in the short space of four years the *Library Assistant* would meet with the sympathy and support which is now accorded it. This support is shown by the fact that the circulation of the present number is twice as large as that of the first, but, with the ambition of youth, we are not satisfied to allow it to remain at this, and we confidently look forward to a large increase in our subscribers' list with the commencement of this volume.

It cannot be denied that concurrently with the existence of the *Library Assistant*, the status and payment of Assistants throughout the Kingdom has gradually improved, but, notwithstanding this improvement, much remains to be done in this direction, and Assistants will best study their own interests as well as the interests of the public they serve, by banding themselves together in the ranks of the L.A.A. for the purpose of increasing their professional knowledge, and thereby qualifying themselves the better to fill the higher positions as they become vacant, for it is now generally conceded—even by librarians—that the assistant of to-day must be the librarian of to-morrow, consequently no stone should be left unturned by the zealous assistant to increase his knowledge of his chosen calling, thereby making himself better fitted to occupy these posts when his turn comes along.

It is not without interest to note that our first two editors now occupy positions as "Chiefs"—Mr. B. L. Dyer at Kimberley, South Africa, and Mr. H. Ogle at Ipswich—whilst of the original publishing Committee, Mr. Caddie is Librarian of Chester, Mr. Clarke of Penge, and Mr. Meaden Roberts of Mile End. In addition to this record, of which we feel justly proud, several of the present members owe their improved positions to their connection with us. It is unnecessary to further emphasize this point than to say that in a recent appointment, a Librarian admitted to the successful candidate that the reason he had obtained the position was due to his connection with the L.A.A. *Verb. Sap.*

When the difficulties under which the *Library Assistant* has to be published are remembered, it more than justifies our gratification upon the completion of our second volume, particularly as its early death was predicted in many quarters. At the same time we are fully cognisant of the great assistance we have received, and are still receiving, from many Librarians and others, and to them we tender our cordial thanks, expressing the hope that they will continue to give us their practical and moral support.

The *Library Assistant* is, we believe, the first and only paper devoted exclusively to the interests of Assistants, and as such marks a turning point in the history of Librarianship, which we hope will in the near future lead up to greater things.

Readers are reminded that only a few back numbers of volumes 1 and 2 remain on hand, and those who want to complete their sets should immediately pen the Editor, who will do his best to supply them with the numbers they require. Already twice their published value is being willingly paid for complete sets, only one or two of which remain in the Editorial Office.

We trust that we can continue to rely upon our readers practical interest in us, not only by their subscribing to the Journal, but also by sending contributions of all matters of professional interest which may come under their notice, for it is only by co-operation of this kind that we can hope to contain many items of interesting news, which would otherwise be lost.

In conclusion we would again urge upon all Assistants the absolute necessity of joining the L.A.A., reminding them that the new Session commences this month, and that all intending members should send in their names to the Hon. Secretary as soon as possible, in order to get the benefit of a complete session.

The *Library Assistant* will in future be published under the direction of Mr. H. Tapley Soper, Sub-Librarian of the Borough of Stoke Newington, to whom all communications should be addressed.

THE LIBRARY ASSISTANTS' ASSOCIATION.

FOUNDED 1895.   SEVENTH SESSION.   YEAR 1901-1902.

Members are requested to read carefully the announcements appearing on this and the following pages, as no further intimation of meetings and other arrangements may be expected.

INAUGURAL MEETING—SEVENTH SESSION.

The inaugural meeting will be held at the Guildhall on Wednesday, October 16th, by kind invitation of Mr. Charles Welch, F.S.A., the City Librarian.

Members are requested to meet at 7 p.m. *punctually*. The proceedings will open with an inspection of this old historic building, arrangements being made for visits to the Crypt, Council Chamber, Museum, etc. This feature alone will prove of much interest to all present.

At 7.45 the meeting proper will take place, when Mr. Welch will favour us with a paper entitled, " The Young Librarian: his training and possibilities."

The Chairman of the Guildhall Library Committee, William Rome, Esq., F.S.A., F.L.S., has kindly consented to preside on this occasion.

At the close of Mr. Welch's address, each member of the L.A.A. will be presented with a copy of Greenwood's " Library Year Book " (1900-01), which the author has very kindly forwarded for distribution amongst our members.

Mr. Rome has intimated his pleasure to invite us to partake of a cup of tea with him at the close of proceedings.

As the hour for meeting is a little earlier than usual, *suburban* members and friends are particularly requested to assist in making this meeting the success which the occasion and the excellent arrangements deserve. Ladies are specially invited.

NOTE.—Formal permission to visit the Guildhall on this occasion is not yet to hand, as the Committee does not meet again until October 7.

NOVEMBER MEETING.

The second meeting of this session will be held at the Croydon Central Library, by kind permission of Mr. L. Stanley Jast, the Chief Librarian, when a paper will be read by Mr. E. A. Savage, the Sub-Librarian. The date will be announced in our next issue.

SEPTEMBER OUTING.

Owing to an insufficient number of promises of attendance at Twickenham being received by the Hon. Sec. Entertainment Committee, it was necessary to cancel the arrangements.

FOURTH ANNUAL DINNER.

Arrangements are being made with reference to the Fourth Annual Dinner, and Mr. W. B. Young, of 63 Leslie Road, Leytonstone, will be glad to receive any offers of vocal or instrumental assistance on that occasion. Further particulars will be published next month.

STUDY CIRCLE.

FOR DETAILS OF THIS SCHEME SEE SEPTEMBER NUMBER.

QUESTIONS ON SEPTEMBER WORK.

SENIOR (1). State what you know concerning the influence of the social conditions of the first quarter of the 19th century upon contemporary literature.

(2). Describe the various methods of book-selection, and discuss their respective merits and demerits.

JUNIOR (1). State what you know of the Lake Poets and their work.

(2). Describe simply the theories of the Indicator and Card-Charging Systems of recording issues, and state wherein they differ.

Students are expected to answer these questions *from memory*, and it is understood that no student will refer to any book for information regarding the questions until after posting his answers. Should any student commit himself by acting in contraversion to these instructions, he will be taking an unfair advantage over his fellow-competitors and thwarting the aims of the S.C. Answers must be received by the Hon. Sec., L.A.A., 236 Cable Street, E., not later than the 16th October, signed with a pen-name and accompanied by a *sealed* envelope containing the real name and address of the student, such envelope to be endorsed on the outside with the pen-name *only*.

Readings for October. (*Period same—First Quarter 19th century*):—

*Brooke's Primer, *Chaps. VII.-VIII.*
*Morley. First Sketch. *Annals to 1837.*
Morley. English Literature in reign of Victoria. *Chaps. V.-VI.*
Saintsbury. Short History of English Literature. *Book X.*
,, Nineteenth Century Literature· *Chaps. III.-IV.*
Ency. Brit. Article on "Periodicals." Vol. XVIII.

Suitable for Junior Division.

It will be necessary to obtain a knowledge of contemporary English History from such sources as are available.

SUMMER PROGRAMME, 1901.

THE AUGUST RIVER TRIP.

As was expected, the L.A.A. outing for August, up the river from Teddington to Walton and back, was very successful, the attendance being much larger than on any previous occasion during the year.

Teddington, although small and of little consequence compared with some other Thames-side places, has yet a few noteworthy features to recommend It. In crossing the town from the station to the lock you pass on your way the parish church of Teddington, a low-roofed structure of considerable antiquity. Its monuments are varied and curious, the most notable being, perhaps, that to the illustrious Peg Woffington.

A start was made from Teddington shortly before four o'clock, the number on board being just over thirty.

The weir, with its bevy of enthusiastic anglers, was presently passed, and here and there one more eager than his mates pursued his hobby bare-legged in the water. He was not at all envied.

Broad vistas of field and woodland now began to open up on either hand, giving way occasionally to noble houses with still, cool green lawns, and to less pretentious dwellings near the water's edge. Nothing could be more lovely or more peaceful than one of those old-fashioned homesteads, embowered in greenery, and situated as it may be in full view of the river, with an ample stretch of flower-flecked lawn bordering paths that lead to all sorts of shady corners and retreats.

Kingston was the next place of interest, a town of some historical importance, as the chroniclers point out, and as the famous coronation stone in the market-place itself will testify. Further on was passed Thames Ditton, well known for its unique angling facilities; and Leigh Hunt, who assuredly was not oblivious to the charms of Nature in any form, says, in his " Lines in a punt " :—

> " Here lawyers free from legal toil,
> And peers released from duty,
> Enjoy at once kind Nature's smiles,
> And eke the smiles of beauty."

Which is all very comforting, but rather exclusive. The views here are extremely beautiful, both on land and water.

Hampton Court was now passed, its towers and turrets in grim silhouette against the evening sky. What a motley array of memories linger about this place! As one looks on, what scenes can the fancy not paint?

Away down the centuries, in one long procession of pomp and splendour, of kings and queens, princes and men of rank, prelates and papal divines, one can see for one's self all the actors in the play—a Wolsey, "lofty and sour to those that loved him not," the despised of Henry in his old age; a Boleyn, a Seymour, a Penn, and a Howard; a Mary walking arm in arm with her Philip along terraces and vine-clad bowers; Elizabeth of gracious memory, with her train of beautiful maidens; a James, of controversial mood, a Charles, and a William; an ambitious George; cardinals, papal legates, statesmen, crafty and cunning; court leeches of great adaptability, and the general hangers-on; young squires from the country, pale youths from the town, all imbued with the one idea of winning fame and the favour of those in power.

Beyond Hampton Court, a short distance, is Garrick's Villa. This choice piece of classic architecture, styled as the "Grecian Temple," puts the finishing touch to an already beautiful scene, which is enhanced by a glimpse—just enough—of the tower of Hampton church through the trees.

The Temple was built by Garrick to provide a suitable home for Roubiliac's statue of Shakespeare, which now reposes in the British Museum.

Hampton itself, and Sunbury with its lock, were soon left behind. Sunbury, a very old, straggling village on the Middlesex side of the Thames, looked very quiet and peaceful seen through the screen of willows by the river-side. It is a rare haunt of fishermen, and on this occasion evidence was not wanting of the fact. But it was a melancholy truth that not once during the whole of the afternoon did any of the party see a single fish landed.

Little more of an interesting nature was seen before Walton was reached. Here an adjournment was made for tea, which was served in the Angler's Hotel, a quaint looking hostelry, with a refreshing view from its comfortable balcony.

By this time evening was well advanced, and when the return journey was commenced darkness was setting in fast. To beguile the time singing was indulged in, several ladies and gentlemen courteously offering their services. After all, there is nothing like music to while the hours away. The multi-coloured lights on the various house-boats—those delightful abodes that seem to have been transported from some enchanted fairyland—enlivened the river in patches here and there all the way down until Teddington was reached, shortly before nine o'clock, when general regret was expressed that the day had not been longer.   J. H.

Mr. J. P. ANDERSON.
Reproduced by kind permission from " The Sphere."

Mr. J. P. Anderson, the subject of our portrait, has recently retired, under the age limit, from the position of Clerk of the Reading Room of the British Museum Library.

His intellectual, yet genial face will be greatly missed by the readers at our great National Library, where his great courtesy and ready help to all have won a host of friends.

Mr. Anderson entered the service of the Trustees of the British Museum in 1860. Since that time he has witnessed many changes in the department where his extensive knowledge of the library has rendered his services in this position invaluable. The present system of collecting and receiving books in the reading room is one of the many improvements introduced by him.

It was in 1881 that Mr. Anderson published his " Book of British Topography." Such has been the demand for this useful and interesting work, that several copies have already been worn out in the British Museum Reading Room. Needless to say, every well-represented reference library contains a copy of this invaluable work.

The bibliographies of the "Great Writer Series," which is such a special feature in these volumes, are from the pen of Mr. Anderson, as are also a great number of other important bibliographies, too numerous to mention.

Mr. Anderson is a man of many and varied interests. He was one of the founders of the London Scottish Border Counties Association, and was the first Chairman of that successful Institution. He was also a Manager of the Westminster Technical Institute from its foundation until it was handed over to the L.C.C. by the Baroness Burdett-Coutts.

The volunteers have claimed him as a member, for he joined the volunteers in the sixties, and was for the last few years of his active service the champion shot of the B. M. Rifle Association. The King of Servia last year conferred upon him the Order of St. Sava in acknowledgement of his contributions to literature.

From his position Mr. Anderson has assisted all sorts and conditions of men, and it has naturally brought him into contact with almost every man and woman of the period noted either in literature, science and art.

It is but left for us to add that we sincerely hope that Mr. Anderson may for many years enjoy the rest he has so well and ably earned.   W. J. H.

THE LIBRARY ASSOCIATION.

The twenty-fourth Annual Meeting was held at Plymouth during the last week of August, under the presidency of G. K. Fortescue, Esq., Keeper of the printed books of the British Museum. The discussions on "Shelf Classification" and on "Catalogues" revealed irreconcilable differences of opinion, and showed that there is not an agreement on even the principles which ought to lie at the foundation of either. With his guides giving directions not uncertain and indefinite, but positive and dogmatic, albeit irreconcilable, what can the Assistant do ? Mr. Taylor thought (according to the report before us) that shelf classification was superior even to a *perfect* catalogue in making the resources of a library on a particular subject available. Mr. Doubleday pointed out the inconvenience of having, as in class guides, a number of separate indexes of portions of a collection, and the absence of title references. He admitted their usefulness to students for whom he was willing to issue them in addition to a dictionary catalogue, which incorporated all their advantages ! Mr. Quinn claimed for the classified catalogue that the schemes of classification now extant enabled a library to be simply and efficiently dealt with, the information being logically arranged and of exhaustive character. The President, recognising that books have not only to be arranged, but found, expressed a very pronounced opinion that an Author Catalogue, with an Index of Subjects, was the solution of the difficulty. The relation of the Reference Library to the educational institutions now at work, and to the Lending Library, was another subject of discussion.

Space forbids us doing more than calling attention to the interesting address of the President on the Catalogue of the British Museum, the greatest printed catalogue in the world, containing as it does between 4,200,000 and 4,500,000 entries.

L.A.A. NORTH-WESTERN BRANCH.

In consequence of the pressure on our space the report of the September meeting is held over.

THE OCTOBER MEETING will be held in the Reference Library, King Street, Manchester, on October 16th, at 8 p.m., when a discussion on the affairs of the Branch will be opened by the Chairman. Suggestions are invited. To be followed by a paper by the Hon. Sec. on "THE EVOLUTION OF LIBRARY ADMINISTRATION :—A PLEA FOR A STANDARD SYSTEM."

NOTES AND NEWS.

Alfred the Great.—In connection with the Millenary Celebration, Mr. John H. Swann, of the Manchester Reference Library, prepared an annotated study-list of books in the Reference Department, which is well worth preserving as a bibliography of Alfred literature.

"**The Aristocrats.**"—We understand that Mrs. Atherton, the author of "Senator North," is the writer of "The Aristocrats," which was recently published anonymously.

Boness, Linlithgowshire.—Mr. Andrew Carnegie has offered £5,000 for a Public Library.

Bradford.—A complete set of the reports of the Challenger Expedition has been secured by the Bradford Public Library.

"**Cassell's Saturday Journal.**"—The issue of September 4th contains an interview with Mr. T. Greenwood, with portrait.

Dalkeith.—Mr. Andrew Carnegie has given £4,000 to the town of Dalkeith, Midlothian, for a Public Library.

Fulham.—The Council have decided to delete the betting news from all newspapers supplied to the Libraries.

Hackney.—The Borough Council has referred to the Law and Parliamentary Committee a letter from a ratepayer, requesting it to take the necessary steps for the adoption of the Public Libraries Acts.

"**Harper's Magazine.**"—The September number contains an article on the influence of Public Libraries on reading in America.

Hull.—The New Central Library is to be opened on November 4th by Lord Avebury.

Hereford.—Under the will of the late Sir Joseph Pulley, formerly M.P. for the Borough, the Library receives £1,000 for the erection of a room to be named after the late Mr. W. E. Gladstone.

Ilkeston.—Mr. Carnegie has offered £7,500 for the erection of a Library on condition that the Council provide the site.

Keighley.—The elevation and plans of the proposed new Library will be found in *The British Architect* for August 30th.

Leadhills.—A visitor to Leadhills has recently given a handsome donation to the miners' library, which is one of the oldest circulating libraries in the Kingdom, having been founded in 1741 by the Allan Ramsay of "Gentle Shepherd" fame, who was born there in 1686.

"The Library World."—The September No. is not up to its usual standard of excellence. Mr. Jast deals in his particular breezy manner with "The treatment of pamphlets," and promises to treat with parliamentary papers next month, which should prove of value, as many libraries now pay special attention to "blue books." "Notes on the Glasgow Exhibition: for Library Assistants," should be read as a supplement to the article which we published on the Exhibition in our July number.

Mold.—The District Council have decided to approach Mr. Carnegie on the question of building a Library for the town.

Public Libraries Act, 1901.—It is not often that one is able to find such a curious mistake in an Act of Parliament as that which occurs in this Act, the full title of which is "An Act to amend the Acts relating to Public Libraries . . . and to regulate the liability of managers of Libraries to proceedings for libel." The clause relating to libel which appeared in the bill promoted by the *Library Association* has apparently been struck out in Committee. But as in law nothing can be taken for granted, one can only wonder whether the King's printers have accidentally omitted this paragraph, or failed to alter the title of the Act. We are curious to know whether it will be necessary to appoint a Royal Commission to set this matter right!

Rylands Library.—We understand that the celebrated collection of illuminated and other MSS. belonging to the Earl of Crawford, has been purchased by Mrs. Rylands.

Shoreditch.—At a recent meeting of the Borough Council it was decided not to proceed with the poll on the question of increasing the Library Rate from $\frac{3}{4}$d. to 1d. in the £, it having been pointed out by the Town Clerk that the limit could be altered by a resolution of the Council under the new Public Libraries Act.

Stepney.—The new Library for the Limehouse District will be opened by the Mayor on November 6th.

Stoke Newington.—At the last meeting of the Borough Council a memorial signed by a number of borrowers from the Public Library, urging the Council to introduce " open access " at the Library was referred to the Libraries Committee for consideration and report.

As we go to press we learn with extreme regret of the death of Mr. Edward Foskett, F.R.S.L., the Chief Librarian of the Camberwell Public Libraries. Mr. Foskett had just returned from his holidays, apparently in the best of health, and died in bed quite suddenly on Friday morning, the 27th September.

CORRESPONDENCE.

[*The Editor solicits expressions of opinion on all matters of interest to the profession, but does not hold himself responsible for the views or opinions of correspondents*].

" DEAR MR. EDITOR, " 6th September, 1901.

" I have just been collating my numbers of the 'Assistant' before sending them to the binder, and I feel I should be ungrateful did I not express some of the happy memories that flooded my mind as the events of the past—although only recently past—come in review before my eyes.

" Harking back to the second number of this second volume, recollections of an exceptionally pleasant meeting in Church Street, Stoke Newington, come to me; members who are the pride of our Association were there, local dignitaries, and oh! such a capital lecturer. What a paper that was!—and how we enjoyed it!—the show of early editions in another room—to say nothing of the refreshments in yet another. Still, there were only a very few there, and of those few one is many hundreds of miles away now, another is librarian in the Provinces—the others I forget.

" Other meetings, large and small, each give rise to recollections of incidents and occurrences for the most part pleasant to dwell upon. They are different now—the old faces have gone, and given place to new—here and there certainly one or two remain whom I remember from my first acquaintance with the Association. It seems to me too, that I miss the presence of some of the seniors—it seems that they are mostly young, enthusiastic members I meet now. But I suppose this is only natural, and as it should be, this is the young people's age, and the old ones sit at the back. The young ones seem to be making things 'go' though, and do some daring things—that trip up the river for instance—but I enjoyed it as much as anybody.

"I rarely miss an ordinary meeting; if I make up my mind to stay away from one, I know I shall regret it, and sure enough if I do some one turns up I wanted to see, or there is something said I should like to have heard. With this feeling so strong upon me, I cannot help but wonder at the very small meetings we sometimes have; if members would only attend regularly, I feel sure they would discover a pleasure in their attendance they would not have suspected.

"However, whether they do or not, *I* shall endeavour to, but I should like it better if I had to pay sixpence extra for 'early doors' in order to avoid the crush!

"Apologising for encroaching so much on your space,

"I am, dear Mr. Editor, Yours truly,

"OLD BOY."

APPOINTMENTS VACANT.

Notice to Library Authorities.—*We shall be pleased to publish under this heading, free of charge, particulars of vacancies if full details are sent to the Editor on or before the 25th of each month.*

ROYAL LONDON OPTHALMIC HOSPITAL, City Road, E.C.—Applications are invited for the office of CURATOR AND LIBRARIAN.

Candidates must be registered medical practitioners. Salary £120. Applications to be sent in not later than 10th October, 1901, to ROBERT J. BLAND, Secretary.

NEW MEMBERS.

BACON, Samuel, St. George, Stepney. (Junior.)
FUREY, J. H., Irlam o' the Heights, near Manchester.
LAMB, Sydney, St. Helens. (Senior.)
LEWIN, Percy E., Woolwich. (Senior.)
NORRIE, Joseph, Walthamstow. (Senior).
USHERWOOD, Victor, Woolwich. (Junior.)
WOOD, Percy H., St. George, Southwark. (Senior.)

Donation to Library.—" Descriptive handbook to the more noteworthy works of prose fiction in the Library of the Midland Railway Institute, Derby," by *E. A. Baker, M.A.*, 1899. Presented by the Author.

NOTICES.

Annual subscriptions to the L.A.A. are now due, and should be sent to Mr. W. Geo. Chambers, *Hon. Treasurer*, Public Library, WOOLWICH.

Communications relating to the Journal and its publishing should be addressed to the *Hon. Editor*, Mr. H. Tapley Soper, Public Library, Stoke Newington, N.

All matter for the November number should be sent in on or before the 19th October.

All other communications should be addressed to the *Hon. Secretary*, Mr. G. E. Roebuck, 236, Cable Street, E.

The Library Assistant:
The Official Organ of the Library Assistants' Association.

No. 47.   NOVEMBER, 1901.   Published Monthly.

THE LIBRARY ASSISTANTS' ASSOCIATION.
FOUNDED 1895.   SEVENTH SESSION.   YEAR 1901-1902.

Members are requested to read carefully the announcements appearing on this and the following pages, as no further intimation of meetings and other arrangements may be expected.

MEETINGS FOR NOVEMBER.

On Wednesday, November 6th, a Special Meeting will be held at St. Bride's Institute, Bride Lane, E.C., at 8 p.m., to consider the following suggested alterations in the Rules of the Association, proposed by Mr. A. J. Philip *(Hampstead)*. Members are requested to give previous consideration to these suggestions in order to facilitate the business of the evening.

> I.—That no junior assistant shall be eligible for full membership and the power to vote at any meeting, until he has a record of at least one year's service, in either a public or private library.
>
> II.—That the Study Circle shall be re-organized or discontinued.
>
> III.—That no measure effecting the status of the Association shall be deemed finally " passed " until it has been announced to, and sanctioned by, an ordinary meeting, and published in the issue of the official Journal of the L.A.A. immediately preceding the announcement.
>
> IV.—That the Annual General Meeting of the Association be fixed to take place some time during the winter session.

On Wednesday, November 13th, the ordinary meeting will be held at the Central Library, Town Hall, Croydon, at 7 p.m., by kind invitation of the Chief Librarian, Mr. L. Stanley Jast. From 7.0 till 8.0 visitors will be able to inspect this successful Free Access Library, a point which should call for a good muster of our members.

The business of the evening will commence at 8 p.m., *sharp*, when Mr. E. A. Savage, the Sub-Librarian, will address the meeting concerning " The Library of the Future." Mr. Jast has kindly consented to preside.

Members are respectfully invited to bring friends. Light refreshments will be provided. Trains to Croydon as follows :—

London Bridge.		Croydon.	Victoria.		Croydon.
6.30 dep.	...	6.53 (New) arr.	6.20 dep. ...		6.52 (West) arr.
6.45 ,,	...	7.7 (West) ,,	*6.50 ,, ...		7.25 (East) ,,
6.55 ,,	...	7.32 (New) ,,	*7.13 ,, ...		7.42 ,, ,,
*7.0 ,,	...	7.25 (East) ,,	7.17 ,, ...		7.53 (West) ,,
7.5 ,,	...	7.26 (West) ,,	Charing Cross.		
*7.22 ,,	...	7.45 (East) ,,	*6.50 dep. ...		7.28 (East) ,,
			Cannon Street.		
			*6.58 dep. ...		7.28 ,, ,,

*Main Line. East, New, and West Croydon are at equal distance from the Library.

VACANCY ON THE L.A.A. COMMITTEE.

A vacancy on the London Committee occurs owing to the resignation of Mr. E. H. Parsons (Stepney), who is compelled to retire owing to unforeseen circumstances.

The Hon. Sec. will be glad to receive nominations for the office on or before the 12th inst. The election will take place, by show of hands, at the Croydon meeting on the 13th inst.

FOURTH ANNUAL DINNER.

The Fourth Annual Dinner will be held at Anderton's Hotel, Fleet Street, E.C., on Wednesday, Nov. 27th, at 6.30 p.m., for 7.

All library assistants are invited, whether members of the Association or not, and the Committee will be pleased to see as many Librarians and other persons interested in the profession, as can be present.

Tickets (3/6 each), should be applied for before November 18th, and may be obtained from Mr. W. B. Young, 63 Leslie Rd., Leytonstone, E., who is still open to receive offers of musical assistance.

NORTH-WESTERN BRANCH.
September Meeting.

The North-Western members travelled to Accrington on Saturday, September 14th, on the invitation of the Librarian, Mr. C. R. Wright.

On arriving at their destination, which was reached about 3.30 p.m., the visitors were shown over the library, where they had an opportunity of witnessing "Open-access" in operation. Modelled somewhat on the lines laid down by Mr. Brown, there are nevertheless several innovations which are due to the energy and enterprise of the librarian.

The members afterwards adjourned to the Mechanics' Institute, when Mr. Wright briefly welcomed the L.A.A., and mentioned that little need be said about the town as good descriptions of the same were to be found in "Red Ryvington," and "The Old Factory," both written by Wm. Westall, a native of the town.

Mr. Wright, having read an apology for absence from Mr. Rowland Hill, of Carlisle, called upon Mr. J. H. Swann to read that gentleman's paper, " Is open access a failure ?" trusting that a thorough discussion would follow.

After the paper had been read, and followed by a good discussion, a hearty vote of thanks was passed to Mr. Hill for the paper, and Mr. Swann for reading it. The visitors then proceeded to inspect the Reading Room, prior to their departure for Whally.

Arriving at the latter place, a visit was paid to the Abbey, after which, tea was partaken of in the De Lacy Hotel.

The proceedings closed with a social hour, during which Mr. Bird kindly officiated at the piano, and the cordial thanks of the meeting having been accorded Mr. Wright, the return journey was commenced. Manchester was reached close on midnight, an unfortunate delay of fifty minutes occurring on the line.

Mr. Wm. Montgomery, Bootle, was elected to the vacancy on the N.W. Committee caused by the resignation of Mr. W. M. McKenzie, now at Aberdeen.

Mr. Hill's paper will be published in a future issue.

N.W. BRANCH OCTOBER MEETING.

The usual monthly meeting of the N.W. Branch was held on Wednesday, Oct. 16th, in the Reference Library, Manchester, Mr. J. H. Swann in the chair.

The chief matter of interest was the discussion of the affairs f the branch, in reference to attendances at the meetings. A esolution was moved by the chairman, "That considering the fact that the bulk of the new members joining the L.A.A. were from out-lying libraries, he moved that in future, meetings be held bi-monthly during the session. Such meeting to be held alternately in one of the towns in the N.W. district where the branch has members."

After many alternate schemes had been considered, it was finally moved and seconded that the chairman's motion be accepted provisionally for six months, commencing with the November meeting and exclusive of the Annual General Meeting. The motion was carried with but three dissenting.

It may be explained that the membership is still increasing, but the fact that there is no general half-holiday as in London, makes it a matter of extreme difficulty to bring so many scattered members together monthly.

Six new members joined the branch during the month.

The meeting unanimously elected Mr. Ed. McKnight, of Chorley, to be first Honorary Member of the N.W. Branch, in consideration of services rendered and his interest in L.A.A. affairs.

The proceedings terminated with a paper on " Library Administration," which was read by Mr. P. D. Gordon, but owing to shortness of time available, the discussion thereon was held over, and the meeting closed with the usual votes.

N.W. BRANCH NOVEMBER MEETING.

The next meeting will be held by kind invitation from Mr. W. E. A. Axon, at his residence, 6 Cecil St., Greenheys, Manchester, on Saturday, Nov. 9th, at 3 p.m.

Mr. Axon will show the members his library, and will speak on a congenial topic.

A large attendance is requested. Members may meet at the Royal Hotel, corner of Mosley Street, at 2.30 p.m., or proceed direct to Mr. Axon's.

NOTE.—*Members are requested to make every effort to attend this, the first of the bi-monthly meetings.*

N.W. BRANCH ANNUAL MEETING.

The Annual General Meeting will take place on Wednesday, Dec. 18th, when the election of Officers and other business will be under consideration. Nominations should be made as early as possible.

SEVENTH SESSION—INAUGURAL MEETING.

The opening meeting of the present session was held at the Guildhall on Wednesday, October 16th, by kind invitation of Mr. Charles Welch, F.S.A., the City librarian. The attendance was very good, over sixty members and friends being present. Miss Hart, the librarian of Trinidad, was amongst the visitors.

Mr. William Rome, F.S.A., F.L.S., chairman of the Guildhall Library Committee, welcomed the L.A.A. to the Guildhall on behalf of his Committee, and having expressed the pleasure it gave him to afford the Association an opportunity of inspecting the grand old building, the most interesting parts were visited.

On the way to the Great Hall, Mr. Rome drew attention to two very interesting collections ; one consisting of the medals and badges of the great City Companies, and the other a collection of his own which he had lent to the Guildhall. This latter comprised Egyptian antiquities ranging from 1800 B.C. to 300 B.C., and numerous Roman coins of inestimable value.

On arrival at the Hall, Mr. Welch pointed out the wooden giants, Gog and Magog, and the canopy under which the Lord Mayor sits at State banquets.

The Chamber of the Courts of Aldermen was next visited. Here are to be seen in the windows and panels of the room, the arms of all the Aldermen who have passed the Chair, and the motto facing it "Audi alteram partem"—Hear all sides.

The Chamber of the Courts of Common Council was entered next. Mr. Welch briefly explained the Council's method of conducting its business.

Passing on, the crypt was reached. Mr. Welch outlined its history and the party then proceeded to the Museum which was the last place of interest to be visited. Here were found numerous antiquities of pottery and glass, coins and other interesting things.

An adjournment was then made to the Reading Room, where the meeting proper was held, Mr. Rome presiding. Mr. Welch read a very interesting paper, entitled "The Young Librarian, his training and possibilities." At the request of Mr. Rees, who thought the paper could be studied with advantage and for the benefit of those members who were unable to be present, Mr. Welch gave permission for the paper to be published in the "*Library Assistant.*"

Mr. Rome was unanimously requested to convey to the Guildhall Library Committee the thanks of the L.A.A. for their kindness in allowing the meeting to be held there.

Replying to a vote of thanks, moved by Mr. Soper, and seconded by Mr. Thorne, for the paper he had read, and the trouble he had taken to make the gathering a success, Mr. Welch said that as chairman of the Summer School Committee in 1895, he had watched with pleasure the formation of the L.A.A.

Sir Edward Verney, in proposing a vote of thanks to Mr. Rome for presiding, said that in his opinion the association was a necessary institution, for it was to the Assistants of to-day that we should have to look for the Librarians of the future.

Mr. Rome thanked those present for their very kind appreciation of the little he had done. In the course of his speech he announced with evident pleasure that after being neglected for over 500 years, Chaucer, who had done so much to crystallize our language, and who had been a City man and a City official, was at last to be suitably honoured by the erection of his bust in the Guildhall.

It was unanimously resolved that the sincere sympathy of the L.A.A. be tendered to Mrs. Foskett in the great loss she had sustained by the death of Mr. E. Foskett, Chief Librarian of the Borough of Camberwell.

A very successful meeting was brought to a close by the

presentation to each member present, of a copy of *The British Library Year Book, 1900-1901*, which had been generously forwarded as a gift by Mr. Thomas Greenwood.

Light refreshments were provided by Mr. Rome at the close of the proceedings. F.P.

STUDY CIRCLE.
QUESTIONS ON OCTOBER READINGS.

Note.—One, if not both, of the questions should be attempted.

1. ENGLISH LITERARY HISTORY.

    Senior.—Briefly trace the rise of periodical literature in England.

    Junior.—Make a list of the works of Sir Walter Scott, placing them in order of date.

2. LIBRARY PRACTICE.

    Senior.—What is the best method of procedure in the event of borrowers returning books from houses containing infectious disease? Does any law exist relative thereto.

    Junior.—Supposing you were asked by a borrower for the best books upon each of the following subjects, which would you recommend? Afghanistan, coins, costume, and the microscope.

READINGS FOR NOVEMBER.

a Brooke's Primer, *Chap. VIII.*
Saintsbury. Short History. *Book XI.*
Birrell. Obiter Dicta. *Series I.*
Also Biographical details concerning the early Victorian philosophic school.

a Suitable for Juniors.

It will be necessary to obtain a knowledge of contemporary English History, from such sources as are available.

The result of the last month's work has been good, but it is hoped that more *provincials* will avail themselves of these courses, which are mainly organized for their benefit. The answers to Library Practice are more satisfactory in the Junior division, than in the Senior.

The best answers in Library Practice are by "Ami" (*Senior*) and "Savoy" (*Junior*). The answers of "Adsum," "Nemo." and "Pro Patria" are insufficient, the two latter students omitting mention of the reviews or guide books. "Quo" is weak in composition, and the answer sent by "Codam" is imperfect in description.

The answers to the Literature questions are on the whole very satisfactory. The best answers are from "Ami" (*Senior*), and "Savoy" (*Junior*). "Adsum" fails to mention the influence of the French Revolution, "Nemo"'s paper is good, but lacks detail, "Pro Patria" errs in giving to England the first place in the political and literary revolution of Europe.

"Puer," "Quo," "Stebenhithe," and "Tamesis II" are all advised to be more careful in composition. "Puer" lacks originality and repeats too aptly the text-book wordings. "Spitzbergen" in a commendable endeavour to be brief, omits many facts that should have been mentioned

Altogether, we are satisfied with our first month's competition.

NOTE.—Students are requested to continue to use the *same* pseudonym, and answer the two questions on *separate* sheets of paper. Also to post their answers in time; one paper arrived 36 hours late, and such will disqualify in future.

The Hon. Sec. is obliged for the numerous suggestions received, all of which, where practicable, will be acted upon. The number of these communications, however, renders direct acknowledgment a matter of impossibility.

Answers to the November questions must reach the Hon. Sec. on or before December 12th.

*THE YOUNG LIBRARIAN: HIS TRAINING AND POSSIBILITIES.

By C. Welch, F.S.A.

I wish to speak to you briefly this evening on three points which I venture to regard as primary duties incumbent upon the young librarian.

These three points are, First:—The duty of reverence for books; Secondly:—The duty of courtesy; and Thirdly:—The duty of self-improvement.

It may perhaps safely be assumed that no one would deliberately *choose* librarianship as a profession if he were not a lover of books, nor could the average mortal be long engaged in the constant companionship of books without coming to regard them as his friends and companions, and treating them in such a way as friendship demands. I have known men who have been book-lovers all their lives, and whose libraries contain among their choicest treasures books which they acquired by saving up the pocket-money of their boyhood. But as a rule the bibliophile (outside, of course, the ranks of librarianship) is a creature of older growth. The librarian has much to learn from him. The care with which he *uses* his books, *binds* them, stores them in well-made bookcases, and impresses on his friends the duty of carefully handling them, has been the means of saving many a precious volume for posterity. What do we not owe to the private owners of libraries, from the noble founders of the Chatsworth and Althorp collections to John Bagford the shoemaker, whose collection of ancient ballads is fitly preserved in the British Museum?

What is a pleasurable instinct in the bibliophile becomes with the librarian, as I take it, a primary duty. He has to hand down his books to posterity, and must see that his generation treats them with all proper respect. This is especially necessary in the case of unique or very rare books and prints. The responsibility becomes in such cases almost a solemn one. But in

* Read at the Inaugural Meeting of the Seventh Session.

dealing with books of ordinary value, it is of the first importance for the assistant himself to set a good example to the public in the care with which he handles or uses books. In times even of great pressure they should not be banged down on the counter or table, or piled up into too high heaps, as this can surely be prevented with a little trouble. A good rule for the Librarian under this head is first, *take care* of your books, be a book-keeper in the truest and best sense of the word. Secondly, let the books, consistently with this your first duty, be placed as freely at the service of your readers as is possible.

I hope I may without giving offence be permitted to insist on the importance of what I regard as the second great duty of the librarian, whether young or old—the duty of courtesy. We look for courtesy as a duty on the part of every Christian man or woman, but may it not be particularly expected from the the librarian ? The object of books and, indeed, their *raison d'être*, is the preservation of all that is most precious and most valuable of the thoughts of men of all countries and times. And surely the effect of such constant companionship should be to soften and elevate, with the result impressed upon us of old in our Latin grammar, " *emollit mores nec sinit esse feros.*" But if necessary " the gentle art of courtesy " must be cultivated, for no librarian will be successful without it. A *library*, to which gentle spirits are naturally attracted, is of all places the most likely where we may entertain angels unawares, and we shall never know what choice gifts many a library has received through the courtesy shown by its officials to some visitor of humble mien. My own experience has been that readers as a rule are most grateful people, and acknowledge any assistance rendered to them with a fervour out of all proportion to the service which it is a duty though not less a pleasure to afford them.

But it is time to turn to my third point—the duty of self-improvement. I know that I am addressing many whose long hours of duty press heavily and make the time of home leisure one on which the first demands should be those of rest and recreation. But I know too that the fact of your membership of the Library Assistants' Association and of your being here to-night gives proof that none of you are going to be content to remain low down on the ladder, if through self-denial and hard work you can reach a higher position.

The duty of self-improvement, though incumbent upon all in whatever profession or occupation they may be engaged, is especially the duty of the young librarian who takes a proper view of the possibilities of his office. The personal advantages it brings to the young student must not be lost sight of. Mental application benefits the whole man by giving increased intellectual vigour, with a further capacity for acquiring knowledge; whilst a better acquaintance with the principles underlying our work gives us a greatly increased interest in its performance.

The material advantages need not so strongly be emphasised: they are patent to us all. Higher qualifications will fit their possessors for promotion to higher posts when these become vacant. They will also ensure that present work, however humble it may seem to be, shall be better done, with greater satisfaction to the assistant himself and greater benefit to the public. This is an age of advancement which makes great demands on individual capacity in every walk of life, and a larger measure of attainment than formerly is not only expected of each one, but is a necessity for those who would hold their own in the struggle not only for success but even for subsistence. There is no shirking these conditions. The librarian must take his place in the general movement. For him at all events there must be no lagging behind—he must rather seek to fit himself for a post among the leaders in the van of progress.

The multiplication of libraries which we have witnessed, especially during the last few years, and the "library spirit" which is so much in evidence at the present day shows that the public mind is deeply convinced of the importance of library work as a part of our national system of education. That system itself is the uppermost subject of domestic concern which now engrosses the attention of our statesmen and of the country at large. Of one thing we may be sure, that the work of the library will in the near future be identified more closely than ever with the great work of education.

Here, then, with the increasing number of libraries and the growing public interest in library work, are strong inducements to all to qualify themselves to the utmost for their professional work. Whilst the present outlook offers a wide scope for the more ambitious among us, it should bring home to every one the importance of the personal influence of the library assistant in the effect produced upon the public in this great crisis of the Library movement.

To turn now to the practical side of my subject. I do no propose to enter into detail as to courses of study. These may best follow the needs and opportunities of the individual. The training of the Summer School and the preparation for the examinations of the Library Association provide an excellent course of professional study, and there is no lack of evening classes at Colleges and Polytechnics for instruction in subjects of general education. Some items of common information suggest themselves as of special use to the librarian. It may be worth while to specify as instances, the order and dates of accession of the English sovereigns, the succession of the earlier Roman emperors, the periods covered by the various styles of our English architecture: the list might be greatly extended. These items of knowledge serve as little pegs on which to hang much other useful information, and serve as keys always at hand to unlock many a puzzle.

In making a choice of special studies, there are some which must be regarded as of first importance to the librarian. The study of heraldry—an elementary acquaintance with it at all events—is almost indispensable. Still more important is a knowledge of palæography, which is most interesting in itself and needs only diligence and practice for its acquisition. Without some proficiency in this study, which may almost be called one of the librarian's tools, the young student will be shut out from much that is of great value in the matters that come before him.

Then there are less nearly allied and more special studies in the choice of which each may best follow his individual taste. To have a private subject of study of which you have gained some hold is to have a very useful possession, whether it be an ancient or a modern language, a department of science or of art, a period of history or literature, a biographical subject or the history of your own locality. Then there are the more practical studies, such as numismatics, architecture, photography, and divisions of archæology, such as earth-works, brass-rubbing, &c.

The knowledge which you will gain by taking up as a hobby some such study as those which I have mentioned will prove most useful to you. It will also be useful to others, and your special study will often come in handy in most unexpected and various ways.

I assume that we shall all work in some corner or another, in the wide field of the great home-science of bibliography, and I cordially recommend the library assistants whom my remarks may reach to respond to the appeal recently made by the Bibliographical Society by taking up the exact study of the output from the press of one of our 17th or 18th century printers. The collection of materials for his life, the preparation of a list of the books which he printed, the careful examination and collection of these as opportunity offers, will prove an excellent training, an interesting study, and a useful piece of work in your profession, and one well within the reach of all whom I address.

I have said enough by way of suggestion—let me add a few words of encouragement. A higher standard will certainly be expected from the librarian in the future, and a wider field for his abilities lies before him. But do not forget that aids to self-advancement exist which were unknown to librarians of a generation since. The programmes of your past sessions afford full evidence of the interest which is felt in the improvement of the position of the young librarian not only by his older colleagues, but also by the members of library committees and all who have at heart the welfare of the library movement.

As in our home politics those who would win the far-off election battle must heed the cry of Register, Register, Register, so those amongst you who would win laurels in your profession must take good heed to Qualify, Qualify, Qualify.

Your meeting here to-night in such good show at the opening of your seventh annual session is sufficient proof that your Association has well recognised the need to which I have chiefly referred in these remarks, and I sincerely hope that the many advantages afforded by the Library Assistants' Association may continue to be enjoyed by a largely increasing band of members.

NOTES AND NEWS.

Back Numbers of "The Library Assistant."—The Editor will be pleased to pay full price (6d. per copy) and postage for any of the following numbers of *The Library Assistant*, viz.—No. 4, April, 1898; No. 8, August 1898; No. 10, October, 1898; No. 11, November, 1898; No. 32, August, 1900; No. 39, March, 1901, and will be pleased to accept as donations to the Association, any other numbers for which readers have no further use.

Australia; Legislature Debates.—The Commonwealth of Australia will be glad to receive at the Victoria Office, 15 Victoria Street, W.C., applications from Librarians who will file the published debates of the Legislature, and faciliate access to them by those of the public interested in the proceedings of the Legislatures of Greater Britain.

NEW MEMBERS.

Senior:—Faraday, J. G. (Hornsey); Sharp, E. (West Ham); Smith, H. J. (Bury).

Junior:—Ashton, J. C. (Wigan); Clayton, C. E. A. (Library of the Royal Medical and Chirurgical Society, London); Gillespie, N. L. (Westminster): King, J. H. (Poplar); Lea, Edith (Wigan); Marsden, J. R. (Mechanic's Institution Library, Burnley); Mee, F. H. (Wigan); Robarts, H. M. (Walthamstow); Rowley, G. F. (Stoke Newington); Welham, H. G. (West Ham).

Reproduced by kind permission from the British Library Year Book, 1900-01.

EDWARD FOSKETT.
AN APPRECIATION.

" All at once they leave you, and you know them."—*Browning.*

It is difficult for those who knew Mr. Edward Foskett, whether their friendship extended for a long period of time, or, as in the case of the present writer, for only a short perid, too realise that he has passed away from the busy professional life of a London librarian. The Borough of Camberwell has lost a good servant, and those who had the privilege of co-operating with him in his daily work have lost a friend; for he brought the element of friendship into a distinct and intimate relationship with the daily routine of library organisation.

He also brought to his work a sincere love of literature, a constructive ability, and a wise restraint. There was a mellowed geniality of temper in his nature which sometimes suggested our conception of the character of Dickens.

Mr. Foskett was appointed by the Camberwell Vestry in 1890, and as Chief Librarian of the Public Libraries of Camberwell, and our branch libraries came within his control and jurisdiction. This entails thought and action of no mean order. Those who can judge of his work from a longer and closer acquaintance would be better fitted to write of his many-sided activity. He was a Fellow of the Royal Society of Literature, and some volumes of verse have been the product of his leisure. In 1886 Messrs. Kegan Paul published a miscellaneous volume, and a second edition appeared in 1887. Much of Mr. Foskett's verse owes its inspiration to Cornish life and Cornish scenery. He had studied to advantage the poetry of Tennyson, and to Tennyson he always rendered a loyal allegiance. His tastes both in life and literature, as Mr. Scott-Scott, Chairman of the Camberwell Libraries Committee justly remarked in moving a resolution of sympathy with the widow and family of Mr. Foskett, were simple, and his ideals were high. His last published volume, " Hugh Trebarwith," a Cornish romance, tells a simple story in clear and simple language, and from it I have chosen two verses from a lyric to illustrate Mr. Foskett's ability as a writer of lyrical verse.

> Time that now defies, is a time that dies
>   With a breath ;
> Love is not a day, for it lives for aye
>   Killing death.
> So in you and me ever may it be
>   Pure and bright,
> Keeping us and one till another sun
>   Brings new light.

The thought of these lines may have occurred to some of those who stood around his grave at Forest Hill to render a last homage to one whose life-work was finished but who has left behind him a tender memory, and to younger men an inspiration for work. Mr. Foskett was 52; to me he always seemed much younger. He was young in spirit, and hopeful of the future; he tried to dignify and honour the calling he had chosen, and now that that busy brain, teeming with many projects, is at rest, we can best honour his memory by emulating his methods.

"Gentleness and cheerfulness, these are the perfect virtues," exclaims Stevenson. The subject of this brief appreciation had happily a large share of these admirable qualities.

C. F. NEWCOMBE.

Inaugural Meeting.—As will be seen from the report published on another page, the inaugural meeting was an unqualified success, and more than fulfilled the expectations of the committee. Of the large number present, over sixty, not more than seven or eight were visitors, amongst whom were Miss Verney, and Miss Hart, the Librarian of Trinidad, who is spending a short time in England. Sir Edmund Verney, who is pleased to claim membership of the Association as a library assistant, was also present, and members from such out-lying districts as Brentford, Hornsey, West Ham, Woolwich, &c., were again able to greet each other after the summer vacation.

The paper by Mr. Welch, which was of a particularly practical nature, and the "running" description of the treasures of the museum and other departments given by Mr. Rome, the Chairman of the Library Committee, as we drifted from one department to another, made us wish that we had more time to spare in order to listen to such an able and courteous enthusiast. It is very gratifying to the Officers and Committee of the L.A.A., who spend a considerable portion of their leisure in the work of the Association, to find at the commencement of a new session, that their labours are so fully appreciated, and they hope that all the meetings during this winter will be as well attended and in other ways successful.

Annual Dinner.—It is hoped that every Assistant in the London District, whether a member of the Association or not, will make a special effort to attend this pleasant annual function. The Committee also extend a cordial invitation to Librarians and others interested in the work of the Association.

Finsbury.—The Finsbury Borough Council has adopted a recommendation from the Public Libraries' Committee to adopt the Public Libraries Act throughout the whole of the Borough, and to raise the limit of the rate from $\frac{1}{2}$d. to 1d. in those parts of the Borough where the lower amount is levied. A month's notice must be given of intention to adopt Acts, and the whole question will come up again on November 7th, on a formal motion to adopt the Acts as above. At the present time the Acts are not operative in the district of St. Luke's and other portions of East Finsbury.

Stoke Newington.—At the last meeting of the Council it was decided, on the recommendation of the Public Libraries Committee, not to grant the petition signed by a number of borrowers asking the Council to adopt "open access."

NOTES AND NEWS.

Leeds. *The Yorkshire Weekly Post* of Oct. 19th, contains an article on the new catalogue and work of the Leeds Public Library, with a portrait of Mr. T. W. Hand, the Librarian.

Woolwich.—The first of the Woolwich Libraries will be opened by Lord Avebury on November 8th. Mr. Henry Phipps, late of Pittsburg, U.S.A., has just given a donation of £100, on condition that the news-room be open for certain hours on Sundays. The offer was made anonymously in the first place through the editor of *The Echo*. We hope to publish a description of the building in our next issue.

Bury.—Lord Derby opened the Art Gallery and Public Library on October 9th. The function was a civic one, the corporation having built the gallery, at a cost of about £30,000, to house the gift of pictures by the Wrigley family in commemoration of Queen Victoria's Diamond Jubilee. The collection is estimated to be of the value of £100,000. *The Bury Times* of October 12th, published a special four-page supplement with illustrations of the buildings and photographs of the principal officials, including the Chief Librarian, Mr. Archibald Sparke, and gives a good account of the rise and progress of the movement which led to the acquisition of this splendid institution. *The Builder* of October 12th, also published an illustration of the building with descriptive letterpress.

Stepney.—The Council has agreed to the report of the Libraries Committee *re* the staffs for the Mile End and Limehouse Libraries, which provides for a first, second, and third assistant, and a porter, at each of the Libraries. The salaries of the assistants are to be as follows, viz :—1st assistant, 30s. per week; 2nd assistant, 20s. per week; 3rd assistant 7s. per week.

APPOINTMENTS AND CHANGES.

*ANDERSON, Mr. A. A. R., St. Bride Institute, to be Junior Assistant, Mile End, Stepney.

CLAY, Mr., Assistant, Upper Norwood, to be Senior Assistant, Limehouse, Stepney.

*HATCHER, Mr. Sydney A., Sub-Librarian, Canning Town Public Library, West Ham, to be Librarian-in-charge.

*HOSIE, Mr. J. A Senior Assistant, Leyton, to be Librarian of Kendal.

LESLIE, Mr., Assistant, Twickenham, to be Senior Assistant, Mile End, Stepney.

*McDOUGALL, Mr. Donald, Senior Assistant, Central Library, West Ham, to be Principal Assistant, Canning Town.

*Moslin, Mr. A. M., Assistant, St. Saviour's, to be Junior Assistant, Limehouse, Stepney.

*Parsons, Mr. E. H., Second Assistant, St. George, Stepney, to be First Assistant, St. George.

*Poulter, Mr. H. W., Assistant, Penge, to be Second Assistant, St. George, Stepney.

Singleton, Mr. J. W., Librarian of Kendal, to be Librarian of Accrington.

*Whitwell, Mr. Charles, Sub-Librarian, Central Library, West Ham, to be Sub-Librarian of the West Ham Public Libraries.

Th following were the candidates selected for the Stepney appointments, viz :—Messrs. *Hatton (Leyton), Clay (Upper Norwood), *Camplin (Shoreditch), *Harper (Stoke Newingto), Norman (Wandsworth), Leslie (Twickenham), Gillespie (Westminster), for the Senior post. Messrs. *Moslin (St. Saviour's), *Anderson (St. Bride Institute), *Pocock (Brentford), *Poulter (Penge), Simmons (Wimbledon), for the Junior post.

*Members of the Library Assistants' Association.

OBITUARY.

We regret to announce the death of Mr. Hanson, the Librarian of the City of London College. Mr. Hanson, who was over seventy years of age, has been ocnnected with the College for over forty years, and was one of the officials in the old premises in Leadenhall Street, and a colleague of the founder, Prebendary MacKenzie.

APPOINTMENTS VACANT.

Notice to Library Authorities.—*We shall be pleased to publish under this heading, free of charge, particulars of vacancies if full details are sent to the Editor on or before the 25th of each month.*

Donations to Library. " Memoirs of Libraries," by Edward Edwards, 2nd Edit., vol. 1, 1901., presented by Mr. Thomas Greenwood, Frith Knowl, Elstree, Herts. " Public and Private Libraries of Glasgow." by Thomas Mason. 1885, presented by Mr. T. Mason, St. Martin's Library, London.

NOTICES.

Annual subscriptions to the L.A.A., excepting North-Western Branch, are now due, and should be sent to Mr. W. Geo. Chambers, *Hon. Treasurer*, Public Library, Woolwich.

Communications relating to the Journal and its publishing should be addressed to the *Hon. Editor*, Mr. H. Tapley Soper, Public Library, Stoke Newington, N.

All matter for the December number should be sent in on or before the 20th November.

All other communications should be addressed to the *Hon. Secretary*, Mr. G. E. Roebuck, 236 Cable Street, E.

The Library Assistant:

The Official Organ of the Library Assistants' Association.

No. 48.   DECEMBER, 1901.   Published Monthly.

DECEMBER MEETING.

The next meeting of this Association will be held on Wednesday, December 11th, at the Central Library, Stratford, E., by kind invitation of Mr. A. Cotgreave.

SPECIAL MEETING.

Members are requested to meet at 7 p.m. for the consideration of the proposed alterations of the Rules, submitted by Mr. A. Philip (*Hampstead*), which were published in our last issue.

The special meeting announced for November 6th, for the consideration of these propositions, was postponed owing to the small attendance.

ORDINARY MEETING.

At 8 p.m. Mr. W. J. Harris (*Hornsey*) will read his "Cotgreave" (1901) Prize Essay, entitled "*How to popularize our Public Libraries.*" This essay should lead to a lengthy discussion. Mr. Cotgreave with his customary generosity, has kindly undertaken to provide refreshments at the close of the proceedings.

NOTE.—All members of the L.A.A. who have not yet received their copies of Greenwood's "Year Book" should be present at this meeting when the *Hon. Sec.* will be pleased to further distribute this valuable donation which the author has kindly sent for our members.

N.W. BRANCH DECEMBER MEETING.

The Annual General Meeting will take place on Wednesday, 18th December at 8 p.m. in the Reference Library, King Street, Manchester, when the Election of Officers and other business will be transacted. Members may send in nominations for the Committee up to and including December 15th to the Hon. Sec.

SPECIAL NOTICE.

By the kindness of the General Committee, a parcel of Greenwood's Library Year Book 1901, has been allotted to this Branch. Every member attending this meeting will receive a copy. Where there are more than one member in a library, copies will be sent to them through their representative present on this occasion.

THE NOVEMBER MEETING.

The second meeting of the Session was held on Wednesday, November 13th, at the Central Library, Croydon, on the invitation of Mr. L. Stanley Jast, the Chief Librarian.

The members assembled about 7 p.m., and found Mr. Jast, Mr. Savage, Mr. Stevenson and other members of the staff waiting to receive them, and anxious to demonstrate the advantages of "Open Access" over all other systems. The building and arrangements generally called for considerable admiration, and the many little devices, for which Mr. Jast has become famous, were examined with interest, and should prove useful to many of those present.

Space will not permit, even if it was thought desirable, to go closely into the merits of the "Open Access" system, which was perhaps seen under the best advantages at this Library, and proved very interesting to the members of the L. A. A. Many had not previously seen it in actual operation, and arrived on the scene with the usual biassed prejudice, but were forced to admit, after putting it to a severe test, by asking for certain books, who had borrowed them, how long had they been out, etc., etc., information which was quickly given, that the system did not seem so difficult in practice as in theory.

After the examination of the building, the members were kindly provided with refreshments by Mr. Jast. About eight o'clock, there being about 30 members present, the meeting proper commenced with Mr. Jast in the Chair, and Mr. Ernest A. Savage was called upon to read his paper entitled, "The Library of the Future." Mr. Savage, in the course of his paper, outlined the future organisation of the public libraries of the country as follows:— There would be a

CENTRAL BUREAU,

which would
(1) Practically control and suggest any legislation with reference to books.
(2) Discuss all methods of service and decide on all forms of "missionary" work; receive, collate, and comment on reports sent in from the libraries of the country.
(3) Catalogue all books published, giving full titles and imprints, informative annotations, and would classify them according to a certain classification; and would distribute the entries throughout the country. If there were anything like uniformity of system among library authorities there would be no difficulty in establishing such a bureau at the British Museum at the present time.
(4) Compile all topical bibliographies, aid in the compilation of local bibliographies, etc.
(5) Discuss and conduct all experiments in library appliances, and employ draughtsmen and pattern makers to work up ideas into plans and models. There will be, in fact, a small body of experts in library furniture and fittings,

open to advise any library authority in the kingdom as to the arrangement and fitting of their building.

(6) Publish all library technical literature, and distribute copies gratuitously to other libraries.

This Central Bureau would be managed by an Executive elected from among the heads of the

COUNTY BUREAUS

which would

(1) Be central storehouses whence travelling libraries would operate in every part of the counties.
(2) Do all binding and similar work, such as the making of pamphlet boxes, printing, and the provision of supplies peculiar to library work.
(3) Act as distributing agencies of the Central Bureau.
(4) Be main agencies for the purchase, and central libraries for the preservation, of local books, which will be lent, if necessary and not in use, to the surrounding libraries.

And so forth.

THE TOWN LIBRARY.

Whose main work would be devoted entirely to service, missionary work, and co-operation with the educational and social institutions of the town.

Mr. Savage was highly congratulated on the quality of his lecture, and for the able manner in which it was delivered. The paper covered a vast area and contained such a wealth of revolutionary ideas that many of those present seemed chary about tackling it. The discussion from a numerical point of view was somewhat poor, but was compensated for by the able manner in which the questions were dealt with by those who took part, which included Messrs. Jast, Potter, Chambers, Hogg, Soper, &c.

The speakers did not favour centralisation of libraries, nor some of the more drastic changes advocated by the lecturer, but many of the suggestions found supporters. The question of removal of the rate limit was met with abundant sympathy, but it was thought that it would not be advisable to press it until the adoption of the Act was made compulsory. Interchangeable tickets was supported, and it was more than noticeable that "Open Access" was not received with that amount of scorn and ridicule which has usually been its lot, and instead of being treated as a huge joke was regarded by all present as a force to be reckoned with—in fact two of the speakers strongly supported it.

Mr. Percy Wood, of St. George-the-Martyr Public Library, was elected to fill the vacancy on the London Committee caused by the resignation of Mr. Parsons.

The meeting concluded with the usual votes of thanks to Mr. Savage for the paper, to the Committee of the Libraries for permission to meet there, and to Mr. Jast for his hospitality, and for the able manner in which he filled the chair.

N.W. BRANCH—NOVEMBER MEETING.

The November Meeting of the N.W. Branch took the form a "Literary Reception" due to the invitation of Mr. W. E. Axon, who asked the members to meet him at his residence on Saturday afternoon, November 9th, when he showed them his fine private collection of literary treasures.

It was singularly appropriate that the members should meet at Mr. Axon's, as, apart from the fact that he is a gentleman whose name is a household word in Manchester—nay Lancashire literary circles, they found in him one who like themselves could once lay claim to the status of a Library-Assistant, so that he could thoroughly and sincerely appreciate their efforts in the work done by them as an association, which, as he smilingly complained, was not in evidence in "his time."

The members assembled in the drawing room when they renewed acquaintance with an old friend in Mr. Green of "Moss Side," who was present, as were likewise that charming hostess Mrs. Axon and her dainty little daughter.

Mr. Axon had arranged in chronological order a large collection of his choice works, representing the progress, or perhaps we should say the decadence of printing, from the earliest times down to the end of the 19th century.

Beginning with a specimen from a Strasburg press dated 1483, Mr. Axon briefly commented on each volume exhibited, explaining the origin and value of his various books, whose histories he further illustrated with many happy little anecdotes concerning their printers, authors and owners, before they became his property.

In addition to his examples of the early printers, Mr. Axon also described what he termed his literary curiosities, exhibiting many rare and curious volumes, some of which are unique owing to their suppression early in their existence, owing their value largely on account of their scarcity. Among others may be mentioned a Spanish jest-book once the property of the poet Southey, one presented by Grattan to Coleridge, and many others equally valuable because of the autographs of famous men inscribed on their pages.

In the course of his remarks on bibliography, Mr. Axon mentioned that there was a splendid field in the matter of English books printed in India which awaited the aspiring Bibliographer and one which so far as he knew had never been dealt with.

After minutely inspecting the books under review, a goodly collection comprising works in English, German, French, Spanish, Latin and Italian, to say nothing of those in various dialects, ranging from a mixture of Spanish, Armenian, Arabic, down to homely and gradely Lancaster, the members proceeded to the library proper, where they were shown the Dewey Classification applied to a private library numbering some eight to ten thousand volumes, which, as could be easily seen were in constant use, and so placed where they could be most readily found, somewhat modifying the niceties of class-distinctions, which as Mr. Axon explained, was one of the privileges which the private book-collector possessed over the public Librarian.

Here Mrs. Axon and little Miss Axon gracefully dispensed tea, while our host showed his fine collections of Autograph Letters and MSS., some of which are of considerable value, nor must we omit to mention that Mr. Axon has one of the smallest if not the smallest volume extant, this being considerably less in size than the famous Bijou Dictionaries, which were so much in vogue a few years ago.

Having exhausted the resources of the library, the proceedings terminated with a hearty vote of thanks to Mr. and Mrs. Axon which was moved by Mr. Swann in a few appropriate words, and supported and seconded by Messrs. Dukins and Haworth.

In reply Mr. Axon expressed the pleasure of himself and Mrs. Axon in meeting the Assistants, who by taking so much interest in their profession showed by their endeavours to improve themselves, that their desire was a sincere one, and no mere flash in the pan, which the existence of the N.W. branch proved. This he thought was a happy augury for the future of the Library Assistants' Association.

P.D.G.

N.W. JANUARY MEETING.

The second bi-monthly meeting will take place on Wednesday, 15th January, 1902. See January "Assistant" for details.

OPENING OF THE WOOLWICH LIBRARY.

The first Library to be erected for the Borough of Woolwich was opened on November 8th, by Lord Avebury. As far back as 1876, an attempt was made to adopt the Acts but was defeated at a public meeting, the supporters being followed to their homes by a howling mob! A poll was taken in 1887 and again in 1888, but on each occasion the opponents had a large majority. In 1896 the Local Board of Health adopted the acts, and the present Library is the outcome of their action.

The building has been erected by a local firm from designs by a ocal architect, and consists of the usual departments, as well as a house for the Librarian. The total cost, including the fittings, which were carried out by the North of England School Furnishing Co. has been £9,800. The building has two frontages, and the elevations are in the Renaissance style, of red brick, Portland stone, and polished granite. The lighting throughout is electric.

Accommodation is provided for 30,000 volumes, 17,000 of which are already in the Library. The "Cotgreave" Indicator has been adopted. Mr. Henry Bond, late of Barrow-in-Furness, Kendal and Lincoln Public Libraries, has been appointed Librarian, and there are also four assistants, all of whom are members of the L.A.A.! Mr. Chambers, our worthy treasurer, being the principal.

The Ceremony of formally declaring the Library open, took place in the Reading Room, after which Lord Avebury delivered an address in the adjoining Polytechnic before an audience of 900 people. In the course of his remarks, his Lordship dwelt upon the great decrease in crime which had been the result of the better education of the people. It was, he said, a fallacy to suppose that a Library meant an increase in the rates, it was an investment. Ignorance cost the country more than education. In 1870 there were 113 prisons, all full, now the number was 55, half empty—several prisons having been turned into Libraries. Continuing, Lord Avebury referred to the value of good reading, as well as the pleasure and profit to be derived from it. It was no exaggeration to say that books, if properly used, endowed them with an enchanted palace of bright and happy thoughts. A Library was a true paradise in which everything was open to them, especially the fruit of the tree of knowledge, for which they were told their mother sacrificed all the delights of the Garden of Eden.

Prior to the ceremony the Mayor (Colonel Hughes, M.P.) entertained a large party to luncheon.

THE PRESIDENT OF THE LIBRARY ASSOCIATION ON "SALARIES."

"Librarianship is a sadly under-paid profession. No phrases can do away with this hard fact. Such a state of things can hardly, one hope, remain long unbettered. There must come a time when librarians, like the members of every other profession, will be paid in some reasonable proportion to their life work of assiduous and always increasing responsibilities. Up to the present time the total want of any such correspondence between the labour and the remuneration has been pitiful if not absurd. Once more I say librarians are underpaid, grossly underpaid, and merely from the view of efficient performance of such work as I am about to describe can anyone doubt that, in their own interest and in the interest of the public, the Municipal authorities of every town in the United Kingdom would do well to increase, and to increase generously, the miserable incomes now paid to those from whom so much is required, and by whom such services are rendered. I feel myself the more free to say this with emphasis since, in saying it, I am not stating my own claims but the just claims of my own friends."—*Library Association Record (September, 1901)*.

THE SOCIETY OF PUBLIC LIBRARIANS.

The Annual Meeting of the above Society was held at the Bishopsgate Institute on Wednesday evening, November 13th. There was a good attendance of members. The Officers elected for the ensuing year were Mr. W. C. Plant, Chairman; Mr. F. Chennell, Vice-Chairman; Mr. H. S. Newland, Hon. Treasurer; and Mr. C. W. F. Goss, Hon. Secretary.

STUDY CIRCLE.

An error occurred in our last issue, the date for receipt of answers to November questions being given as *December* 12th, in mistake for *November* 12th.

In consideration thereof, the Education Committee has agreed to allow students to send in answers, for *both* this and last month's questions provided both sets of answers reach the Hon. Sec. L.A.A., 121 De Beauvoir Road, Kingsland, London, N., on or before December 12th. Kindly use the same pen-name.

QUESTIONS ON NOVEMBER WORK.
Students are advised to answer one if not both of the questions.

SENIOR. 1.—State what you know of Thomas Carlyle and his place in English literature.
2.—If a museum is attached to a Public library, and supported from the one general rate, does Library Law place any definite limit to the financial support of the museum.

JUNIOR. 1.—Write what you can concerning the " Idylls of the King."
2.—What is the best binding for (a) Reference Books, (b) Fiction, (c) Pamphlets.

READING FOR DECEMBER.
*Brooke's Primer. Chapter vii.
Morley's First Sketch (Annals) to 1825.
Chambers's Cyclopædia Eng. Liter. pp. 568-92.
Saintsbury. Short History. Bk. x. ch. iv.
*Suitable for Juniors.

NOTES AND NEWS.

The Annual Dinner was held at Anderton's Hotel on November 27th and proved in every way a thorough success. A full account will be published in the January issue.

Australia ; Library Statistics.—An Australian circulating library has been reckoning up its readers' tastes for one year. The results are rather curious. Thackeray heads the poll easily. Bulwer Lytton is second in popularity, with Sir Walter Scott close on his heels. Dickens is only fourth, and is not far ahead of Captain Marryat and Charles Lever. Our colonial cousins would seem to be somewhat old-fashioned and conservative in their literary likings.

" Book-binding and the care of books."—Mr. Cockerell, who will be remembered by many Assistants as the genial lecturer on Book-binding, in connection with a recent series of L. A. classes, and by others for his excellent paper read before the Society of Arts on the Treatment of Leather, has just published a book which will form a useful addition to Assistants' private libraries. It is issued as No. 1 of " The Artistic Crafts Series " by John Hogg, at 5/- net.

Early Printed Books at the British Museum.—The Exhibition of Early Printed Books, at present on view in the King's Library of the British Museum, has furnished the authorities with an opportunity of issuing an illustrated guide to the works. The arrangement is chronological, beginning with admirable illustrations of types and woodcuts, showing the art of printing in its first rude stages. Some notes on famous bindings are another feature in a guide which possesses a permanent value to the bibliographies. The guide is published at the low figure of 6d, and we should advise all our readers to procure a copy.

Festiniog.—The Urban Council of Festiniog has decided to close the branches at Conglywal and Tanygrisian owing to lack of funds.

Ipswich.—The newly-organised Reference Library of 5,000 volumes was opened on November 8th by the Mayor of Ipswich, who was supported by the Members of Parliament for the Borough, the Chairman and Members of the Committee and other gentlemen. The books are housed in a handsome new room with excellent accommodation for students.

Kimberley.—In spite of the unsettled state of affairs in South Africa, the Kimberley Library, under the direction of our late Editor, Mr. B. L. Dyer, is making what little progress is possible. No. 1 of the " *The Library Record,*" which has just reached us, shows that a goodly number of well-selected books have been purchased during the last 15 months. There is plenty of room for improvement in the "get up" of this little *Record*, which has evidently been produced as cheaply as possible, but we are pleased to be able to congratulate Mr. Dyer on the introduction in his far away "sphere of influence," of this method of communication with borrowers which has proved so helpful to readers in our "tight little island."

Lambeth.—Dr. Garnett recently unveiled the London Millenary Tablet to Alfred the Great, presented to the Brixton Library by Mr. Richard C. Jackson, a well-known local antiquarian.

"The Library Association Record."—The September issue, published about the middle of November, is made up of the report of the annual meeting and is the best and fullest report of any annual meeting of the L.A. that we can remember. The address of the newly-elected President is a model one, and should be read by all library assistants. We quote on another page a particularly interesting extract on "Salaries."

"The Library World."—In conjunction with the above should be read the report of the annual meeting published in this Journal, in the October issue, and the two pungent editorials entitled "*At Plymouth*," and "*Crisis or Opportunity.?*" The account of the annual meeting of that mystic Association, *The Pseudonyms*, published in the same issue, to those who can read between the lines, is full of sarcasm of the most acrid order. The promised article by Mr. Jast, on Parliamentary papers, to which we referred in our October issue, has apparently been forgotten.

The November issue contains an interesting "editorial" on Mr. Howell's article "On the Influence of Public Libraries on Reading in America, to which we recently called our readers' attention. The first instalment of an instructive comparison drawn from *Two Reports on Open Access*, a discussion by the "Pseudonyms" on "*Librarianship under Three Heads*," viz., *Financial, Administrative and Literary*, and a good batch of miscellaneous news.

A New Book on Library Economy.—The care of books is a matter that appeals to all bookmen. Mr. John Willis Clark, who is Registrar of the University of Cambridge, has written an essay which bears upon it. He calls his volume an essay because he wishes to indicate that it is only an attempt to deal in a summary fashion with an extremely wide subject. This subject is the development of libraries and their fittings from the earliest times to the end of the eighteenth century. Mr. Clark writes of the monastic library, showing its relationship, through its fittings, with the collegiate libraries of Oxford and Cambridge. He also dwells on the value of illuminated manuscripts as illustrating the life of a mediæval student.

"**Martello Tower,**" is the pseudonym of Commander F. M. Norman, R.N.

"**Maxime Gorky.**"—We understand that this is the pseudonym of Alicksici Marksimovitch Pieshkov.

Newington.—Mr. T. A. Gilbert, a member of the Libraries' Committee, has presented to the Library a very rare portrait of John Revoult, Master of the Walworth Academy, engraved by Ward, after Sir William Beechy, R.A., 1798.

Novel Reading in Russia.—It is said that in the Free Libraries of Petersburg, the novels of Mayne Reid are more in demand than any other foreign writer. After Mayne Reid, Fenimore Cooper comes next in point of popularity.

The People's Palace.—The Governors having decided to close the Reading Room and Library in consequence of lack of funds, and the nearness of the Library about to be opened by the Stepney Borough Council in Bancroft Road, it is proposed to hand over to the latter Institution the reading stands and books which number about 12,000.

Poplar.—*The Building News*, November 8th, contains the plans and elevation of the recently opened Library at Bow.

Rare Books.—The November issue of the *Pall Mall Magazine* contains an excellent article on the prices realized at sales for rare books.

St Bride Institute.—In connection with the Conversazione held to commemorate the 7th anniversary of the opening, and the presentation of a bust of Samuel Richardson, by J. Passmore Edwards, Esq., the Governors issued a beautifully printed and illustrated pamphlet, to which Mr. Lange, the Librarian, contributed a short account of the life of " The Father of the English novel."

Stamping *v*. Defacing Books.—A useful hint is conveyed in a letter we have received from an old frequenter of the British Museum Reading Room. After mentioning a certain Jewish liturgical work, in which is an engraving by Holl, after the portrait by Slater, of the Rev. Solomon Hirschell, for forty years (1802-1842) the Chief Rabbi of the German and Polish Jews in England, he remarks:—" The face of the learned dignitary, who was of very imposing presence, and is said to have been fully conscious of the fact, is marked, however, by lines and figures which would invite the suspicion that he had been tatooed in a red pigment as elaborately as if he had been a Maori chieftain. But this appearance is of a deceptive character, and is seen to be produced by the partial but vivid transference of the stamp which identifies the volume as the property of the British Museum. The stamp and the face exactly coincide when the book is shut."—*Daily Chronicle*.

Stepney.—The Library about to be fitted up for the blind will shortly be in active operation at the St. George's Library.

The Building News of November 1st contains an illustration with plan of the Limehouse Library opened on November 6th, and the *Municipal Journal* of November 8th, an excellent illustrated article on the growth and opening of this Library.

The Mile End Library has received a donation of £50 from Mr. Spencer Charrington, M.P.

Windsor.—The Royal Library at Windsor Castle is to be enlarged. A room adjoining it, hitherto used by the Lord-in-Waiting, will be thrown into the inner print room. This will enable many thousands of volumes to be added to the hundred thousand valuable works now on the shelves. Some books of little importance have been disposed of to make room for the King's books. The electric light is now fully installed in the library, and when the additional space has been procured the library will rank as one of the finest in the world. The King has left the entire arrangement of valuable works and extensive collection of prints and drawings in the hands of his experienced librarian, Mr. Richard Holmes.

BOOKS, &c., RECEIVED.

Chorley Public Library. Catalogue of the books in the Library (Reference and Lending Departments). pp. 329. 8vo. Brevier and Nonpareil. Compiled by Edward McKnight, Librarian.

A neatly printed and carefully compiled Dictionary Catalogue of 10,000 volumes. Prefaced by a list of donations and an account of the opening proceedings. A laudable attempt is being made to form a collection of books and pamphlets relating to the locality. The provision of technical books appears to be limited, especially in respect of local industries, but otherwise the collection of books is an admirable one.

Some attempt at condensation might have been made with profit, and the information conveyed in titles occupying five and six lines given in half the number.

Catalogue of the Reference Department of the Hornsey Central Library. Compiled by Thos. Johnson, Chief Librarian and Secretary. pp. 134 and xiii. Sm. 8vo. paper covers, price 3d.

A classified catalogue arranged upon the Brown "Adjustable" Classification, the first, we believe, issued on this system, with subject and author indexes. Many of the entries could, with advantage, have been abridged, which would have allowed more space for annotations. The Catalogue is carefully and neatly compiled and nicely printed, and is not disfigured with advertisements. Users of the "Dictionary" Catalogue will at first find the references difficult, but this would have been considerably lessened if the class letters and section numbers had been repeated as a head line to each page of the classified list. The number of volumes catalogued is not given.

We are glad to have had the opportunity of handling this Catalogue, and congratulate Mr. Johnson on its production.

REPORTS RECEIVED.—Metropolitan Borough of Finsbury, 1900-1. City of Gloucester, Second Annual, 1900-1. Leyton, Eighth Annual, 1900-1.

NEW MEMBERS.

Senior.—LITTLE, C. (Penge); PICK, E. A. (Shoreditch); SAVAGE, E. A. (Croydon).

Junior.—CHIVERS, P. W. (Croydon); DAVIS, J. (Penge); JACKSON, C. P. (Woolwich); STEWART, J. D. (Croydon); WARNER, J. (Croydon).

APPOINTMENTS AND CHANGES.

SURETIES, Mr. G. H. Sub-Librarian, Hornsey Central Library, to be Librarian-in-charge, Highgate Branch Library.

APPOINTMENTS VACANT.

[**Notice to Library Authorities.**—*We shall be pleased to publish under this heading, free of charge, particulars of vacancies if full details are sent to the Editor on or before the 25th of each month.*]

METROPOLITAN BOROUGH OF POPLAR PUBLIC LIBRARIES.

The Council of the above Borough is about to appoint for the Public Libraries a Junior Assistant with not less than two years' experience in library work, at a commencing salary of £45 per annum. Applications, in candidates' own handwriting, stating age and qualifications, together with testimonials, must reach me not later than December 7th.

Council Offices, High Street, Poplar.   LEONARD POTTS,
November 23rd, 1901.   *Town Clerk.*

ERRATA.

Page 17, " Hear all sides," for " all " read " both." Page 22, 7th line from foot, for " collection " read " collation." Page 25, 9th line from top, " and our branches came within his control," delete " and," and for " our " read " four." We regret that in announcing the Stepney appointments in our last issue we used the terms " Senior Assistant " and " Junior Assistant " instead of " First Assistant " and " Second Assistant."

NOTICES.

Annual subscriptions to the L.A.A., excepting North-Western Branch, are now due, and should be sent to Mr. W. Geo. Chambers, *Hon Treasurer*, Public Library, Woolwich.

Communications relating to the Journal and its publishing should be addressed to the *Hon Editor*, Mr. H. Tapley Soper, Public Library, Stoke Newington, N.

All matter for the January number should be sent in on or before the 18th December.

All other communications should be addressed to the *Hon. Secretary*, Mr. G. E. Roebuck, 121 DE BEAUVOIR ROAD, KINGSLAND, N.

The Library Assistant:
The Official Organ of the Library Assistants' Association.

No. 49.   JANUARY, 1902.   Published Monthly

THE LIBRARY ASSISTANTS' ASSOCIATION.
FOUNDED 1895.   SEVENTH SESSION.   YEAR 1901-1902.

Members are requested to read carefully the announcements appearing on this and the following pages, as no further intimation of meetings and other arrangements may be expected.

JANUARY MEETING.

The January meeting of the L.A.A. will be held at Battersea Public Library, Lavender Hill, S.W., on Wednesday, January 15th, at 8 p.m., by kind invitation of Mr. Lawrence Inkster, the Borough Librarian.

Members will be addressed by Mr. F. E. Chennell, Librarian of Willesden Green, on the *Pleasures of Librarianship*, and it is hoped that there will be a large attendance of library assistants, whether members of the L.A.A. or not.

MR. GREENWOOD'S PRESENTATION TO OUR MEMBERS.

Each member of the L.A.A. who has not yet received a copy of Greenwood's "Year Book" should make early application to the Hon. Sec., such application to be accompanied by four penny stamps to defray postage.

DECEMBER MEETING.

The sessional meeting for December was held at the West Ham Central Library on Wednesday, December 11th, at the invitation of Mr. Cotgreave, who, as is his wont, entertained his guests right royally.

Every facility was given the members for inspecting the working of a successful indicator library, and following so closely the visit to Croydon, gave them an excellent opportunity of comparing the two systems and weighing their relative merits.

Prior to the ordinary meeting, a special general meeting was held to consider a number of proposals brought forward by Mr. Philip, particulars of which were published in our November issue. After consideration the first three motions were lost, the fourth one, altering the date of the Annual Meeting from the summer to the winter, being carried by a majority of two.

At 8 p.m. the ordinary meeting commenced, Mr. Cotgreave welcoming the members, and expressing his pleasure at seeing them there from year to year in ever increasing numbers. The "Cotgreave" 1901 Prize Essay, entitled, "How to popularise a Public Library," was then read by Mr. Harris, the successful competitor, and provoked a good discussion, although some disappointment was felt that a number of important points, owing to the 1,000 words limit, had not been dealt with at greater length. In order to allow further scope, Mr. Cotgreave has suggested that the limit should be increased to 2,000 words, and has generously offered to increase the 1902 prize to two guineas. Particulars of this competition will shortly be issued.

On the motion of Mr. Soper, seconded by Mr. Coutts, a hearty vote of thanks was accorded to Mr. Harris for having read his paper.

Mr. F. Meaden Roberts moved a vote of thanks to Mr. Cotgreave for his presence that evening, and for the innumerable other things for which we were indebted to him. This was seconded by Mr. Pickard and carried by acclamation.

Prior to the close of the meeting, the Chairman (Mr. Rees) announced his election to a seat on the Council of the *Library Association*, an announcement which was received with loud applause. Mr. Rees said that he very much appreciated this honour, and that he knew the members of the L.A.A. would take it as a recognition of the work of their Association, for he felt sure that it was on account of his official connection with the Library Assistants' Association that he had been elected to a seat on the Council of the older and more important Association. The Chairman was heartily congratulated upon the honour bestowed upon him.

Before leaving, Mr. Cotgreave entertained his guests to light refreshments, and presented to each a copy of his valuable *Guille-Alles Catalogue*, a gift which, needless to say, was greatly appreciated. A most enjoyable and profitable evening came to an end all too soon.

By special permission from Mr. Cotgreave, we are enabled to present with this issue an excellent portrait, with a fac-simile autograph, of the genial Chief of the West Ham Libraries.

W. G. C.

N.W. BRANCH ANNUAL MEETING.

The third Annual Meeting of the North-Western Branch was held on Wednesday, December 18th, in the Reference Library, Manchester, Mr. J. H. Swann presiding.

The annual report was laid before the meeting, and, together with that of the Hon. Treasurer, was adopted. The report of the Treasurer showed a small balance on the right side.

It is gratifying to report that although eight members have left the Branch for various reasons during the past year there is a gain of ten members over previous records.

The election of officers resulted in the Chairman being unanimously re-elected, and a Vice-Chairman (Mr. J. W. Dickens) was also appointed. The Hon. Secretary having asked to be relieved of his duties, Mr. W. Quarmby was elected to fill the office. Mr. W. Crompton was re-elected Hon. Treasurer, and the following members were elected to serve on the Committee :—Messrs. H. W. Kirke (Chetham Hospital), A. Baker (Chester), H. Percival, P. D. Gordon (Manchester), W. Montgomery (Bootle), W. H. Shawcross (Bury), and W. Berry (Oldham).

The retiring Officers and Committee having been accorded a hearty vote of thanks, the proceedings terminated, and the distribution of copies of the "British Library Year Book," presented to the Association by Mr. Thomas Greenwood, took place.

N.W. BRANCH JANUARY MEETING.

The next meeting will be held in the Athenæum (George Street entrance), Manchester, on Wednesday, January 15th, when members are requested to contribute short papers, or to make brief remarks on such subjects as "The Sunday opening of Libraries," "Library Hints," etc., etc. Intending contributors should intimate the subject of their paper or remarks to Mr. W. Quarmby, Hon. Sec., on or before January 13th.

Those members who did not attend the Annual Meeting may have a copy of the "British Library Year Book" on remitting postage to the Hon. Secretary, or they will be obtainable at the January meeting.

N.W. BRANCH SUBSCRIPTIONS.

Subscriptions to the N.W. Branch for 1902 are now due, and should be forwarded to the Hon. Treasurer, Mr. W. Crompton, Y.M.C.A. Library, Manchester, as early as possible. All other communications should be addressed to the Hon. Secretary, Mr. Wilfred Quarmby, Central Public Library, Oldham.

FOURTH ANNUAL DINNER.

The Fourth Annual Dinner of the Association was held at Anderton's Hotel, Fleet Street, on Wednesday, November 27th. About 40 members and friends of the Association sat down, among them being Mr. W. Bridle, of East Ham ; Mr. A. Cotgreave, of West Ham; Mr. C. J. Courtney, of the Minet Library; Mr. R. A. Peddie ; Mr. Roberts, of St. Saviour's; and Mr. Taylor, of St. Giles. Letters of regret at inability to attend had been received from several gentlemen, among them being Mr. Fortescue, Dr. Garnett, Mr. Greenwood, Mr. Henry Ogle, Mr. Pacy, and Mr. Tedder. The Chair and Vice-Chair were occupied by Mr E. G. Rees (Westminster), and Mr. S. A. Hatcher (West Ham) respectively.

The loyal toasts having been honoured, Mr. H. D. Roberts proposed the toast of "The Library Assistants' Association." In the course of a very happy speech he said that he had always taken a great interest in the Association. The first meeting they held in a Public Library was at St. Saviour's, and he was the first Public Librarian to read a paper before them. He hoped the Association would continue to progress. It had come to stay, and its membership was a stepping stone to something higher. He recommended all to work for and obtain the certificate of the Library Association. He hoped to see all senior appointments fall to certificated men, and that the Association would impress upon its members the advisability of working for it.

Mr. Rees, in replying, expressed pleasure that it had been proposed by a gentleman so well known to the library world, and that many librarians were present. At the last moment Mr. Welch, of the Guildhall, had been prevented by a severe chill from attending. Librarians should be glad to see their assistants members of the Association, and should encourage them to join. Apart from its educational influence it gave them opportunities for interchange of experience, for seeing other libraries, and hearing addresses from men well able to teach them. They would thus become better assistants, and better work would be done.

The toast of " Our Provincial and Colonial Colleagues " was proposed by Mr. W. G. Chambers. The large growth of the Association in the provinces during the third year of its existence, he said, was due to the inauguration of " The Library Assistant." The provincial membership was now 82, of whom 56 belonged to the North-Western Branch. The establishment of other branches was only a question of time. Several officers of the L.A.A. had started their library careers in the provinces, including the present, and at least two past secretaries. The Colonial influence was started by the translation of Mr. Dyer to Kimberley. The outcome of his appointment being the election of three Kimberley assistants as members. He looked forward to the time when they would have branches in South Africa and other British colonies.

Mr. Soper in a particularly witty speech proposed " The Visitors," saying that they were always pleased to see librarians at their festivals, as it showed that the Association had their sympathy. As editor of " The Library Assistant " he had always received the utmost courtesy from them. He saw many gentlemen present who had not that pale and careworn expression denoting the librarian. He hoped they were borrowers. His examples of the questions with which assistants are assailed during the course of a day caused much amusement. Mr. Taylor, Librarian of St. Giles's

Public Library, briefly replied, thanking the Association for the invitation, and expressing the pleasure it would give him to invite them to the Holborn Libraries.

Mr. Cotgreave also responded, and in the course of his remarks said that as he remembered several happy meetings he felt that he really must accept this invitation. No one had a more sincere wish for the Association's progress than himself. He hoped they would all do their best to be present at the meeting which was shortly to be held at West Ham, when he hoped that they would feel that they were coming to see a friend. He had known Mr. Rees ever since he came to London, in 1888, and was pleased to see him in the chair.

In proposing the toast of "The Chairman," Mr. Peddie said that he had had the honour of once holding that position, which was now an easy job compared with what it was in the early stages. He regretted he could not attend the ordinary meetings. He managed to attend two events in the year, the Annual Meeting and the Annual Dinner. The Annual Dinner was one of the most pleasant functions and one to which he looked forward during the preceding months. He considered that the speech of Mr. Dyer, at the First Annual Dinner, had opened out a new era for the Association. It started in great difficulties, and had to fight a large number of opponents. Mr. Roberts and one or two more had stood by them. He himself took the bull by the horns, and read a paper on the L.A.A. before the Library Association. They had to say something about the L.A.A. in reply, and that had to be something good. Then Mr. Dyer came along with his fighting programme, which he maintained was the saving of the Association. It might have dropped for lack of energy. It was now a living force in the profession. Mr. Rees had the interests of the Association at heart, and he was prepared to back it up.

Mr. Rees, in reply, said it was the second year the Association had made him Chairman, and he felt the honour very much. The officers of the Association had always worked well with him. It was said when the journal started, "It will go on while Dyer's here, but who will take it up when he goes." Mr. Ogle and Mr. Hatcher had both done well, and since Mr. Soper had had it in hand the *Library Assistant* had not lost in health and vigour. He had been in the profession 25 years, having been appointed at Westminster in 1876, and he regretted that there was no Library Assistants' Association in those early days. He concluded by proposing the health of the Vice-Chairman.

Mr. Hatcher acknowledged the toast in a few words, saying that he could not claim to have been in the profession so long as

Mr. Rees. He had only seen nine years' service, and that in one library, where he had always felt at home. Since he had been a member of the Association he had taken a greater interest in his work.

Between the various toasts the company were entertained to a very varied and excellent programme of vocal and instrumental music, contributed by Mr. F. C. Chidgey, Mr. A. Cogswell, Mr. Cuthbert Collins, Mr. C. J. Courtney, Mr. A. H. Crouch, Mr. W. J. Harris, Mr. George Hiles, Mr. Walter Rees, Mr. D. P. Steed, Mr. H. P. Steed, Mr. W. B. Thorne, and Mr. W. J. Vellenoweth, Mr. H. P. Steed accompanying at the piano. The toast of "The Artistes" having been drank, the evening concluded with the singing of "Auld Lang Syne" and the "National Anthem" W. B. Y.

LIBRARIANSHIP IN SOUTH AFRICA.

At an early meeting of this session will be read a paper with the above title which has been contributed by the Librarian of Kimberley, and which will form a useful supplement to the article by the Librarian of Buluwayo, which appeared in Volume I of this journal, when it was conducted under the editorial ægis of Mr. Dyer.

From our Appointments column it will be seen that for the third time within a period of fifteen months a South African appointment has been given to an assistant from the ranks of our members. It is, we believe, the first assistant-librarianship in the Colonies which has been filled from a London Public Library staff. The salary we understand, is £120 per annum, which in spite of the increased cost of living in the Colonies, as compared to that at home, seems a substantial increase on the salaries paid at present in London Libraries.

That more appointments will fall to the members of the L.A.A. is our sincere belief, and it will be well if all the members who desire an improved position in their profession, keep an eye on possibilities of openings under the Southern Star.

A sign of the times that is at the least significant appears in the 1900 Report of the Committee of the East London Public Library, where, after recording that there were some 9,000 volumes in stock, that the income was £857, and that plans had been drawn up for a new Library building to cost £4,200 the Committee adds the following paragraph :—

"In concluding this report, your Committee bring to notice the desirability of having a professional Librarian. It is with no grudging spirit you are assured that the time and labour required to be spent in the service of this institution is already beyond what any body of unleisured persons could be called on to bestow, and there also exists need for competent knowledge of the book market and trained experience in library management."

A further sign is that at Salisbury the Victoria Memorial Committee have decided that the memorial to the Queen-Empress shall take the form of a Public Library.

The field for trained Librarians in South Africa should be a wide one and our members have already done so well in securing recent appointments that we trust even more may find good appointments in the Dark Continent that is being so rapidly developed.

LIBRARY ASSOCIATION SUMMER SCHOOL.

The prizes for the best reports of the lectures on subjects connected with Library administration delivered at the meeting of the North-Western Summer School, held at Wigan in June last, have been awarded as follows :—First Prize, Mr. SYDNEY A. FIRTH, of the Public Library, Birkenhead. Second Prize, Mr. F. W. B. HOWARTH, of the Public Library, Manchester.

STUDY CIRCLE.
GENERAL REPORT FOR NOVEMBER.

The best answers to the Literary History questions were those of " Ami " (*Senior*) and " Mowgli " (*Junior*), whilst to the questions in Library Practice, " Nemo " (*Senior*) and " Quo " (*Junior*) contributed the answers of highest standard.

The Literary History " Bonne foi " was careless in composition, and " Pro Patria's " meaning is obscure in places. " C. A." " Puer," " Quo " and " Scott " having simply transcribed their answers, were disqualified. " Spitzbergen " mentions no dates, and " Tamesis II." sent too short an answer.

In Library Practice the senior answers are open to grave objection, principally in that they rely upon the borrowers notifying cases of infectious disease. The only safe method is to have notifications sent direct from the Medical Officer for the district. The junior answers are also unsatisfactory, students giving too much prominence to the " Encyclopædia Britannica." Several modern works relating to Afghanistan are almost entirely neglected. Only one student mentions Raverty, and several of the books suggested are antiquated and superseded.

GENERAL REPORT FOR DECEMBER.

The best answers to the Literary History questions are from " Bonne foi " (*Senior*) and " Puer " (*Junior*), whilst the best answers to Library Practice are those from " Pro Patria " (*Senior*) and " Savoy " (*Junior*).

In Literary History "C.A." is weak in composition, "Spitzbergen's" paper shows lack of thought, and "Tamesis II.," again, is too eager to condense his answer. "Quo" answered the question very intelligently. In Library Practice "Ami" and "Bonne foi" overlook the "Museums and Gymnasiums Act." "Nemo" mentions this, but is not quite conversant with the powers of the Act. The junior answers may satisfy the letter but not the spirit of the question. Only "Savoy" gives any reason for the choice of material. The answers of "C. A." and "Puer" are insufficient.

RESULTS OF THIRD SESSION.
Number of Marks obtained.

Senior Division.		Junior Division.	
"Nemo"	451 marks	"Savoy"	555 marks
"Ami"	442 ,,	"Quo"	435 ,,
"Pro Patria"	405 ,,	"Puer"	405 ,,
*"Bonne foi"	285 ,,	"Spitzbergen"	375 ,,
†"Adsum"	143 ,,	*"Mowgli"	355 ,,
		"C.A."	340 ,,
		"Tamesis II."	305 ,,
		†"Coddam'	170 ,,
		†"Stebenhithe"	110 ,,
		†"Scott"	50 ,,

* 2 month's work.   † 1 month's work.

The Education Committee therefore award the Senior Prize, Morley's "Victorian Literature," to "Nemo," Mr. Richard Iveson, of the Leeds Public Libraries, and the Junior Prize, "Scott's Poetical Works" to "Savoy," Mr. Douglas A. Gillespie, of the Westminster Public Libraries.

GENERAL PRIZES TO S.C. STUDENTS.

The United States Bureau of Education have forwarded to the Hon. Sec. a copy of Cutter's "Rules for a Dictionary Catalog" for *each* student, and all who have contributed papers to the Study Circle will receive a copy upon forwarding two penny stamps to the Hon. Sec., L.A.A, not later than Jan. 21st.

FOURTH SESSION.
READINGS FOR JANUARY.

*Brooke's "Primer of English Literature." *Chap.* viii.
Morley's English Literature in the reign of Victoria." *Chap.* vii.
Saintsbury's Nineteenth Century Literature. *Chap.* iii.
Also contemporary biographical matter (*Senior and Junior divisions*).
* Junior.

QUESTIONS ON DECEMBER READINGS :—
 1. Literary History.
  Senior. "Give a brief account of the early Nineteenth Century essayists."
  Junior. "State the most important historical works written in the first quarter of the nineteenth century."

2. Library Practice.
   Senior. "Mention such as you can of the most important systems of classification and state wherein they differ."
   Junior. "Should Public Library books be stamped?"
   NOTE. Students should attempt *one*, if not both of the questions, in order to obtain marks for the *Annual* Prize. The loss of a prize is honourable, but lack of perseverance is a bad quality in any library assistant.
   Answers to this month's questions must be sent to the Hon. Secretary on or before Saturday, January 18th.

* HOW TO POPULARISE A PUBLIC LIBRARY.
By WILLIAM J. HARRIS.

Many and various are the methods which may be employed, though too often left unemployed unfortunately, to popularise our Public Libraries, which without the skilful steerage of a masterhand at the helm show but a sorry result for the money that is spent upon them. Libraries require as much advertising in their own particular way as any business, and the Librarian should look to it (as of course the energetic and zealous librarian does) that his library, *though not himself*, is kept well before the public's eyes. Then with judicious administration and thoughtful organisation, the library should do some good work.

With regard to situation, the library should be placed as near as possible in the centre of the town or district which it is intended to serve, and should occupy a prominent position in a main or business thoroughfare. It is desired to place knowledge within easy access of the ignorant, not to make them search for it in hidden places. How often is a Public Library stowed away in some by street, while the earnest stranger enquires, often with small success, its whereabouts of the surrounding yet apathetic borrowers.

One great influence which tends to make a library popular is the friendly and helpful courtesy with which a librarian and his staff meet the public. It should be the ever earnest endeavour of the library staff to make the stranger welcome, by instructing him or her in the principles upon which the library is worked.

The administration of the library should be reduced to simplicity from the borrowers' point of view, and the fewer the rules the better. As most librarians with experience know, the public are not fond of rules; therefore the wise librarian will meet them as far as possible on this point as on all others.

The library should be fully catalogued, and the catalogue kept up to date by the means of a card cabinet. This saves

* "Cotgreave" (1901) Prize Essay.

endless unnecessary enquiries. Every library should set aside a special section for young readers, and the age limit should be as low as possible. Juvenile readers should be invited and encouraged by the providing of a good selection of sound and wholesome literature for their use, and the preparation of a special catalogue by means of which their choice may be guided, and the work of selection made lighter for them. Neighbouring schoolmasters' co-operation should be solicited to complete the valuable work of attracting the young to the library. Some libraries circulate boxes of books in the neighbouring schools, under the supervision of one of the masters, and the boxes are changed periodically.

No library is complete without its musical section. This adds much to the recreative side of the utility of public libraries. The selection should consist of standard operas, oratorios and orchestral scores, besides works on the theory and practice of music.

The librarian should persuade the local papers (and this is not difficult where tact is used) to publish the newest list of books added to the library. Few local editors would prove obstinate if approached in the right spirit. Lists also should be prepared of books dealing with the topics of the day. Statistics of library work should be sent to the local papers, thus keeping the library in public notice. It is advisable, too, to study the syllabuses of the local literary and scientific societies, and to bring before their notice a list of books contained in the library, dealing with their special subjects. This would probably secure members' patronage, besides assisting and advancing them.

Readers and borrowers should be interested in the history and topography of their own neighbourhood. Collections of prints and sketches of the district should be hung on the walls of the reading room, and supplemented in the reference library by all possible local literature.

Some libraries are conducting series of lectures by professional lecturers. This interests and attracts the public.

The contents of all the magazines, etc., taken in the library should be placed on a convenient notice board in the various rooms for the benefit of intending readers.

Writing tables with accessories, such as pens, ink, pencils, etc., placed under proper supervision, should be an advantage and assistance, which the public would not be slow to seize.

The issuing of *bulletins*, either quarterly or bi-monthly, when properly or intelligently conducted, unquestionably tends to arouse public interest in the library.

The lending department, the most important side of the

library, should contain only the best works, and these in ample quantity. No books should be harboured on the shelves which do not circulate. These should be removed to the basement, and replaced by books which will circulate. Books are not ornaments for shelves, but tools for readers. Many present existing libraries would be the better for such a clearance and replacement.

The one great ideal of the librarian should be, to *give*, or assist to give, *culture*, which before he can give, he must possess. Librarians cannot attach too much importance to the acquisition of culture. A librarian should also make the library bright enough to attract all classes of the community. And here a word might be added. A library will never become popular or well patronised without it contains in abundance those three great essentials to comfort: *warmth*, *light* and *cleanliness*. However well stocked the library may be with books, the librarian will never induce his public to sit in cold and draughty, or ill-lighted and uncleanly rooms. Therefore let him look to it that his library attract his public in this respect. Let him, also, be ever ready to help the ignorant in their choice of books, and ever courteous to all, and thereby gain both his readers' respect and popularise the library.

NOTES AND NEWS.

Study Circle.—With this month's issue begins the Fourth Session of the Study Circle. This is the commencement of a new year's work, and intending students should make themselves acquainted with the particulars contained in our September and October issues.

Donation to the L.A.A. Library.—Mr. Cockerell has presented a copy of his recently issued text book on "Book binding and the care of books," to which we drew attention last month.

Society of Public Librarians.—At a meeting held at the Bishopsgate Institute on Wednesday evening, December 4th, Mr. C. Whitwell (West Ham) read a paper entitled, "Notes on juvenile literature of the 18th and 19th centuries."

Mile End.—The Library is to be opened on January 9th by Canon Barnett, Warden of Toynbee Hall.

NEW MEMBERS.

Senior.—BUDDERY, E. E. (West Ham).
Junior.—BEER, F. A. R. (West Ham): BLACKMORE, C. F. (Stoke Newington); LEIGHTON, T. (West Ham).

APPOINTMENTS AND CHANGES.

*CHAMBERLAIN, F. Arthur. Transferred from Rotherhithe to Bermondsey Central Library as 2nd Assistant.

*HARRADINE, F. C. Junior Assistant, Leyton, to be Assistant, Poplar Library, E.

*MATTOCKS, S. G., Assistant, Hampstead, to be Assistant Librarian, Kimberley Public Library, South Africa.

*Members of the Library Assistants' Association.

BOOKS, &c., RECEIVED.

Leyton Public Libraries Magazine (Quarterly), No. 13, November, 1901. *Edited* by Z. Moon, F.R. Hist. S., Librarian.

Manchester Public Libraries, 49th Annnal Report, 1900-1.

West Ham Public Libraries Quarterly Notes, July-September, 1901. *Edited* by A. Cotgreave, F.R. Hist. S., Chief Librarian.

Stoke Newington Public Second Supplementary Catalogue, 8vo., pp. 1-11 and 112 price 3d. Contains the titles of 3,500 volumes added during the period, Aug. 1900-Nov. 1901.

APPOINTMENTS VACANT.

[**Notice to Library Authorities.**—*We shall be pleased to publish under this heading, free of charge, particulars of vacancies if full details are sent to the Editor on or before the 25th of each month.*]

BOROUGH OF LEWISHAM.
PUBLIC LIBRARIES COMMITTEE.

The Committee require the services of a Sub-Librarian at a salary of £100 per annum to take charge of the Branch Library at Lee. Previous experience in Public Library work and organisation essential. Applicants must not be under 21 or over 25 years of age.

Applications in candidate's own hand writing to be made on printed forms to be obtained from the undersigned, accompanied by copies of not more than three recent testimonials, which are to be sent in and endorsed "Application—Sub-Librarian" on or before Monday, January 13th, 1902.

The appointment will be made subject to the rules and regulations of the Council from time to time in force, and subject to medical examination.

Canvassing is prohibited.

EDWARD WRIGHT,
Town Clerk.

LEWISHAM TOWN HALL,
CATFORD, S.E.
19th December, 1901.

NOTICES.

Annual subscriptions to the L.A.A. are now due, and should be sent to Mr. W. Geo. Chambers, *Hon. Treasurer*, Public Library, Woolwich. Members of the N.W. Branch should send their subscriptions to Mr. W. Crompton, Y.M.C.A. Library, Manchester.

All matter for the February number should reach the Hon. Editor on or before 20th January.

All other communications should be addressed to the *Hon. Secretary*, Mr. G. E. Roebuck, 121 DE BEAUVOIR ROAD, KINGSLAND, N.

The Library Assistant:
The Official Organ of the Library Assistants' Association.

No. 50.   FEBRUARY, 1902.   Published Monthly

THE LIBRARY ASSISTANTS' ASSOCIATION.
FOUNDED 1895.   SEVENTH SESSION.   YEAR 1901-1902.

Members are requested to read carefully the announcements appearing on this and the following pages, as no further intimation of meetings and other arrangements may be expected.

FEBRUARY MEETING.

The next meeting of this Association will be held at the Newington Public Library, Walworth Road, S.E., on Wednesday, February 26th, at 8.0 p.m. The Librarian, Mr. R. W. Mould, F.S.A., Scot., to whom we are indebted for this kind invitation, has further favoured us by promising to address the meeting. Mr. Mould's paper will be entitled "Our Work," and will form a continuation of the paper read by him at a meeting in a former session.

NOTE.—This will be the third meeting held in South London this Session, the Committee being desirous of arranging the programme for the special advantage of Assistants south of the river. It is earnestly hoped that a good attendance will show an appreciation of Mr. Mould's kindness and the endeavour of the Committee to meet the wishes of all members of the L.A.A.

SOCIAL GATHERING.

The Annual Social Gathering of members and friends will take place at St. Bride's Institute, Bride Lane, Ludgate Circus, E.C., on Wednesday, **March 25th**, at *7.30 p.m. sharp.*

The evening's entertainment will consist of a concert and dance.

It is hoped that members will keep this date open and attend with as many friends as possible, ladies being especially welcome.

Admission will be by programme, to be obtained at the Hall on the evening.

THE JANUARY MEETING.

The January meeting was held on Wednesday, the 15th, at the Central Public Library, Battersea, on the invitation of Mr. Lawrence Inkster, the Chief Librarian. Mr. Rees, who occupied the chair, in opening the meeting, explained that it was hoped that Mr. Inkster would preside, but owing to an official engagement he was sorry that he would be unable to do so. He sent his best wishes for the continued prosperity of the Association, and hoped the meeting would be an enjoyable one, and that he would be able to be present when the Association again visited Battersea. Mr. Chennell, Librarian of the Willesden Green Public Library, on rising to read his paper, explained that since the announcement of the meeting in the *Library Assistant*, he had decided to read a paper on "The Woes of a Librarian." "The Pleasures of a Librarian," he thought, would be more fitting for a future paper, the woes of all professions, and especially that of Librarianship, having to be counted with first, and the pleasures came as a sequel. From a synopsis of the paper, which will be found on another page, it will be seen that it was of a very entertaining nature, and came as a pleasant contrast to the previous papers of this session. About 30 members were present, and a short discussion took place, in which Messrs. Chambers, Harris, Hogg, Soper, and P. H. Wood took part. Mr. Chennell, in replying to a vote of thanks, regretted that owing to the limited accommodation at Willesden Green, he was unable to invite the Association there, but hoped that when the projected extensions were completed, he would be able to do so. He thanked those present for the pleasure it gave him to lecture to the Association, and for the attention given to his paper. The meeting concluded with a hearty vote of thanks to Mr. Inkster for the use of the room, which Mr. Hogg, the Sub-Librarian, kindly undertook to convey on behalf of the Association.

N.W. BRANCH—JANUARY MEETING.

The second bi-monthly meeting was held in the Athenæum Library, Manchester, on January 15th, 1902, Mr. J. H. Swann in the chair.

In response to the invitations for short papers, etc., the Chairman read a short paper on "Librarianship as a profession," in which he compared librarianship with the recognised professions, and pointed out the radical differences.

This paper was followed by another from Mr. W. Quarmby, entitled, "Bettering ourselves." A vigorous discussion arose upon each paper, chiefly on raising the status of librarianship, and providing means to improve the prospects of assistants, the following members taking part in the debate:—Messrs. P. D. Gordon, Hy. Seed, J. D. Dickens, W. H. Berry, F. W. B. Haworth, W. H. Shawcross, Hy. Percival, and Geo. Fletcher.

Mr. Gordon placed before the meeting a copy of Mudie's new classified Fiction Catalogue for inspection. Owing to the time having been fully taken up by the preceding business, this did not receive the attention it deserved, but we may have another opportunity for discussing the merits of classified fiction.

W. Q.

N.W. BRANCH. MARCH MEETING.
The third bi-monthly meeting of this Branch will be held in the Central Library, Oldham, on Wednesday, March 19th. For times of trains and other arrangements see March number. Members who have not yet applied for a copy of the *British Library Year Book* are requested to do so without delay.

OPENING OF THE MILE END LIBRARY.

Thursday, January 9th, was an important day in the annals of Mile End, for the inhabitants saw fulfilled in the opening ceremony of the Public Library their hopes and aspirations of six years ago.

It was on February 5th, 1896, that the Public Libraries Acts were adopted. For three years previously the Governors of the People's Palace had been negotiating with the late Vestry of Mile End Old Town for the transfer to the latter body of the library at the above institution, but it was found that there were legal difficulties in the way, and in 1899 negotiations were finally abandoned.

In April of last year the Stepney Borough Council directed the Libraries Committee to consider if the Vestry Hall in Bancroft Road could be adapted for a Public Library. The Committee submitted plans prepared by the Borough Engineer, which were adopted by the Council, and the alterations have been carried out, and bookcases and newspaper stands provided, at a cost of £250.

The Library occupies two floors, and consists of lending and reference departments and reading room. In the lending department provision has been made for the shelving of about 12,000 volumes. The reference department will seat 20 readers and will accommodate 3,000 volumes. The reading room, which was formerly the Council Chamber, is lighted on three sides by lofty windows, and is undoubtedly one of the finest reading rooms in London.

Mr. F. Meaden Roberts, who organised the St. George-in-the-East Library, has been appointed Librarian, and hopes to have all the departments in proper working order in the course of a few weeks.

The opening ceremony was performed by the Rev. Canon Barnett, Warden of Toynbee Hall, and the pioneer of Public Libraries in East London. The Mayor (Alderman E. Mann, J.P.) presided, and was supported by most of the influential gentlemen of the Borough.

Canon Barnett in the course of his remarks said that they had given him a very pleasing duty; they had given him an inspiring subject. Books had played a great part in the making of nations. He looked forward to the future when generations to come would look back upon England and look on her as great, not because of her millions, but because of her Shakespeares. A book in a very intimate way was a man's best friend, and a library was a court where Kings and Queens were always on their thrones. And that court was open to all comers, and those who entered it might come into close contact with Kings and Queens. In a library one becomes conscious of the higher passions which were at work all around, and the higher aims which were in the minds of people, and he hoped the people of Mile End would enter that library and feel themselves refreshed.

This addition to the Public Institutions of the East End completes the circle of Libraries for the Borough of Stepney, the others being situated at Limehouse, St. George-in-the-East, and Whitechapel, thus making Stepney one of the best equipped as far as Libraries are concerned, of the London Boroughs.

B. J. H.

GLASGOW PUBLIC LIBRARIES.—RANKIN READING ROOM.

The Rankin Reading Room was opened to the public on 15th January, and will now be open daily from 9 a.m. till 10 p.m. This public reading room has been established in execution of a bequest by the late Mr. John Rankin, portioner, of Armadale Street, Dennistoun, who died 27th March, 1897, leaving to the Lord Provost and Magistrates property of about £3,000 value to be devoted to some object of public utility in the old Second Ward of the City. The testator specified a public bath or a public reading room as among the purposes to which the bequest might be applied, and his benevolent intention has been realised by the co-operation of the Magistrates with the Committee on Baths and Washhouses and the Committee on Libraries. A suitable though small reading room has been provided in the extensive new Baths building in Whitevale Street, the cost of the construction of the room being paid out of the Rankin bequest. The balance of the bequest has been transferred by the Magistrates to the Committee on Libraries, by whom it will be used as a partial provision for the cost of maintenance and administration, the cost over and above the produce of the bequest being defrayed from the rate levied for public library purposes.

THE WOES OF A LIBRARIAN.
BY FRANK E. CHENNELL.
[*Synopsis of a Paper read at the January meeting of "The Library Assistants' Association."*]

It is with much hesitancy and doubt that I approach my subject. Can I reasonably expect that Assistants will see other than *pleasure* in the position of Librarian? and dare I hope that they will acknowledge that *their* respective Chiefs encounter any *woes* in the exercise of their duties? I would ask you as Assistants *not* to claim a monopoly of our professional tribulations, but to bear with me while I endeavour to expound a few of those that trouble the soul of the Librarian.

I have entitled my reading—"A Librarian's woes," and trust the expression is not too strong for the petty troubles I relate. I must confess that I have chosen it for much the same reason as that which constrained "Sam Slick" to shave with a black-lead brush; he could find no other brush, and I—could find no other title.

We are all aware that the general opinion on the side of the counter that is not ours, is, that the Librarian's position is one of ease, if not of luxury,—that he has no woes, no troubles, no tribulations. I have said I fear even Assistants share this opinion. Every Librarian is acquainted with the Reader who imagines that the only onerous duties we have to perform are those of handing a borrower a book over the counter in much the same way as a shop assistant across the way will proffer him a packet of tea. Oh! that he could but lift the veil a wee bit, and experience himself a few of the sorrows that assail the Librarian!

My remarks, in this paper, apply more particularly to the young Librarian recently evolved from a Senior Assistant. One of your members addressed you at your last meeting upon the best way to organize, and more especially to popularize our Libraries. I simply intend to remind you of a few of the troubles the organizer will encounter when he may be considered to have completed the initial portion of his organization.

His treasures being safely housed, the first woe which will befall him is the preparation of a Catalogue. Classification and other minor details will not trouble him to any great extent. In matters such as these, he will probably follow the system he has been conversant with under his late Chief.

The Catalogue is, however, quite another matter, and may cause him endless worry. It is generally found that a newly-fledged Librarian pins his faith to the Catalogue compiled upon the dictionary system. For a small, or indeed a medium-sized Library, it is no doubt the best form of index to the contents of the shelves. Having, however, made up his mind upon this point, here commence a few of his woes. There are so many points to bear constantly in mind, so many pitfalls to avoid, if the Catalogue is to lay claim to consistency. Should his Library be above the average size of the Institution to which an Assistant generally succeeds, he is hampered and hindered in his compilation by fears lest his Catalogue should get too bulky. He has nightmares of disagreeable Committees over its excessive cost. Then, he remorsefully cuts, prunes, and generally mutilates his copy until his fond dream of an ideal Dictionary Catalogue loses itself in the horrid reality of a printer's heavy bill.

Should it be an Institution with a meagre stock of books, say seven to ten thousand volumes, then the advocate of the Dictionary Catalogue is in his element. He is an astute man and sees clearly how easily his pint of peas can be made to fill a quart measure. Subjects are multiplied and cross references ingeniously inserted. A book upon the Grey Parrot for instance offers him boundless visions of expansion. It can be placed under parrot, ornithology, birds, with cross-references, until it would seem that the most obtuse reader, desirous of consulting the book, cannot but find "pretty poll."

From a reader's point of view—and we should aim to study readers—this after all is the way to catalogue. The Librarian must only beware lest from excess of zeal he should be tempted to emulate the indexer employed by St. George Mivart. The last named gentleman, a few years ago, wrote a book entitled "The origin of human reason." Many of you possess a copy of the work in your respective Libraries. In it there is an amusing story of a Cockatoo. The reader who looks at the index cannot fail to find all about this wonderful bird. The anecdote is indexed in no fewer than 15 places. Please do not imagine that I think either of you would go to this extent in cataloguing, but seriously, what a source of worry and trouble cross references are. There are those to avoid, and those to be inserted at all hazards. Those appropriate, and those decidedly inappropriate. In the latter category we must place the entry, which appeared in a catalogue, a short time ago, God *see* Fiske, which, to my mind gives an unduly exalted position to the humble author of "The idea of God as affected by modern knowledge," and implies a corresponding abasement of the Deity. Cross-references have, moreover, a deplorable habit of wandering from the subject they are desired to point to.

Then there is the unutterable worry caused our Librarian by the printer. Most worthy typographer! Many of us have had sad experience of his manifold pranks. Many of you, gentlemen, have yet to experience them. The clean revise passed for press, and, later on, the almost miraculous appearance of errors which did not exist in any earlier proof. The dropping of a letter, a word, or errors due to wrong distribution are excusable. Everyone who dabbles in print suffers from such accidents. Even a prominent London daily newspaper a short time ago wound up an article in favour of women's rights with an impassioned appeal in support of women's tights! This is a digression. To return to the main point I must say that many of the printer's vagaries pass beyond one's understanding.

While talking of Catalogues I should like to mention that errors must frequently exist in the Librarian's "copy." The following are a few errors, taken at random, from a recently published catalogue of a provincial library. I think you will admit they are not mistakes to be imputed to the printer :—

Confessions of St. Agustine. *Edited by Routledge & Sons.*
Hermit in London. The ditto in the Country (all in one line).
Leaves from the journal of our life in the *Islands*
     More ditto
W. Musters apprenticeship (Author unknown but Transl. by
     Carlyle)
Paris and its scences!
Teachings of Epicteus!
Essays on various subjects by *the Lord of* Montaigne!

Though I know but little about *you* the acquaintance with the work of the Librarian cited compels me to unhesitatingly suggest that future catalogues of this Institution would be better entrusted to Assistants.

Of course errors exist in every catalogue, and living as I do, in an extremely frail glass house, I am very loth to throw stones. I can only hope that you will agree that the errors I have cited are blemishes of negligence, and not accident.

May I also suggest that many are perchance due to faulty handwriting? Please do not deem even this matter beneath your notice. I am convinced that one sure way to avoid these errors is to ensure that every catalogue slip is not only correctly, but legibly written. It is true Hawthorne was proud of his illegible scrawl and fancied it author-like, and that Byron, Hugo and others took pride in their spider-like endeavours at writing. We need not emulate them, nor indeed need we copy Hawthorne's American friend who once wrote an undecipherable epistle to his son at Yale University. To help him to make some sense of the scrawl the lad called in a fellow student, who must have been somewhat of a wag. His only remark was to the effect that it looked remarkably like a Doctor's prescription and suggested consulting a Chemist. They hied forthwith to an apothecary, who threw a quick glance over the letter, stood some moments in subdued thought, and then began to pour from several bottles into a phial. The phial was now half-full. Then came a dubious pause. The Clerk scratched his head and finally baffled, appealed to the proprietor of the store. A short, low dialogue took place. Then, the Chief with an air of superior wisdom, uncorked another bottle, filled the phial with an apocryphal liquid, and labelled it in proper form. " Fifteenpence for the cough mixture " he said with a friendly smile!

Apart from the worry connected with the printer, there is another woe appertaining to the catalogue. After carefully estimating that our proposed catalogue will make, say, 100 pages and cost £60, with what trepidation and woe begone faces do we submit the final account to the Committee when we discover that the venture has reached 170 pages and the bill swelled to nearly £100.

Passing rapidly on there is a matter which no doubt distresses Librarians, and if they are conscientious in their work, causes them much anxiety. I refer to the selecting of books for purchase. When preparing lists of proposed additions I often ponder and wonder what methods other Librarians have for the choice of fit and proper books to augment their Libraries. What are their guides to the good, the bad, the indifferent. We are all led, to a great extent, indeed, in many instances, entirely, by reviews, and I am tempted to enquire, what is the true value of the majority of these press notices. How frequently do we find, what the "*Saturday*" flays the "*Spectator*" extols, what the "*Academy*" condemns the "*Athenæum*" lauds. If we trust entirely to reviews and reviewers, then, I think, we must beware of pitfalls. Reviewers are but human. Could we fathom the reasons for many a harsh criticism there would be found, no doubt, motives which could compel us to admit the criticism as unjust. Among the motives, religious differences, political divergencies, and too often disappointed ambition. But in these matters we are, I fear, between "The devil and the deep sea." If we fail to read reviews, we may, among other evils, place upon our shelves works of doubtful morality published under the guise of fiction. If we do read them then I contend it is too often a most difficult task to discriminate among the variety of opinions expressed concerning one and the same book. What can we now think of the Edinburgh Reviewers and their treatment of Keats, Shelley, Byron, and Wordsworth; the great Macaulay was called an "insolent puppy" and "one of the most obscure men of the age" because forsooth his opinions did not coincide with those held by the publishers of the reviews. What can we now think of Voltaire's opinion of Milton—"A barbarian who constructed a long Commentary on the first chapter of Genesis in 10 books of harsh verse." This latter was not a review, but, what a striking example of the utter worthlessness of the press notice, is the position in literature now held by the former. There is ample scope for a paper upon the value of reviews. I throw the subject out as a suggestion to any ambitious member of the Assistants' Association in need of material for a Reading. In my opinion there is only one way out of this review quandary, and that, to ignore so far as possible any notice that is not author-signed, and to seek these notices in periodicals of the highest repute. This special woe of the Librarian includes so many minor details. There are, as I have stated, books to be purchased new. Reviews, such as they may be will aid him here. There are, however, in addition, one thousand and one works, which he must watch, and wait, and pray for. Standard works out of print, and which can only be procured by closely scanning the catalogues of second-hand books. Upon the acquiring of these the Librarian must be prepared to expend a vast amount of time. Should he, even, through these means obtain a desired volume he has to guard against imperfections, and collating is a worry and trouble—a work which in instances such as these the Librarian must personally undertake. He is further called upon to distinguish between the original edition and the artful, subtle reprint. He has to guard against spurious editions. The catalogue of literary forgeries is a long one.

Then there is a "Woe" which until this morning, I had no intention of introducing into my reading. It, however, keenly affects Assistants, and, a woe, I am sorry to say, Librarians are often responsible for. I refer to the increase of lady workers in the Library. I am by no means opposed to the employment of female assistants in—exceeding moderation. I received, however, this morning, a letter from which I learn that it is generally understood that when a male senior leaves a certain Library his place is to be filled up by the appointment of a female junior assistant—reserving, I suppose for the mere man the post of Sub-Librarian and Chief Assistants. Now whether this be fair to Librarians does not interest me. The ubiquitous female now competes in every calling. The Assistants' remedy is to outstrip them in efficiency, or,—marry them. What does concern me is the effect it may have upon a profession which has still to be numbered among those called learned. If many Libraries follow the example of the one I have cited the number of training schools for future librarians will slowly decrease. The number of coming men will be thinned. Competition for senior positions will therefore be less keen because fewer qualified candidates will be available. A fall in competition invariably entails a lower standard of efficiency. We need a higher standard, the Assistants' Association exists I believe, to further this. Their "libraical" battle-cry is the same as the recent political one—"Efficiency."

Another of our woes is the Assistant himself, and here I know I am treading on dangerous ground "where Angels fear to tread." However, it is not my intention to use strong language against these gentlemen, nor do I wish to "damn with faint praise." There are Assistants, and Assistants. Taken as a body, I firmly believe they are as hard working and ambitious a school of strivers as one could desire in any profession. I do not say this because I am addressing assistants. It is a conviction which must force itself upon every Librarian. The class of youngster I wish to mention is the careless inconsequent youth fresh from the palatial buildings, an extravagant government now erect for a system of cramming without parallel in the history of our country. The youth, who even Mr. Philip deems unworthy to exercise himself in your deliberations; "He's an absent-minded beggar and his weaknesses are great," and to Kiplingize still further "We have to take him as we find him." But what a source of worry he too frequently is. Of course the lad progresses in point of age, ability and intelligence, and (if he joins the Assistants' Association) soon commences to take a deep interest in his work and in the Institution. Here, however, is where our woe commences. The income of the library will not permit of a salary at all commensurate with his age and usefulness and he quickly seeks new and greener pastures. Or, if we try, as I hope we all do, to do our duty by the lad we assist him to promotion in another, and a larger library. In either case the result is the same—we have to enlist and to train a raw recruit. To librarians in large or well staffed institutions this woe will not commend itself. They probably hand over the new comer to a Senior Assistant. To others, who must for years remain poorly staffed the discomfort and worries are, believe me, apparent and serious. The difficulty, I need hardly say, is merely a financial one.

The limited income precluding not only the quantity but the quality. So much for the Assistant woe, and I must hurry on. But another "woe," paradoxical though it may seem, is the Librarian himself. Please do not think I am specially criticising anyone. It is to a great extent self analytical. I really think that, as Librarians, we are too prone to fence ourselves around with an amount of reserve. A deep knowledge of literature is possessed by few, indeed, it can nowadays only be held by those whose daily avocation is centred in books, or whose hobby is their collection and study. A librarian's knowledge, from mere handling alone, is sure to be extensive and we are perhaps too ready to deride the unfortunate borrower who demands "The Autocrat at the breakfast table," by Sherlock Holmes or "Oliver Goldsmith" by the Vicar of Wakefield! I have myself heard Librarians, and indeed Assistants sneer at the reader who has given utterance to similar lapses, much to the latter's discomfort, but sadder, to his discouragement. I admit the temptation to do so is great. The British public credits our profession with but slight erudition. When, therefore, a member of the Great B P does slip, it is perhaps difficult to restrain from acquainting him with his fall. Let us, however, be tolerant in these matters and not smile at the ignorance of many of our readers in matters literary. If any profession should be renowned for broadmindedness in word, thought, and deed, I think, Gentlemen, it should be ours.

[*Owing to the limited space at our disposal it was found necessary to considerably abridge Mr. Chennell's paper, which will account for its discontinuity.*—ED. "L.A."]

STUDY CIRCLE.
REPORT ON JANUARY WORK.

The best answers to the Literary History questions are those of "Alfaro" (*Senior*) and "Livre" (*Junior*). The adjudicators specially commend the answers of "Quiver" and "Black Ink" and "Leno." "R. Peggio" does not mention Hallam. The best answers in Library Practice are from "Simple Simon" (*Senior*) and "Leno" (*Junior*), "Bonne foi" overlooks several important systems of classification, although the particular description given in his paper is accurate. "Black Ink" and "Mystax" are advised to be more careful with composition and spelling. The answer from "Jorrocks" is very good.

FOURTH SESSION.
QUESTIONS ON JANUARY WORK.

Senior 1.—Give a general sketch of the literary history of England from 1800 to 1825. (Not to exceed 1,000 words.)
    2.—Do you consider lectures in libraries to be a legitimate extension of library work? State your reasons.

Junior 1.—State what you know of Percy Bysshe Shelley and his work.
    2.—Define the meaning of a "cross-reference," and tabulate as far as you can the instances where cross-references are needed.

READING FOR FEBRUARY.

Commencement of 2nd period of 19th century literary history—1825-1850.
*Morley. "English Literature in the reign of Victoria." *Chaps.* I-VI.
*Saintsbury. "Nineteeth Century Literature." *Chaps.* III. V. & VI.
    *Both divisions.

MR. MACALISTER'S ANNUAL S.C. PRIZES.

On the inauguration of the Study Circle, Mr. J. Y. W. Macalister very kindly offered an annual prize of £1 to the student who gained the highest number of marks during the year. Mr. Macalister has since further favored our students by offering TWO prizes of £1 each, such to be awarded to the Senior and the Junior who have attained the highest position in their respective divisions. In addition to this, he also offered Vol. I. of the " Library " as second prizes (one for each division). The Education Committee therefore announce Mr. Alfred Edwards, of the Liverpool Public Libraries, as *Senior* winner of the £1 prize, and Mr. J. McKnight, of the Wigan Public Libraries, as *Junior* first-prizeman. The two copies of the " Library " are awarded to Mr. P. D. Gordon (our late Hon. Sec. N.W. Branch), and to Mr. F. Dallimore, of the Wigan Public Libraries, they having gained the second highest number of marks in their respective divisions. We heartily congratulate these gentlemen, and feel sure that the fact that such marked interest in S.C. results being taken by the heads of our profession will add largely to the competition in this and future sessions. The L.A.A. are very grateful to Mr. Macalister for his practical interest and assistance.

NOTE.—Particulars of competition are given in our September and October issues, or may be had from the Hon. Sec. L.A.A., to whom all answers must be sent *on or before* Friday, February 14th.

Cutter's Rules will be sent to those members who competed in *last* session's work, on receipt of two penny stamps to defray postage. Please apply early.

NOTES AND NEWS.

Battersea.—The Council has adopted the Museums Act, which will come into force in April next.

Brentford.—The Committee has arranged an excellent course of popular lectures on literary and antiquarian subjects. Mr. Chas. Welch, F.S.A., Librarian of the Guildhall, Mr. A. A. Barkas, Librarian of Richmond, and Mr. F. Turner, F.R. Hist. S., Librarian of Brentford, are amongst the lecturers.

Colonial Appointments.—From a New Zealand paper we gather that the Wellington Council recently advertised for a Librarian at £200 per annum. Previous experience is not mentioned as a qualification, so we conclude that there is a lack of trained men in this progressive Colony. We venture to think that many a trained man from the mother country would have been glad of the opportunity of applying for this vacancy had time permitted.

Edward Edwards.—A monument, the gift of Mr. T. Greenwood, is to be erected over the grave at Niton of the pioneer of the Public Library movement. Dr. Garnett will perform the ceremony on Feb. 5. Mr. Stanley Jast is conducting a party from London.

Hackney.—The Council has, by a majority of four, postponed the question of adopting the Public Libraries Acts for twelve months.

Leyton.—Among the many excellent little magazines which have of late years been issued from our Public Libraries, the Leyton "Library Magazine" takes a prominent place. We have before us the current number, which contains, besides a well-catalogued list of additions, an article entitled, *Aaron, the son of the devil*, and the continuation of a biographical index to the County of Essex. The former is interesting as referring to the earliest dated portrait of a Jew, which was "drawn on a forest-roll of the County of Essex," and which is reproduced with the article. The index is a very praiseworthy attempt to compile a list of Essex celebrities from the earliest times, and its exhaustiveness is shown by the fact that the end of letter "b" has not yet been reached, although it has been running through the last six numbers.

Montrose.—By the Provost's casting vote the Acts have been adopted, thus giving the town the advantage of Mr. Carnegie's offer to provide a building.

Oldham Free Lectures.—Members of the N.W. Branch, present at the meeting at Oldham last year, when Mr. Chas. Walters gave his lecture on Wm. Morris, will be pleased to hear that he is to lecture on Feb. 8th at seven o'clock, on "Tennyson's choice of Friends."

St. Pancras.—The motion for the adoption of the Public Libraries Acts has been withdrawn until a more favourable opportunity occurs.

Society of Public Librarians.—A meeting was held at the Bishopsgate Institute on Wednesday evening, Jan. 15th, 1902, when Mr. Z. Moon (Leyton) read a paper entitled "Langland and his work."

"Views and Memoranda of Public Libraries."—Mr. Cotgreave, the author of this useful work has intimated that he will supply members of the L.A.A. with copies at a reduced price of 7/6, if orders are sent direct to him.

Wandsworth.—The Acts have been extended to Tooting, and a reading room is to be opened there at an early date.

APPOINTMENTS AND CHANGES.

*CLARE, A. Junior Assistant, Oldham, to be Senior Assistant.

DAY, B. To be Junior Assistant, St. Saviour's Public Library.

ELLACOTT, H. To be Second Assistant, St. Saviour's Public Library.

HATCHER, A. To be Junior Assistant, Leyton Public Library.

*Member of the Library Assistants' Association.

NEW MEMBERS.

Senior.—NEESHAM, E. W. (Kendal).

Junior.—BOWRING, W. (Kensington); DAVISON, C. E. (Bermondsey); HARWOOD, W. (Stalybridge); ROBINSON, S. C. (Poplar).

BOOKS, &c., RECEIVED.

Chorley Public Library, Second Annual Report, 1900-01.
Penge Public Library. Final Report of the Commissioners to 31st March, 1901.
Manchester Public Libraries. Quarterly Record, Vol. V., No. 3.
Pratt Institute. Monthly. No. 2. Vol. X. December, 1901.
Views and Memoranda of Public Libraries, By Alfred Cotgreave, F.R.Hist.S. 4to. pp. I.-VI. 1-326. 450 illustrations. ports. and plans. 10 6.

The author does not claim anything of a literary character for this book, but hopes that as, owing to the munificence of many well-known gentlemen, and the public spirit of many corporations and local authorities, public libraries are springing up all over the country, such a work, the only one published of the kind, will be of considerable utility to library committees, librarians, architects, and all who are interested in these institutions. In arranging for the external appearance or planning of the various departments of a library, a work giving views and plans of many of the largest and most famous libraries, as also of smaller ones of every degree and kind, should prove useful in many ways. There is also a very useful statistical table giving the income, work, hours, etc., of all rate-supported libraries in the United Kingdom. Another feature which will be of great interest to many of our profession is the large number of excellent photographs of librarians of London and provincial libraries.

APPOINTMENTS VACANT.

[**Notice to Library Authorities.**—*We shall be pleased to publish under this heading, free of charge, particulars of vacancies if full details are sent to the Editor on or before the 28th of each month.*]

METROPOLITAN BOROUGH OF BERMONDSEY.
Applications are invited for the post of Librarian-in-Charge of the St. Olave Library. Previous experience essential. Salary £120 per annum. Applications, stating age and experience, with not more than three recent testimonials, endorsed " Librarian," to reach FREDK. RYALL, *Town Clerk*, Town Hall, Bermondsey, not later than February 8th.

NOTICES.

Annual subscriptions to the L.A.A. are now due, and should be sent to Mr. W. Geo. Chambers, *Hon. Treasurer*, Public Library, Woolwich. Members of the N.W. Branch should send their subscriptions to Mr. W. Crompton, Y.M.C.A. Library, Manchester. Other communications respecting the N.W. Branch should be addressed to Mr. W. Quarmby, Hon. Sec. Central Public Library, Oldham.

All matter for the March number should reach the *Hon. Editor* on or before 20th February.

All other communications should be addressed to the *Hon. Secretary*, Mr. G. E. Roebuck, 121 DE BEAUVOIR ROAD, KINGSLAND, N.

The Library Assistant:

The Official Organ of the Library Assistants' Association.

No. 51.　　　　MARCH, 1902.　　　　Published Monthly

THE LIBRARY ASSISTANTS' ASSOCIATION.

Founded 1895.　　Seventh Session.　　Year 1901-1902.

Members are requested to read carefully the announcements appearing on this and the following pages, as no further intimation of meetings and other arrangements may be expected.

MARCH MEETING.

The next Meeting of this Association will be held at Woolwich Public Library on Wednesday, March 19th, at 7.30 p.m., by kind invitation of Mr. H. Bond, the Borough Librarian.

A paper on "South African Librarianship," from the pen of our Colonial colleague, Mr. B. L. Dyer, of Kimberley, S.A., should insure a large attendance. Ladies and Library Assistants *not* members of the L.A.A. are cordially invited.

Refreshments will be provided.

Note.—At this meeting the vacancy on the Committee caused by the resignation of Mr. Macdougall (West Ham) will be filled.

Stations—South Woolwich on the G.E.R., Woolwich Arsenal on the S.E.R. The Library is situated in William Street.

SOCIAL GATHERING.

The Annual Social Gathering of members and friends will take place at St. Bride's Institute, Bride Lane, Ludgate Circus, E.C., on Wednesday, **March 5th (not March 25th, as announced last month)**, *at 7.30 p.m. sharp.*

The evening's entertainment will consist of a concert and dance.

It is hoped that members will keep this date open and attend with as many friends as possible, ladies being especially welcome.

Admission will be by programme, to be obtained at the Hall on the evening.

FEBRUARY MEETING.

The fifth meeting of the session, was, by permission of the Libraries' Committee of the Borough of Southwark, held at the Newington Public Library on February 26th.

The members were received by Mr. R. W. Mould, F.S.A., Scot., the Librarian, and were introduced to the Chairman of the Committee, Mr. Councillor Bryan, M.A., who had very kindly offered to conduct the Members over Browning Hall, now used as a Working Men's Club, but formerly an Independent Chapel.

This feature of the programme proved very interesting, and more particularly because it came as a surprise to most of those present.

Mr. Bryan explained that the Hall, the shell of which comprised part of a chapel built about 1790, derived its name from the connection of the Browning family with the district. Robert Browning, the father of the poet, married a Sarah Ann Wiedeman, who was a member of the congregation. The father of the poet lived at that time in Camberwell where, in 1812, the poet was born. In his early days Browning was a constant attendant at the chapel, and it would prove interesting to compare the influence of the teachings of the minister of that time on the writings of the poet. The Rev. Mr. Clayton held the pastorate in Browning's time, and it is recorded that he once publicly rebuked the poet from the pulpit for laughing and playing with his sister during the sermon. Southwark is naturally very proud of this and other notable literary connections. In the case of Browning, the Registers of the Parish proving these connections are still extant, but they nearly shared the fate of many similar registers, and were only rescued at the last moment by Mr. Bryan from a heap of rubbish which was about to be carted away. These were examined by the members present with considerable interest.

David Livingstone, the explorer, who at one time lived at Aldersgate, married the daughter of Dr. Moffat, who was connected with Browning Hall, and in the person of Captain James Wilson they had a churchwarden who in his early years boasted of his infidelity and his record as a pirate. He was reclaimed in middle life by the influence of the chapel, and acted as Hon. Captain of the ship which took the first missionaries, sent out by the London Missionary Society, to the South Sea Islands.

The members also visited the Public Baths, the largest of which is used in the winter by the Libraries' Committee for a series of lectures, which is a special feature of Mr. Mould's scheme.

Returning to the Library they partook of refreshments

generously provided by Mr. Mould, and afterwards adjourned to the spacious and comfortable Reference Library to listen to his excellent paper entitled *Our Work*. This proved a veritable well of information on Librarianship, and particularly of the departures made at Newington in order to thoroughly adapt the Library to the needs of the locality. We have obtained permission from Mr. Mould to publish a synopsis of his paper in an early issue for the benefit of our provincial members

An interesting evening closed with a vote of thanks, proposed by Mr. Soper and seconded by Mr. Chambers, to Mr. Mould for his kindness and for his useful paper, and to Mr. Councillor Bryan for presiding, proposed by Mr. Rees and seconded by Mr. Percy Wood.

Mr. Councillor Bryan in replying said that he had learnt many interesting and surprising facts concerning the work of a Librarian and his Assistants during the time he had been Chairman of the Committee, particularly from their able and energetic Librarian concerning the styles of catalogues, classification and other details, which he had never associated with the work of a Librarian. He thought it was little short of disgraceful that the men who had charge of the storehouse of knowledge and introduced to the public the thoughts of the great authors of all ages are not paid higher salaries than is paid to the men who collect the rubbish from the roads. He promised that when an opportunity presented itself he would do his best to alter this unsatisfactory state of affairs.

There were about forty members present.   H.T.S.

N.W. BRANCH—MARCH MEETING.

The next meeting will be held in the Central Library, Union Street, Oldham, on Wednesday, March 19th, at 7.45 p.m., when a paper will be read by Mr. C. Owen, Librarian in charge of the North-Moor Branch, entitled " The Free Library: the Workingman's University."

A short discussion will take place prior to the above on "The Notification of Diseases." Members intending to be present are requested to bring forms, used for such purposes, for distribution.

As the Spring Exhibition of Pictures is now open, members and their friends wishing to take this opportunity of visiting the same can travel from Manchester (Victoria) by any of the trains the times of which are given below.

Trains Out.					Return.				
Manchester.					Oldham.				
(Vict.) dept.	6.8	6.27	6.50	7.15	(Cenl.) dept.	9.33	9.37	10.12	
Oldham.					Manchester.				
(Cenl.) arr.	6.34	6.53	7.16	7.39	(Vict.) arr.	9.55	10.8	10.34	

EDITORIAL.
The Library Association Classes.

We notice with extreme satisfaction the alterations respecting the examinations which the Library Association announce in connection with the classes in Cataloguing and Classification which commenced last week. Soon after the end of the classes, we are informed, the official examination of the Library Association will be held. There will be no usual class examination, but all students will be expected to present themselves at the official examination in Section 2—Cataloguing, Classification, and Shelf Arrangement. This is a far more satisfactory arrangement than that previously in vogue. Under the old order successful students were not granted a certificate, but had to fall back upon the list of successful candidates published in *The Library Association Record* when occasions arose for them to prove that they had been through this important test of their abilities.

Of course we take it for granted that the Association will grant Provisional Certificates for each subject, and that when a student possesses a certain number of Provisional Certificates he will be entitled to the Associations' Professional Certificate.

This plan of holding examinations for Library Assistants has been strenuously advocated by this Association since its inception, and is regarded as a direct outcome of a communication which the Committee addressed to the Education Committee of the Library Association nearly twelve months ago, in which this plan, amongst other suggestions was embodied. We have received no official communication to this effect, but feel sure that our surmise is correct, and in order to show our appreciation it is hoped that many members of the Library Assistants' Association will endeavour to attend these classes, which are organized principally for their benefit, after a deal of hard work by the Library Association's Education Committee and its indefatigable Hon. Secretary, Mr. Henry D. Roberts. The subjects are two of the most useful and practical which could be dealt with, and it is doubtful if men more capable than Mr. Quinn and Mr. Barrett, both Public Librarians of many years experience, could be found to deal with these subjects from a Public Library Assistant's point of view.

The only thing which we regret is that these classes were not established on this sound basis when they were started some four or five years ago. If this had been done it would have saved the time of a number of students who will now have to go over the same ground again in order to gain a certificate. To many, for various reasons, this is impossible, some are not now able to give the time, while others have been transferred from London,—two, at least, whom we remember as successful students being as far off as South Africa, while others are two or three hundred miles away in the provinces.

TITLES OF HONOUR IN CATALOGUES.
By P. Evans Lewin.

Carlyle had a supreme contempt for titles of honour. "Sartor Resartus" is a scathing satire on such "dry-as-dust" vanities. Yet it is the lot of the cataloguer, fortunate or unfortunate according to the constitution of his mind, to have to record the names of men (not their deeds) in the most useful form. He is bound down by certain "rules" which often clash one with the other, and contain little to guide him in the matter of titles. Sovereign princes, princes of the blood, pontiffs, saints, etc., are entered under the Christian name; but the question at once arises "what is a sovereign prince?" or "who is royal?" It is the purpose of this paper to answer some of these questions.

English titles are simple enough. We have our dukes, marquesses, earls, viscounts, barons, baronets, and knights. There is often, however, some confusion between baron and baronet. The former is entitled to be called Lord, and the latter, Sir. Mistakes constantly appear in the treatment of the titles of peers. Thus in a well-known catalogue Lord Macaulay appears as Macaulay, Lord T. B., the proper entry being Macaulay, T. B. Lord, as he was a peer, and not merely the son of one. It is only the sons of dukes and marquesses who are by courtesy (though only esquire by law) called Lord Thomas or Lord John, those of peers of lower grade being the Hon. Thomas or the Hon. John. Another catalogue has Brassey, Lady Annie, instead of Brassey, Annie, Lady; thus making her the daughter of a peer instead of the wife of one. And yet another has Cadogan, Adelaide Lady, instead of Cadogan, Lady Adelaide, thus making the writer, though only a peer's daughter, a peeress.

These little points are always arising. Thus many catalogues have Herbert, Lord, of Cherbury, instead of Herbert of Cherbury, Lord, giving the poet a local instead of a territorial distinction. The old Scotch feudal designations are a constant stumbling-block. Graham of Claverhouse (Viscount Dundee) is very often entered Graham, of Claverhouse. There is no need for the comma, as Graham of Claverhouse is his full name, just as is the case with Ross of Bladensburg, the "of Bladensburg" being an addition granted to the family for deeds of valour, and therefore an integral part of the name. Of course it is well understood that a man should be entered under his best known title and not necessarily under his highest distinction. Thus no one would put Lord Bacon under Verulam, Viscount; but Sir Thomas Erskine May is often wrongly entered under Farnborough, Lord, a title he only bore for a few weeks and not known to the general public. After all it is their convenience a cataloguer should study, and by being finically correct he may detract from the usefulness of his catalogue. It is well, however, to be up-to-date in the matter of promotions. A man may receive a title and yet retain his surname, as is the case with Viscounts Goschen and Peel. It would be obviously wrong to enter them now as Goschen, G. J., and Peel, A. W.

Foreign titles are exceedingly complex and require careful attention. It is safe in many cases to ignore them altogether and stick to the surname, but this cannot always be done. In France the assumption of titles has been steadily going on. It is computed that 60,000 persons have titles, the great majority with no right whatever. Who will decide off-hand under what heading to put the following?

J. P. de *Saint Martin* d'Aglie, Marquis de Rivarol.
C. de *Besançon* de Bazoches.
Henri Gratien, comte *Bertrand*.
L. A. *Berthier*, prince de Neufchatel et de Wagram.
J. *Bernadotte*, prince de Ponte Corvo (Napoleon's General).
F. P. *Langlois* de Longueville.
Mme. M. de *Leprince* de Beaumont.
T. *Geoffroy* Saint Hilaire.

I have italicised the proper entry in each case. The general rule is "under the first part of a foreign double name, unless it be a Christian name," but Geoffroy *is* also a Christian name. It will be seen that sometimes the name comes first and the title last, and sometimes *vice versa*: how then, is one to decide? A reference to one of the well-known French biographical dictionaries, of which there are several in the British Museum, will settle the question. "De Courcelle's Dictionnaire des Généreaux Français," Hennequin's Biographie Maratime," "Bayle's Dictionnaire Historique," "Firman-Didot's Biographie Générale," and "De Magny's Le Nobiliare Universel" (an invaluable and monumental history of the noble houses of Europe, in 22 vols.) are among the best; and the "Almanach de Gotha" should not be overlooked. It is quite safe to ignore the titles granted by Napoleon. No one would think of looking for a book on Marshal Ney under Elchingen, duc d', prince de la Moskowa; or for one on Marshall Macdonald under Tarente, duc de. But again there are exceptions to French titles; thus, the Duke of Berwick (which may be considered a French title although the first Duke was an English Peer) would not go under Fitz-James, nor the Duke of Mayenne under his surname; etc. Another confusing practice is that father and son often apparently bear the same title, being, say, Comte de Saint Hilaire and Vicomte de Saint Hilaire respectively, and the book may be easily attributed to the wrong man. The particule de, now so universal, is often assumed unlawfully. Jean Lebrun will perhaps call himself Lebrun de Nevers. Of course, he must still remain Lebrun.

But there are two French titles which cannot be ignored, Monseigneur and Madame, the former being as well as a royal title an ecclesiastical designation, as Mgr. d'Hulst, and the latter a royal title, as Madame Elizabeth. The French titles of nobility are, in order of rank, duc, prince, comte (highest of all when born by a royal personage), vicomte, baron, and the old title, sire or seigneur (chieftain), as the Sire de Coucy.

There is nothing, however, to equal German titles. To an Englishman they are caviare, often unpronouncable, more often without apparent meaning. It is impossible to enumerate all. Some of them, in due order, are, grand duke, elector, duke, palatine, margrave, landgrave, all designating sovereign lordship, prinz (prince of blood royal), fürst (prince by creation, as Prince Bismarck), count, and baron. The von has the same meaning as in France. Palatine is a title which leads to confusion, for I have found Elizabeth, Princess Palatine, entered under Palatine.

Then there are the "ruling" titles of all nations. Cæsar, which was originally a surname, became the title of the Roman Emperors, and it is therefore correct to place C. Julius Cæsar under Cæsar, but not his successors under that name. From Cæsar we get Czar. Incidentally there are Doge, Protector, Sultan (mighty man), Statholder, Caliph (substitute), Khedive, and Emir, or Amir, the last really being the designation of all descendants of the Prophet, beggars or princes, who are entitled to wear a green turban, but not in the presence of the Sultan, who cannot claim Mahomet as an ancestor. Finally come Bey or Beg, Pasha (governor), Sheik (village chieftain), and many others.

As it is the rule to put the eldest sons of kings under their Christian names, it may be well to mention some of the chief of these titles. They are Prince of Orange, Prince of the Asturias, Duke of Brabant, Don N. of Alcantara, Duke of Sparta, Comte de Paris, Duke of Beza. Infant and Infanta are of course correct designations for a catalogue. We have at the present day the Infanta Eulalie.

This is only the fringe of the subject, but it is of interest to ibrarians, as in cataloguing a large reference library strange titles crop up, and it is necessary to have some idea of their meaning so as to give them a correct entry. Selden in his "Titles of Honour" treats exhaustively of the subject, but things have changed since his day, for Dukes have become Grand Dukes, Grand Dukes Kings, and Kings Emperors. No longer is a King "Your Highness," but "Your Majesty," and if things still progress Kings will become "Your Celestial Enormity"; dukes "Your Majesty"; lesser fry "Your Highness"; baronets will be "Serenities"; and we, the commonalty, shall all become baronets at least. Then will the intelligent cataloguer rejoice.

STUDY CIRCLE.
QUESTIONS ON FEBRUARY READING.
Senior. 1.—State the characteristics of the work of Robert Browning.

2.—Draw up the form of an estimate for the printing of a catalogue of 60,000 entries (*annotated*).

Junior. 1.—Give an account of the life of Charles Dickens, and, so far as you can, a chronological list of his works.

2.—Compile a list of works of fiction relating to the Elizabethian Period introducing actual historical personages.

REPORT ON FEBRUARY WORK.

Literary History. The best answers in this division are those of "Alfaro" (*Senior*), "Livre" and "Pontifex" (*Junior*). The last-mentioned tie with results. The senior papers show a decline in standard compared with last month. "Othello" is weak in grammar and "Leno's" answer is disjointed. *Library Practice.* The best answers were contributed by "Spero" (*Senior*) and "Livre" (*Junior*). Senior papers are of a rather perfunctory nature, the Junior papers showing far more serious attempts to adequately answer the divisional questions. "Black Ink" should have given more examples. "Mystax" gave none and thereby lost many marks. The answer by "Pontifex" was inadequate. "R. Peggio's" spelling is weak. He also errs in considering Cataloguing outside the preparatory range of Junior Assistants.

READING FOR MARCH (as last month).

Answers to be sent to Mr. G. E. Roebuck, 121, De Beauvoir Road, Kingsland, N., on or before Saturday, March 15th.

NOTE.—We regret to announce an error in the results of Mr. Macalister's competition, Junior Division. Mr. Dallimore is First-prizeman, and Mr. McKnight, Second.

NOTES AND NEWS.

Items of Interest to the Profession.—The *Editor* will be glad if readers of this Journal will forward to him any items of interest to the library world which come under their notice. Notices of the adoption of the Acts, New Features in Administration, Appointments and Vacancies, and important Donations will be especially welcome, together with copies of Publications for notice in the " Books Received " column. Readers are also reminded that the columns of this Journal are open for the discussion of topics of interest to the profession. The only restriction being that communications should be brief and to the point, as space is an important consideration.

Resignation of the Hon. Sec. of the L.A.A.—It is with much regret that we announce the resignation of Mr. G. E. Roebuck, who has held the post of *Hon. Secretary* of the Library Assistants' Association during the last twelve months. During this time Mr. Roebuck has rendered considerable service to the L.A.A., giving especial attention to the development of the Study Circle. In tendering his resignation to the Committee Mr. Roebuck said he was sorry that he was obliged to take this course, which was due to certain alterations which had taken place at the Library with which he is connected, and which had not left him sufficiently free on Wednesdays to carry out the duties in connection with the Association. Under these circumstances the Committee was reluctantly compelled to accept his resignation, and passed a resolution thanking him for the able manner in which he had performed the duties during his term of office.

Mr. Radcliffe, of the East Ham Public Library, has kindly undertaken to fill the vacancy until the next election of officers and committee.

Library Journals.—This form of communication between Librarian and Readers is deservedly becoming more popular than ever. We have before us specimens from Chorley, Finsbury, and Willesden Green. The first mentioned contains an interesting little article on *Ancient Crosses of the Leyland Hundred* with an illustration, *Topical Lists* of books in the Library on *Richard I., St. Francis of Assisi, Louis IX, Thomas Wentworth, Earl of Stafford, Milton, and Cromwell*, illustrating a series of Lectures organized by the newly-formed Chorley Lecture Society, to be given by Mr. G. C. Henderson, M.A., of Balliol College, Oxford, and a number of jottings. The Willesden Green issue contains a number of *Library Notes*, a classified list of *Some Notable Books of the last few years in the Library*, and quite a new feature in the form of a leaflet on the *Art of Biography*, with extracts from speeches by Mr. Asquith and Lord Rosebery bearing on the subject, together with an excellent list of *Some Great Books of Biography and Auto-Biography in the Library*. These are the most useful specimens of Library Journals which we have seen for some time. The next issue of the Willesden Green Journal will run to 2,000 copies and be distributed gratis. Both the Chorley and Willesden Green Journals are well patronized by advertisers, which is a great consideration to Libraries with small incomes.

The Finsbury Journal consists chiefly of a classified list of recently added books of the quality of which only a Library with a large income can afford to purchase. The chief feature of this Journal being the excellent annotations. We should advise Assistants to procure a copy and study Mr. Brown's excellent specimens of this branch of cataloguing.

Aberdeen.—Mr. Carnegie has offered £6,000 for the establishment of three Reading Rooms.

Edmonton.—The Library authority for this district is evidently suffering from a bad attack of panic, and has taken the unprecedented course of stopping the circulation of books from the Lending Library, on account of a recent outbreak of Small-pox of not a particularly virulent character. This drastic course is in our opinion quite unnecessary in view of the fact that a case of infection carried through the medium of books has never been proved, and the London Medical Officers generally agree that if the usual course of notifying the Librarian of all infected houses and taking the ordinary precautions is adopted this is all that is necessary.

Edward Edwards.—The monument presented by Mr. Thomas Greenwood, who, by the way, is engaged on a detailed life of Edwards, was unveiled at Niton, Isle of Wight, by Dr. Garnett, C.B., on February 8th. A large party assembled to witness this interesting ceremony, and included a number of prominent Librarians. Dr. Garnett delivered an interesting panegyric, in which he pointed out how eminently useful had been the life of Edwards.

Fulham.—The Public Libraries Committee has recently been the recipient of two most valuable and interesting donations. Mr. Charles J. Feret, the author of *Fulham old and new* has presented the entire manuscript of his work to the Libraries. His book was published in three volumes sm. fo., and contains a vast store of information, of much value both from historical and antiquarian points of view, upon Fulham, its streets, churches, buildings, antiquities, the Bishop of London's Palace, etc., etc., and is embellished with many illustrations. It is quite in the front rank of local histories, and represents the work of many years. About one third only of the matter collected by Mr. Feret was published, and as the whole is contained in the manuscript, the value of the gift may be readily appreciated.

Mr. W. Hayes Fisher, M.P. for Fulham, has also made a most valuable donation. The collection consisting of about 2,000 prints, photographs, maps, drawings, etc., made by Mr. Feret for the purpose of illustrating his book, *Fulham old and new*, was purchased by Mr. Fisher for presentation to these Libraries.

Greenwich.—We understand that the question of the adoption of the Public Libraries Acts is to be considered at an early date by the Council.

Mr. Thomas Greenwood.—The issue of *Great Thoughts* for February 8th, contains an article by Mr. F. M. Holmes on "The growth of Municipal Libraries," with an appreciation and portrait of Mr. Greenwood.

London County Council.—A library for the use of members has been established at the County Hall.

Southwark.—The Council has decided to erect seats at St. George-the-Martyr Library, and on the adjoining vacant land, to be let for the purpose of viewing the Coronation procession, the object being to raise sufficient funds to erect another Library.

Stepney.—The Council has decided by a majority of 16 not to adopt the Museums and Gymnasiums Act. The Libraries Committee is paying special attention to the details of a scheme for the supply of books in Braille type for the blind, which is to be carried out in conjunction with the British and Foreign Blind Association, who hope in time to extend it to other parts of the Metropolis.

Stoke Newington.—Owing to the falling off in the issue of books from the Lending Department, caused by the Small-pox scare, the Libraries' Committee has issued a circular assuring the public that no danger of infection is to be feared from the circulation of books. The Librarian receives notice of every case of infectious disease occurring in the Borough, and in houses where borrowers reside the books are collected by the Sanitary Authority and thoroughly disinfected. In all cases of Small-pox the books are destroyed.

Wolverhampton.—The *Municipal Journal*, Feb. 8th, contains an account of the opening of the New Library with an illustration.

BOOKS, &c., RECEIVED.

Chorley Library Journal: a quarterly magazine, V. 1., No. 6, *illus·* Ed. by Edward Mc Knight.

Finsbury Public Libraries' Quarterly Guide for Readers, V. 9, No. 31.

Walthamstow Public Library Report, 1900-1901.

Willesden Green Public Library Quarterly Record and Guide for Readers, New Series, V. 1, No. 4, *Ed.* by the Librarian (Frank E. Chennell.)

NEW MEMBERS.

Senior. HAWKINS, W. G., Public Library, Fulham; HOBSON, Alfred, Reference Library, Peel Park, Salford; SEIDEL, F. L., Public Library, Willesden Green; SMITH, J.H., Reference Library, Peel Park, Salford.

Junior. BARNFIELD, Thomas, Public Library, Irlam O' the Heights, Salford; ELLISON, J. B., Institute of Science, Art & Literature, Leeds; GARNER, E. W., Public Library, Boro' Road, S.E.; KERSHAW, James, Public Library, Weaste, Salford; SHAW, John, H., Public Library, Bury; WADSWORTH, A., Reference Library, Peel Park, Salford.

APPOINTMENTS AND CHANGES.

BARNES, W., Senior Assistant, Battersea, to be Sub-Librarian in charge of the Lee Branch of the Lewisham Public Libraries.

BLAKEY, ARTHUR, Junior Assistant Bermondsey Central Library to be 2nd Assistant St. Olave Branch Library.

DAVIDSON, CHARLES, Junior Assistant Rotherhithe Branch of the Bermondsey Libraries to be 1st Assistant St. Olave Branch Library.

DICKSON, J. G., late of Aberdeen, to be Librarian of Beaconsfield, S.A.

GARDINER, WILLIAM, Junior Assistant Bermondsey Central Library to be Junior Assistant Rotherhithe Branch Library.

GILL, A. K., Assistant Librarian, Northampton, to be Librarian of the St. Olave Branch of the Bermondsey Libraries.

The following were the selected candidates for the Lewisham appointment, viz: Messrs. Barnes (Battersea), *Chambers (Woolwich), *Faraday (Hornsey), *Mc Dougall (West Ham), *Vellenoweth (Minet), *Young (Leyton). Mr. Chambers withdrew.

A new feature about this appointment was the fact that the selected candidates had to undergo a very careful medical examination at the hands of the Medical Officer of Health for the district before being interviewed by the Committee. They all passed !

The first selection for the Bermondsey appointment consisted of Messrs. Barnes (Battersea), *Chambers (Woolwich), Cousins (Wandsworth) +Fletcher (Ashton-under-Lyne), Gill (Northampton),*Montgomery (Bootle), *Soper (Stoke Newington), +Young (Leyton). Mr. Barnes withdrew and the Committee selected the following, viz:—Messrs. Gill, *Montgomery, and +Soper to appear before the Council.

Members of the Library Assistants' Association.

APPOINTMENTS VACANT.

[**Notice to Library Authorities.**—*We shall be pleased to publish under this heading, free of charge, particulars of vacancies if full details are sent to the Editor on or before the 28th of each month.*]

NOTICES.

All matter for the April number should reach the *Hon. Editor* on or before 20th March.

All other communications should be addressed to the *Hon. Secretary*, (*pro. tem.*), MR. J. RADCLIFFE, Public Library, East Ham, E.

The Library Assistant:
The Official Organ of the Library Assistants' Association.

| No. 52. | APRIL, 1902. | Published Monthly |

THE LIBRARY ASSISTANTS' ASSOCIATION.
FOUNDED 1895.   SEVENTH SESSION.   YEAR 1901-1902.

Members are requested to read carefully the announcements appearing on this and the following pages, as no further intimation of meetings and other arrangements may be expected.

APRIL MEETING.
The next Ordinary Meeting will be held at the Central Public Library, 126 High Street, Poplar, on Wednesday the 16th April. Mr. W. B. THORNE will open a discussion on *Printing for Public Librarians.* Mr. H. ROWLATT, Borough Librarian (to whom we are indebted for permission to visit the Library) has kindly consented to occupy the Chair.

ANNUAL SOCIAL GATHERING.
The Annual Social Gathering took place at the St. Bride Foundation Institute, on Wednesday, March 5th, about 80 members and friends were present.

An excellent musical programme had been arranged and was greatly appreciated, the Rialto Mandoline Band, the cornet solos of Mr. A. H. Crouch, and the duets of Messrs. Gamgee and Loveland of the Westminster Nigger Troupe being particularly well received. Songs were also rendered by Miss F. North (with violin obligatto by Miss Vivian), Mr. A. Cogswell, Mr. W. J. Vellenoweth, and Mr. W. B. Young. After the concert the remainder of the evening was spent in dancing until shortly after 11, when the singing of *Auld Lang Syne* brought a very pleasant evening to a close.

Mr. Arthur Stanley Crouch presided at the piano, and the Committee desires through these pages to express its thanks to him and the other artistes who so kindly gave their services on this occasion.   W.B.Y.

MARCH MEETING.
Members of the L.A.A. to the number of about 30 met at the Woolwich Public Library on March 19th, when a paper by Mr. B. L. Dyer, Librarian of Kimberley, entitled, *War and the Library: Stray Notes,* was read by the Hon. Treasurer. Mr. P. Evans Lewin also contributed a paper on *Some Systems of Classification.*

Councillor C. H. Grinling, B.A., Chairman of the Libraries' Committee, occupied the chair and was supported by several members of the Committee. Prior to the Meeting members had an opportunity of inspecting the Library, the interior of which is considered to be one of the prettiest in South London. They were also entertained to refreshments by Mr. and Mrs. Bond, who had generously made very ample provision for their comfort. Mr. A. W. Crockford, Sub-Librarian of Richmond, was unanimously appointed to fill a casual vacancy on the Committee.

Mr. Grinling delivered an address to the members and said:

I am one of those who live rather in the future than in the present or past, and I felt that I could not do better than say a word or two as to the librarian's future. I believe myself that librarians in the future will hold—as indeed I believe they hold now—one of the most recognised and important positions in any community. Wherever I look round I see signs of the development of the library movement. I have taken an interest in it as far back as I can remember. In my student days at Oxford I remember I used to wander round the Union Library seeing what details I could pick up, and now I find that the more I am brought into contact with the library movement the more clear I grow in my mind that there is a great future for the Librarian.

Now what I would suggest is that all of you who are on the lower steps of the library ladder should aim at moulding your lives not so much from the point of view of the present position of a librarian but from the point of view of the position in ten or twenty years time.

In estimating the value of the character of any post in life the right thing is to consider into which of two classifications it falls. There is the position which we may call the disinterested position, and there is that other one—the interested position.

When I speak of the disinterested position, we may take as a type the position of a clergyman, and the position of a teacher. Those would be a sufficient illustration of what I mean. When I was up at Oxford I used to look at all the people I met and ask myself whether they really cared most for a disinterested position or for an interested one from the financial point of view, from the point of view of fame, honour, or of dignity. I liked to know men who did care very much indeed about the development of their own lives and about the development, the brightening, the uplifting, of the lives of those around them. I have a very robust faith that that type is to be a dominant type of the future. I have that faith and conviction that the type of man, the type of woman, who are going to care mainly for the development of life and character of those around them will become the dominant type and will gradually wear away the majority—the type of those who only desire to get on in the world. I do not mean for one moment to disparage any earnest striving after success, but the one is the higher and the other the lower on the ladder of development. I am very jealous indeed that the ideals of the rising race of librarians shall be of a disinterested type. I have a strong belief in the great importance of keeping your ideal of life as a harmonious whole. I think it is in the first chapter of Herbert Spencer's Social Statics that he sketches out the various biases that affect every man. We all have many biases, some of which we are conscious of, but of many of which we are completely unconscious. If we would have a harmonious and well regulated life we must always be careful to swing back the pendulum to the contrary direction of the biases of our life, and if we would have a well balanced life it seems to me that we must seriously consider how that is best going to be balanced. I understand that there is a well recognised tendency in the library movement to estimate that. I understand that in some libraries the times of attendance are so arranged that the librarians and their assistants have a choice whether they will get off so much time on certain days or get a clear day in the week. I should never hesitate for one moment in choosing. I believe that it is in getting long stretches off, a day at a time or a week-end whenever possible, that those off-times become among the most valuable of all our lives. They bring us that opportunity of bringing that balance into our lives which we all need. I rejoice in all these opportunities which bring us right away, by cycling or walking, into completely other fields. I think the finest direction for the helping of a librarian may be suggested to us by a saying of John Ruskin. It runs something after this style: For every hundred men who can speak you will only find one man who thinks, and further, for every thousand men who think you will only find one man who sees. That is a most important truth, for the whole field of our knowledge needs testing by every one, and in every generation you will require those *individual* tests. No knowledge is of the slightest value to us which we take for granted. The only knowledge worth having is the knowledge we have *made* our own. It is by the five senses that we submit to the test the knowledge of the greatest men of all time, and it is on our days off, on our week-ends, that we have the finest opportunity of putting this test to our own knowledge by using all our senses and especially our hearing and sight. The whole realm of natural science which you have stored up in a few books needs a constant individual test by every one of us. How few of us, when we go out for the short walk which may be the only thing possible for us in the way of exercise, use our eyes, to look at the clouds, to look at the trees, to see the faces of passers by, and to read the thoughts and the feelings behind the faces of the people around. It is only when we are going to use our own senses that we shall get that balance which will make our life one harmonious whole.

I think if we always aim at developing every day more clearly to ourselves what is our main aim in life, if we always ask ourselves whether our life is to be one of the disinterested or one of the interested lives, and if, above all, we picture the possibilities of life for ourselves and others by the great drift and trend of things which we see and can feel and think out for ourselves day by day, then I feel that that ideal and aim of life will be, it *must* be, of the utmost daily help to us and for each individual department of the world around us.

The discussion on Mr. Lewin's paper was taken part in by Messrs. Wood, Soper, Chambers, Stevenson, and Bond, the principal points raised by it being the relative value of the various systems of classification now before Librarians, and the desirability or otherwise of close classification on the shelves.

The Chairman in his closing remarks referred to the fact that he had been associated with Mr. Dyer at Toynbee Hall, and that he himself had prepared the first catalogue.

The meeting which was very successful broke up shortly after ten, hearty votes of thanks having been passed to Mr. and Mrs. Bond, the Chairman, and to the readers of the papers.

P.E.L.

N.W. BRANCH MARCH MEETING.

The March Meeting was held in the Central Library, Oldham, on he 19th inst., when, after inspecting the Libraries, etc., and viewing the pictures in the Spring Exhibition, a paper, "The Free Library: the working man's University," was read by Mr. C. Owen, of Oldham.

During the course of his paper Mr. Owen sketched an ideal institution, which was intended to help the working classes to improve themselves by placing within their reach the best books on every subject, and providing them with courses of lectures such as the University Extension Lectures or the Ruskin Hall Series.

N.W. BRANCH MAY MEETING.

The next meeting will be held by the kind invitation of H. Guppy, Esq., M.A., in the John Ryland Library, on a Tuesday evening during May. For date see the May Journal.

It is earnestly requested that as many members as can possibly attend will endeavour to do so, when Mr. Guppy will take for his subject, "The Story of the English Bible." As his library is very rich in its collection of Bibles, the meeting should prove interesting.

It is the Committee's intention to organise a class in Bibliography, with Mr. Guppy as Lecturer, if they can secure that gentleman's services and obtain the requisite number of students. Further particulars will be published with the North Western Annual Report shortly to be issued.

The following gentlemen have kindly consented to become Vice-Presidents of the North-Western Branch:—

Mr. R. BATEMAN, Chief Librarian and Curator, Oldham.
„ P. COWELL, City Librarian, Liverpool.
„ W. R. CREDLAND, Deputy City Librarian, Manchester.
„ HY. GUPPY, M.A., John Ryland Library, Manchester.
„ C. MADELEY, Chief Librarian, Warrington.
„ B. H. MULLEN, M.A., Chief Librarian, Salford.
„ G. T. SHAW, The Athenæum, Liverpool.   W. Q.

OUR WORK.

BY RICHARD W. MOULD, F.S.A., SCOT.

[*A Paper read at the February Meeting of the Library Assistants' Association held at the Newington Public Library*].

On the occasion of your former meeting at this Library the subject of the paper submitted was, as in the present case, "OUR WORK," but it dealt more especially with that portion of our work involved in the establishing, organising, and generally making ready of a new Institution for the public use. It therefore left untouched, except by incidental references, the less heroic and exciting, but none the less important, work of the

" Daily round, the common task " that follows the throwing open with more or less *éclât* of the doors of the new Library, an occasion which, by-the-way, can be turned to very good account if, immediately after the departure of the royal or other distinguished personage who has kindly performed the inaugural function, the people are forthwith invited to enter and inspect their new possession. This was done at Newington, and during the evening 10,000 persons passed through the building; more than three hundred copies of the catalogue were sold, and four thousand borrowers' forms were issued to applicants. To adapt Shakespeare, the occasion is a flood-tide in the affairs of libraries which, taken advantage of, leads on to success.

My paper to-night, designed as a continuation of the former one, concerns itself with some of the items of every-day library work, but having regard to the many agencies in operation for imparting instruction in the details of library practice, of which permit me to say that your own Association, based on the admirable principle of self-help, is not the least important and commendable, I must be careful to avoid those points which to dwell upon in the present instance would be tantamount to the obviously belated labour tersely described in a familiar saying, but poetically elaborated, as follows :—

> " Teach not a parent's mother to extract
> The embryo juices of an egg by suction ;
> That good old lady can the feat enact,
> Quite irrespective of your kind instruction."

Your own personal experiences in the various important libraries with which you are associated, your own individual quest of knowledge that will be professionally useful—and what knowledge is otherwise in a profession like ours that is so comprehensive in its range of interests and requires that its representatives shall be something of the character of animated encyclopædias ?—and your organised efforts to the same end, give you, I am glad to acknowledge, a position that makes the avoidance I have intimated difficult for me to maintain. As at the annual meetings of the Library Association, the value to the delegates, and through them to the Libraries they represent, lies not so much in the papers read and discussed, for a contribution of any marked originality or particular force is of rare occurrence, as in the stimulus of meeting with fellow workers in the same cause and the consequent revival of waning enthusiasm and declining ideals ; so, though little that is new to you in Library practice may be gathered from my paper, renewed interest in our work may result from a brief survey together of some of its branches.

The first duty of a Public Librarian is to study his locality, its history, its industries, its aspirations, and particularly the occupations and character of its people.

Upon that study must be based every development or retrenchment. It must guide in the selection of additions for the Library, and of papers for the Reading Rooms, it must have some influence in the decision as to the printed catalogue, and even in the question of binding. The character of the Lectures, if any are given, must be wholly determined by it.

It is generally found that the poorest people have the largest families, and it happens, too, that the poorest localities from the point of view of the Library rate, generally have the largest populations, Newington, for example, where the penny rate produces £2,145, has a population of 120,000 packed away within a square mile, while another parish within the borough, St. Saviour's, has an income from the Library rate of about half that of Newington, but only a tenth of the population. Again, one Library district may be compact and of a small area like Newington, which is an advantage as enabling the authorities to devote their resources to the building up of one large Library in a central situation, while another may be long and straggling like Lambeth, which makes the provision of several small Libraries preferable to one large one. The difference in local circumstances must manifestly be recognised and met by different methods if the people of every district are to have equal return for their outlay. And it is well to remember in this connection that the social derelict, the overworked widow, the worn-out workman, the unconsidered costermonger, and even the redoubtable Hooligan himself, that occupy so large a place in the living pictures that the cinematograph of untoward circumstance and physical and mental failure throws upon the dingy screen of our poorer thorough-fares, contribute their share to the maintenance of the institution ostensibly established to ameliorate their condition and lift them up towards better things; and they must be provided for in the Library—and it is in proportion to the extent to which our work reaches and influences the submerged section of the people that it is truly valuable and successful.

In poor working-class districts the Librarians' object must be to provide many popular, recreative and entertaining books that will appeal to the people who are likely to be attracted to his Library by light mental refreshment rather than by the more solid and costly food suitable for more vigorous and intellectual appetites. And if in the circumstances the Librarian finds that imaginative literature is most in demand he should not be unduly sad, for a liking for the ideal rather than the real is not a bad trait of character, and after all the ideal that is visible only to the mental vision is always pleasanter and more profitable to contemplate. The old monks thought so and lived up to their belief, for in the libraries of the monasteries there were more copies of the works of the early writers of Romance than of more serious authors, and judging from the numerous entries of the work in the catalogue which is preserved in the Library of Trinity College, Dublin, the *Gesta Guidonis de Warewick* was an especial favourite with the monks of St. Augustine's at Canterbury centuries ago, and even to-day men of education, the clergymen and others who work for and live with the people and see so much of the distressful life, are often glad to turn for relief to works of fiction. And in this connection the story of an incident that occurred in quite recent years at an Irish convent is interesting.

At the local bookseller's a volume was seen by the short-sighted Mother Superior, and she, thinking it to be by a favourite dignitary of the church— one Canon Doyle—bought it in order that it might be read aloud to the novices, and in the usual course the reading of it was begun. The first chapter astonished them. Never had love-making been so openly propounded within that saintly sanctuary. The novices were visibly moved.

"Well, well," said the Mother Superior, "the dear Canon is preparing us for a miracle of grace. The frivolous flirt, by the mercy of Heaven, no doubt ends by taking the veil."

Then came the revelation that the book was not by Canon Doyle at all, but by one Conan Doyle. Of this the Mother Superior was informed.

"Very well," she said; "the bookseller where we bought the book is a pious man, and now that we have paid for it we should be very wasteful not to read it through to the end."

The charm enshrined in a tale, a novel, a poem, acting upon the grey gloom of dreary common-place life, like sunrise upon the mists of night, suffuse it with revivifying warmth and brightness; and I am not sure that even Librarians and Library Assistants have not a taste for such literature as distinct from books of mere instruction; but there is this saving grace for them—every book they read helps them in their work. So we ought not to be too sad if the fiction percentage is higher than some think it ought to be. There must be, of course, besides imaginative literature a good selection of Travel, Biography, Popular Science, Natural History, and also good technical works suggested by an examination of the returns of the occupation of borrowers. Our Reading Rooms should be made attractive by the popular character of the magazines and papers provided, by pictures on the walls, and a general air of comfort and brightness; and in the case of the Boys' Room it is not desirable or necessary to attempt to usurp the function of the schoolmaster or tutor by giving definite instruction to the frequenters, but it is most important that the appointments of the room, and the books and papers provided therein, should be of such an attractive character that the room of itself will exert a magnetic influence and draw the boys to it. There should be nothing in the room to suggest school and lessons: boys have generally had enough of them before the room is opened in the evening. All the same, by using the room they are unconsciously increasing their knowledge and training themselves to use the other departments of the Library in after life. Our purpose should be to interest and to attract from downward courses, rather than to impart definite instruction.

A word as to the Reference Library. The special advantage of such a department over the Lending Library is that the books are always available. But, further than providing a selection of the best comprehensive works of an encyclopædic character, very little is possible in this direction in poor districts except by the co-operation of neighbouring Library authorities, every one contributing towards the establishment of a Reference Library that shall be worthy of the name and a credit to the locality such as those of many provincial centres.

And in passing permit me to remark that at present there is not a great free Reference Library such as gives distinction to many prominent towns anywhere in South London, or indeed, apart from National and special Libraries, and the Guildhall Library, anywhere in London; but the excellent use that is made of such as there are, of which the Library of St. Martin in the Fields is perhaps the best in London, is ample proof of the need for better provision. In every one of the new Boroughs there should be a really first-rate Reference Library. And the need for immediate action is becoming more urgent every year, for books of standard interest, and sets of important publications that should form the foundation of every good Reference Library are becoming more and more scarce and costly owing to the insatiable appetite and unlimited financial resources of our kin across the seas who to-day are the best and most welcome customers of the English second-hand booksellers. Our country is being drained of irreplacible books, complete sets of the Annual Register, publications of learned Societies, for example. A set of Notes and Queries similar to that acquired for this Library two or three years ago for £24 is priced £40 in a recent catalogue. It is therefore part of our work to secure whenever possible these books for our own Libraries.

In building up the Reference Library, regard must be had to books in special demand, though not exclusively, for there are many excellent books of which the general public know nothing whatever, and it is part of our work to introduce them. A bookseller who supplied one Library had never heard of the Annual Register, and how few there are who know of the Index to the Times.

Meanwhile, if the existing Libraries were in telephonic communication with each other, the whole of their present resources on any particular point could be readily made known to a reader who fails to get what he requires at the Library he happens to call at first.

Now, dare I introduce the thorny question of the Catalogue, which came within the scope of the first part of my paper, but is of sufficient importance to be touched upon again. Save the Indicator and Open Access, I do not know a more stimulating topic for a meeting of Librarians, and I am sure that a vote would result pretty much as it did in the case of the six young mothers who agreed to form themselves into a committee to decide which of their respective babies was the prettiest. Each child got one vote! So every Librarian stands by his own catalogue, and so long as it is the one best suited to his particular public he has every right to do so. But there should be no difficulty in generally admitting that in poor districts costly catalogues are a mistake. Perhaps no publication is of necessity more ephemeral in character than the printed catalogue of a popular Lending Library. It is out of date almost as soon as it is issued. Therefore the less elaborate and bulky the better, though to issue a catalogue that might fairly be described as a mere hand-list is no doubt a big sacrifice of ambition, and catalogues, like more important things, are often judged by mere bulk or appearance. It was not a little interesting to note, some time back, that the two London library catalogues selected for notice in a French bibliographical work were the largest London librarians have ever produced.

A cheap catalogue finds its way into the homes of the people more readily than a dear one, and becomes there a permanent advertisement of the Library, and it gives that submerged section of the public to which reference was made above a chance to possess a copy, equally with their fellow-citizens in better circumstances. Personally I should be glad if they could be quite free so that no class of borrower could possibly have an advantage over another in the use of the Library. These considerations had weight in the decision as to the Newington Catalogue, or handlist, I am indifferent as to its title, and subsequent experience justified the course taken. The original catalogue, dealing with 9,500 volumes, was sold at fourpence a copy, and within five months the entire edition of 2,100 copies was in the homes of the people of the parish. A catalogue of some 6,000 additions was issued twelve months ago at twopence a copy, and 1,300 copies have been sold. The first edition realised a small profit, and in the very difficult financial position of the Library it was eminently desirable that the catalogue should pay for itself as it did. The plan of the Newington catalogue is, I believe, unusual. In the main it is a single entry catalogue or list in one alphabet, the entries being under the author or subject according to the character of the work. In brief, works of fancy which are an author's own creation such as fiction, poetry, drama, and belles lettres generally are entered under the authors' names where everyone would be likely to look for them, and works of fact such as biography, history, science, art, travel and geography are entered under the subject, where I think they would generally be expected to be found. The original catalogue was quite experimental, and put forth with some fear and trembling, but as it seemed to meet the general requirements of the borrowers, and moreover, as it seemed to be a step towards the solution of the printed catalogue problem of large and growing Libraries in working-class localities, where the alphabetical must be preferable to the classified catalogues and where the catalogue must be cheap I am encouraged to adhere to its main principle, though, of course, in each successive edition strengthening by concise cross references the points wherein it may have proved weak. As supplements special subject lists should be issued from time to time.

At Birmingham the idea of a cheap catalogue has lately been adopted, the price being no more than one penny for most of the catalogues. This, to my mind, is progress. *The* catalogue of a large Library can never be the printed one. It must be the Librarian's Catalogue behind the counter either in card or book form, according to choice or circumstance, and which without cost but that of labour can be made to answer any question as to the resources of the Library that any borrower can possibly ask. That catalogue should include every subject represented by complete books or articles in general works and magazines in every department of the Library and its branches, if any, and in the latter case there should be an exact counterpart of the catalogue at every branch. It can have annotations, bibliographical data, and every conceivable particular the Librarian may desire to give or what may possibly be useful, but which in the printed catalogue would involve more expense than is consistent with the impoverished circumstances of many Libraries and would make its selling price prohibitive to the majority of borrowers. Its usefulness can be very materially increased by including whenever possible the result of other Librarians' labours, as I am doing by incorporating in the special catalogue the useful Contents-Catalogue lately issued by the Librarian to whom the profession generally must accord grateful acknowledgments for his devoted labours n the production of acceptable Library aids,—Mr. Alfred Cotgreave of West Ham. This will enable the Librarian and his staff to develop other useful aids to our work: such for example as a title list of all the plays and poems in the Library, a bibliography of local literature or other exhaustive lists of special subjects of local or general interest in which the Library may be unusually rich. After all, the published catalogue never shows the entire resources of a live Library. For the latest additions enquiry must be made at the Library itself. Here I might be allowed to say a word as to showing recent additions to the Library. The books themselves are first shown in a case on the counter, and entries of them are made in the catalogues for public use. These catalogues, which show the complete contents of the Library up to date are in the form of guard books half bound in pigskin. The printed catalogue is cut up and mounted with spaces left at intervals for additions. It is mounted down the middle of the page, leaving wide margins on either side of the printed matter also available for new entries. This arrangement, which I believe is new, has the advantage of preserving the strict alphabetical sequence of the entries almost indefinitely, but like the secret of perpetual motion the art of making the materials of which Catalogues are made wear for ever has not yet been discovered. Of course it entails the labour of writing up as many catalogues as may be required for counter use. But to write or otherwise prepare cumulative lists so that the latest list embodies all the additions up to date in perfect order which would be the only useful alternative save the card catalogue would be equally laborious but less advantageous. The card catalogue is, I think, out of the question for public use in a busy lending library. It is certainly less readily or conveniently consulted than a book catalogue, a page of which shows some fifty entries at a glance. The card catalogue is unsurpassed for staff use and the Reference Library reader of leisure.

Library lectures are not yet a generally recognised feature of our work. But in poor districts they appear to be the lever that will help to lift the people to the level of the Libraries. If popular and attractive in character and not ostensibly "with a purpose," they help to achieve the end that the original promoters and pioneers of the Library movement had in view, viz: to make free libraries an effective part of the machinery employed for bettering the condition and character of the people. It is to be regretted that the attitude of the Government auditor towards expenditure in this direction is unsympathic and discouraging. The position he takes is quite illogical. An authority on any subject may write a book on his subject, and any required number of copies of that book may be bought for the Library. But if he were asked to lecture to the Library borrowers on that same subject at a cost much less than the price paid for his books, and with the advantage of immediately reaching a far larger number of persons in one night than could be reached by means of his books in a year, exception would be taken to such expenditure. And the same applies to humorists and other entertaining writers and lecturers such as Max O'Rell. But the advantage to the public does not end with the lecture. The special lists of books in the Libraries for the distribution of which the lecture is an excellent opportunity and excuse, draw the people to the Library for further information on the subject in which the lecture has created or revived interest. These lists are made permanently useful by insertion in the Catalogues on the counter. That is our experience here where lectures and recitals have formed part of our work for several years, and the accommodation in the Library building has been outgrown and the great Public Hall which you saw to-night has to be used for that purpose. As a consequence the people of Newington begin to feel that the Library is an institution for their use and benefit, and are making good use of it in every department. Another point in connection with the lectures in this district should be mentioned. The population is a migratory one, changes taking place in the course of three years that are equivalent to an entire clear out of its immense population. In order to meet this our work must be kept well before the public so that the large body of newcomers may know of it. And this can hardly be more effectually done than by the lectures which must be widely advertised in the locality. I am not sure that this work by attaching residents to their local institutions will not cause them to become less disposed than they are at present to "flit" at the first opportunity, and more willing to remain and help to make the borough more and more attractive. We know that propinquity to a Free Library is now often used as a recommendation for their property by House Agents in their advertisements.

So far I have dealt with "Our Work" in its adaptation to local conditions. Those details of which the public have no knowledge, which fill up the long day and the result of which manifests itself in that part of our work that meets the public eye, but which are as a rule so smoothly carried on that the ratepayers will sometimes wonder how on earth the Library staff while away the time, such details are practically the same in every Library. The due warming and ventilation of the rooms to suit all constitutions and temperaments must be everywhere attempted, though this is not generally one of the most successful features of our work. Tidiness, order, cleanliness, ready service, good lighting, and similar features of good administration are as essential in one district as in another, though the Librarian of an unfashionable locality will have to contend with the local standard with regard to some of these points. I know of a Librarian so situated who wanted his Library renovated. "But," objected an authority, "it was done three or four years ago; my establishment has not been done out for ten years!" "Sir," the Librarian urged, "is the Library to be conducted according to the standard of your establishment or to one which shall make the Library a model for the people of the district to live up to?" Even clean windows exert a salutary influence and aid in our work more than may be apparent, and we cannot afford to economise in such matters.

But our work has its interesting features, and there is not a detail which is unimportant, though there be many that are of a nature that occasionally makes one think that Johnson's definition of a lexicographer as "a harmless drudge" might be applied with equal force to a Librarian—including of course the Assistant. The "atmosphere" of a Library—the word is not to be taken too literally, mind—the very presence of books suggesting so vast a world to be explored, every one a highway or byway to regions of wonder and delight, have a charm that make the rest quite tolerable even for the most junior of the juniors if he have the root of the matter in him. The lowest grade of our work, and here let me say that I think personally attending to the public one of the highest, is of value to us if we have a disposition to pick up unconsidered trifles of Library knowledge. Even the cutting, stamping, labelling and repairing of books are occupations that can be made to contribute materially to our professional education and usefulness. The collating of books is exceedingly important work, and though some binders give such work to young girls who do it mechanically, the Library assistant to whom such work falls ought to consider himself highly favoured, for, even more than cataloguing, it gives him an opportunity to acquire a knowledge of books more intimate and personal than that which most folk possess regarding members of the aristocracy—their titles. The careful collator who makes notes, mental or otherwise, of special features of the books that pass through his hands, is likely to be of great service in the still higher work, viz., that of personally attending to readers, though that higher work has now to be done, owing to limited staff, with the disturbing consciousness of other work running into arrear the while. This patient personal attention to the requirements of individual readers and students is the highest form of Library service and will be required of the generation of Librarians who succeed the present men who, working under all the difficulties and disabilities of pioneers can only see the better things from afar. When the Public Libraries are free from debt and that portion of the income from the penny rate which is now swallowed up in capital charges can be devoted to the employment of an adequate number of qualified assistants, a time which many present to-night will enter upon, then Librarians will have their opportunity. At the same time much will be expected of them, for a higher level of popular education will have been reached. The young men in the profession to-day for whom that good time is coming will therefore do well to see that they are fully equipped for their work, and this they will be likely to do if they make the most of the advantages their own Libraries offer, usefully employ their leisure and steadfastly concern themselves with the question not "what do we require of 'Our Work,'" but "What does 'Our Work' require of us."

NOTES AND NEWS.

The L.A. Examinations.—By the courtesy of the Hon. Sec. of the Education Committee we are enabled to enclose with this issue a copy of the revised syllabus of the L. A. Examinations. We also print an interesting letter in reply to our Editorial of last month. Owing to pressure on our space we reserve our comments on the foregoing until next month.

Honours for Librarians.—At the last meeting of the L.A.A. Committee, a resolution was passed congratulating Messrs. Guppy and Sutton on the honour conferred upon them on the occasion of the visit of the Prince of Wales to Owens Coll., Manchester, when they were invested with the degree of M.A.

The Hon. Sec. of the L.A.—The appointment of Mr. Lawrence Inkster, chief librarian of the Battersea Public Libraries, to this important post should give satisfaction to all. We heartily congratulate Mr. Inkster on his election. The vacancy caused on the Council by Mr. Inkster's elevation has given another public librarian the opportunity of securing a seat, viz:—Mr. Plant, Chief of the Shoreditch Public Libraries.

The L.A. and the L.A.A.—Mr. Evan G. Rees, Chairman of the L.A.A. has been elected a member of the L.A Education Committee.

Birmingham.—The Birmingham Memorial to Ruskin is to take the form of a Library, Museum and Art Gallery.

Buckley.—At a recent meeting of the Buckley (Flintshire) Urban Council it was announced that Mr. Carnegie would give twenty times as much as one penny rate would produce towards the erection of a free library at Buckley, that the Hawarden Estate had offered a site, that Mr. Herbert Gladstone would give £500, and the Rev. Harry Drew £100, and that Mrs. Drew would be responsible for £200. The chairman gave notice that at the next meeting he would move the adoption of the Public Libraries Act.

"**The Boys' Own Paper**" of February contains an article on librarianship as a profession, entitled "*What shall I be?*"

Ireland.—Mr. Andrew Carnegie has expressed his intention of giving a handsome grant towards the establishment of a free library in Omagh, co. Tyrone.

Mr. S. W. Kershaw of Lambeth Library, contributes an interesting article to the March issue of *The Sunday at Home*, on 'La Rochelle and its Story.'

Library Architecture.—*The Builder* of March 22nd contains an abstract of a paper on *The planning of some recent Library Buildings in the United States*, read before the Royal Institute of British Architects by Mr. Sydney Greenslade.

Mutilating a Newspaper.—*James Little*, 28, was charged with wilfully damaging a newspaper at the Camberwell Central Library, Peckham Road. The librarian said such acts frequently occurred at public libraries, and were very difficult of detection. Mr. Francis remarked that public libraries were kept for the benefit of people who would use them properly. This was not the proper way to use a library, and the prisoner would have to pay a fine of 10s. or go to prison for seven days.

Southwark.—The following resolution has been adopted by the Council on the recommendation of the Public Libraries Committee:—" That secretaries or duly authorised persons of registered societies, institutions, trade unions, &c., be accepted as guarantors."

Wood Green.—The Wood Green District Council is negotiating with the Alexandra Palace Trustees for the use of a room in the Palace for the purpose of establishing a branch library.

STUDY CIRCLE.
QUESTIONS ON MARCH READING.

Senior. 1. Give an account of the work of James Anthony Froude and contemporary historians.

2. In arranging architectural details for a new library, what system of heating would you advocate? Give reasons for preference.

Junior. 1. Who was the author of "Ivry" and which are his most important works?

2. State what is meant by the terms "fixed location," and "movable location." Detail the differences.

All answers must be sent to Mr. G. E. Roebuck, 121 De Beauvoir Road, Kingsland, N., on or before April 11th. New pseudonyms to be used.

REPORT ON MARCH WORK.

1. *Literary History.* The best answers in this section were contributed by "Alfaro" (*Senior*) and "Livre" (*Junior*). The adjudicators are very pleased with "Alfaro's" paper which shows a considerable grasp of the subject. "Spero" sent a good paper, which was, however, somewhat disconnected. The work of "Bonne foi" and "Sartor" was commended. The standard of the juniors' work was extremely good.

2. *Library Practice.* The best answers in this section were those by "Bonne foi" (*Senior*) and "Black Ink" (*Junior*). The adjudicators announce that the Senior papers were all of good standard, each being sufficiently correct for the purpose required. The appended reasons given by "Bonne foi" gave his paper the slight prominence over other contributors. The junior assistants (with the exception of "Black Ink," "Mystax" and "Livre") do not appear to have taken much pains to secure a good result. It is astonishing to observe how little juniors know concerning the historical novels of England's most interesting era.

READING FOR APRIL (*as last month*).

QUARTERLY REPORT. FOURTH SESSION.

The following is a list of the total number of marks obtained by students (Jan. to March, 1902).

Senior Division.		Junior Division.	
Alfaro	558	Livre	645
Spero	510	Black Ink	470
Bonne foi	506	R. Peggio	465
Simple Simon	337	Mystax	410
Sartor	195	Leno	345
		Othello } Pontifex }	195
		Quiver	180
		Jorrocks	155

The Education Committee declare

"Alfaro" Mr. A. Edwards (Liverpool) and
"Livre" Mr. F. Dallimore (Wigan)

to be divisional prizemen, and the prizes will be sent to these students at an early date.

One more appeal is made to assistants throughout the country, members or otherwise, to give more support to this most important branch of our Association's work.

"COTGREAVE" (1902) AND "L.A.A." JUNIOR (1902) PRIZES.

A prize of £2 is offered by Mr. A. Cotgreave for the best essay of not less than 1,700 or more than 2,000 words, entitled, *Anticipated Developments of Library Practice*. This competition is restricted to *senior* assistants. A *junior* competition is also open. A prize of £1 is offered for the best essay of not less than 700 or more than 1,000 words, entitled *How to make the L.A.A. more useful to junior assistants*.

All papers must be sent to Mr. J. Radcliffe, Public Library, East Ham, not later than May 25th, signed with a pseudonym, and accompanied by a *sealed* envelope bearing on the outside the pseudonym *only*, and containing within the name and address of the contributor.

CORRESPONDENCE.

[*The Editor solicits expressions of opinion on all matters of interest to the profession, but does not hold himself responsible for the views of correspondents. Communications should be written on one side of the paper only, and should be as brief as possible.*]

To the Editor of the "Library Assistant."

Dear Sir,

In the editorial of your March number you have fallen into the error of confusing the class examinations with the professional examinations of the Library Association. The former were restricted to the absolute work of particular classes, the latter cover the whole of the syllabus of the professional examination. The subjects and the standard are very different. The examination to be held in May will not be on the work of either of the classes now being held, for neither class pretends to cover the whole of the ground. What we do hope is that the classes may be of some help to students intending to present themselves for the professional examination. The idea of holding the examination directly after the end of the classes this year is, as you rightly suppose, in consequence of representations which your Committee made on the subject. It was just because if certificates had been issued in connection with these Class examinations, they would have been confused with the professional certificate, that the Council decided not to issue any at all. That they were wise in doing so is evident, because to produce a certificate of having passed a class examination would be a totally different thing to being able to show that one had passed the professional examination.

Of course, you are right in presuming that provisional certificates will be granted for each subject. When a student has passed in all the subjects, he will obviously get the full certificate. Formerly the candidates were obliged to take the examination in three sections. Under the new syllabus they may now do so in five, surely a great boon to would-be certificated persons.

I must join issue with you at once on your last paragraph. My previous remarks apply, but you surely miss the very point of these classes. It is not expected that a student will attend the classes, and straightway forget all he has learnt. If past students have gained any good by the classes at all, and were in a position at the end of a series to obtain the professional certificate if examined, they should surely be able to do so now, otherwise what permanent good would the classes have done them, and of what real value would a certificate be? As to students being in South Africa and in the provinces, I shall be glad to arrange for candidates to be examined in any centre out of London, provincial or abroad, which may be convenient to them.

I sincerely trust that all the students in the present classes, and many other of your members, will present themselves in the professional examination in section 2, Cataloguing, Classification and Shelf Arrangement, to be held in May.

Yours faithfully,
HENRY D. ROBERTS.

Fulham Public Libraries,
London, S.W.
23rd March, 1902.

Dear Mr. Soper,

You have asked me to give you notes of a few books bearing upon the subject matter of my lectures on "Classification" for publication in the "Library Assistant" for the guidance of the students of the class in their private reading. I therefore append the titles of a few of the books which have proved to be of the most service to myself. I regret that I am not able to send to you a better considered list.

Though there is much scattered literature upon the subject of classification; there is exceedingly little which is co-ordinated or which can in any sense claim to approach towards completeness or exhaustiveness.

Yours faithfully,
FRANKLIN T. BARRETT.

PRACTICAL.

Brown, James D. Manual of library classification and shelf arrangement. London, 1898. (Contains the "Adjustable" system.)

Cutter, Charles A. Expansive classification. Boston. 1891 (in progress).

Dewey, Melvil. Decimal classification. Boston, 1899.

Edwards, Edward. Memoirs of libraries, vol. 2. London, 1859.

Richardson, Ernest C. Classification, theoretical and practical. New York, 1901. (Contains brief notes of many systems; and a considerable bibliography).

And many scattered articles in the English and American professional journals.

THEORETICAL.

Welton, J. Manual of logic. London, 1896. 2 vols. (Especially Book 1, dealing with terms, predicables, categories, division and classification).

Fiske, John. Outlines of cosmic philosophy. Vol. 2. London, 1874. (Contains a most valuable exposition and review of the Spencerian system).

Flint, Robert. Classification of the sciences: in the Presbyterian review, vols. 6 and 7.

Jevons, W. Stanley. Principles of science, a treatise on logic and scientific method. 1877. (Especially ch. XXX on classification).

Pearson, Karl. Grammar of science. London, 1900. (A chapter on the classification of the sciences).

Shields, Charles W. Philosophia ultima, Vol. 2. New York, 1889.

The above list contains what I believe to be the best; the few titles which follow are of books, which are, for the present purpose, of lesser value, though containing suggestive matter.

Bain, Alexander. Logic. New York, 1886. (Containing in the chapter on the classification of the sciences, much pregnant though brief criticism of the various theoretical systems.)

Comte, Auguste. Positive philosophy, freely translated and condensed by H. Martineau. 1875. 2 vols.

Encyclopædia Britannica; article on Encyclopædias.

Encyclopædia Metropolitana; introduction on method, by Samuel Taylor Coleridge.

Fumagalli, Giuseppe. Della collocazione dei libri nelle pubbliche biblioteche. Firenze, 1890.

Graesel, Arnim. Grundzuge der Bibliothekslehre. Leipzig, 1890.

Maire, Albert. Manuel pratique du bibliothecaire. Paris, 1896.

Mivart, St. George. An enumeration of the sciences; in his Groundwork of science, a study of epistemology. London, 1898.

Petzholdt, Julius. Bibliotheca bibliographica. Leipzig, 1866.

NEW MEMBERS.

Junior.—BLAKELY, A. A. (Bermondsey); BURGESS, John (Salford); DIXON, Miss L. (Leyton); HENLEY, Charles (Poplar); PAYNE, E. J. (Bow).

ERRATA.

Page 70, line 2, for "Lord Bacon under Verulam, Viscount," read "Lord Chancellor Bacon under Verulam, Lord, or under St. Albans, Viscount."

BOOKS, &c., RECEIVED.

Birmingham Free Libraries: Books, Pamphlets, and Magazine Articles on British South Africa. Occasional Lists, No. 2.

Croydon Public Libraries: The Reader's Index, v. 4, No. 2.

Leyton Public Libraries: Class List No. 8. The Bible. Library Magazine, v. 4, No. 14, *ed.* by Z. Moon, Librarian.

Manchester Public Free Libraries; Quarterly Record, v. 5, No. 4.

Willesden Green Public Library: Quarterly Record and Guide for Readers, n. s., v. 2. No. 1, *ed.* by the Librarian.

APPOINTMENTS VACANT.

[**Notice to Library Authorities.**—*We shall be pleased to publish under this heading, free of charge, particulars of vacancies if full details are sent to the Editor on or before the 28th of each month.*]

The City and Guilds of London Institute are about to appoint a Librarian at the Institute's Central Technical College, Exhibition Road. Salary £100. Particulars will be sent on application. Applications to be sent in not later than April 7th.

NOTICES.

All matter for the May number should reach the *Hon. Editor* on or before 19th April.

All other communications should be addressed to the *Hon. Secretary*, (*pro. tem.*), MR. J. RADCLIFFE, Public Library, East Ham, E.

The Library Assistant:

The Official Organ of the Library Assistants' Association.

No. 53. MAY, 1902. Published Monthly

THE LIBRARY ASSISTANTS' ASSOCIATION.

Founded 1895.   Seventh Session.   Year 1901-1902.

Members are requested to read carefully the announcements appearing on this and the following pages, as no further intimation of meetings and other arrangements may be expected.

MAY MEETING.

The next Ordinary Meeting will be held by the kind invitation of Mr. W. A. Taylor, Librarian of the St. Giles' Public Library, in the Council Chamber, Municipal Offices, 197, High Holborn, W.C., on Wednesday, May 7th., at 7.30. p.m., when Mr. R. A. Peddie will address the meeting.

The chair will be taken by Mr. Councillor A. Moresby White, chairman of the Holborn Public Libraries Committee.

Light refreshments will be provided.

The meeting place being fairly central, a good attendance of members and friends is specially requested.

At this meeting two members will be elected to audit the accounts of the Library Assistants' Association.

ANNUAL MEETING.

The Seventh Annual Meeting will be held by the kind permission of Mr. J. Y. W. MacAlister, F.S.A., at 20 Hanover Square, at 8 p.m., on June 18th, next.

All nominations for Officers and Committee, and all notices of motion and proposed amendments to the Rules of the Association, must be made in writing to the Hon. Sec., *pro. tem.*, on or before May 15th, in order that they may be sent out with the Annual Report in the June No. of the *Assistant*.

Nominations for Chairman, Hon. Secretary, Hon. Treasurer, ten London, and ten non-London Members of Committee may be made by any Member.

APRIL MEETING.

The April Meeting of the L.A.A. was held in the Poplar Public Library at the kind invitation of Mr. Rowlatt, the Chief Librarian. The subject for the evening was a paper contributed by Mr. W. B. Thorne (St. Bride Institute) entitled *Printing for Librarians*.

Mr. Rowlatt being voted to the chair, after a few preliminary words of welcome, called upon Mr. Thorne to read his paper, which showed evidence of much careful and thoughtful preparation. All the essential points in the arrangement of MS. for the printer were thoroughly dealt with in a very practical manner.

In the discussion which followed, Mr. Rowlatt explained his method of preparing MS., and advocated, where a good printer is employed and the MS. has been carefully prepared, the use of first proofs in page form. This, he said, saves much time and labour both to the printer and librarian, but where constant additions are inserted as the catalogue is in progress, it is unfortunately not possible. Mr. Baxter's interesting suggestion that corrections should be made in red and black ink by the librarian seems to overcome to some extent the difficulties of overcharges. The following members also contributed some interesting and practical remarks to the debate: Messrs. Rees, Soper, Pickard, Hatcher and Harris.

Mr. Harris proposed and Mr. Law seconded, that the best thanks be given Mr. Thorne for his interesting paper. Mr. Thorne suitably replied.

A vote of thanks was then proposed by Mr. Rees, thanking Mr. Rowlatt for his kind reception, and was carried with acclamation.

A pleasant evening was brought to a close by the thoughtful consideration of Mr. and Mrs. Rowlatt who entertained the company with light refreshments before leaving.

There were 30 members and visitors present.   W. J. H.

N. W. BRANCH MAY MEETING.

The next meeting will be held in the John Rylands Library, Manchester, on Tuesday, May 27th, at 7 p.m., when Mr. Guppy will speak to those present on *The History of the English Bible*, and will illustrate his remarks by the exhibition of some of the Bibles contained in the fine collection at the John Rylands Library.

It is particularly requested that as many members as can possibly attend will do so.   W. Q.

LIBRARY ASSOCIATION EXAMINATION.

The next official examination, Section 2—Cataloguing, Classification and Shelf Arrangement only, will be held on Wednesday, May 21st. Names of candidates, accompanied by the fee of 10s. (which may be returned at the discretion of the Education Committee), must be sent to Mr. Henry D. Roberts, Hon. Sec. of the L.A. Education Committee, on or before May 14th. Further particulars will be forwarded on application to Mr. Roberts. Local centres will be arranged wherever necessary.

EDITORIAL.

THE LIBRARY ASSOCIATION'S REVISED EXAMINATION SYLLABUS.

It will be seen by the revised syllabus of the Library Association, which we were privileged to issue with our last number, that several changes in the *modus operandi* of holding examinations have been formulated. The class examinations, for which no certificate was granted, have been abolished. From the ambitious Assistant's point of view this is a very proper step. Without a certificate or recognition in some tangible form, as proof of one's ability and knowledge, these examinations were useless. Not that we advocate the passing of examinations merely for the sake of becoming the possessor of a piece of parchment, but as a weapon to fight one's way into the front rank of our profession, and as a guarantee that we are properly qualified and capable of filling these positions, and, in addition, as a protection against the non-professional, and generally non-efficient, applicant for public appointments, which should be by virtue of training and service the monopoly of the present-day Assistant. This is an age of degrees and certificates, and library authorities, like other authorities, rightly look for evidence of this kind as a guarantee of the professional ability of would-be public officers. It is to the L.A. that we have a right to look for these credentials, indeed, it is part of its duty under its Royal Charter to supply them, and to provide the necessary means for obtaining them.

In past examinations the questions set have generally been of a nature beyond the province of the work of Assistants or Librarians of rate-supported libraries, and in many instances excessively theoretical and often pedantic and useless. It will be interesting to judge by the questions set at the examination to be held this month whether the Council has thoroughly realised that the controversy which has for a number of years raged in connection with this matter was born of, and stimulated by, a real grievance on the part of Library Assistants, and we trust that the examiners will carry out to its fullest, the statement contained in the syllabus that " the special object of the examination as a test of the practical competence of a candidate is held in view by the examiners in setting the questions."

" In future it will be possible to take the examination in five sections instead of three. This will considerably lessen the tax on the very limited time which Assistants have for the study of the important and extensive subjects which the examination embraces, and we would suggest that the rule which provides for section 1 to be taken in parts should also be applicable to sections 2 and 3. Certificates *pro tanto* will, we are pleased to note, be granted for each section.

Another important point, and one which has ever been a *casus belli* between this Association and the L.A. is the question of the policy of the " open door." It will be seen that under the new scheme this grievance has been considerably minimized, the door is no longer wide open, it has been put " upon the chain." The new clause provides that " all candidates for the professional examination must have been engaged in practical library work during the three years previous to their attending any examination." The effect of this, however, is somewhat marred by the next clause, which provides that " the Council, through the Education Committee, reserve to themselves the right to suspend this regulation at their discretion." In spite of the last clause, however, this is an important and graceful concession on the part of the Library Association Council. The Library Assistants' Association has worked hard to close the " open door," and has received valuable assistance and support from prominent librarians from all parts of the country, but it is to the N.W. Branch of the Library Association that the greatest credit is due for the final attainment of this most desirable reform. It will be remembered that some two or three years ago, by the influence of this progressive and practical body, a resolution was carried at an annual meeting against the admission of outsiders. It is undoubtedly owing to this important and praiseworthy action on the part of the N.W. Branch that the Council has been forced to come to this compromise. All we can hope is that the chain which now holds the door ajar will become so rusty that any attempt to open it for the admission of the outsider will prove futile, and that the Council having embarked upon a policy of protection for its members, and the profession with which they are connected, will eventually be convinced of the necessity of carrying it to its full and logical conclusion.

WAR AND THE LIBRARY.—STRAY NOTES.
By Bertram L. Dyer,
Librarian of Kimberley, S.A.

A hasty glance through the publications of the Library Assistants' Association makes an irresistible impression that there are few topics of interest to the Librarian of the future which have not already, in some form, been brought before one of the meetings in one or other of the seven successful sessions the doings of which your publications record.

Librarians who are now honoured with invitations to address you may be pardoned some little envy of the almost limitless choice of subject which lay before the more fortunate contributors to the programmes of your earlier sessions—

"That rapturous time,
When the feelings were young and the world was new,
Like the fresh bowers of Eden unfolding to view."

From parochial to prison libraries, from first editions of Shakespeare, Milton, or Marryat, to penny literature, from smallest detail of charging system to high matters of professional education and status, from the origins of books down to the question of Fiction—from great to small, from grave to gay, and from important questions of principle to trifling items of detail, your varying addresses have passed in review, in one or other aspect, all librarianship.

But stay—there is one subject that as yet appears to have been overlooked, and it would seem as if, "like the angel Pity" libraries shunned "the walks of war," and that with the commencement of the "pride, pomp and circumstance of glorious war" the Librarian's occupation was gone!

The large totals of the various war funds have evidenced that the angel Pity has not shunned the battle-fields of Britain Beyond the Seas, and the publication of a Cape Parliamentary Blue Book, containing the 1900 Library returns, together with the receipt of a smaller return issued by the Librarian of Durban, shows that in Cape Colony and in Natal the existence of an invading force in portions of the Dominions of Her late Majesty did not give pause to the work of the Public Library, even amid the din of a battle, or during the rigours of a siege.

Cut off, as some of these South African Libraries have been from all the world for periods of varying duration, by invading battalions, or by marauding bands of disaffected Colonists who have thrown in their lot with the Transvaalers, still the Libraries have struggled on—crippled a little by the inevitable circumstance of martial law—but yet doing the best within the circumstances to fulfil all the functions of a Library.

Some few stray notes which have been set down at odd times may perhaps be of some little interest to you, as describing things abnormal in your present experience, and therefore having some little claim on your attention.

The endless stream of printed matter which has been written around questions South African since the eyes of the Empire have been focussed on this part of the Dark Continent, makes one hesitate before adding more to the burden, lacking that chief qualification of complete ignorance of the subject which has been mainly that of most of the ephemeral writers, the speed of whose pens has only been equalled by the hastiness of whose conclusions as to the ultimate destinies of all Africa South of the Zambesi.

There is a very general impression that there are no Public Libraries in South Africa, and that in these things the Old Country is far ahead of her Cape daughters. But South Africa has a Library System, which in many things can give points to the home system—more especially in the way it develops and fosters local effort in the smaller towns and the scattered villages.

This system is however of very modern establishment, and even as there were Public Libraries in England before Mr. Ewart laid the foundations of that legislation which has so extended their benefits, there were Libraries in the Colony which have by legislation specially suited to Colonial requirement extended to all the more populous places of the Colony the benefits of a state-aided Library system.

So far back as 1761, one, Joachim N. von Dessin bequeathed to the Consistory of the Dutch Reformed Church at Cape Town, "a large and most valuable collection of books" to serve as the nucleus of a Public Library, together with a very small annual sum for their upkeep. The number of volumes amounted to upwards of four thousand, in the Dutch, French, German, and Latin tongues, and the donation may be usefully compared with that bequeathed at about the same date, by John Dawson to the Vicar and Churchwardens of St. Leonard, Shoreditch. It is interesting to note that while Shoreditch is the only Municipal Public Library in the County of London which can claim to have received the nucleus of her present Public Library in the eighteenth century, it was not until well into the last quarter of the nineteenth century that any steps were taken to properly house or extend that gift of a former century, while Cape Town had claimed its books from the Consistory, and housed them in a special building so far back as 1818! This was six years before the Corporation of the City of London took steps to found her Guildhall Library, and nearly half a century before the sister City of Westminster parted with her heritage of the Tenison Library to the musical sound of the auctioneer's hammer!

Twenty years after Cape Town had re-housed her Library, Swellendam established a Library to be followed by George in 1840, Graaf-Reinet in 1847, Cradock in 1850, Colesberg in 1852—links in a chain, many another of which has been forged since the Legislature commenced to give grants in aid of Libraries.

In 1851, Pietermaritzburg, in Natal, led the way in the sister Colony, by the foundation of the Natal Society, to be followed in 1853 by Durban, with its Mechanics' Institute, reconstituted in 1873 as its Public Library, which enjoys the distinction of being the only Public Library in South Africa to which all residents of a Town have access for borrowing privileges, it being handsomely subsidised by the Municipality for this purpose.

As curiously illustrative of the value and importance of the Cape Town Library in the first half of the nineteenth century, there is an interesting passage in "The Life and Times of Sir John Molteno," who "had come out to the Cape as assistant in the Cape Town Library, but whose occupation at the Library gave him an opportunity of becoming acquainted with the country, and soon proved too narrow and restricted an opening" for the man who was destined to become the first Premier of Cape Colony.

Writing about 1844 to his mother in England he says:—

"I much wish you could obtain a proper account of the Cape, perhaps you may be able to get the loan of some recent work, there are several. If you were so fortunate as we are at the Cape, in having a Public Library of 30,000 volumes to resort to, you would experience no difficulty in this respect."

Ex-Library-Assistant Molteno was instrumental in extending to the whole of Cape Colony the benefits that he so highly appreciated, for in 1874 provision was made in the Annual Estimates of the Colony for the encouragement of Public Libraries and Reading Rooms in all parts.

Says his filial biographer:—" This has been a most successful measure, and under it, Libraries of a very valuable character have come into existence in every important town in the Colony." But it is yet more remarkable that a village which one might be justified in calling petty, and which in England would certainly not have a Library unless it had a Verney living adjacent to it, out here has a Library, and receives governmental aid for such Library.

The main principle of the South African System of Libraries, is that no voluntary or compulsory rate is levied for Library purposes, and that the residents of a Town are not mulcted alike, whether they be users of the Library or not. The actual users of the Libraries pay into the funds of the local Library, subscriptions which are graduated in most places according to the number of books required to be borrowed at one and the same time, or according to the number of persons in the household who use the Library rooms. Then, in most cases, for every pound of Annual Subscription the government adds another pound—but this pound for pound grant may not exceed £100 per annum. In the case of large Towns, each Library is considered on its merits, and a fixed grant is made in aid of general revenue, while special grants may be made in aid of Building Funds, Reference Libraries, etc.

In addition, the Acts constituting the various larger Municipalities contain a provision that the Corporations may, out of general funds, vote sums in aid of Schools, Hospitals, and Libraries.

The main income is, however, derived locally from subscriptions, and the subscribers elect from themselves the Committee of Management, and directly control the Libraries.

For the purpose of fixing the individual grants, Annual Returns have to be made after the Library Accounts have been duly audited, which Returns must be signed by the auditors, and by the Civil Commissioner of the district, and from these Returns annual statements are compiled which are issued as Parliamentary Blue Books.

Nine Libraries receive special grants, Grahamstown, Cape Town, Cradock, East London, Graaf-Reinet, Kimberley, King Williamstown, Port Elizabeth, and Queenstown. No less than 98 other Libraries received pound for pound grants in 1900, while of four others no details were to hand. It is true that only six new names this year appear on the list, while seventeen names have dropped out as compared with 1899, but in the especial circumstances, it would not have been surprising if there had been an even greater decrease. Libraries deriving their main income from so fluctuating a source as voluntary subscriptions would naturally be supposed to shew by their financial returns the effects of an incursion of an enemy, or a general disturbance of the community they were supported by. But the names that have dropped out of the list are those of small and unimportant places—villages you would almost call them. For instance, Mafeking has dropped out, but Mafeking only started its Library in 1898, and no details appear in the 1899 return, so that the beginning can hardly be said to have been made. Vryburg and Griquatown too have gone from the Return, but the latter of these had only 2000 volumes, collected only £10 in subscriptions, and had a total income of £60.

Comparing the Returns for 1897 with those for 1900, there appears a general increase in the sums of money raised locally for the Libraries, and though there are fluctuations such as always must occur, the influence on the Libraries generally, of the disturbed state of affairs has not been of anything like so serious a nature as one would have imagined. Cape Colony has kept her Libraries intact, but Dundee, in Natal, was "Looted by the Boers" and is at present closed.

Of the part that individual Libraries have played in the war, it were almost impossible to attempt a record. Cape Town, Port Elizabeth, and East London, in the Colony, and Durban and Pietermaritzburg in Natal, have temporarily gained additional subscribers from the residents of the new Colonies that have perforce been away from their permanent homes. Here too, this cause has affected our work.

All the Libraries of the Colony have done the very best that they could to make welcome Tommy Atkins and his Officer, and one of the pleasing sights which work in a South African Library affords, is the rush that Tommy, —just in from march " on column," dusty, weary, and soiled,—makes in the reading-room, for the files of his beloved paper, be it English, Scotch, Irish, Australian or Canadian. Then, too, the evident pleasure of being able to write a letter home with clean ink, clean pen, and clean paper, at a decently steady table, instead of on the least windy side of a dust-storm swept Kopje—or amid the discomforts of a tent through whose canvas is beating the penetrating tropical rain of South Africa.

A cynical officer recently observed that it were useless for the enemy to attempt to enter the block-houses on account of the huge barricades which Thomas Atkins could shelter himself behind, composed of the literature which well-meaning persons showered on the guardians of these "guarders of Communication "—but there never has been any slacking in the demand for reading matter of all kinds, for block-houses, hospitals, and camps—and a failure to supply it brings early reminder.

Ministering to the wants of the soldier is a pleasant duty, but the military authorities do not always display equal pleasure in ministering to the wants of the Library, and more especially in the inland towns where permits are necessary before goods from the coast may be forwarded. Library books, may, strictly speaking, not be necessaries of life, but judging from the use both officers and soldiers make of them, it is vexatious to have to wait weeks or months while the carefully selected box of books from London lies at the port of entry " waiting permit."

The censorship of the Military Censor is a thing rather to be suffered under with patience than with gladness. The vexatious delays with regard to foreign papers, of such standing as the " Revue des Deux Mondes " are inexcusable. as also the complete stoppage of purely scientific papers from America,—such as " Cassier's Magazine," and the " Scientific American "— to say nothing of " Public Libraries."

Until recently there was an order enforced, that all South African newspapers should be delayed three weeks from date of posting, because it had been discovered that communications of a supposed treasonable nature had been sent in newspapers to avoid the probable opening of letters by the Censor. The delay of three weeks meant practically that the South African newspapers were delivered after the newspapers of even date that were published in England had come to hand—and a more vexatious regulation was never promulgated for so weak a reason—for it must be manifest that newspapers addressed by a publishing office to a public institution could not be used for treasonable communications. Certain newspapers organised a parcel delivery through the Cape Government Railway for such towns as had sufficient subscribers resident in them, but for many papers and places this was impossible. Fortunately this regulation has now been rescinded.

Of forbidden books and newspapers—things placed on the military *index expurgatorius*—it were perhaps unwise to attempt a list just at present, but in years hence these things will form matter for wonderment.

In closing these disjointed and stray notes, it were well to remind all of you who are interested in the development of South African Libraries that in 1897 our very good friend, Mr. MacAlister published in the "Library," a most interesting article from the pen of the Hon. Mr. Justice Laurence, Judge President of the High Court of Griqualand, and for nearly a score of years chairman of this Library. This article, with an interesting address on this Library have been reprinted in a volume of "Collectanea," published by Macmillan in 1899, and both are well worthy the attention of all those interested in the Library movement in South Africa.

Now is neither the moment nor the opportunity for other than this rough and disjointed paper, but at a future date some more experienced librarian of this continent may be able to lay before you a proper view of all the South African Libraries, from the "shank end" to "the Empire up North," from the German territories to the Portuguese, whence all the knowledge that is mine, is the brief word "discontinued" on a returned letter asking for information as to the Library of Lourenco Marques, but until such date, the information contained in the very useful table which Mr. Miller, of Bulawayo contributed to Volume I. of your journal requires little supplement.

If it does nothing else, this table may serve to prove that the Public Libraries of South Africa are trying, even in war time, their best to live up to the words of that other South African Ex-Library-Assistant—Thomas Pringle—the as yet greatest poet of South Africa :—

"For in this wilderness there is work to do—

. . . .

"Something for Africa to do or say,
If but one mite of Europe's debt to pay."

STUDY CIRCLE.

Report on April Work :—

LITERARY HISTORY. The best answers in this section were sent by "Bala" (*Senior*) and "Liber" (*Junior*), "Bala," however, omits mention of several very important historians of the period. "Saturn" confuses the two Froudes, and the answer by "Dust" is very disconnected. "Poohbah" runs "Liber" very close for top marks.

LIBRARY PRACTICE. The best answers are those from "Saturn" (*Senior*) and "Poohbah" (*junior*). The standard of the papers sent in is very fair, but junior assistants have been rather given to explain the system which they are accustomed to, treating all others somewhat neglectfully.

Readings for May.

Senior.—Saintsbury. 19th Century Literature, ch. IV. Morley. Victorian Literature, ch. IV.

Junior.—Morley Victorian Literature *only*. Last portion of ch. IV.

Questions on April Reading.—Literary History.

Senior.—Give an account of the life and work of Sydney Smith.

Junior.—State what you know of the works of Walter Savage Landor.

Library Practice. *Senior.*—What method of operation with the Public Elementary Schools do you consider most preferable, and why? *Junior.*—What books would you recommend as containing the best information concerning the first six King Edwards?

NOTE.—All answers must reach Mr. G. E. Roebuck, 121 De Beauvoir Road, Kingsland, N., on or before May 16th.

NOTES AND COMMENTS.

Battersea.—A Juvenile Reading Room has been opened in the Mantua Street Board School.

Bermondsey. OPENING OF A NEW BRANCH.—On April 7th a Branch Library for the St. Olave's District was opened to the public by Mr. Henry Vezey, the Vice-Chairman of the Libraries' Committee, in the absence through illness of the Mayor.

The Library is at present located in a portion of the St. Olave Institute. Only the Reading Rooms are available at present, but the Lending Department, which will start with 8,000 volumes, will be opened shortly.

Greenwich.—At the last meeting of the Council, the Acts were adopted for the whole of this Borough, and will come into operation immediately. The Mayor stated that it was only proposed to levy a ½d. rate at present, realising £500 per annum. This sum, he believed, would be sufficient to start with. It is proposed to rent a house for £100 per annum, and the remainder of the £500 is for salaries and general maintenance!

The first Library is to be at East Greenwich, and branches are to be opened at West Greenwich, Charlton, and St. Nicholas, Deptford. Fortunately for Greenwich, the Council realises the necessity for the early appointment of a Librarian, which will be one step towards the abandonment of the idea of being able to maintain even a medium-sized Library on the ridiculously inadequate sum mentioned.

Ilford.—The Council has decided to put the P. L. Acts, which were adopted in 1892, into operation. A penny rate will amount to between £500 and £600.

"Liberty Review."—We cull the following from the *Liberty Review* for April :—

"WOULD NOT BE BRIBED TO STEAL.—Mr. Carnegie offered to Loanhead £12,000 towards a public library if the ratepayers would adopt the book-stealing Acts. The ratepayers preferred to remain honest and refused to adopt the Acts."

Can any of our Readers tell us what are the "book-stealing Acts," and why they are so called !! The *Liberty Review* evidently has views of its own on the question of Public Libraries.

"Library World."—In the April number of this Journal we are informed that :—

"In order to commemorate his tenure of office as Mayor of Eastbourne the Duke of Devonshire has presented to the Borough a site near the station for a technical institution and Public Library."

This information was published in the issue of the *Library Assistant* of August, 1898!!! Our contemporary contains, amongst other interesting information, an excellent and practical article on *News Room Arrangement*, by Mr. Burt, Sub-Librarian of the Fulham Public Libraries.

Southend.—The Coronation Committee has under consideration the adoption of the P. L. Acts for the celebration of the King's accession.

Steeple Claydon.—Lady Verney recently laid the foundation stone of a new Public Library and Village Hall, which is being erected at a cost of £1,500 at the expense of Sir Edmund Verney, Bart.

BOOKS, &c., RECEIVED.

BISHOPSGATE INSTITUTE (Chas. Wm. F. Goss, Librarian). Report for the year ended March 25th, 1902.

This Report records the classification of the Library on the Dewey Decimal System and the much advertised change which has taken place in connection with the method of issue. An excellent programme of concerts and lectures has been carried out during the year. The report also contains a useful list of the large collection of Directories contained in the Library.

"EDWARD EDWARDS: the Chief Pioneer of Municipal Public Libraries" by *Thomas Greenwood*, xii. + 246 pages, gilt top. Scott, Greenwood & Co. 2/6 nett.

KIMBERLEY PUBLIC LIBRARY (Bertram L. Dyer, Librarian). Nineteenth Annual Report, 1901.

The unsettled circumstances alluded to in the last two Reports have, unhappily, not being without influence on the year's work, but nevertheless the report shows an all-round improvement on the two preceding years, and nearly equals 1898, the best year in the recent history of the Library. We are pleased to see that the Committee think that any photographs or printed matter bearing on local affairs should be preserved in the Library, and have started a local collection.

LIBRARY ASSISTANTS' ASSOCIATION (NORTH-WESTERN BRANCH). (W. Quarmby, Hon. Sec.) Third Annual Report to December, 1901.

This Report shows a steady increase in the membership and in the usefulness of the Association. Unfortunately, as with all small Associations, the state of the exchequer holds back any new projects, the Committee remarks that "the income will have to be supplemented, from other sources than subscriptions if further progress is to be recorded.

PASSMORE EDWARDS PUBLIC LIBRARY (SOUTHWARK), (Thomas Aldred, Librarian), Supplementary Catalogue, 1—48 + i—viii, double columns, 8vo.

This is a carefully compiled piece of work arranged on the "Cutter" classification, the first catalogue on this system in England. A departure has been made from the usual course adopted in public library catalogues, viz : that no call numbers are given to the books. The borrower simply asking for the book required by its short title, *e.g.*—Hedin's, "Through Asia," and we are given to understand that the assistants have no difficulty in finding what is wanted as the whole library is closely classified on the shelves. A repetition of the main divisions at the top of each page, would, we think, have proved a useful addition.

OBITUARY.

The news of the death of Mr. Sydney G. Mattocks has come as a shock to all who knew him, and especially to those who enjoyed the privilege of his society in the family circle of Mr. and Mrs. Dyer, both of whom were deeply attached to him. His pleasant and genial disposition endeared him to all with whom he came in contact, to which he added a keen and intellectual interest in his profession. He was successful in several of the Library Association examinations, and in 1898 was awarded a "Greenwood" prize offered through the Library Assistants' Association for an essay entitled *My Professional Studies*.

He received his early training in the Kensington Public Libraries, and was afterwards appointed to a more important post in the Hampstead Libraries. Early in the present year he left England to take up the appointment of Assistant Librarian at the Kimberley Public Library under his old colleague, Mr. Bertram L. Dyer. Within three weeks from his arrival at Kimberley he developed typhoid fever, contracted during his journey "up country," from which he succumbed on March 10th.

He was born at Rainham, Kent, in 1882, and was thus only in his 20th year.—" His mind was perfect and his purpose true."

At the last meeting of the L.A.A. Committee a vote of condolence was unanimously passed, and copies of the same directed to be sent to Mr. and Mrs. Mattocks and Mr. and Mrs. Dyer.

APPOINTMENTS AND CHANGES.

BROWN, J. WILSON. Senior Assistant, Cardiff Public Library, and late of the Kendal and Shoreditch Public Libraries to be Assistant Librarian, Kimberley Public Library, South Africa. Mr. Brown held the office of Hon. Sec. of the L.A.A. previous to his appointment to Cardiff.

NEW MEMBER.

Junior.—Smith, Aloysius (Salford).

NOTICES.

All matter for the June number should reach the *Hon. Editor* on or before 20th May.

All other communications should be addressed to the *Hon. Secretary*, *(pro. tem.)*, MR. J. RADCLIFFE, Public Library, East Ham, E.

The Library Assistant:

The Official Organ of the Library Assistants' Association.

No. 54.   JUNE, 1902.   Published Monthly

THE LIBRARY ASSISTANTS' ASSOCIATION.

FOUNDED 1895.   SEVENTH SESSION.   YEAR 1901-1902.

Members are requested to read carefully the announcements appearing on this and the following pages, as no further intimation of meetings and other arrangements may be expected.

ANNUAL MEETING.

The Seventh Annual Meeting will be held, by the kind permission of Mr. J. Y. W. MacAlister, F.S.A., at 20 Hanover Square, at 8 p.m. on Wednesday, June 18th.

The report of the Committee and the balance sheet will be submitted; the Officers and Committee for the ensuing year will be elected; and any business, of which notice has been given, will be considered.

All nominations received will be found on the ballot paper enclosed herewith to all members qualified to vote. The ballot papers will be opened and counted at this meeting.

Members are earnestly requested to be present at this meeting, and subscribers to this Journal and others interested in the Association are cordially invited to attend.

SUMMER PROGRAMME.

An afternoon excursion to Brighton will take place on Wednesday, July 9th, when it is hoped that arrangements will be made to visit, among other places of interest, the new Public Library.

The party will travel by the V.E.C.A. express, which leaves Victoria at 12.30 p.m., Clapham Junction at 12.35, and East Croydon at 12.50. Railway tickets (2s. 6d.) may be obtained in advance from MR. W. B. YOUNG, 63 Leslie Road, Leytonstone,

E., or direct from the Secretary, V.E.C.A., 64 Cheapside, E.C. If purchased at stations on the day, tickets will be 3s.

In order to facilitate the necessary arrangements, all intending to join the party are requested to inform Mr. Young as early as possible.

PROPOSED CONFERENCE.—PRELIMINARY NOTICE.

It is proposed to hold a General Gathering of Members of the L.A.A., from all parts of the country, at Wolverhampton this year. A suggested date is September 10th.

Wolverhampton is fairly central. An Industrial and Art Exhibition is now being held there, and will continue during the summer months. The principal Railway Companies are running excursion trains thereto at reduced fares.

The *Hon. Sec.*, Mr. J. Radcliffe, Public Library, East Ham, E., will be glad to hear from members and friends who intend joining the party.

If a satisfactory number reply no effort will be spared to ensure a successful meeting and to provide an attractive programme.

It is particularly requested that communications on this subject should reach the Hon. Sec. not later than the 30th June.

"COTGREAVE" (1902) AND "L.A.A." JUNIOR (1902) PRIZE ESSAYS.

Members of the L.A.A. and Assistants generally are particularly requested to note that the date for the receipt of essays for the above prizes has been EXTENDED to TUESDAY, JUNE 10th, in the hope that a larger number of assistants than have already done so will be induced to compete. Full particulars appeared in the April Number of the *Assistant*.

FAREWELL SUPPER TO MR. J. WILSON BROWN.

At a cosy restaurant within a stone's throw of the favourite Fleet Street haunt of Dr. Johnson, about a dozen members of the L.A.A. dined together on Wednesday, April 30th. The guest of the evening was Mr. J. Wilson Brown, a former secretary, who sailed for Kimberley on the Wednesday following. Our whilom leader and esteemed colleague the Kimberley Librarian on hearing that Mr. Brown was leaving Cardiff immediately gave evidence of the confidence he had in Mr. Brown's work and ability by offering him the post of Chief Assistant at Kimberley.

It is worthy of note that Mr. Brown is the second Secretary and third member of the L.A.A. to go to Kimberley. We wish him God speed and every success in his new sphere of labour.

THE MAY MEETING.

The May Meeting of the L.A.A. was held by invitation of Mr. W. A. Taylor, Librarian of St. Giles' Public Library, in the Council Chamber adjoining the St. Giles' Library, on May 7th. The chair was occupied by Councillor A. Moresby White, chairman of the Holborn Public Libraries Committee, and amongst those present were Mr. W. A. Taylor and Mr. Hawkes, Librarian of the Holborn Public Library, refreshments being kindly provided by Messrs. Hawkes and Taylor. Messrs. Law and Thorne were appointed auditors of last year's accounts.

The Chairman, on behalf of the Holborn Borough Council and the Libraries' Committee, welcomed the Association and said that the real object for which public libraries exist is to teach and instruct the public, to point out obvious sources of information, and to supply that information. Their object is not merely to amuse or provide recreation. That is the debasing, the lowering, the degrading of a high ideal. Librarians and Assistants should form a walking index to the books so as to put the reader on the track of other works and thus lead from one thing to another, and from one study to a higher one. It is all very well to erect a great building, but if sufficient sums are not set aside for the payment of capable officials, and sufficient sums to attract men of brains and intelligence, men who will work towards the realization of a high object, then the result aimed at fails, and these grand buildings, these municipal palaces, might as well have been pigsties, lunatic asylums, washhouses, or anything else. Capable and efficient service must be provided for or the whole fails. Misguided individuals who want to hand their names down to posterity are not doing any very great service unless they bear in mind that large buildings must include efficient service and that efficient service can only be purchased by sufficient pay. The salaries of library assistants are miserably inadequate when compared with the rate of wages paid to other persons in the service of local authorities. He hoped that it would be borne in mind that the end of an association like the L.A.A. is not merely to advance its own interests, much as he sympathised with that, but also to advance the public interest, and that librarians and assistants are the custodians of the public mind and the future will look to them for the improvement of the general stock of wisdom and the happiness of the people.

Mr. R. A. Peddie then addressed the Meeting on the *Past, Present, and Future of Public Libraries*, and said that, like everything else that was good, the Public Library movement began in Scotland, and that it was a Scotsman who circularized the whole of the boroughs of that kingdom in the year 1700. But the efforts made between the years 1840 and 1850 were the cause of the passing of the Act; yet this was preceded by the Baths and Washhouses Acts. He thought that in the conjunction of these two questions, Baths and Libraries, the Baths first, the Government must have had for once something sensible in mind. When people had washed *then* they should read. The public library has not yet crystallized into its final form. The original idea was to provide newsrooms and collect books, no matter what, anyhow, haphazard, without any idea of co-operation. We are beginning to get beyond that. In referring to indicators and open access, he said that sufficient initiative was not allowed to assistants, and the public was either turned loose into an enclosure or had to go to the catalogue. He believed the reference library to be the most important department of any library. The public library was too often a mere circulating library and this was partly due to the decadence of our periodical literature which forced people to read novels, whereas in Germany and Italy, which possess magnificent libraries in every town, the circulating library is almost unknown. There the people study their books and do not merely read for amusement. The periodical literature of this country renders it essential that circulating libraries should exist in England in order that people may be weaned from reading " such pernicious stuff." He advocated co-operation between the libraries of London. The national library should be the centre of bibliographical research, of historical research, the working office of our great thinkers and scholars; then there should be the Library of the Province such as that at Manchester, which might be made to feed a network of towns, and this should be established in all populous centres such as the Tyneside district. The City Library should remain for the ordinary reader and the ordinary student, but there should be rural Libraries which might be worked on the plan of the American Travelling Libraries tried in Massachusetts. We are just now on the eve of a great educational revolution, and librarians should keep a sufficient grasp on this question to bring them more in touch with the educational machinery. Before long the schoolmasters of the country might be officials of the same Council and then both would work together, the schoolmaster to teach and the librarian to train the children to read. The library assistant must also train himself, not necessarily by examinations but also by attending classes, and he might even be able to "assimilate knowledge through the pores of the skin." He considered the L.A.A.

deserving of great credit and it was an association differing from all others as its members were constantly changing. In spite of this its useful work continued.

A discussion followed and was taken part in by Messrs. Soper, Thorne, Chambers, Lewin, P. H. Wood, Pickard and McDouall, and votes of thanks were passed to the Holborn Borough Council, Councillor A. Moresby White, and Messrs. Taylor and Hawkes. P. B. L.

STUDY CIRCLE.

READINGS FOR JUNE (*as last month*).

QUESTIONS ON MAY READINGS.

LITERARY HISTORY.

Senior. Give an account of Charles Lamb and his contemporaries.

Junior. State what you know of the work of Isaac Disraeli.

LIBRARY PRACTICE.

Senior. What methods are most preferable for the systematic preservation of local historical and topographical matter, not in volume form.

Junior. Write a short article on the filing of newspapers and periodicals.

NOTE.—The above questions conclude the Fourth Session of the S. Circle, which will be discontinued during the holiday season. The opening of the Fifth Session (in the Autumn) will be duly announced, and the Committee trust that more support will be extended to this most useful section of the Association's work.

Answers to the above questions must reach Mr. G. E. Roebuck, 121 De Beauvoir Road, Kingsland, N., on or before Saturday, June 14th.

CORRESPONDENCE.

[The Editor solicits expressions of opinion on all matters of interest to the profession, but does not hold himself responsible for the views of correspondents. Communications should be written on one side of the paper only, and should be as brief as possible.]

Dear Sir,

In your last issue you congratulated the Library Association on the increased interest it was showing in the education of library assistants, and the keener sense of its duties and responsibilities to the profession in this respect. Your congratulations were previous and undeserved, for the Education Committee of that body is now proposing what can only be characterized as a gross betrayal of the interests of assistants, and a dereliction of its duty of education. It has passed a recommendation to the Council that the technical instruction of library assistants should be handed over to the Technical Education Board of the London County Council through its School of Economics. Originally intending to ask merely for a grant in aid of their classes, the Education Committee has been induced to consent to what is practically a transfer, to this alien body, of their power and moral duty of education under their Royal Charter. It is perhaps needless for me to say that the London School of Economics, in proposing the transfer, is not actuated by any high motive of public duty, or of regard for the interests of the library profession. It sees a means to secure students for neglected portions of its own syllabus, and, consequently, increased grants of public money. Its ideas of the proper education for the young librarian will be regarded with amazement by assistants. The scheme comprises such subjects as Palæography and Diplomatic (great importance is attached to this), General Economics, Methods of Statistics, General History and Organization of Local Government! These are of vital importance to library assistants, are they not? Our municipal libraries naturally abound in Anglo-Saxon manuscripts and state papers of Henry VIII. The study of statistics will of course prove of invaluable aid to an assistant in reckoning the day's issues; and how can one expect him to catalogue a book properly unless he can recite the provisions of the first Local Government Act? These people apparently have a vague idea that Bibliography means the compiling of short lists of books on special subjects. They would be quite willing to give this instruction—in fact their lecturers make a point of giving their students rough lists of books. This view of the study of Bibliography will interest those assistants who remember with gratitude Mr. Guppy's admirable lectures. The School of Economics naturally does not attach much importance to the subject of "Library Administration, including Cataloguing, Methods of Printing and Bookbinding, etc." (all lumped together), but if the Library Association will defray the expenses of this particular class, they will consider the question of adding it to their syllabus. But there is another subject in which these importunate library assistants are clamouring for instruction—Literature! Really, says the School of Economics, we cannot be bothered with such minor points, they must get this elsewhere. Besides, what do library assistants need with literature if they have a sound instruction in Diplomatic and the History of Local Government! And anyhow, we should have to pay a special lecturer for that. So literature is dropped. Surely, Mr. Editor, this is exchanging King Log for King Stork with a vengeance. The Library Association's classes were ludicrously inadequate, but good so far as they went. We lose this little and get in return—Palæography and Diplomatic!

The Education Committee seriously proposes to hand us over to the tender mercies of this College of Laputa. They would be relieved of a little expense and a great deal of trouble. There is only one serious criticism they have to offer on the scheme, and that is worthy of it and them. The School of Economics, with all its Chinese ideas, does not consider that its theoretical education is all-sufficient to turn out a competent librarian. Curiously enough, it thinks that this education should only be supplementary to practical experience in a public library. But this is against all the traditions of the Library Association! This controverts our most sacred principles! This is rank Trades Unionism, the Closed Door, the Protection of Incompetents! This is what that pestilent little Library Assistants' Association has been making such a fuss about. Oh! this will never do! So they gravely insert an amendment providing for the negation of this clause at their will, and then, with the warm glow of a keen sense of moral rectitude and duty well done, send up the proposal with their blessings to the Council.

I am afraid, Mr. Editor, that the Education Committee does not concern itself much about the views of library assistants on the matter of their education. It would be too much to expect that the disapproval of our little Association could disturb the self-complacency of these Mandarins. But we ought not to allow this most shameful betrayal to pass without a word of protest. I can hardly believe that the edict of this Tsung-li-Yamen has the approval or acquiescence of its erstwhile energetic Honorary Secretary, who, alone among his fellows, has by his action on previous occasions led library assistants to think that he had their interests sincerely at heart. But if I am mistaken, and it is that he has abandoned his lone furrow, then we have little hope but in our own unaided efforts. It may, however, be not too late to make an earnest appeal to Mr. Roberts to re-commence once more his Sisyphean labours, and to remind him that labour, like virtue, is sometimes its own reward.

I am, yours, etc.,
A LONDON LIBRARY ASSISTANT.
To the Editor of the " Library Assistant."

*EDWARD EDWARDS.

Truly a prophet has little honour in his own country. The melancholy story of " Edward Edwards, the Chief Pioneer of Municipal Public Libraries," illustrates once more the fact that more often than not recognition comes too late to stay " the iron in the soul " of disappointed hopes. Yet this was not altogether the case with Edwards, for though he himself lived neglected and forgotten, the recipient of a stranger's bounty, he saw the splendid edifice of which he had laid the foundations rising step by step; an abiding monument for the ages and not merely that column trophied for triumphal show from which the inscription is worn in a generation. Edwards has raised his own monument.

The little volume just issued by Mr. Greenwood, dedicated to the Forgotten Benefactors of Humanity, is a token that the new century recognises in Edwards one of that little

---

*EDWARD EDWARDS, by *Thomas Greenwood*, xii. + 246 pages, gilt top, 2/6 net. (Scott, Greenwood & Co.)

band of workers in the cause of education which daily grows larger. That Mr. Greenwood should have done so much to rescue Edwards' name from oblivion is appropriate; it is the tribute of one lover of the library movement to another. The little we glean of the personal life of Edwards from this volume makes us desire more. The introductory chapter compels our attention, and the sad details of the last chapter, narrating the old age of Edwards, alone yet not friendless, draw our sympathy towards him more than any amount of biographical details would have done. It is to be regretted that the materials Mr. Greenwood has had to work upon have been so very few, and yet had Edwards' character been less retiring that touch of nature which makes the whole world kin would not have been so strong and we should have been the less drawn to the man. It is unnecessary here to allude to the literary quality of the book before us. The greater part is taken up with the history of Edwards' connection with the British Museum and the Manchester Public Library, and with his work on behalf of the library movement, a subject interesting to the student of that movement, but not one lending itself to review. The purely personal details of the volume are those which will delight the reader. The descriptions of the man as he was will touch the chord of sympathy. ." He had the scholar's stoop, and always wore a frock coat with a silk hat, with neckties of a blue or green colour." Perhaps not much in that little touch, but the chord is struck in the following:—" The frock coat and silk hat ultimately turned very shabby and became a mark for the fun of the village boys." That is the pathos of his life; his forgotten old age when he barely subsisted on a small government pension.

He is likened to Francis of Assisi in the preface, and certainly he had many of the saintly qualities: his disregard of poverty, his lack of personal ambition, and his enthusiasm for the cause he had taken up; but we cannot help thinking that Mr. Greenwood is ill advised in calling marked attention to Edwards' religious views. "He began life as a Nonconformist," he says, "and ended it as an earnest Episcopalian. To this early training in dissent he owed whatever of true spirituality there was in his inner religious life." Such a sentence might very well have been left out, as it savours too much of the very fault with which Edwards himself is charged.

Space does not permit of a longer notice of this admirable book, which, in addition to its bearing on the Public Library movement, has a still higher claim to esteem by its appeal to our sympathy. The preface contains an admirable suggestion as to a tribute to Edwards' work—he wants no memorial; these we already have all over the country. An Edward Edwards Librarians' Home of Rest at Niton, and an Edward Edwards Library School are both put forward as tentative suggestions for future benefactors. At the end of the book will be found Dr. Garnett's feeling and scholarly address given at Niton in February last, when a stone was raised over the hitherto unmarked grave. The general public, and especially librarians, should indeed be very grateful to Mr. Thomas Greenwood for thus honouring the memory of Edward Edwards.

No Public Library will be complete without at least one copy of this work on its shelves, and the low price at which it is published brings it well within the scope of the modest amount which Library Assistants are able to spend on their private collections. P. E. L.

NOTES AND COMMENTS.

Sydney, N.S.W.—The report of the Public Library contains some interesting reading. A fiction and juvenile percentage of 57.4 is apologised for, though this would compare very favourably with many English and American libraries. The system of fines for over-detention has recently been introduced into the lending department, and appears to have been much resented by the borrowers, as more than 1000 surrendered their tickets rather than pay the fines. Notwithstanding this, the results are regarded as being eminently satisfactory.

A competitive examination for three cataloguers for the reference library resulted in the success of three ladies, out of fourteen applicants divided equally between the sexes.

Stepney.—The Chairman of the Committee (Councillor F. C. Mills) has very kindly offered to take the Public Libraries Committee, together with the whole of the libraries staff, upon a visit to Oxford and its Colleges on Saturday, the 31st May, and in order to carry out his wishes the Public Libraries in the Borough will be closed on that Saturday.

Stratford-on-Avon.—The Public Libraries Acts have been adopted and Mr. Carnegie is presenting a Library. The Mayor headed a subscription list with £100 towards the purchase of books, &c.

Tipton, Staffordshire.—The Tipton Free Library Committee has improved on the principle of blacking out betting news. It is offering to let the spaces taken up by betting transactions to tradesmen whose advertisements will be gummed over the spaces.

LIBRARY ASSISTANTS' ASSOCIATION.

SEVENTH ANNUAL REPORT.

To be presented at the Seventh Annual Meeting, at 20 Hanover Square, W., on Wednesday, 18th June, 1902.

The Committee beg to submit the Seventh Annual Report on the work of the L.A.A. The year under review has been one of steady progress and considerable success.

The Sixth Annual Meeting was held on June 19th 1901, again by the kind invitation of Mr. MacAlister, at 20 Hanover Square. Mr. Evan G. Rees was, for the second time, elected Chairman of the Association, Mr. W. G. Chambers was again elected Hon. Treasurer, and Mr. G. E. Roebuck Hon. Secretary. The Annual Report was adopted, the names of the members elected to serve on the Committee made known, and the results of the Prize Essay Competitions announced. The suggestion by Mr. Hogg that a Circular setting forth the advantages of membership of the L.A.A. was considered and, with slight alteration, carried. Several suggested alterations of Rules were discussed resulting in the alteration of section D of Rule 3.

On December 11th a Special Meeting was held to consider a number of proposals brought forward by Mr. A. J. Philipp. Of these, one altering the date of the Annual Meeting from the Summer to the Winter was carried by nine votes to seven.

The opening Meeting of the Session was held at the Guildhall on October 16th by kind invitation of Mr. Charles Welch, F.S.A., the City librarian, over sixty members and friends being present. Mr. W. Rome, F.S.A., F.L.S., Chairman of the Guildhall Library Committee, welcomed the L.A.A. on behalf of his Committee, and expressed the pleasure it gave him to afford the Association an opportunity of inspecting the grand old building, the most interesting parts were visited; Mr. Rome drawing attention to, and explaining the valuable works of Art and Antiquity, while Mr. Welch kindly outlined the history of the Hall, the Chambers of the Courts of Aldermen and Common Council, and the very interesting Crypt. At the meeting proper, Mr. Welch read a very instructive paper entitled, "The Young Librarian: his Training and Possibilities," Mr. Rome presiding.

The Ordinary Meetings have been regularly and successfully held each month from October to May, and the best thanks of the Association are due to the Lecturers, the readers of the papers, the gentlemen who have presided at the meetings, and to the Librarians and Library Committees who have enabled us to visit their Libraries, and have so kindly given us their hospitality. On another page is given particulars of the meetings.

The Committee is indebted to the Governors of the St. Bride Foundation Institute, and to those Librarians who have placed rooms at our service for Committee Meetings.

The North-Western Branch reports continued progress during the past year. A complete list of the valuable and varied papers read before this Branch, together with the names of the Lecturers, etc., appears on page 118.

The Committee note with much satisfaction that in addition to Mr. C. W. Sutton, M.A., the Hon. President, the North-Western Branch has enlisted the interest and support of the following gentlemen, who have consented to become Vice-Presidents:—Messrs. Bateman (Oldham), Cowell (Liverpool), Credland (Manchester), Guppy, M.A. (The John Rylands Library), Madeley (Warrington), Mullen (Salford) and Shaw (Liverpool Athenæum).

The L.A.A. Committee will be happy to entertain proposals from Assistants in other parts of the country, with a view to the formation of other Branches.

The social side of the programme has, as usual, been in the hands of the Entertainment Committee, which organised in the Summer a visit to Rochester, where, under the guidance of Mr. G. Payne, F.S.A., and Mr. Protheroe (Librarian of Rochester), to whom the thanks of the Association are due, a very enjoyable and instructive half-day was spent. Later in the summer a pleasant launch trip to Walton-on-Thames took place. The Fourth Annual Dinner, held at Anderton's Hotel in November, was attended with the usual success, as was the Annual Conversazione held at the St. Bride Foundation Institute in March.

During the past year the Study Circle has been regularly worked to a re-organised programme, the main principle of which has been the study of *two* subjects—Early Nineteenth Century Literature, and Library Practice. The first item has been closely and systematically dealt with, whilst the questions set in Library Practice have been of a most practical nature.

The quarterly results have been published in due course, the prize-winners being:—

THIRD SESSION:—*Senior*.—Mr. R. Ineson (Leeds).
Junior.—Mr. D. A. Gillespie (Westminster).

Fourth Session :—*Senior*.—Mr. A. Edwards (Liverpool).
Junior.—Mr. F. Dallimore (Wigan).

The Committee has again been generously assisted by Mr. MacAlister, who has supplemented his previous donation of £5 by £1 and two copies of Volume I. of "The Library" for the Annual Prizes which were gained by :—

First (*Senior*).—Mr. A. Edwards (Liverpool).
First (*Junior*).—Mr. F. Dallimore (Wigan).
Second (*Senior*).—Mr. P. D. Gordon (Manchester).
Second (*Junior*).—Mr. J. MacKnight (Wigan).

The Committee heartily congratulate the prizemen, and thank the several adjudicators for their valuable assistance.

The general results of the Study Circle at the close of this, the second year of its existence, indicate the advantage of correspondence classes, and although much more support might reasonably be expected, the Committee is generally well-satisfied with the results of this department of its work.

The Hon. Librarian reports that 32 books and pamphlets have been added to the Library during the year, bringing the total up to 288 volumes. Thirty-eight volumes have been borrowed during the same period, mostly by provincial members. For the additions to the Library thanks are due to Mr. E. A. Baker, M.A., Mr. Cockerell, Mr. Cotgreave, Mr. Greenwood, Miss James, Mr. MacAlister, Mr. Mason, and the Library Association. Donations of books and professional Literature would be welcomed, particularly parts of periodical publications needed to complete the sets now in the Library, and of which particulars can be obtained from the Catalogue issued with this Journal for October and November 1901.

In February the Committee had, with very much regret, to accept the resignation of Mr. G. E. Roebuck, the Hon. Secretary. Mr. Roebuck has the sincere thanks of the Committee for the considerable service he has rendered us during his twelve months of office. At the request of the Committee, Mr. J. Radcliffe, of the East Ham Public Library, very kindly undertook to fill the vacancy until the annual election of officers.

The Association now numbers 230 members, of whom 135 are Seniors, 85 Juniors, and 10 Honorary Members, being a net increase of 34 compared with last year; 61 of these members are accredited to the North-Western Branch. A complete list is appended.

The Finances of the Association remain in a satisfactory condition, and the Committee desires to offer its thanks to the following gentlemen who have given donations during the year, viz. :—Mr. Hy. Ogle, 10s. 6d. ; and Mr. G. Preece, 10s. 6d.

The " Library Assistant " has been regularly published during the past year, and the Committee is glad to be able to report that owing to its popularity and larger subscription list the issue and size have been increased. The increase has afforded the long-wished for opportunity of publishing regularly, and almost in their entirety, the papers read at the monthly meetings. It is hoped that another extension will be practicable at an early date which would allow of the publication of papers read before the meetings of the North-Western Branch, and further inclusion of topics of interest. A new feature, which it is hoped will be fully developed during the coming year, has been the free insertion of advertisements of appointments vacant.

On the retirement of Mr. Ogle from the Editorship of the Journal in May last, Mr. S. A. Hatcher kindly undertook, temporarily, to conduct it. In August Mr. H. Tapley Soper was appointed Editor.

In December last the Chairman, Mr. Evan G. Rees, was elected to a seat on the Council of the Library Association. His election by the Council we regard as a pleasing recognition, by that body, of the work of the L.A.A.

We note with satisfaction several changes made by the Council of the Library Association in the professional examinations, and we venture to think that these alterations are, in a measure, the outcome of a communication which the L.A.A. Committee addressed to the Education Committee of the Library Association about a year ago.

Signed on behalf of the Committee,

EVAN G. REES, *Chairman.*

J. RADCLIFFE, *Hon. Secretary.*

18th May, 1902.

PROGRAMME OF MEETINGS.

Seventh Session, 1901-2.

LONDON.

Date.	Lecturer.	Paper or Business.	Where held.
1901			
June 19		Sixth Annual Meeting	20 Hanover Square
July 10		Excursion to Rochester	
Aug. 28		River trip to Walton	
Oct. 16	Mr. C. Welch, F.S.A.	"The Young Librarian: his training and possibilities"	Guildhall.
Nov. 13	Mr. E. A. Savage	"The Library of the Future"	Cent. Lib. Croydon.
Dec. 11	Mr. W. J. Harris	"How to popularize our Public Libraries"	Cent. Lib., West Ham.
1902			
Jan. 15	Mr. F. E. Chennell	"The woes of a Librarian"	Cent. Lib., Battersea.
Feb. 26	Mr. R. W. Mould	"Our Work"	Newington Pub. Lib.
Mar. 19	Mr. B. L. Dyer	"War and the Library"	Woolwich Pub. Lib.
,,	Mr. P. E. Lewin	"Some systems of Classification"	do.
Apr. 16	Mr. W. B. Thorne	"Printing for Public Librarians"	Poplar Pub. Lib.
May 8	Mr. R. A. Peddie	"The Library of the past, present and future."	Municipal Offices, Holborn.

N.W. BRANCH.

Date.	Lecturer.	Paper or Business.	Where held.
1901			
June 29		Visit to Knutsford	
Sept. 14	Mr. R. Hill	"Is open-access a failure?"	Accrington P. L.
Oct. 16	Mr. P. D. Gordon	"Library Admistration: a plea for reform"	Reference Library, Manchester.
Nov. 9	Mr. W. E. Axon	"Bibliography"	6 Cecil Street, Moss Side.
Dec. 18		Annual Meeting	Reference Library, Manchester.
Jan. 15	Mr. J. H. Swann	"Librarianship as a Profession"	Athenæum, Manchester.
,,	Mr. W. Quarmby	"Bettering ourselves"	Ditto
Mar. 19	Mr. C. Owen	"The Free Library: the working-man's University"	Cent. Lib., Oldham.
May 27	Mr. H. Guppy, M.A.	"The Story of the English Bible."	John Rylands Library, Manchester.

OFFICERS AND COMMITTEE, 1901-1902.

CHAIRMAN:
[b][d] Evan G. Rees, Westminster.

COMMITTEE:
Baker, A., Chester.
Brown, J. W., Kimberley, S.A.
[a][d] Bullen, R. F., Poplar.
[c] Burt, A. G., Fulham.
Crockford, A. W., Richmond. (Elected March, 1902).
Gordon, P. D., Mudie's, Manchester.
[a][c] Green, T., Shoreditch.
[a] Hatcher, S. A., Canning Town.
[a] Hogg, J. F., Battersea.
[c] Mc Douall, W. B., Shepherd's Bush.
[c] Mc Dougall, D., Canning Town (Resigned February, 1902).
McKenzie, W., Aberdeen.
[c] Parsons, E. H., Stepney (Resigned October, 1901).
Radcliffe, J., East Ham.
[b] Rivers, J., Hampstead.
[a][d] Soper, H. Tapley, Stoke Newington.
[b] Stevenson, R., Croydon.
Swann, J. H., Manchester Reference.
Vellenoweth, W. J., Minet.
[c] Wood, P. H., St. George the Martyr, Southwark. (Elected November, 1901).
[b] Wood, R. B., Westminster.
[c] Young, W. B., Leyton.

HON. SECRETARY.
G. E. Roebuck, Stepney. (Resigned February, 1902).
J. Radcliffe, East Ham. (Elected February, 1902).

HON. TREASURER.
[b][d] W. Geo. Chambers, Woolwich.

HON. EDITOR.
[a][d] H. Tapley Soper, Stoke Newington.

HON. LIBRARIAN.
A. H. Carter, Westminster.

a Branches Sub-Committee. b Education Sub-Committee.
c Entertainment Sub-Committee. d Journal Sub-Committee.

LIST OF MEMBERS.

HONORARY MEMBERS.

Samuel J. Clark.
Bertram L. Dyer.
Richard Garnett, C.B., LL.D.
Thomas Greenwood.
Miss M. S. R. James.

J. Y. W. MacAlister, F.S.A.
Henry Ogle.
R. A. Peddie.
F. Meaden Roberts.
Charles Welch, F.S.A.

ORDINARY MEMBERS.

*Anderson, A. A. R., Stepney.
Anderson, G. C., West Ham.
Ayton, J. G., Poplar.
Bacon, S., Stepney.
*Bailey, E., South Shields.
Bain, R., Glasgow.
*Baxter, W. D., *Library of Wynne Baxter.*
Beer, F. A. R., West Ham.
Benson, W. E. H., Cripplegate Institute.
Blackmore, C. F., Stoke Newington.
Blakely, A. A., Bermondsey.
*Bonner, F. H., Croydon.
Bowring, W., Kensington.
*Brace, W., Shoreditch.
*Bradley, C. A., Lambeth.
*Brown, E. C., Bristol.
*Brown, J. W., Kimberley, S.A.
*Buddery, E. E., West Ham.
*Bullen, R. F., Poplar.
Burbidge, P. W., West Ham.
*Burgoyne, F. J. P., Battersea.
*Bursill, P. C., Westminster.
*Burt, A. G., Fulham.
*Bushnell, F. C., Fulham.
Cameron, A. E., Croydon.
Camplin, P. W., Shoreditch.
*Carter, A. H., Westminster.
*Carter, W. A., Cripplegate Inst.
*Chamberlain, F. A., Bermondsey.
*Chambers, W. G., Woolwich.
Chivers, P. W., Croydon.

*Clarke, A. L., R. Med. & Ch. Soc.
Clayton, C. E. A., R. Med. & Ch. Soc.
Clinch, C. H., Ealing.
*Cogswell, A., Wandsworth.
*Coltman, W. L., Derby.
*Coutts, H. T., Croydon.
*Crockford, A. W., Richmond.
Davis, J., Penge.
Davison, C. E., Bermondsey.
*Denne, G. E., Richmond.
*Dinelli, H. P., Hammersmith.
Dixon, Miss, Leyton.
*Eidmans, F., Bermondsey.
Ellison, J. B., Leeds (Inst. of Sci., Art & Lit.)
*Ewing, J. C., Glasgow.
*Faraday, J. G., Hornsey.
*Farnell, W. J. C., Wallsall.
*Gabbatt, G. W., Barrow.
Garner, E. W., Southwark.
*Gentry, E. J., Lincoln.
Gillespie, D. A., Westminster.
*Gillespie, N. L., Westminster.
*Glazier, T. W., Wandsworth.
*Gray, T., Carlisle.
*Green, T., Shoreditch.
*Hall, S. B., Lambeth.
*Harper, B. J., Stoke Newington.
Harradine, F. C., Poplar.
*Harris, W. J., Hornsey.
*Hatcher, A. W., West Ham.
*Hatcher, S. A., West Ham.
*Hatton, A. E., Leyton.

*Hawkins, W. G., Fulham.
Henn, F., Imperial Institute.
Hirst, L., Kensington.
*Hogg, J. F., Battersea.
Henley, C., Poplar.
*Ineson, R., Leeds.
Jackson, C. P., Woolwich.
Jones, G. P., Stepney.
*Kettle, B., Guildhall.
King, H. J., Poplar.
*Law, W., Battersea.
*Lawler, E. A., Westminster.
Lawrence, E. W., Lambeth.
Leighton, T., West Ham.
*Lewin, P. E., Woolwich.
*Little, W. H., Penge.
*Lloyd, J., Kensington.
Loney, R., Stepney.
Lubritski, H., Stepney.
*McDouall, W. B., Hammersmith
*McDougall, D., West Ham.
McDougall, O., West Ham.
*McGill, W., Glasgow.
*MacKenzie, W. M., Aberdeen.
Margetts, J. G., St. Bride Inst.
Maule, A. C. S., Hornsey.
May, E., Kimberley, S.A.
Morgan, Miss G. M., Shoreditch.
*Moslin, A. M., Stepney.
*Nash, A., Wandsworth.
*Nash, M. H. B. Croydon.
*Neesham, E. W., Kendal.
*Norrie, J., Walthamstow.
Packington, L. J., Lambeth.
*Parsons, E. H., Stepney.
Payne, E., Poplar.
*Peplow, W. A., Croydon.
*Philip, A. J., Hampstead.
*Pick, E. A., Shoreditch.
*Pickard, W., Bermondsey.
Pocock, F., Holborn.
Polley, G. E., Westminster.
Pottinger, H. G., East Ham.
*Poulter, H. W., Stepney.
*Proctor, W., Leeds.

*Radcliffe, J., East Ham.
*Rees, E. G., Westminster.
*Rivers, J., Hampstead.
Rix, H. J., West Ham.
*Roach, Miss, Kimberley, S.A.
Robarts, H. M., Walthamstow.
Robertson, R., Glasgow.
*Robinson, F., Ipswich.
Robinson, S. C., Poplar.
*Roebuck, G. E., Stepney.
Rowley, G. F., Stoke Newington
*Savage, E. A., Croydon.
*Seidel, F. L., Willesden Green.
*Seward, F., Bromley, Kent.
*Sharp, E., West Ham.
*Sharphouse, D., Leeds.
Sheppard, R. W., Day's Library.
*Simnett, W. E., Inst. of Civil Engineers.
*Smith, Miss A., Kensal Town.
*Smith, H., Bishopsgate Inst.
*Soper, H. Tapley, Stoke Newington.
Steed, Miss A. M. J., Shoreditch.
*Steele, H., Carlisle.
*Stevenson, R., Croydon.
Stewart, J. D., Croydon.
Stone, O. W., East Ham.
*Strother, G. W., Leeds.
Sunley, W. H., Leyton.
*Sureties, H. G., Hornsey.
*Thorne, W. B., St. Bride Inst.
*Tilling, A. E., Bristol.
*Treliving, N., Leeds.
*Tumath, A. J., Holborn.
Turner, F., Kimberley, S.A.
Usherwood, V., Woolwich.
*Vellenoweth, W. J., Minet.
*Verney, Sir E., Middle Claydon.
*Waite, C. H., Kensington.
*Walker, J. W., Leeds.
*Ward, A. T., Cripplegate Inst.
*Warman, A. J., Newport, Mon.
Warner, J., Croydon.
Weber, A. J., Poplar.

*Welch, H. C., Guildhall.
Welham, H. G., West Ham.
*Whitwell, C., West Ham.
Willis, F. G., Carlisle.

*Wood, P. H., Southwark.
*Wood, R. B., Westminster.
Yates, A. H., Hornsey.
*Young, W. B., Leyton.

* *Senior Members.*

NORTH-WESTERN BRANCH.

PRESIDENT:
Mr. C. W. SUTTON, M.A.

VICE-PRESIDENTS:
Mr. R. BATEMAN.   Mr. H. GUPPY, M.A.
„ P. COWELL.   „ C. MADELEY.
„ W. R. CREDLAND.   „ B. H. MULLEN.
Mr. G. T. SHAW.

CHAIRMAN: J. H. Swann.   VICE-CHAIRMAN: J. D. Dickens.

HON. SEC.: W. Quarmby.   HON. TREASURER: W. Crompton.

ORDINARY MEMBERS.

Alley, Miss J. T. F., Manchester.
Ashton, J. C., Wigan.
‡*Baker, A., Chester.
Barnfield, T., Salford.
‡*Berry, W. H., Oldham.
*Briars, G. C., Sale.
Burgess, J., Salford.
Clare, A., Oldham.
Credland, Miss I., Manchester.
*Crompton, W., Y.M.C.A., M/c.
Crook, B., Chorley.
*Cunningham, W., Athenæum, Liverpool.
Dallimore, F., Wigan.
*Dickens, J. D., Athenæum, M/c
Eastwood, T. R., Oldham.
*Edwards, A. H., Liverpool.
*Evans, E., Northwich.
*Fletcher, G., Ashton.
*Furey, J. H., Salford.
*Galloway, H., Mudie's, M/c.
*Goodier, S., Lyceum, Oldham.
‡*Gordon, P. D., Mudie's, M/c.
Harwood, W., Stalybridge.

*Haworth, F. W. B., M/c.
Haworth, H., Accrington,
Hesketh, A., Accrington.
*Hobson, A., Salford.
*Irwin, R., M/c.
Kershaw, J., Salford.
‡*Kirk, H. W., Chetham's Coll., M/c.
*Lamb, S., St. Helen's.
Lea, Miss E., Wigan.
*Luke, E., M/c.
McAdam, J., Bootle.
McKnight, J., Wigan.
Marriott, E., M/c.
Marsden, J. R., Burnley.
Mee, F. H., Wigan.
*Mellor, C., Ashton.
‡*Montgomery, W. T., Bootle.
*Moorhouse, T., Stalybridge.
*Nicholson, F. B., M/c.
*Parkinson, H. J., Warrington.
‡*Percival, H., Owen's Coll., M/c.
Phillips, P. H., Chester.
*Pomfret, J., Blackburn.

*Pyne, O. M., John Rylands, M/c
*Quarmby, W., Oldham.
*Seed, W. H., Accrington.
Shaw, J. H., Bury.
*Shawcross, H. W., Bury.
Smith, A., Salford.
Smith, H., Wigan.
Smith, H. J., Bury.
Smith, J. H., Salford.

*Smith, T., Salford.
*Sutton, O.J., John Rylands, M/c.
*Swann, J. H., M/c.
Wadsworth, A., Salford.
*Whittinghame, E., Lyceum, Liverpool.
Williams, W., Bootle.
*Young, E., Athenæum, L'pool.

* *Senior Members.*   *Members of Committee.*

ATTENDANCES OF COMMITTEE.

NAME.	GENERAL COMMITTEE.		SUB. COMMITTEES.		TOTAL.	
	Conv'd	Atten.	Conv'd	Atten.	Conv'd	Atten.
Bullen, R. F.	12	8	15	12	27	20
Burt, A. G.	12	6	11	5	23	11
Chambers, W. Geo.	12	12	20	17	32	29
*Crockford, A.W. (elected Mar. 1902)	3	—	—	—	3	—
Green, T.	12	8	5	4	17	12
*Hatcher, S. A.	12	11	5	4	17	15
Hogg, J. F.	12	9	4	2	16	11
McDouall, W. B.	12	7	1	1	13	8
*McDougall, D. (resigned Feb. 1902)	8	2	8	5	16	7
Parsons, E. H. (resigned Oct. 1902)	4	1	4	2	8	3
*Radcliffe, J.	12	10	20	17	32	27
Rees, E. G.	12	10	20	16	32	26
Rivers, J.	12	1	8	3	20	4
Roebuck, G. E.	12	8	25	21	37	29
Soper, H. Tapley	12	12	15	15	27	27
*Stevenson, R.	12	8	8	5	20	13
Vellenoweth, W. J.	12	4	—	—	12	4
Wood, P. H. (elected Nov. 1901)	8	6	5	5	13	11
Wood, R. B.	12	9	9	9	21	18
*Young, W. B.	12	10	11	11	23	21

* *Local Members of the Non-London Committee.*

RULES.

1. NAME.—The Association shall be called "THE LIBRARY ASSISTANTS' ASSOCIATION."

2. OBJECTS.—Its objects shall be to promote the social, intellectual, and professional interests of its members, by meetings of a social character, by discussions, and in such other ways as may be suggested from time to time.

3. MEMBERS.—(A) All persons engaged in library administration, other than chief librarians, shall be eligible for election. Applications shall be made in writing to the Hon. Secretary, and shall be considered at the next meeting of the Committee (B) When a member is raised to the status of chief librarian, or leaves the profession, such person shall cease to be a member six months afterwards. (c) The Committee shall have power to elect honorary members, such members not having the right of voting. (D) The Association shall have power to expel, at an ordinary meeting, after one month's official notice of expulsion shall have been given, any member by a vote of 20% (twenty per cent.) of the total number of members of the L.A.A. (or the affiliated branch to which he belongs), in favour of that course.

4. SUBSCRIPTION.—(A) The Annual Subscription shall be 5s. for Senior, and 2s. 6d. for Junior Assistants, payable in advance on October 1st. (B) Members being 6 months in arrear with their subscriptions shall cease to belong to the Association.

5. OFFICERS.—(A) The Officers of the Association shall consist of a Chairman, Treasurer, Secretary, and a Committee of ten London and ten non-London members, who shall be elected at the Annual Meeting. (B) In the event of any of these offices falling vacant, the vacancy shall be filled at the next Ordinary Meeting of the Association.

6. MEETINGS.—(A) There shall be an Annual General Meeting of the Association fixed to take place some time during the Winter session. (B) Ordinary meetings shall be held monthly from October to May at such times and places as shall be decided by the Committee. (c) Special General Meetings shall be called on the requisition of twenty members of the Association, such meeting to be held within six weeks from the date of receipt of such requisition by the Hon. Secretary.

7. BRANCHES.—Application for the formation of a branch shall be made in writing to the L.A.A. Committee, by not less than 10 members in the proposed district.

Each branch shall be bound by the Rules of the Association, but may formulate special rules for its local government, providing the same are confirmed by the Committee of the L.A.A. All proposed local rules must be deposited with the Hon. Secretary of the Branches' Sub-Committee for approval. Members of a branch shall pay their subscriptions to the treasurer of the branch, who shall remit to the treasurer of the L.A.A. for every Senior Member 3/6, and for every Junior Member 2/-, to cover the cost of the official publications.

8. PROCEDURE.—(A) Amendments to these rules shall only be considered at the Annual General Meeting, or at a Special General Meeting convened for that purpose.

NOTES AND COMMENTS.

Mr. Carnegie's Gifts.—We copy the following from the *Daily News* of May 24th:

SIR,—During the time I was in Washington, in the first week of the present month, what seemed to be an authorative statement was given by an American writer of Mr. Carnegie's gifts in the United States and the United Kingdom and Ireland. The gross sum is put down as 67,212,923 dols., or considerably over thirteen millions sterling, given to libraries and other institutions. Mr. Carnegie's gifts are far more numerous in America than on this side of the Atlantic.

He has, I understand, recently stated that he is willing to give a library in this country wherever a site is provided and permanent maintenance is undertaken by the local governing body.

Municipal authorities, and others with influence, should see to it that this side of the Atlantic is well represented in Mr. Carnegie's public generosity, and make their applications direct to him.—Yours, etc.,

THOMAS GREENWOOD.

Frith Knowl, Elstree, Herts, May 23rd, 1902.

Greenwich.—Mr. Carnegie has given £10,000 for the erection of Public Libraries.

Kingston.—It has been decided to erect a new building at a cost of £6,000. Under the powers of a Local Improvement Act of 1888 the rate is to be raised to 1½d.

Leeds.—*The Architect* of April 26th contains an illustration of the elevation and plan of the Public Baths and Library recently erected in York Road.

Wandsworth. — The Mayor of Wandsworth has given £5,000 for the erection of a Library at Tooting.

STATEMENT OF RECEIPTS AND EXPENDITURE, 1901-2.

RECEIPTS.	£	s.	d.	EXPENDITURE.	£	s.	d.
Balance	12	16	8	Printing and Stationery ...	56	2	6
Members' Subscriptions ...	29	15	0	Prizes (Prize Essay Scheme)...	2	1	0
,, ,, N.W. Branch	8	12	0	Study Circle Prize ...	1	0	0
Advt. in, and sale of "Library Assistant"...	51	7	6	Postages	16	19	7
Donations	1	1	0	Bookbinding	0	9	9
				Expenses at Meetings ...	1	14	0
				Pamphlet Cases... ...	0	10	6
				Miscellaneous	0	5	6
				Balance	24	9	4
	£103	12	2		£103	12	2

ENTERTAINMENT SUB-COMMITTEE, 1901-2.

	£	s.	d.		£	s.	d.
Tickets for River Trip ...	7	5	0	Hire of Launch	5	5	0
38 Dinner Tickets @ 3s. 6d. ...	6	13	0	40 Teas @ 1s.	2	0	0
Sale of Programmes (Conversazione)	1	6	0	34 Dinners @ 3s. ...	5	2	0
Balance	0	2	3	Printing	0	16	0
				Postage	1	2	3
				Hire of Hall for Conversazione	1	1	0
	£15	6	3		£15	6	3

ASSETS AND LIABILITIES.

	£	s.	d.		£	s.	d.
Balance carried down ...	24	9	4	Printing " Library Assistant"	20	3	6
Advertisements	5	10	0	Stationery	3	0	0
Donations (promised) ...	2	0	0	Study Circle Prizes ...	4	0	0
Members' Subscriptions ...	4	15	0	Postages	6	10	0
Sale of "Library Assistant"...	3	0	0	Balance of Assets over Liabilities	6	0	10
	£39	14	4		£39	14	4

WILLIAM LAW, } Auditors.
W. B. THORNE, }

May 21st, 1902.

W. GEO. CHAMBERS, Treasurer.

NOTES AND COMMENTS.

Library Aids.—A lady library assistant, writing in the *Library Record of Australasia*, draws attention to the latent possibilities of the common or household brick as a library aid. Covered with cloth or brown paper it makes an effective book support. White paper may be pasted on the end of the brick, this will be found useful as a shelf register, etc., etc. The covers of discarded exercise books are also recommended for magazine cases. We never thought of this before. There is evidently a crying need for the "refining hand of woman" in our public libraries.

American Libraries.—Some of the American Public Libraries, with commendable enterprise, have taken to bold advertisement of their wares. Attractive posters are fixed in the cable cars, between the soap and the pill advertisements. After learning how to cure that tired feeling, the passenger can glance through the list of latest accessions at the local library, before going on "to the soaps."

Mr. Carnegie's Gifts.—The *Commercial Advertiser* publishes a summary of Mr. Andrew Carnegie's public gifts as recorded up to the present time. Since Mr. Carnegie began disbursing the total has reached 67,000,000 dollars (nearly £14,000,000), of which 52,000,000 dollars has been given in the United States, 13,735,000 dollars in the United Kingdom, chiefly in Scotland, and 876,000 dollars in Canada.

Glasgow.—Designs have been invited for a Branch Library for the Anderston District.

Ilford.—We regret to hear that the Council has postponed putting the Acts into force owing to the financial state of the District.

McKnight, Mr. Edward, Librarian of the Chorley Public Library, has been invited by the Congregational Union of England and Wales to read a paper on "The Old Hall," Gainsborough, at the celebration in June, of the foundation of the first Separatist Church, from which sprang the Pilgrim Fathers. Mr. McKnight has made a special study of the history of the Pilgrim Fathers, and recently published a *brochure* entitled, "Myles Standish, the Captain of Plymouth."

BOOKS, &c., RECEIVED.

BATTERSEA. (LAWRENCE INKSTER, Librarian) 15th Annual Report, 1901-2.

BOOTLE. (C. H. HUNT, Librarian). *What shall I read?*

CROYDON. (STANLEY L. JAST, Librarian). *The Reader's Index.* V. 4, No. 3. May and June, 1902.

FULHAM. (FRANKLIN T. BARRETT, Librarian). 14th Annual Report. 1901.

STEPNEY—St. George's Library (G. E. ROEBUCK, Librarian), Catalogue of Books in the Juvenile Department.

This is an admirable list, and reflects much credit upon the compiler, Mr. G. E. Roebuck. A serious and commendable attempt is made to increase the educational value of the children's library by cataloguing the stories and tales under subject headings, and by adding, under the author entry, a brief note. The excellent chronological list of historical tales, sub-divided into the great dynastic periods, which appears under the heading "England and the Empire," deserves especial praise. No better method could be devised to arouse an intelligent interest in the study of English History. Co-operation with the local school teachers should be a feature of this library. With regard to the form of the catalogue, much space might have been saved by an occasional use of double column. We are pleased to notice that the list is sold at the nominal price of one penny.

WATERLOO-with-Seaforth. (EDITH G. TAYLOR, Librarian). 4th Annual Report, 1901-2.

APPOINTMENTS AND CHANGES.

MINTO, Mr. John, M.A., Librarian of Perth to be Librarian of Brighton.

The other selected candidates for this appointment were Messrs. E. A. Baker, M.A. (Midland Railway Institute, Derby) and R. Bateman (Oldham).

*POCOCK, Mr. F., Assistant, Brentford, to be Second Assistant, St. Giles P.L., Holborn.

* *Member of the Library Assistants' Association.*

NEW MEMBERS.

Senior.—BUSHNELL, F. C., Fulham.   NASH, M. H. B., Croydon.

Junior.—CAMERON, A. E., Croydon;   POLLEY, G. E., Westminster;   YATES, A. H., Hornsey.

APPOINTMENTS VACANT.

[**Notice to Library Authorities.**—*We shall be pleased to publish under this heading, free of charge, particulars of vacancies if full details are sent to the Editor on or before the 28th of each month.*]

NOTICES.

All matter for the July number should reach the *Hon. Editor* on or before 20th June.

All other communications should be addressed to the *Hon. Secretary*, MR. J. RADCLIFFE, Public Library, East Ham, E.

The Library Assistant:

The Official Organ of the Library Assistants' Association.

No. 55.   JULY, 1902.   Published Monthly

THE LIBRARY ASSISTANTS' ASSOCIATION.

FOUNDED 1895.   SEVENTH SESSION.   YEAR 1901-1902.

Members are requested to read carefully the announcements appearing on this and the following pages, as no further intimation of meetings and other arrangements may be expected.

ANNUAL MEETING.

On Wednesday, June 18th, by kind invitation of Mr J. Y. W. MacAlister, the Seventh Annual Meeting of the L.A.A. was held, at 20 Hanover Square.

There were over 50 members present. Mr. E. G. Rees having taken the Chair, the proceedings opened with the reading of the minutes of the Sixth Annual Meeting, and the Special General Meeting held at West Ham, on December 11th 1901, which were confirmed.

The Chairman, in moving the adoption of the Annual Report, pointed out that during the past year steady progress had been made, both in the number of those who had paid subscriptions to the Journal, and those who had joined the Association, but regretted that out of the large number of Assistants throughout the Kingdom so small a proportion thought it worth while to join the Professional Association.

The Report having been adopted, the Chairman declared the following Officers elected, without opposition, for the ensuing Session :—

MR. E. G. REES, *Chairman.*
„ W. G. CHAMBERS, *Hon. Treasurer.*
„ J. RADCLIFFE, *Hon. Sec.*

The result of the poll for the Committee was then declared to be as follows :—

LONDON MEMBERS OF COMMITTEE.

Elected.		Not Elected.	
Soper, H. Tapley	101	Philip, A. J.	58
Hogg, J. F.	90	Pocock, F.	51
Bullen, R. F.	83		
Green, T.	83		
Wood, R. B.	81		
Parsons, E. H.	72		
Wood, P. H.	72		
Burt, A. G.	71		
McDouall, W. B.	66		
Bradley, C. A.	63		

NON-LONDON MEMBERS OF COMMITTEE.

Elected.		Not Elected.	
Swann, J. H.	82	Pomfret, J.	53
Gordon, P. D.	77	Berry, W. H.	51
Quarmby, W.	74	Crockford, A. W.	50
Cunningham, W.	68	Ewing, J. C.	49
Stevenson, R.	67	Percival, H	48
Harris, W. J.	64	Brown, J. W.	47
Hatcher, S. A.	63		
Baker, A.	57		
Montgomery, W.	57		
McKenzie, W.	56		

The Chairman then declared the result of the Cotgreave Prize Essay Competition, the winner being Mr. T. W. Glazier, of the "Tate" Library, Streatham, Mr. W. Harris, of the Hornsey Public Libraries, last year's prizeman, coming a very good second. The pseudonyms of the remainder of the competitors are set out below in order of merit as decided by the adjudicators :—Third —" Mercury," fourth—" Ferrex and Porrex," fifth—" Grapheus." For the Senior Prize there were only five entries, and the Chairman hoped that in future more interest would be taken in these competitions. The winner of the Junior Prize will be announced at a later date.

Mr. Peddie congratulated the Association on the Report, and thought it a sign of the increased interest taken in the Association that so much as one guinea had been paid for the first volume of *The Library Assistant*. He also noticed the growth of the professional library, and thought that 288 volumes collected in so short a time was highly satisfactory. The growth of the N.W. Branch was an especially bright feature, for the real hope of the Association lay in the Provinces, and he hoped to see the methods of branch organisation extended in the future.

There could be no doubt that the Association ought to have a majority of library assistants in its ranks. The Association has filled a place in the profession which was distinctly empty, and its monthly Journal is of great value because it is often able to touch on matters of great interest likely to be overlooked by other journals. He saw no reason why some of the papers should not be published in volume form, thus making a valuable addition to the professional literature. He congratulated the Association on its continued progress, and on the interest which was taken in it by men who were able and willing to help, and he pointed out that if any member had bright ideas his connection with it would bring him into contact with those who would help him to carry them out. Speaking of the educational work of the L.A., he said they had not done all they should have done—and the rest of the Litany. But he felt that until some radical alteration was made in the governing body of a certain Association, matters would continue as they were. He believed that a very large number of the members of the L.A. were agreed that something more should be done—and he thought they would get their way.

In accordance with the Agenda, Mr. W. G. Chambers then moved:—

"That the Resolution of the Special General Meeting of December 11th, 1901, altering the Annual Meeting from the Summer to the Winter Session, be, and is hereby rescinded."

This was seconded by Mr. R. B. Wood, and opposed by Mr. Pickard, who thought the Winter Meeting should be given a fair trial. He was supported by Mr. P. H. Wood. The motion was carried by 21 votes to 14.

Mr. F. Pocock then moved:—

"That in future a report of the meetings of the Committee of the L.A.A. be published in the *Library Assistant*."

This was seconded by Mr. Hatcher, but was opposed by Mr. Soper, who pointed out that there was little room for more matter in the Journal, and that it was not usual for proceedings of Committees to be published, though he supported the principle because they had nothing they wished to hide as suggested by a previous speaker. Any important work done by the Association is immediately published in some form or other. The motion was also spoken on by Messrs. Hogg, Pickard, Peddie and others, but was defeated by 21 votes to 11.

Mr. Thorne then moved a vote of thanks to the Committee, which was seconded by Mr. Parsons and carried unanimously.

Mr. W. G. Chambers in replying, said the work was often hard and made considerable inroads on time and pocket, but that when their work was appreciated in the way it had been it became a pleasure.

A vote of thanks to Mr. MacAlister for the use of the room, moved by Mr. Rees, and seconded by Mr. Soper, having been carried with applause, Mr. Harris then proposed a vote of thanks to the chairman, and said that the success of a meeting very largely depended on the Chairman, and therefore he had the more pleasure in proposing this vote. This was seconded with some pleasing remarks by Mr. Hogg, and Mr. Rees briefly replied, and in thanking the Association for again electing him chairman said his work was always pleasant, though at times it was not easy. He had much satisfaction, however, in finding his efforts had been appreciated. P. E. L.

N.W. BRANCH—MAY MEETING.

On Tuesday evening, May 27th, a meeting was held at the John Rylands Library, Manchester, on the kind invitation of Mr. H. Guppy (Chief Librarian). Ten members were present, and when assembled in the Bible Room Mr. Guppy gave a very interesting address on the Bible, and, in particular, the history of the English version. He expressed regret that the meetings of the Branch were not better attended, and said that apart from the educational value to be derived, the members who endeavoured to attend regularly, thereby showing interest in their occupation, would necessarily come under the favourable notice of librarians at whose libraries meetings were held, and thereby increase their chances in the future.

Turning to the subject of the evening, Mr. Guppy pointed out the pre-eminent position of the Bible in literature, which, apart from any theological considerations, renders it a book of whose history every librarian and assistant ought to have a satisfactory knowledge.

Something should be known of the various codices, of the principal translations—especially the English version—and of the chief results of the searching criticism to which the Bible has been subjected in modern times.

Dealing with the history of the English version, Mr. Guppy referred briefly to the partial translations made by Bede, King Alfred, Richard Rolle and others; then coming to Wycliffe's translation he pointed out that it is now held to have been partly done by Wycliffe's friend, Nicholas of Hereford. This translation was made from the Latin Vulgate. A contemporary manuscript copy was shown.

The version by John Tyndale was the next to be considered, and Mr. Guppy went into considerable detail in telling the life story of this remarkable and not fully appreciated man. The spread of the New Learning in Europe brought with it the Greek Testament of Erasmus, the Brescia Hebrew Bible, and the Complutensian Polyglot, and with the facilities given by the art of printing greatly increased the study of the Bible among scholars. John Tyndale desired to render it accessible to the English people in their own tongue, and after much persecution he lost his life in the endeavour. His translation of the New Testament (1525) was made direct from the Greek. In 1537 appeared the "Matthew" Bible which was edited by John Rogers, Tyndale's literary executor, and contains Tyndale's translation of the Pentateuch and New Testament, and a translation of Joshua to the 2nd Book of Chronicles also, in all probability, by him. Tyndale's work was thoroughly done and forms the basis of the later versions, including the Authorised (1611) and the Revised, thus making an organic connection throughout. Time would not permit more than a brief mention of the later versions, but we venture to hope that Mr. Guppy will deal with those on another occasion. The splendid collection of Bibles, one of the glories of the Library, enabled Mr. Guppy to illustrate his address in a striking manner.

Owing to the holiday season there will be no meeting in July or August. The next being fixed for late in September, for date and place see August Journal.

J.H.S.

SUMMER PROGRAMME.

An afternoon excursion to Brighton will take place (provided that a sufficient number of promises to attend are received) on Wednesday, July 9th. The party will travel by the V.E.C.A. express, which leaves Victoria at 12.30 p.m., Clapham Junction at 12.35, and East Croydon at 12.50, arriving at Brighton about 2.30, and returning therefrom at 8.30, thus allowing 6 hours at the sea-side. A brake drive to the Devil's Dyke and back is proposed (fare 1/6), returning to Brighton in time for tea, after which the Royal Pavilion will be visited, a charge of 3d. per head being made for admission.

Unfortunately, the Library Buildings are still in the hands of the contractors, so the proposed visits to that institution and to the Museum and Art Gallery, must be abandoned.

Railway tickets (2/6) may be obtained in advance from Mr. W. B. Young, 63 Leslie Road, Leytonstone, E., or direct from the Secretary, V.E.C.A., 64 Cheapside. E.C. If purchased at the stations on the day, tickets will be 3/-

Will all who intend joining the party kindly send their names to Mr. Young (if they have not already done so), together with an intimation as to the number of friends by whom they will be accompanied, at once, so that all necessary arrangements may be completed.

CORRESPONDENCE.

[*The Editor solicits expressions of opinion on all matters of interest to the profession, but does not hold himself responsible for the views of correspondents. Communications should be written on one side of the paper only, and should be as brief as possible.*]

THE LIBRARY ASSOCIATION.
Education Committee.

ST. SAVIOUR'S PUBLIC LIBRARY,
44a SOUTHWARK BRIDGE ROAD, S.E.
20th June, 1902.

DEAR SIR,

I am directed by the Education Committee to inform you that the statements contained in a letter signed "A London Library Assistant," which appeared in the June number of your journal, are in many cases erroneous, and, the whole subject being still *sub judice*, the publication of any facts is premature.

Yours faithfully,
HENRY D. ROBERTS, *Hon. Sec.*

The Editor, "Library Assistant."

DEAR MR. EDITOR,

Among the few pleasures of life that fall to the lot of library assistants must certainly be counted the amusement they frequently derive from contemplating that source of innocent merriment—their chiefs. I am moved to this reflection by the announcement, in the June *Library Association Record*, of a proposed alteration of the bye-laws of that Association. It will be remembered that the *Sturm und Drang* of recent years culminated, at the Plymouth meeting, in a volcanic upheaval which violently ejected the Hon. Secretary from office and scattered his supporters to the four winds. The exciting agent was a suggestion to "automatically remove" what were picturesquely termed the old fogies of the Council by rendering, each year, a proportion of its body ineligible for re-election for twelve months, the members retiring by rota. But now these clamourers for new blood are in power, the idea that they themselves should be automatically removed does not appeal to them quite so strongly. Their idea of suitable subjects for removal is "the members who receive the least number of votes." This is a stroke of genius, worthy of ex-President Kruger himself! Naturally, at such elections, the members who tail the poll are the new members, the unknown new blood. These reformers, these "eight fresh young fellows," *vide* Mr. MacAlister, will be politely invited into the Council and as politely kicked out again in alternate years, while the old fogies who so strongly approve of this influx of new blood, will not be automatically removed but by the gentleman with the hourglass and scythe!

" DIFFICILE EST SATIRAM NON SCRIBERE."

The Editor, "Library Assistant."

[To the Editor of "The Library Assistant."]

SIR,

I was very glad to see Mr. Greenwood's letter in your last issue. It would be a good thing if you were to give Mr. Carnegie's address* so that library authorities could write to him direct. I hope that Mr. Carnegie in making his gifts will not forget the Public Libraries already

---

†Skibo Castle. Sutherland, N.B.—*Ed.*

established, and whose usefulness is crippled through having heavy loans to pay off.

To my mind those Libraries who adopted the Library Acts years ago, without any incentive in the shape of gifts, should be the ones to receive help. Unless this is done, Libraries now being established through Mr. Carnegie's munificence are on a better footing than the old ones, having no loans to pay, and are able to pay their Assistants better salaries. This should not be so. I hope, Mr. Editor, you will bring this before Mr. Carnegie.

I believe a certain English Library philanthropist refuses to help Libraries already established, only giving to places on condition that the Acts are adopted. To my mind this is wrong: help should be given to those who have helped themselves. ASSISTANT.

STUDY CIRCLE—RESULTS OF FOURTH SESSION.

Senior.				Junior.			
Name	Lit. Hist.	L. Prac.	Totals	Name	Lit. Hist.	L. Prac.	Totals
Bala ...	270	180	450	Liber ...	275	200	475
Saturn ...	230	200	430	Y Byldwr	90	210	300
*Dust ...	68	40	108	*Poohbah	115	60	175
				*Critic ...	95	20	115
				*Thor ...	95	—	95

* 1 paper submitted

REPORT.—The work submitted for the Fourth Session of the Study Circle was of a good standard, and the adjudicators complain only of the low number of papers sent in. Throughout the Session "Saturn" has run "Bala" very closely for the top place, and although "Bala" secures the prize, his papers on Library Practice are not up to the standard of those from "Saturn."

The results of inconclusiveness are rather sharply marked in the Junior Division. "Poohbah's" papers for the first month were certainly as good as any, and a continuance of the same standard would perhaps have resulted in the acquisition of the prize.

As will be seen from the above schedule, the highest marks were obtained by "Bala"—Mr. A. Edwards (Liverpool), and "Liber"—Mr. F. Dallimore (Wigan), and the Committee declare these competitors prizemen for the Fourth Session.

NOTES AND COMMENTS.

Mr. Carnegie's Gifts.—During the past month we have been inundated with information from all parts of the country concerning the gifts of this munificent Crœsus. It is said that the Court of Crœsus was the Asylum of Learning. Mr. Carnegie appears to be desirous of outshining his classic prototype by carrying out the principle on a much larger scale. Surely if such generosity continues the United Kingdom will become a veritable land of pedants. Below is a list of donations since our last issue, it is too much to hope that it is complete—such a compilation seems impossible—for before one's ink is dry more cheques are on their way to cheer the troubled hearts of Committees, trying to carry out on the mere pittance produced by a penny rate the noble ideas of a far seeing educationalist of the middle of the last century. But our legislators have not yet caught up to his cycle. This list tots up to the respectable sum of £77,500.

Brentford	£5,000	Northampton	£5,500
Brierley Hill	£2,000	Patrick, Glasgow	£10,000
Kettering	£8,000	Poplar	£15,000
Lewisham	£9,000	Selly Oak	£3,000
Maidenhead	£5,000	Walkeley	£2,000
Merthyr Tydvil	£6,000	Workington	£7,000

Books, &c., received.—Owing to the pressure on our space we are compelled to leave over until our next issue the usual list and comments on the many books and pamphlets received during the past month.

Wolverhampton Conference.—Members and friends who intend to take part are requested to send in their names *immediately*. This meeting will take the form of a *one* day excursion, and will not extend to three or four days as generally supposed. Full particulars will be found in the June number. Final arrangements will be notified in the August issue.

APPOINTMENT.

SOPER, H. Tapley, Sub-Librarian, Stoke Newington, to be Librarian, City of Exeter.

The other selected candidates were Messrs. JONES (Cardiff), and HAGGERSTON (Norwich).

NEW MEMBERS.

Senior.—DOCKRAY, C. F., Salford. KNIGHT, Miss L. E., Blackpool. **Junior.**—FRANCE, Miss E. Blackpool. HARRISON, Miss M., Blackpool.

APPOINTMENTS VACANT.

[**Notice to Library Authorities.**—*We shall be pleased to publish under this heading, free of charge, particulars of vacancies if full details are sent to the Editor on or before the 28th of each month.*]

NOTICES.

All matter for the August number should reach the *Hon. Editor* on or before 20th July.

All other communications should be addressed to the *Hon. Secretary*, MR. J. RADCLIFFE, Public Library, East Ham, E.

The Library Assistant:
The Official Organ of the Library Assistants' Association.

No. 56.   AUGUST, 1902.   Published Monthly

THE LIBRARY ASSISTANTS' ASSOCIATION.

FOUNDED 1895.   SEVENTH SESSION.   YEAR 1901-1902.

Members are requested to read carefully the announcements appearing on this and the following pages, as no further intimation of meetings and other arrangements may be expected.

AUGUST EXCURSION TO EPPING FOREST.

It has been arranged that the next excursion of the L.A.A. will take place on Wednesday, August 13th, to Epping Forest. It is hoped that this outing will prove a success. There is every prospect of a pleasant holiday if only sufficient members will attend. Ladies are especially invited. The proposed programme will be :—A general assembly at Liverpool Street Station (Smith's bookstall) at 2.15 p.m., train to Chingford, and from there, a pleasant ramble to High Beech through the glades of the Forest. A visit to Queen Elizabeth's Lodge will form an item of the ramble. By this time it is hoped that all will have cultivated a suitable appetite for tea at The King's Oak Hotel.

After exploring the beauties of the neighbourhood, and visiting the ancient earthworks of the Loughton Camp, a return ramble will be made to Loughton Station.

Endeavours have been made to suit this excursion to the pockets of Junior Assistants, so Juniors please notice, and come in your numbers. You will be heartily welcomed. Will those wishing to join kindly send a post card to Mr. William J. Harris, Branch Library, Stroud Green, N. Train leaves Liverpool Street for Chingford at 2.32. Return fare to Chingford, to return *via* Loughton, 1s. Tea, 1s.

NORTH-WESTERN BRANCH.
SEPTEMBER MEETING.

The next meeting will be held by the kind invitation of Ben H. Mullen, Esq., M.A., at the Central Library, Peel Park, Salford, on Wednesday, September 10th, 1902, when it is expected Mr. Mullen will address the meeting.

For further particulars see September Journal.

"L.A.A." JUNIOR (1902) PRIZE.

The delay in the announcement of the result of the above competition has been due to the difficulty felt by the adjudicators in arriving at a decision, in consequence of the very equal merit of many of the essays sent in. It was finally decided to award the

FIRST PRIZE to Mr. F. Dallimore, Wigan.

SECOND PRIZE to Mr. F. Pocock, Holborn.

The following are commended:—"Marmion," "Ulysses," "Tertius," and "Book-Lover."

NOTES AND COMMENTS.

Change of Editor.—The Editor has to announce that, owing to what has been termed his "elevation to the Upper House," it becomes necessary for him to relinquish his office. It is with feelings of considerable regret that he takes this unavoidable step, for during his tenure of office he has made many friends, to all of whom he tenders his best thanks for the assistance they have rendered from month to month in the production of this Journal. Mr. W. B. Thorne, of the St. Bride Institute Library, has been unanimously elected to succeed him in the editorial chair, and it is hoped that he will be able to count on the same generous assistance which has enabled the retiring Editor to bring the Journal to its present popular, and it is hoped efficient, standard.

Birkdale.—Mr. C. J. Weld Blundell, Chairman of the District Council, has offered, as a Coronation gift to the town, a site for a public library and reading-room and £1,000 towards the erection of the building.

The Brighton Excursion.—On July 9th a number of members and their friends joined in an excursion to Brighton. The attendance was below the average, doubtless because the new Library buildings were not in a sufficiently advanced state to repay inspection, but the party quietly enjoyed the refreshing sea breezes and other attractions of London-by-the-Sea, and much appreciated their respite from the torrid Metropolis.

Finsbury.—It has been decided to black out the betting news from the daily papers. The resolution was carried by a large majority and one of the members remarked that if by their action they minimised the temptation to the youths of the Borough they would be doing good.

Mr. Carnegie's July Benefactions.—July proved another busy month for the self-appointed adjuster of Legislature deficiencies, as the subjoined list of donations will illustrate:—

Eastbourne	... £10,000	Leicester	...	£12,000
Fenton ...	... £5,000	Londonderry		£8,000
Finsbury	... £13,000	Mansfield	...	£3,500
Grays (Essex)	£3,000	Northampton		£5,500
Hammersmith	£10,000	*Paddington	...	£15,000
Haworth	... £1,500	Rawtenstall	...	£6,000
Lambeth	... £12,500	Rushden	...	£2,000
Larne...	... £2,500	Stirchley	...	£3,000
	Woolwich	... £14,000		

* This offer is made upon condition that the Acts are adopted.

Kimberley.—By the same boat which brought home the gallant K. of K. we received a copy of the *Diamond Fields Advertiser*, from which we learn that, the Army having completed its Herculean task of pacification, the Library Authority is following close behind with an offer for educational advancement. It is a pity that the Municipal Authority could not see its way to accept the generous offer made by the Library Authority. The suggestion was that if the grant was increased the subscription system should be abolished. Had this been accepted the Library would have been put on a firm municipal footing similar to those of the Mother Country. But it was not to be. What we hope will prove to be the next best course was resorted to, and the subscription reduced to a figure which will bring the advantages of the Library well within the means of all but the poorest, the hope of course being that with a much larger subscription list the Institution will be worked at a cheaper rate. This is not altogether satisfactory. The Public Library should be established on a firm municipal basis, and be free to all comers in order to accomplish its maximum of good. We hope that our old friend and colleague, Mr. Dyer, will bring his well-known powers of perseverance to bear until he sees the whole of South Africa equipped with a complete system of Library Block Houses established on a principle equal to, if not better than, that in vogue in the United Kingdom.

Wolverhampton Conference.—The Committee regrets to have to announce that owing to the very few guarantees of attendance received, it has been reluctantly compelled to abandon the project.

SOME SYSTEMS OF CLASSIFICATION.
By P. Evans Lewin.

Read at the April Meeting of the Library Assistants' Association.

The classification of books may be briefly summed up as of two kinds—bibliographical and philosophical. It is not necessary here to do more than touch upon the bibliographical side of the question. A bibliographical and material classification must necessarily rank inferior to a scientific and philosophical classification. A child may attempt a classification of his playthings by putting together round objects such as marbles and chestnuts, and square objects such as toy bricks and wooden dominoes; but the help of the scientific man is required in order that the child may learn that the substance of marbles and bricks belongs to the mineral, and that of dominoes and chestnuts to the vegetable kingdom. In the same way books may be classified in a catalogue according to date, language, country, and the presses from which they issued; or on the shelves according to their size, colour, binding, or any other peculiarity which may take the librarian's fancy, and his fancy may sometimes run riot, as was the case with the naturalist who classified the whole order of fishes according to the various peculiarities of one fin.

It will be seen that the classification of books may have a dual nature: they may be classified on the shelves or in the catalogue, the two not necessarily going together. To this day some librarians adopt a mere material shelf classification for their books, without having a classified catalogue; generally, of course, dividing the books into main classes according to their contents; beginning with the smallest book at the top of the case and continuing down to the largest by minute gradations. As a mere matter of convenience in the shelving arrangements or pleasingness to the eye, this scheme of arrangement is very well—

"The rows of books in silence stand,
And catch the passer's eye,"

yet this studied order of size is *not* classification.

Other librarians attempt to make their shelf classification coincide with their catalogue classification, and to me this system seems the most commendable. It is generally worked with a modified form of size classification, the folios, quartos, octavos, and sometimes the smaller books, being placed on different shelves for convenience.

But for the purpose of this paper I shall endeavour to give a statement of the different systems of philosophical classification which have been, or are now, in use.

It seems that like many other things connected with books, the earliest scheme of classification originated with the Chinese. Long before the invention of printing in Europe they had divided the field of knowledge into about twenty main classes with their sub-divisions. It scarcely seems credible, however, that the books of the Alexandrian libraries were not classified and apportioned to the different schools of thought which collected in that metropolis. The enlightened Ptolemies could hardly have allowed a hap-hazard arrangement at the institutions they founded and supported, nor could the philosophers, from Ptolemy Philadelphus to the illfated Hypatia, in whose days the books received their crowning desecration at the hands of Cyril's most Christian monks, have tolerated confusion in the libraries they loved so well.

It is, however, to Conrad Gesner*—a name that should always be honoured among librarians—that Europeans are indebted for the first practical system of classification. Gesner, who was born at Zurich in 1516, and became a professor in its University, has been called the Pliny of Germany. Undoubtedly the position he occupies in the literature of his age is a very high one, for there are no less than 171 entries in the British Museum Catalogue relating to this one man, and he wrote on all kinds of subjects including botany, pharmacy, medicine, natural philosophy, grammar, and history. It is in the Supplement to his Bibliotheca Universalis,† which, being a list of Greek, Hebrew, and Latin books with short criticisms and remarks, may perhaps be looked upon as a forerunner of the annotated catalogues of our own day, that we find his system of classification. It is divided into six main groups, of which Sermonales embraced (with others) Philology and Poetry; and Mathematicæ included Arithmetic, Music, Astronomy, and the allied scientific and fine arts. Most of these groups are largely extended—thus, the first one, " De Grammatica," has 21 sub-divisions, some of which are again divided. Gesner died in 1565 of the plague, and when he found his end approaching desired that he

---

* Gesner was preceded by at least one other classifier, Alexo Vanegas de Busto, of Toledo, 1540, and was closely followed by Florian Trefler, a Bavarian monk, 1560 ; John Rhodius, of Padua, 1631 ; François de Araoz, 1631 ; and Claudius Clement, of Madrid, 1635. Systems of classification had been in use in monastic libraries from an early date, i.e., at S. Riquier in A.D. 831, and at S. Emmeran zu Regensburg (Ratisbon), 1347. The elder Aldus and Robert Estienne published classified catalogues in 1498 and 1546 respectively, and Andrew Maunsell, of London, published one in 1595. Petzholdt in his Bibliotheca Bibliographica, 1866, gives a list of the systems then known.

† Pandectarum sive Partitionum universalium Conradi Gesneri Tigurini, medici et philosophiæ professoris, libri xxi. Tiguri [Zurich], 1548.

might be carried into the Museum with which he had been connected for so long a time, and thus die amidst his pupils and surrounded by the monuments of his labours.

He was followed by a Frenchman, Christopher de Savigny, the forerunner of many other French classifiers who flourished in France in the 17th and early 18th centuries—a period of great activity in that way across the Channel, but an almost barren epoch in England.

Savigny, in a large folio work published in 1587,* gives "for the edification and profit of the young" a table of all the arts divided into 16 main divisions, with many sub-divisions. That he entered on his work in earnest is shown by the fact that grammar alone has 78 divisions and ethics 66; others being in like proportion. He is lauded by the French bibliographers as the forerunner of Bacon, who is accused of having to some extent founded his system on Savigny's.

It is to Bacon, however, that we as Englishmen must look for our first system of classification. In his Advancement of Learning he produces a scheme which, crude and vague as it is, must yet be regarded as the father of English classifications. Human knowledge he divides into three great classes—Memory, Reason, Imagination; and names them History, Philosophy, Poetry. History was divided into two main headings—Natural and Civil: Philosophy into three—God, Nature, Man. A restriction of the sense of the word Philosophy has somewhat changed the use of his classification, for we no longer look upon philosophy as inclusive of natural science, but as being the study of that which is non-material, or the working of the mind—a signification which is even now undergoing change as the connection between mind and matter is more and more demonstrated. One cause, therefore, for the modification of all "arbitrary" classifications is the gradual changing of the signification of words. The system of Bacon has been made the groundwork of other schemes by Regnault-Warin, Laire, Peignot, and D'Alembert.

After Bacon comes the system of Samuel Taylor Coleridge, though other attempts were made in England, I believe, before his time. Then Edward Edwards propounded a scheme which had the advantage of being a natural progression of knowledge; thus Theology, Philosophy, History, followed one another.

---

* Tableau accomplis de tous les arts libéraux, contenant brièvement et clèrement, par singulière méthode de doctrine, une générale et sommaire partition des dicts arts, amassez et reduicts en ordre pour le soulagement et profit de la jeunesse. Paris, 1587.

Perhaps the best known English system is that in use at the British Museum.* It has been tried for many years, but is found wanting in this—that it does not go far enough because the immense number of books dealt with requires a more extended classification than is attempted. It is to be understood, however, that the British Museum System is probably only of value to the Museum itself, and is not suitable for an ordinary public library. Though philosophical it is practical. Too many systems seem philosophical without having the latter virtue; that is, the ordinary man is unable to understand them, and they therefore fail because they do not bring the ordinary educated reader in touch with the books classified. It seems to be thought by the general public that the British Museum offers no scheme of classification whatever because they are, at present, only brought into contact with an author catalogue. But this is not so. There exist all the materials for a classified catalogue in the shelf registers. The books in the Museum are classified on the shelves and in an order which is at least philosophical. They are divided into 10 main classes. First of all comes Theology as the most ancient and the most natural of beginnings, starting with the Bible arranged first under its original languages, and then under Greek and Latin, followed by their derived languages in due pedigree order; then the Slavonic tongues, and finally the Oriental. Theology or Divine Law is most justly followed by Human Law called Jurisprudence, followed by the knowledge of Nature called Natural History and Medicine. Then, though not such an obvious progression, comes Archæology and Arts, followed by Philosophy and Sciences (Bacon's old division, be it observed). Then comes History, collected works first, and the others geographically arranged. Sandwiched in between History and Biography is Geography, an arrangement open to objection. Finally, Belles Lettres (including Encyclopædias and Fiction) and Philology. These ten main divisions are divided into about five hundred sections.

Three other important schemes must be dealt with, two originating in the United States (Cutter's and Dewey's), and one in England (Brown's).

American librarians, and to a large extent English and Continental, seem to have followed the lead of Dewey. Whatever may be said about his system of classification—and it is open to objection in some places—there can be no two opinions about the excellence of his decimal system of notation. First come the ten main classes which are sub-divided to the hundredth

---

* To be found in the Transactions of the Conference of Librarians, 1877.

number, and by means of decimal points may be extended to as many sub-divisions as desired. The main advantage of this is that when a science and a literature on that science spring up they can at once be assigned a position without affecting the rest of the classification. Thus *M.* Santos Dumont on Balloon Steering need not be left out in the cold. Dewey's is the most minute system of classification yet published (what lurks in the brains of other librarians we know not), and the extensive index is probably the chief cause for its more general use. But like everything of mere human origin it has its faults. Religion is especially weak, giving little provision for Comparative Religion. Literature seems a general dumping ground, for it includes Classics, Letters, Poetry, Fiction, etc., and History, Biography, and Travel are conjoined in one class, but without doubt the necessary limitation of the number of classes to ten accounts for this.

The relative popularity on the Continent of Dewey's and Cutter's systems may be tested by the fact that there are books and pamphlets in the British Museum on Dewey in the following languages—English, French, German, Spanish and Italian, and not one on Cutter.* Perhaps I should mention the American language too, for a perusal of the introduction to Dewey's Decimal System of Classification will reveal many peculiarities which might have gladdened the heart of the late Sir Isaac Pitman, but which are scarcely pleasing to an English eye. Even the British Museum authorities are constrained to place that expressive little word " sic " after one of the most trying examples.

The other American system—that of Cutter—is still in process of formation. So far it has been divided into six classifications—and a bit. The first is only suitable for a very small library, and the sixth is supposed to do for a library of a million volumes. Some of the classes of this sixth classification have again been expanded very largely, notably religion, and form the "bit" I have alluded to. There is a small subject index to the sixth classification, and to parts of the now forming seventh classification, but for usefulness it cannot be compared to Dewey's index. Cutter's Expansive Classification is divided into 36 main classes, with room for additional classes by means of other letters or symbols. Each class is known by a letter, and in addition to letters figures are used in some cases. Thus 45 always stands for England, and 60 for Asia, and by expansion

---

* Cutter's System is in use at the Passmore Edwards Public Library, Borough Road, and an examination of the Supplementary Catalogue will give a very fair idea of its application.

6899 for British Burma, and so on *ad infinitum.* 39 stands for France, and so 39An3 for Andorra. But let us look at some of Cutter's own descriptions of books, for they are weird in the extreme—and yet so simple that the originator says he has found no difficulty when they are once explained. But oh, the explanation! Here is a book called Hughes' Windsor Forest: G45W72.H8; and here is Martin's Old Chelsea, G45C41.M3., and in some American libraries books are asked for under these symbols. Now for the explanation. G stands for Geography, 45 for England, W for Windsor, 72 is from an alphabetical order-table of Cutter's own invention, and H8 stands for Hughes. Here is another example, a very mild one—YfOl 35ag. This represents Mrs. Oliphant's "Agnes," Yf for fiction, Ol 35 for Oliphant, and ag for Agnes. We seem to be back in the old days of mnemonics when by some long forgotten jargon our fathers learned that William the Conqueror was crowned in 1066 and that Queen Elizabeth died in 1603. The explanation, you see, is perfectly simple, but of all the devices for bewildering the borrower and assistant, I regard this as the most soul-stirring. Cutter's classification I have heard described as more scientific than Dewey's, and it is very highly spoken of by Dr. Richardson in his "Classification." It may be so, I am no judge; yet its dress is most unbecoming, and if there is any practical use, save that each book gets a different symbol, for such a super-ingenious device as YfOl 35ag I shall be delighted to hear of it.

There is one English system that needs mention, that of J. D. Brown. I do not know this system, except that the classes are designated by letters and the sub-divisions by figures. I have been told that it is concise and practical, but much shorter than the other systems.

There are other minor systems in use: one at Melbourne, which builds up a classification on the smallest foundation, beginning at sponges, and so on through Biology to other subjects arranged on (to the originator) a strictly philosophical basis; others, which have been published in America, by Fletcher, Harris, Schwartz, and Perkins; several systems originating in Italy; one by Lord Lindsay; and that used by Sonnenschein.

The great drawback to close classification seems to be this: that whereas knowledge can be minutely classified, books cannot. So many main divisions with their chief sub-divisions seem to me all that is necessary for the classification of books on the shelves of a small library. Few books deal with one subject only. A book on the circulation of the blood will probably touch on other allied matters, and therefore cannot fall under one of those minute divisions so dear to the Deweyite. Books on specialized subjects become rarer as time goes on (though, paradoxical as it may seem, they increase titularly year by year), for all knowledge is so intimately connected and interbound that it is almost impossible nowadays to keep to the defined minutiæ. The difficulty of strictly classifying books of the 15th, 16th, and 17th centuries is too well known to need enlarging upon. It therefore becomes apparent that books which are too closely classified are, so to say, lost sight of. The specialist has his own libraries, the doctor, the divine, the lawyer, the chemist, the engineer, where the books may be classified and re-classified until they will bear the process no longer; but for the general reading public a few main divisions with their natural sub-divisions suffice.* Whether it is wise for the librarian to rely too much on someone else's minute classification rather than follow his own well thought-out plan is an open question. For all libraries to be administered on one plan, for all their books to be classified on the ideal system (which will never be invented), as many ideal librarians will be required as there are libraries unless the librarian is to be a mere figure-head and his assistants clockwork mechanisms. Individuality is, to my mind, even though it have its cranks and fads, far better and of a far higher order than any pattern, rule-of-thumb conduct, without personality, without characteristic and without interest. The pattern librarian of the future, about whom we hear so much, who is worked from a central bureau, I hope never to see; for the man who accepts meekly the decision of a central authority as to where he shall place a book, without question and in perfect faith, is a terrible possibility of the "coming" centralisation of libraries, which may or may not take place *ad Calendas Græcas*.

---

* I allude to the too minute classification of works of a technical, scientific or philosophical nature, often dealing incidentally with closely allied subjects which the librarian sometimes ignores. It is impossible for a librarian to have a sufficient technical knowledge of the contents of books of such a nature, and thus the classification is too often by title only.

APPOINTMENTS.

CRAIGIE, Mr. James, Librarian, Arbroath Public Library, to be Librarian of the Sandeman Public Library, Perth.

The other selected candidates were Messrs. Ford, *Glasgow*; *Law, *Battersea*; and McDonald, *Dumbarton*.

HARGRAVES, Mr., Sub-Librarian, Hull Public Library, to be Librarian, Stockport Public Library.

*HARPER, Mr. B. J., Senior Assistant, Stoke Newington, to be Sub-Librarian.

*Members of L.A.A.

OBITUARY.

We regret the event which makes it our duty to record the demise of the well-known writer on the History and Practice of Typography—Mr. John Southward. Born sixty-two years ago in Liverpool, he was apprenticed to his father, a printer in that city, who published a local paper. Here he not only learned the art of the printer, but was also initiated into the mysteries of journalism.

At one time he made a journey through Spain and contributed to the "*Printers' Register*" a series of articles on the printing offices of that country. For several years he edited the "*Printers' Register*," which is one of the oldest trade papers now existing. In the early years of the Library Association he read a paper on the necessity for providing our public libraries with a proper proportion of the best technical works, of which in those days they were in many cases sadly deficient. As is well known to members of the L.A.A. he delivered two courses of lectures on the History of Printing in connection with the Library Association Technical Education Classes, and those who were privileged to hear either will remember the interesting manner in which he treated a somewhat dry subject, and the never failing courtesy with which he answered questions or cleared up difficulties.

His contributions to the literature of typography are too numerous to be fully detailed in a short notice of this description, but mention must be made of the most notable. His principal work is undoubtedly *Practical Printing*, of which the fifth edition has lately been published. *Modern Printing*, in four volumes, was the last practical work from his pen. The article *Typography* in the ninth edition of the *Encyclopædia Britannica* he wrote, as well as works on *Artistic Printing, Printing Machinery,* and *Authorship and Publication*. He was also responsible for a large part of Bigmore and Wyman's *Bibliography of Printing*, and compiled, with the assistance of the Librarian, the annotated catalogues of the typographical collections in the St. Bride Institute. At the time of his demise he was preparing for press a new work on the *History of English Printing*, which was also to trace the development of the Art in the Colonies. The manuscript is finished, and publication was expected in the autumn season.

Mr. Southward had been ailing for some time, and recently underwent an operation at St. Thomas' Hospital, from the effects of which he gradually sank and expired on July 9th. As Goethe says, Death is a commingling of eternity with time; in the death of a good man eternity is seen looking through time.

NEW MEMBERS.

Junior.—Messrs. F. EARL and J. M. WORMALD, Tate Library, Streatham.

APPOINTMENTS VACANT.

[**Notice to Library Authorities.**—*We shall be pleased to publish under this heading, free of charge, particulars of vacancies if full details are sent to the Editor on or before the 28th of each month.*]

METROPOLITAN BOROUGH OF WOOLWICH.

JUNIOR ASSISTANT LIBRARIAN.

The Council of the Metropolitan Borough of Woolwich require the services of a second Junior Assistant Librarian.

Salary commencing at £70 per annum. Applicants to be between 19 and 26 years of age, and preference will be given to those who have had previous experience in Public Library work.

Applications in candidate's own handwriting, enclosing copies of three recent testimonials, to be endorsed "Junior Assistant Librarian," and to be sent addressed to me at the Town Hall, Woolwich, not later than Thursday, August 28th.

Candidates will be required to devote the whole of their time to the duties of their appointment.

Canvassing the Members of the Council will disqualify.

By Order,
ARTHUR B. BRYCESON, *Town Clerk.*

TOWN HALL, WOOLWICH,
July 26th, 1902.

NOTICES.

All matter for the September number should reach the *Hon. Editor*, Mr. W. B. THORNE, St. Bride Institute, Bride Lane, E.C., on or before 20th August.

All other communications should be addressed to the *Hon. Secretary*, MR. J. RADCLIFFE, Public Library, East Ham, E.

The Library Assistant:

The Official Organ of the Library Assistants' Association.

No. 57. SEPTEMBER, 1902. Published Monthly

THE LIBRARY ASSISTANTS' ASSOCIATION.

FOUNDED 1895.   SEVENTH SESSION.   YEAR 1901-1902.

Members are requested to read carefully the announcements appearing on this and the following pages, as no further intimation of meetings and other arrangements may be expected.

AUGUST EXCURSION.

Owing to the inclemency of the weather, this outing, which it was hoped would have been one of the most successful ever arranged, had to be abandoned at the last moment.

INAUGURAL MEETING—OCTOBER.

It is hoped that the inaugural meeting of next session will be held at the London School of Economics, early in October. The Committee are endeavouring to arrange for some prominent member of the profession to give an address on the Technical Education of Library Assistants, with special reference to the Classes which are to be established at this School in connection with the Library Association.

NORTH-WESTERN BRANCH.
SEPTEMBER MEETING.

The next meeting will be held at the kind invitation of Ben H. Mullen, Esq., M.A., in the Central Library, Peel Park, Salford, on Wednesday, September 17th, at 7.30 p.m., and not the 10th, as previously announced.

Mr. Mullen will read a Paper, and afterwards conduct the members round the Library and Museum.

Will those intending to be present on this occasion kindly acquaint Mr. Mullen on or before the 16th inst.

LIBRARY ASSOCIATION CLASSES.

The next professional examination of the Library Association will be held in January, 1903, at centres to suit the convenience of candidates. Full particulars may be obtained from the Hon. Secretary of the Education Committee. Copies of the syllabus and questions set at recent examinations may also be seen in the "Library Association Year Book," the 1902 issue of which is now ready. It may be obtained from the Assistant Secretary of the Association, Whitcomb House, Whitcomb Street, Pall Mall East, S.W.

The next series of classes will commence on October 15th, and will be held at the London School of Economics, Clare Market, E.C. A course of ten lectures on "Elementary Bibliography" will be given by Mr. J. D. Brown, and also on Wednesdays during the Michaelmas term a course of lectures on "Bibliographies of special subjects" will be given by various specialists. The Library Association will pay half the fees of any students nominated by one of its members.

Further particulars of these lectures may be had on application to the Hon. Secretary of the Education Committee, or to the Director of the London School of Economics.

STUDY CIRCLE.

The Committee has pleasure in announcing that the work of the Study Circle will be continued in the ensuing session, in a modified and, it is hoped, improved form. It has been thought desirable to bring their efforts more into line with the work of the Education Committee of the Library Association, to supply, as far as their means allow, the needs of those assistants who are unable to attend the classes. The syllabus of the Library Association will be taken in detail, commencing with "Library Management," and questions will be set monthly, similar in scope to the questions set at the professional examinations. The text-books are those recommended by the Library Association in the current "Year Book." Further details will be given next month.

JOHN DURIE, THE LIBRARIANS' APOSTLE.
By P. EVANS LEWIN.

"The Thing that hath been, it is That which shall be," and "there is no new Thing under the Sun," saith the Preacher. Yet it will be a matter of surprise to some that as far back as the year 1650, a pamphlet was published containing a plea for the better payment of librarians, and that at a time when Britain was behind all the Continental nations in her treatment of literature, its author should have been a Scotsman. At the present day the position of a librarian and his importance to the community are better recognized, but in the seventeenth century he was regarded, in Britain at any rate, as a mere keeper of books, whose sole duty it was to be responsible for the *safe keeping* of the books placed under his care. With, perhaps, the exception of the Bodleian Library, then but a small collection, England possessed no public libraries which could compare to the Royal Library at Paris, the University Library at Prague, the Imperial Library at Vienna, the Libraries of the Escorial and the Vatican, those at Lyons and Heidelberg, and others which then formed the nucleus of those grand libraries which now exist in almost every town of any importance on the Continent.

It is not to be wondered at, therefore, that the office of librarian was held in small esteem in England, then the least progressive country in science, art, and literature, and credit is due to John Durie for endeavouring to arouse some interest in the matter. In a tract entitled "The Reformed Librarie-Keeper," published in the year 1650, he brings forward a scheme, at a period convulsed by political agitation, for the better management of libraries.

John Durie was born at Edinburgh in the year 1596, forty years after a more celebrated man, the occult philosopher John Dee, had sent in his memorial to Queen Mary for the recovery and preservation of ancient writings and monuments, and for the erection of a "library royal." Dee, like Durie, had lived much out of England, travelling from Court to Court, and in his wanderings he had seen those collections of books which were the glory of Europe. Dee himself had collected four thousand precious volumes, which became the prey of an ignorant mob during one of his journeys on the Continent. It is to be noted that these two men were equally cosmopolitan and erratic in their tastes, Dee inclining to the study of the almost untrodden paths of natural science, Durie keeping to the broad way of religious tolerance and building up for himself a name in history by his lifelong endeavours to promote a union of all Christian Churches. Durie came of a good stout Scottish stock, being the grandson of that John Durie, associated with Knox, who, though a Preacher, was fond of athletics, for "the gown was no sooner off and the Bible out of hand in the Kirk, when on went the corselet and up fangit was the hagbut; and to the fields." He was educated at Sedan, and later visited Oxford for the purpose of study at the Bodleian. His Continental education seems to have broadened his mind, for he laboured strenuously throughout his life for the Union of Christendom, making incessant journeyings with that end in view. Received with much favour by Gustavus Adolphus, he was ordered out of Sweden by his celebrated daughter and successor Queen Christina, that lady who, on occasion, donned male attire and called herself "King," and was finally in her turn forced to quit Sweden by her rebellious subjects. There is no doubt that Durie often let his zeal outrun his discretion, for his writings show him to have been a singularly hard-hitter. After his expulsion from the Court of Christina we find him engaged as Domestic Chaplin to Mary, Princess of Orange, daughter to Charles I. and mother of William III., but tiring of this he returned to England, and in the year 1645 preached before Parliament, " Israel's Call to March out of Babylon," a sermon which gained considerable attention. In the year 1650 at a time when the fate of what forms the nucleus of the Royal Collection in the British Museum, then kept at St. James' Palace, was trembling in the balance, he was appointed deputy to Bulstrode Whitelocke, afterwards Chancellor, in the office of Librarie-Keeper at St. James'. There can be small doubt that to the exertions of Durie and Whitelocke we owe the preservation of what then constituted our National Collection, which some of those old iconoclasts in their blind zeal for the destruction of all that savoured of royalty and antiquity, would have converted into hard cash and shipped beyond the seas.

About this time Durie wrote the tract which is the subject of this paper. In it he expressed views greatly in advance of those current. " The Librarie-Keeper's place and office, in most countries, are looked upon," he says, " as places of profit and gain, and so accordingly sought after and valued in that regard ; and not in regard of the service which is to bee don unto the Commonwealth of Israel, for the advancement of Pietie and Learning. For the most part men look after the maintenance and livelihood settled upon their places more than upon the end or usefulness of their emploiments, and so they subordinate to the advantages of their places to purchase mainly two things thereby, viz : an easy subsistence and some credit in comparison of others, nor is the last much regarded if the first is to bee had," and, he continues in words almost applicable to the present day, " their places are but mercenarie, and their emploiment of little or no use further then to look to the books committed to their custodie that they may not bee lost—and that is all." Then Durie goes on to complain that at Oxford " the settled maintenance of the Librarie-Keeper is not above fiftie or sixtie pound per annum," the assistant, we learn from Edwards' Memoirs of Libraries, getting but £10, and a servant £4, in the money of that day, and he urges " that their places might not be made, as everywhere they are, mercenarie, but rather honorarie, and that with a competant allowance of two hundred pound a year (a much larger sum then than it is now) som emploiments should bee put upon them further then a bare keeping of the books." This further work he describes as follows:—The Librarian is to be "a Factor or Trader for helps to Learning and a Treasurer to keep the books, and a Despenser to applie them to use, or too see them well used, or at least not abused; and to do this, first a Catalogue is to be made to be 'ranked' in the order most easily to be found which is that of 'Science and Languages,' when first of all the books are divided into the *subjectam materiam* whereof they treat, and then everie kinde of matter sub-divided into their several languages .... and a reference is to bee made to the place where the books are to bee found in their shelves or repositories." For the increase of the stock "correspondence should bee held with those that are eminent in everie science, to trade with them for their profit," for the exchange and purchase of books, the librarian to give an account of his trading once a year. The Catalogue of additions is to be written and then put in print every three years. Might not all this have been written in the middle of the nineteenth century instead of in the middle of the seventeenth?

It will be seen from the foregoing extracts that Durie's endeavour was to raise the status of a Librarian, so that instead of being a caretaker he should become not only a help to the learned, but a scholar himself. At the same time that the "Reformed Librarie-Keeper" was published another pamphlet, but not in such a happy vein, appeared, named "The Reformed School," which contains Durie's peculiar views on education. The model youths of those days were "in winter to be waked at five, in summer at four of the clock in the morning," and to be safely in bed by nine at night. "The usher shall cause them to rise, which whiles they are adoing and putting on their clothes, he shall with a previous short ejaculation, reade some part of the Scriptures unto them. This is to bee don within the space of half-an-hour, to bee measured by a sandglass, after which every-one shall go abroad for the space of another half-hour to stretch, wash and cleanse himself, till the whole family be called togither; the women and girls shall be in one room by themselves, and the men and boyes in another, so that they shall not see one another and yet be both able to hear him who shall read prayers." After the arduous duties of the day were accomplished "those that desired them should not be refused bread and beer of good quality," and no doubt the little victims of the Reformed School appreciated this part of the daily drudgery. Other times other manners.

To Librarians John Durie should have a peculiar interest, and not less so to Assistants, for he was one himself. He is the apostle of better salaries, and probably the first Englishman who has pleaded for their office. Therefore no apology is needed for including in these pages the meagre particulars here supplied of one who was the friend of such men as Milton, Baxter, Mede, and Hall, the confidant of Gustavus Adolphus, the correspondent of half the theologians of the Continent, the writer of a very voluminous literature, and last but not least, from our point of view, a Library Assistant. Probably in the Valhalla of Librarians he is addressed as "Saint Durie"; at any rate he deserves a memorial of some sort, and this I have endeavoured to offer.

NOTES AND COMMENTS.

New Hon. Member.—To signify their hearty appreciation of the valuable services rendered to the Association by Mr. H. TAPLEY SOPER, both as Committee-man and Hon. Editor, the Committee have unanimously elected him an Hon. Member on his appointment to the librarianship of Exeter. The Committee believe that their action in thus honouring one who entirely deserves the honour will meet with the approval of all members. They also wish him a prosperous and successful career in his new position.

Brierley Hill.—Permission has been asked to raise a loan for the establishment of a Free Library and Technical School, Mr. Carnegie having given £2,000 towards the cost.

Cockermouth.—Mr. E. L. Waugh, son of the late Liberal member for Cockermouth, has presented the borough of Cockermouth with a site for a public library in Main Street, in order to enable the district to claim Mr. Carnegie's gift of £1,000.

Eastbourne.—Including Mr. Andrew Carnegie's gift of £10,000, the Corporation have decided to spend £35,000 on the erection of a public library and technical institute.

London Library.—Mr. George Meredith has been elected vice-president of the London Library, in place of the late Lord Acton.

Soldiers' Libraries.—The system of regimental libraries seems to be a very complete one in Germany. The Kaiser has himself looked after the matter and made it a personal business. He first contributed 60,000 marks out of his private purse, and then raised the sum to 80,000 marks, and subsequently to 120,000 marks, and appointed a special commission to select and purchase 400,000 volumes, to which ample additions are made from time to time. By an ingenious plan, there is an exchange of books between regiment and regiment; so that one good library serves for all. This way of improving the spare hours of soldiers has so impressed General André, the French Minister of

War, that he too has inaugurated a similar system in the French Army.

Stornoway.—At a meeting of the Town Council of Stornoway on Friday, a promised contribution of £3,500 from Mr. Andrew Carnegie, for the erection of a building to be used as a public library at Stornoway was unanimously accepted. The condition of the gift was that the borough contribute the sum of £120 annually towards the expense of maintaining the library.

Woolwich.—Plans for the Plumstead District Library have passed the Council, and the erection of the Library is to be pushed on without delay. The selection of a site for a branch at Eltham is also under consideration. It is hoped that it will be possible to open both these Libraries free of debt, as it is estimated that the donation of £14,000 from Mr. Carnegie plus the accumulated rates which the Council has in hand will be sufficient to defray the cost of erection.

The Editor will be glad to receive particulars of any instance where a site has been given by a borough council or other local body for the erection of a library.

Membership of the L.A.A.—Members are requested to note that they can, upon application to the Hon. Sec., obtain circulars explaining the objects of the Association. It is hoped that applications will be made for these for distribution with a view to obtaining new members.

Donations to the L.A.A. Library.—From Miss JAMES, Library Bureau, Boston, U.S.A., Plummer's "Hints to Small Libraries," 3rd Ed., 1902.

From THE UNITED STATES GOVERNMENT. A Handbook for the Cataloger. Part 1. Compiled by A. R. HASSE. 1902.

CORRESPONDENCE.

DEAR SIR,

Although I always read with pleasure my "Library Assistant" when it comes, curiously enough I did not notice until to-day a letter signed by a gentleman with a long Latin pseudonym, which appears on page 134 of the issue for July. As he mentions my name in a connection that seems to suggest I am in some way responsible for the resolution which is to be put forward in the name of the Council at the next Annual Meeting, I trust you will allow me to say that not only am I in no way responsible for the resolution, but (while willing to accept it on the principle of the thin-edge-of-the-wedge) I strongly disapprove of it as a compromise, which is bound to fail, unless it is merely the beginning of legislation in that direction. I think the number of seats to be automatically vacated each year is too small, and the proposal that those members of the Council (*almost certainly new members*) who receive the smallest number of votes shall retire, is most unfair.

Believe me, faithfully yours,

J. Y. W. MAC ALISTER.

THE EDITOR,
LIBRARY ASSISTANT.

BOOKS, &c., RECEIVED.

NOTE.—*The Editor will be pleased to receive Library and other publications for notice in this column.*

Glasgow Corporation Public Libraries (FRANCIS THORNTON BARRETT, Chief Librarian). Index Catalogue of the Gorbals District Library. 1902.

A first-rate example of a *multum in parvo* dictionary catalogue, with several innovations by way of introduction, one being a capital classified table of the subject-headings occurring in it, based on Dewey's Decimal System. Another is a List of Writers in Foreign Languages, in which, under German, we are surprised to find William Shakespeare, and while the works of Dante, Petrarch, and Tasso are represented in the Library, no mention is made of them under the heading "Italian." We presume that what is really meant is a list of *books* in foreign languages. For the rest, the Catalogue is nicely produced and wonderfully cheap.

Limehouse Public Library (G. H. MCCALL, Librarian). Descriptive Catalogue of books in the Lending and Reference Departments. 1902.

Manchester Public Libraries (C. W. SUTTON, Chief Librarian). Classified List of Books placed in the Reference Library. Edited by Ernest Axon, Assistant Librarian.

REPORTS, READERS' GUIDES, ETC., have been received from the following libraries:—Bootle, Croydon, Hereford, Hornsey, Kensal Rise, Leyton, Lincoln, Stoke Newington, West Ham, Westminster, Willesden Green.

APPOINTMENTS.

Cass, Mr. A. R., Second Assistant of the Tottenham Public Library, to be Senior Assistant at Stoke Newington Public Library.

*Law, Mr. W., of the Battersea Public Library, to be Assistant Librarian and Clerk at the Brighton Public Library.

Robertson, Miss R. (untrained), to be Assistant at the Haggerston Branch of the Shoreditch Public Libraries.

Thompson, Mr. H. M., Junior Assistant of St. Bride Foundation Institute, to be Second Assistant at Poplar Public Library.

* Member of the L.A.A.

NEW MEMBERS.

Junior.—Messrs. H. S. LUMSDEN, Aberdeen. PERCY FERMAGE, Kimberley. EDGAR TERRY, Woolwich.

APPOINTMENTS VACANT.

[**Notice to Library Authorities.**—*We shall be pleased to publish under this heading, free of charge, particulars of vacancies, if full details are sent to the Editor on or before the 28th of each month.*]

NOTICES.

All matter for the October number should reach the Hon. Editor on or before 20th September.

All other communications should be addressed to the *Hon. Secretary*, MR. J. RADCLIFFE, Public Library, East Ham, E.

The Library Assistant

The Official Organ of the Library Assistants' Association.

No. 58.   OCTOBER, 1902.   Published Monthly

THE LIBRARY ASSISTANTS' ASSOCIATION.
FOUNDED 1895.   EIGHTH SESSION.   YEAR 1901-1902.

Members are requested to read carefully the announcements appearing on this and the following pages, as no further intimation of meetings and other arrangements may be expected.

INAUGURAL MEETING.

The first meeting of the session will be held at the London School of Economics, Clare Market (top of Clements Inn, west side of Law Courts), on **Wednesday, October 8th,** at 8 p.m. Mr. H. D. Roberts, has kindly consented to give an address on the Technical Education of Library Assistants, with special reference to the classes which are to be established at the above school in connection with the Library Association. Mr. Lawrence Inkster will occupy the chair, and an interesting and profitable evening is anticipated. Visitors are invited, and every member is requested to do his utmost to attend, so that the ensuing winter's work may have an encouraging and successful send-off. A vacancy on the Committee will be filled at this meeting.

FIFTH ANNUAL DINNER.

Arrangements are being made for the Fifth Annual Dinner, which will be held at Anderton's Hotel, Fleet Street, E.C., on Wednesday, November 19th. Tickets 3/6 each as usual. In order that all assistants may have an opportunity of attending, the ordinary meeting for the month has been cancelled. Any suggestions or offers of musical help will be gladly received by Mr. W. J. Harris, Branch Library, Stroud Green, N., who has the management in hand.

MEMBERSHIP OF THE L.A.A.

A circular explaining the objects of the Association and benefits of membership has been prepared with a view to obtaining new members. Copies may be had from the Hon. Sec and it is hoped that they will be judiciously distributed, so that a large increase in our numbers may result.

NORTH-WESTERN BRANCH.
SEPTEMBER MEETING.

This meeting was held as arranged at Peel Park, Salford, where Mr. Mullen presided over a very good gathering of members, who were fortunate in having read to them by Mr. Mullen the paper he had prepared for the Birmingham Conference of the Library Association.

The paper dealt with a scheme for reducing to a minimum the misplacement of books on the shelves in a reference library. This he proposed doing by substituting, instead of the usual gilt number, a series of four coloured circles, four squares, and two triangles, known as "Major Indices," each representing one of the main headings of the Dewey classification, and "Minor Indices" in the form of smaller coloured circles for the sub-divisions. Thus a volume wrongly shelved would be easily detected by the form, colour or position of the "Indices." After discussing the various points of the paper, and a reply from the writer, a vote of thanks was passed to Mr. Mullen for his kind invitation, paper and hospitality. The members then adjourned to visit the Reference and Lending Libraries, and before dispersing were entertained to light refreshments by Mr. Mullen.

As this paper will no doubt be published in the L.A. Conference Report, members are referred to that for fuller details of Mr. Mullen's scheme.

The next meeting will be held on November 15th, at the Free Library, Warrington, by kind invitation of C. Madeley, Esq., chief librarian. Times of trains and all particulars will appear in the November issue of the "Assistant."

STUDY CIRCLE.

As announced in the September journal, the work of the Study Circle commences this month. The subject chosen is "Library Management," interpreted in its widest sense. No monthly course of reading will be given, as it is realised that the subject is not one that can be studied from text-books alone ; but questions will be set with a view to test the knowledge gathered from practical experience of work in a public library. Students should not, of course, entirely neglect what few text-books there are that deal directly or incidentally with the subject, but it must be understood that the questions should be answered from memory, and that no reference to any book should be made between reading and answering the questions.

QUESTIONS.

(1). Give a list of works of reference (excluding ordinary encyclopædias) that you consider indispensable for an average public library ; also mention some others usually found in such libraries that you think may be dispensed with. Give reasons in each case.

(2). Describe and give rulings for (a) Binding Book, (b) Cash Receipts Book, (c) Lending Library Stock Book, (d) Withdrawals Register.

Answers should be sent, not later than the 21st inst., to Mr. R. B. Wood, Public Library, Buckingham Palace Road, London, S.W., signed by a pseudonym, and with the real name of the student enclosed in an envelope on which is written the pseudonym.

ENEMIES OF BOOKS.

It may be remembered that at a Congress of French Librarians, held in August, 1900, it was resolved to offer a prize of £40 for an essay on the preservation of books from the attacks of insects, and the destruction of the latter. At the same time two other prizes of £40 and £20 respectively were offered for further papers on the same subject.

We now learn that twenty-three essays were received, the Congress prize of £40 being awarded to Herr Johann Bolle, an agricultural chemist, of Gontz, Austria. The other £40 prize was not awarded, but the £20 was given to Monsieur Constant-Houlbert, a Professor at the Lycée of Rennes. Both these gentlemen agree in recommending that the books be fumigated with sulphuret of carbon, first placing them in a hermetically sealed box. They consider this method superior to treating with superheated air, which has a tendency to warp the covers.

It is noticeable that neither prize was secured by a librarian; and we regret the fact that neither of the successful competitors was an Englishman.

PUBLIC LIBRARIES AND CHILDREN.

We notice some very interesting matter on this subject in the *Sunday School Chronicle* for August 21st. Rightly thinking the subject one of sufficient public importance to warrant a special investigation, the Editor arranged for a symposium of the opinions of some of the principal librarians of this country. The questions asked amounted to "What guidance is given?" "Who selects the books for the juvenile department?" The replies to the first query show that while every effort is made by the staff to assist juvenile readers, no carefully planned out system is practised as in America. It would seem that Battersea has done most in this direction, a separate room specially furnished having been set apart for their use. The Editor of the "S.S.C." is very concerned about the constitution of book committees where they exist, and where they do not he says "an enormous responsibility is placed upon the librarian, and it is to the credit of these public servants that our libraries are so well managed." It is an all-important matter, and we earnestly appeal to all assistants to patiently endeavour to lead young readers to occupy themselves with those books which will foster a love for only the best of the great literature in their keeping.

A hero and a fight or two,
 A villain forced to grovel;
An ad., a magazine review,
 And there's your modern novel.
American Stationer.

PRINTING FOR LIBRARIANS.

[NOTE.—*Read at a Meeting held at the Poplar Public Library in April last, to open a Discussion on the subject.*]

I venture to think that it would be as well if all of us were to endeavour to obtain at any rate a superficial knowledge of the practice of printing. I mean enough to be able to recognise and distinguish the different sizes of type, whether a page is leaded or set solid, and items of that character.

During these remarks it will be more convenient if we imagine that the work to be printed is a catalogue, and not a class list, monthly guide, or other small publication

In the first place, it is usual to advertise for tenders for the work of printing. Specifications of what is required should be prepared, and all printers applying furnished with a copy. Mr. Quinn in his " Manual of Cataloguing " gives a very full and useful scheme for a specification which is well worthy of study. It will be seen there how every detail is set forth, and this should be done, not only in fairness to yourself, but to the printer also. In selecting your printer it is wise to bear in mind that the lowest figure is not always the cheapest. Pay a fair price for your article and you can demand a fair article in return, but if your sole thought is cheapness, believe me, you will regret your choice before the work is out of hand. A well printed catalogue is an advertisement to the library and an encouragement to the reader, while one that is badly produced will cause in many minds suspicious thoughts to arise as to the general efficiency and up-to-dateness of the institution. Every properly prepared work is arranged on a certain conventional and fixed plan, and the author or compiler of a catalogue desirous of avoiding the appearance of inexperience must prepare his copy accordingly. The several parts of a book follow in this order:—Half-Title, Title, Dedication (if any), Preface or introduction, Body of Work, Index (if any). It ought to be here stated that the text portion of a work is always printed first—the title etc., being left to the last. This practice is useful, because it gives the compiler an opportunity of alluding in his preface to points which have arisen during the process of printing, some of which probably could not have been anticipated.

About preparing MSS. for the press, I shall say nothing, as Mr. Quinn has familiarised you all with the process in his handbook, in a manner far more understandable than I could put it before you. Having passed your copy on to the printer, you will, in the course of a short time, receive from him " slip proofs " to correct. The length of these proofs is sometimes somewhat surprising. The reason of their length (as you all probably know), is that as the compositor fills his " stick " with type, so he places it on a long wooden tray known as a " galley." When this galley is full, the type is just loosely tied up with a fine cord, and two or three impressions, which constitute the proofs, are pulled. This reminds me of the story of the lady who, when she received slip proofs for the first time, informed the printer that she did not want her book to be such an awkward shape! and also that she wanted it printed on both sides of the paper, which latter she thought should be of a better quality. The printer's reply is not recorded!

Correcting proofs is an interesting and at the same time wearying employment. If you attempt to do it single-handed, the strain on the eyesight, caused by constantly changing from copy to proof, is very painful. Having a second person to read the copy is not so satisfactory as may be supposed, but as it is somewhat quicker, and certainly a saving to the eyes, I think that whenever possible this help should be employed. When this task is on hand, it should always be remembered that any alterations or additions made in the proof other than printer's errors and literals will be charged extra for. So that it is wise to see that your copy is, as nearly as possible, if not quite, as you want it to appear in print, otherwise you will find your charges for corrections mount up alarmingly. Too much care cannot be taken in reading proofs. Errors creep in in all sorts of unexpected places, and unless searched for diligently will escape unnoticed, only to appear when the work is completed, making blemishes which will prove an eyesore. If possible, always let two persons read the proofs, and if both are fairly vigilant, the majority of mistakes will then be run to earth. I find it a good rule never to be satisfied until I have found a mistake, and confess to disappointment when repeated readings fail to show one. With the weird and curious signs of correction, I take it the majority of you are familiar; if not, I again refer you to Mr. Quinn's Manual, where he gives most of them, a verbal explanation being difficult without illustrations. As the work progresses you will receive from the printer the matter made up into page form; on this must be written the first three letters or first word of the first and last entries of each page, as a key to their contents. A final revision, to see that all errors have been corrected and that no fresh ones have crept in, must also be made. As each batch of proof is returned to the printer the date must be written upon it, together with the initials of the person responsible for its correction. This simple precaution is a satisfaction to all parties. It should be mentioned that if you write anything on the proof which you do not wish to be printed, such as an instruction to the printer, either write it in red ink or draw a circle round it; otherwise, there is a chance of it being incorporated, however irrelevant it may be to the adjoining text. I would also say a word here on behalf of the printers' reader. Frequently you will find he will query certain entries, dates, or names. Never scorn these queries, as the man is very often a highly intelligent individual, and knows quite well what he is doing. His remarks are always worthy of consideration, as is abundantly testified by many of the leading writers of the day.

I think now I have said sufficient on the matter of proofs and corrections, and must hark back a bit to other items. It is a great point to decide judiciously whether the pages of a book shall be set solid or leaded. When the object is to crowd as much matter as possible into a page the type should be solid, that is, the lines should be set as closely together as the type will permit. When the pages are required to be light and elegant the type should be leaded, that is, the lines are set a little apart from each other by the insertion between them of small slips of metal, technically called leads. Whenever possible the pages should be leaded, as they then present a much more attractive appearance than if set solid. The selection of type is of course a difficult matter, and while circumstances have a lot to do with it, it mainly depends on the ideas of the responsible person what face shall be used. I will only mention one face which is very popular and serviceable—that is, "Long Primer." It is largely used in bookwork as a medium letter, combining the advantages of legibility, typographical elegance, and economy of space. It admits of the crowding into a page of a large amount of matter; at the same time its appearance is light and bold, and by no means calculated to fatigue the eye. The leaders and editorial articles in newspapers and magazines are usually in Long Primer, as are many of the elegant 8vo. and 12mo. volumes issued by high-class publishers.

The Linotype Machine has recently been brought into use for Catalogue work, the St. Bride Institute being, I believe, in spite of other claims, among, if not *the* first to use it. I am unaware that any particular advantage accrues from its employment—composition, I suppose, is cheaper—but as certain modifications have to be made on account of its somewhat limited capacity, I doubt its supreme utility for such work, at least at present. The lines of type, or "slugs," as they are called, can indeed be purchased by the library and kept standing for future editions of the catalogue, and I believe it costs less to acquire these than it does to buy type which is hand composed. When a new edition of the catalogue is required, the additions are cast on the machine and inserted in their proper order, but of course the whole has to be re-arranged to bring it to proper page size again.

One difficulty with the Linotype is the corrections—every line being solid, it necessarily follows that if there is a correction to be made, the whole line must be re-cast, if only to insert a single comma. In consequence corrections are very costly.

Some of the large American libraries possess their own type-casting machines, which are operated by the staff. I do not know that this has been attempted in England.

Another type casting and setting machine which is being now boomed considerably in the printing trade is the Lanston Monotype. It casts single types, as its name indicates, and composes them suitably for all kinds of work, and is furthermore, so I am told, specially suitable for catalogue setting. It is truly a wonderful machine, and to see it at work one marvels at the ingenuity of man. The types being cast separately, alterations can be made of course in the same way as in hand composition, and here it gets a distinct advantage over the Linotype. Moreover, it carries a greater variety of faces than the Linotype, heavy and italic types being included. Its use is not very general yet, but one cannot help thinking there is a great future before it.

In conclusion, I would say a word on *good* printing. Many there are who cannot distinguish good from bad. The type, the ink, and the paper may be of the best quality, and yet the printing bad. On the other hand, those materials *may* be inferior and the printing good, although few printers who pride themselves on good workmanship care to use inferior materials. Let it not be supposed, however, that because so few readers can discriminate between good and bad printing, the typography of a book is of minor importance. The prominent characteristics of bad printing are:—

1st.—*Unequal Spacing.* In some lines the words are set too closely together, in others too far apart. This want of uniformity is a great eyesore. It is not always the fault of the compositor. It results very frequently from alterations being made in a page after it is in type.

2nd.—*Lavish use of hyphens at the end of lines.* A good compositor justifies or adjusts his lines so as to avoid as much as possible using hyphens, which are as unsightly in a catalogue as in a letter.

3rd.—*Careless Punctuation and Orthography.* A compositor or reader will, unless he has strict injunctions to the contrary, rectify faults of punctuation, and correct such clerical errors as are made even by those most accurate, especially in proper names, etc. On the other hand, indifferent compositors will not only suffer a *lapsus calami* to become a printed error, but will also pervert a word in a ludicrous but provoking manner.

Strive to avoid these faults, and to the extent of your avoidance so far will you have a well-printed catalogue.

W. B. T.

NOTES AND COMMENTS.

Battersea.—Mr. Carnegie's offer to give £15,000 for building three branch libraries, on condition that the Borough Council provides the sites and raises additional taxation for their maintenance, has been accepted by 27 votes to 13.

East Ham.—Mr. Carnegie has offered East Ham £10,000 for the erection of two additional Public Libraries.

Exeter.—We notice that our friend Mr. Soper has soon begun to make things lively at the Royal Albert Memorial College, where he was recently appointed. In a report to the Governors on the present condition of the Library, he said the system now in use was both antiquated and unreliable, and advised the adoption of open access in both Lending and Reference Departments, as well as a re-classification of the whole Library on the Dewey system. Several Governors spoke in support of the scheme, and as, apparently, there was no opposition, the report was adopted. Here is another victory for the "Open Access Party," who are to be congratulated on having such a vigorous supporter as Mr. Soper.

Gladstone Memorial Library.—The St. Deniol's Memorial Library at Hawarden is to be opened on October 14th by Lord Spencer, as chairman of the Gladstone National Memorial. Other distinguished men are expected to attend the ceremony.

Glasgow.—A reference library of about 4,300 volumes has been bequeathed by Mr. Jeffery, of Johnstone, Renfrewshire, to the Mitchell Library, for public use and service. It is reported to be particularly rich in works on art, archæology, topography and natural history.

Lower Sydenham.—A site for the new Public Library which has been presented by Mr. Carnegie was offered to the Lewisham Borough Council by a local builder. In consequence of its not being centrally situated, a good deal of objection has been raised, and the Council are to be petitioned in the matter at their first sitting after the recess.

Sir Edward Russell on the Carnegie Gifts.—Speaking at the opening of a bazaar at Criccieth recently in aid of the proposed public library, towards which Mr. Carnegie has contributed £800, Sir Edward Russell said the Welsh people were very fond of reading, of music, and of art generally, and he wished that similar feelings were more general in Britain. The proper ideal was to regard education not so much as a means of personal advancement and of getting on, but of giving sweetness, excellence, happiness and worthiness to whatever life we live. They had an illustration in the generosity of Mr. Carnegie of the fact that there were some men on the very heights of financial prosperity who perceived that one of the best philanthropies which they could exercise by means of their great wealth was to afford to the whole population those means of study and of the enjoyment of art which Mr. Chamberlain had once said that, properly provided to the public, would equalise the intellectual enjoyments of the poor with those of the rich. Practically Mr. Chamberlain's ideal had been largely realised in all great towns, and all should desire that it should be realised also in every sort of district in the country.

NEW MEMBERS.

Juniors.—Miss Olive Marsden, Darwen; Messrs. Walter Cook, Croydon; W. G. Henderson, Aberdeen; F. W. McLaren, Walthamstow; John Smith, Mitchell Library, Glasgow.

APPOINTMENTS VACANT.

[**Notice to Library Authorities.**—*We shall be pleased to publish under this heading, free of charge, particulars of vacancies, if full details are sent to the Editor on or before the 28th of each month.*]

METROPOLITAN BOROUGH OF POPLAR.

The Council of the above-named Borough invites applications from candidates for the post of SECOND ASSISTANT LIBRARIAN. Salary £120 per annum. Applicants must have had practical experience in Library work, including Cataloguing, and must be competent, under the supervision of the Borough Librarian, to take charge of a Library establishment.

Applications, stating age and previous library experience, in candidate's own writing, accompanied by copies of three recent testimonials, under cover, endorsed "Application—Second Assistant Librarian," must reach the undersigned not later than October 6th, 1902.

LEONARD POTTS,
Council Offices, High St., Poplar, E.   Town Clerk.
15th September, 1902.

BOOKS, &c., RECEIVED.

NOTE.—*The Editor will be pleased to receive Library and other publications for notice on this page.*

Borough of Bootle: Second Supplement to the Catalogue of the Free Public Library, with a reprint of the entries in the First Supplement. Compiled by Charles H. Hunt, Librarian, and William T. Montgomery, Sub-Librarian. 1902.

A nice, plain, easily understood dictionary catalogue in three sizes of type, a praiseworthy feature of which is the addition of the sub-librarian's name to the title page. We wish more honour was given in this respect, where honour was due. At the end of each letter are interesting quotations on books and reading. We notice some inconsistency in the matter of real names and pseudonyms, and we do not like the use of foreign equivalents for "volumes" in an English catalogue.

Reports, Readers' Guides, etc., have been received from the following libraries:—Bootle; Croydon; Royal Albert Memorial College, Exeter; Kendal.

APPOINTMENTS.

Bagguley, Mr. W. H., to be Librarian of the Great Western Railway Mechanics' Institution, Swindon.   [103 applications].

*Coltman, Mr. W. L., Derby Public Library, to be Second Assistant, Public Library, Woolwich.

Hosie, Mr. John, Librarian of Kendal, to be Librarian of Arbroath Public Library.

*Member of the L.A.A.

NOTICES.

All matter for the November number should reach the Hon. Editor on or before 20th October.

All other communications should be addressed to the *Hon. Secretary*, MR. J. RADCLIFFE, Public Library, East Ham, E.

The Library Assistant:
The Official Organ of the Library Assistants' Association.

No. 59.   NOVEMBER, 1902.   Published Monthly

THE LIBRARY ASSISTANTS' ASSOCIATION.
FOUNDED 1895.   EIGHTH SESSION.   YEAR 1901-1902.

Members are requested to read carefully the announcements appearing on this and the following pages, as no further intimation of meetings and other arrangements may be expected.

OUR SUPPLEMENT.

We wish to call special attention to our supplement and to record our indebtedness to the proprietors of " Punch " for the great privilege they have bestowed upon us in allowing us to issue it. Permission to publish " Punch " cartoons, except after the expiration of several months, is so rarely given, that we cannot value too highly the honour accorded to us. We may safely say this is the first time a " Punch " cartoon has been presented with a professional periodical such as this, a fact which our readers will doubtless appreciate. The motive of the cartoon is one which will appeal to those engaged in public library work, and all will admire the able manner Mr. Bernard Partridge has expressed it in his drawing.

FIFTH ANNUAL DINNER.

The Fifth Annual Dinner will be held at Anderton's Hotel, Fleet Street, E.C., on Wednesday, November 19th, at 7 p.m. It is hoped that all assistants will make an effort to attend, juniors being especially invited. An interesting musical programme is being arranged. The Committee will be pleased to welcome as many librarians as can be present, and other persons interested in the profession.

Applications for tickets (3/6 each) should be made to Mr. William J. Harris, Branch Library, Stapleton Hall Road, Stroud Green, N., who is still open to receive offers of musical help.

NORTH-WESTERN BRANCH.
NOVEMBER MEETING.

This meeting will be held on the kind invitation of C. Madeley, Esq., at the Museum and Library, Warrington, on Saturday, November 15th. Will members who intend being present please notify Mr. Madeley on or before the 12th. Train from Manchester Central 2.30 p.m., arriving at Warrington 2.48 p.m.

ANNUAL MEETING.

The Annual Meeting will be held in the Reference Library, Manchester, during December. Nominations for Chairman, Secretary, Treasurer, and eight Committee men, should be made to the Secretary by November 15th. If a sufficient number of nominations are received, ballot papers will be forwarded to all members of the Branch, otherwise the election will take place in the usual way. It is essential that the majority of the nominees should be assistants within a short distance of Manchester, in order that a quorum can easily be formed.

Any notices of motion for this meeting should be given in at the Warrington meeting.

PRESENTATION TO MR. P. D. GORDON.

At a special meeting of the Committee on October 1st a presentation in the form of an Elizabethan Copper Writing Set, was made to the former Hon. Secretary on the occasion of his marriage, and in recognition of the untiring energy he displayed while he held that position.

LIBRARY ASSOCIATION EDUCATION COMMITTEE.

We announce with pleasure that the Council of the Library Association have elected on their Education Committee Mr. Evan G. Rees and Mr. Reginald B. Wood, as representing the Library Assistants' Association. This is a very gratifying result and recognition of the efforts of our Association for the improvement of the professional efficiency of library assistants. It cannot but be productive of benefit both to the Education Committee, who will thus learn at first hand the views and opinions of assistants as to their technical education, and to the Library Assistants' Association, who, apart from the satisfaction the members will feel at such an important endorsement of their *raison d'être* will receive advantage in being brought into closer touch with a body working in the same direction. For instance, it may be possible to interest the Education Committee in the question of extending to provincial assistants the benefits metropolitan assistants now derive from the classes—a work this Association, far less able, has been endeavouring to do for some time. Our Study Circle does not supply a tithe of the need, and if the L.A. Education Committee will take over the task, the L.A.A. Education Committee will cheerfully sing their Nunc Dimittis.

STUDY CIRCLE.

The response to the questions set in the October Journal has been fairly satisfactory, but the Committee thinks that a much larger number of assistants ought to attempt the work. It would point out to those senior assistants who evidently consider it not worth their while, that the answering of these questions will prove invaluable practice for the " Library Management " section of the Professional Examination, as they are modelled on questions previously set and likely to be set again at these examinations. It would also point out that the Professional Certificate is likely to attain much more importance in the near future than has been attached to it, and that at any rate the more practical sections of it will probably soon be regarded as an indispensable qualification.

The replies to the October questions will be commented upon in the next number.

QUESTIONS.

(3) Give reasons for and against the practice of inflicting fines for overdetention of books. State what you consider to be the fairest scale of fines. How would you record fines so as to be able to check at any time any disputed fine.

(4) Draw up an imaginary Binding List of not less than twelve items, giving full instructions to binder. The list should include all probable varieties of orders.

Answers should be sent not later than the 21st inst., to Mr. R. B. Wood, Public Library, Buckingham Palace Road, London, S.W., signed by a pseudonym, and in the case of new students, with the real name enclosed in an envelope on which is written the pseudonym. Former students are requested to retain the same pseudonym throughout the Session.

INAUGURAL MEETING.

The first Meeting of the Eighth Session was held at the London School of Economics, Clare Market, when some fifty members and friends were present, including Sir Edmund Verney, Mr. Stanley Jast, Mr. W. W. Fortune, and Mr. F. Meaden Roberts. Mr. Lawrence Inkster occupied the Chair, and Mr. H. D. Roberts read a paper (which appears elsewhere in this issue) on "The Technical Education of Library Assistants."

In his opening remarks, the Chairman said the Library Association had not abandoned the Technical Classes, as had been suggested, but had done what they thought best in holding them in connection with, and at this School. After referring to the system of providing Classes with funds out of the rates, adopted in America, and announcing that Mr. E. G. Rees would read a paper on the same subject before the Library Association at the January 1903 Meeting, he called upon Mr. Roberts.

Considerable discussion followed the paper, and was opened in a capital speech by Mr. R. B. WOOD (St. George, Hanover Square), who said he thought the Education Committee was rather intolerant of criticism from assistants, although they professed to invite it. He did not agree that the Classes about to commence would be satisfactory to all. He only asked that the Education Committee should give assistants thorough and continued instruction in the subjects of the Syllabus of the professional examinations, and arrange the Classes so that at the end of a series the Student could sit for the corresponding section of the examination. At present there was no connection between the instruction and the examination. He did not see why the Library Association need call in the aid of the School of Economics. They were well able to bear the expense, judging from their financial statement. He could not see the practical value to assistants of the subjects in Group II. of this programme, and regarded them as the price they had to pay the School of Economics for Group I. The library assistant was not an accountant or a statistician. Local Government, Political History, Economics, Palæography, and Diplomatic had no particular interest for him. He had more to do with modern printing than ancient writing. He simply wanted instruction in Public Library Administration, and that was apparently the one subject the School of Economics thought unnecessary for his education. It was not to the credit of the Library Association that they abandoned the charge of the professional efficiency of assistants to an alien body of peculiar views, and salved their consciences by the application of a £10 note in paying half their fees.

MR. FORTUNE said he was pleased to be at a meeting of the L.A.A. again. He was sorry Mr. Wood had taken the attitude he had, as it would be discouraging to the L.A. Education Committee. Assistants' educational facilities were much greater now than they were years ago, and they should be grateful for what was now offered them. He was sure Mr. Brown's lectures would be very valuable, and would like to attend them himself. Public libraries, he said, should be worked on a purely business footing. If some businesses were carried on in the manner some libraries are, they would be bankrupt in a very short time.

MR. CHAMBERS (Woolwich) was disappointed with the Syllabus. Failed to see that Group I. would be of much use, and thought Group II. of no use at all. Assistants would not come from the suburbs to hear lectures on history and diplomatic, when they could get them at their local polytechnic.

MR. F. M. ROBERTS (Mile End) sympathized with Mr. Wood. The L.A.A. had attacked the L.A. in the early days on this question, and now they had got so far, after several snubbings. He also wondered what the use of the subjects in Group II. would be to the average assistant. If they became thoroughly acquainted with all those subjects, they would consider themselves much too good for librarianship. The assistants of to-day would make as good librarians as those at present occupying that position, but they must be better in the future. He suggested that some members of the L.A.A. should sit on the L.A. Education Committee.

Mr. S. Jast (Croydon) did not agree with the objections offered, thought they were mythical. The L.A. Council should know exactly what the attitude of assistants was. Pointed out assistants need only attend those Classes most helpful to them. It was important that a University, such as this School was, should recognize library subjects. The short Classes in Cataloguing and Classification could be extended next year. These were only a foundation on which a much more elaborate structure might be built. Thought the suggestion that some assistants should be on the L.A. Council very good. Was of the opinion that assistants should study in their own libraries as well as at the Classes, and also that librarians should be *made* to teach their own assistants, and also buy all library literature for their use.

Mr. Rees (Westminster), Mr. Stevenson (Croydon), Mr. Pickard (Bermondsey), and Mr. McKillop (Librarian of the School) also added their views. Mr. Chambers proposed a vote of thanks to Mr. H. D. Roberts, which was seconded by Mr. W. J. Harris.

Mr. Roberts, in reply, said that the L.A. Education Committee had been unanimous in their decision to arrange the Classes in connection with this School. He had no doubt whatever, that the Council would welcome assistants among their number. He believed the suggestion had never been made before, or he was sure that several assistants would have been elected on that body. Regarding "outsiders," he said he had received letters from two or three ladies asking " if they attended the course of lectures would they be guaranteed a situation at the end" (laughter).

He pointed out that the Classes were for assistants in *all* libraries, and not only for those in public libraries, so that some of the subjects would appeal to those in private or institution libraries, which would not be so necessary for the others. He echoed Mr. Jast's remark, that it was an important fact worthy of notice, that the London School of Economics, which was a branch of the London University, should provide Classes in library subjects, and students should consider it an honour to be allowed to attend them.

Mr. Rees proposed a vote of thanks to the Chairman, and after he had suitably replied, Mr. H. D. Roberts said he had received a letter from Professor Dixon, President of the L.A., wishing the L.A.A. and the Classes every success, and regretting that he could not be present.

NOTES AND COMMENTS.

Committee Vacancy.—At the October Meeting Mr. W. B. Thorne was elected to fill the vacancy on the Committee caused by the resignation of Mr. H. Tapley Soper.

"Sketch."—An illustrated interview with Mr. Carnegie appeared in the "Sketch" of October 8th, 1902.

Belfast.—An offer of £15,000 from Mr. Andrew Carnegie towards the erection of three branch libraries in Belfast has been accepted.

Bodleian Library.—The Tercentenary of this famous library was celebrated on October 8th and 9th, when upwards of two hundred distinguished guests from all parts of the world gathered together. A number of honorary degrees were conferred.

Brighouse.—The borough of Brighouse is one of the many places that have made application to Mr. Andrew Carnegie for a grant towards a proposed free library. The town has already a capital free library, towards which the rate contributes £330 per annum. But Brighouse wants to have a branch library at Rastrick. The reply which has been sent to the request for help is as follows:—" Dear Sir,—Yours of the 12th instant received. You state that the revenue is insufficient for the present library, there being nothing for books, etc. Being so, why need another building ? Besides, in view of the number of applications before Mr. Carnegie—some 400 since July—nearly all wanting attention, he could hardly establish a precedent of giving a branch library to districts of 22,000 people, who have already one library.—Respectfully yours, James Bertram, Private secretary."

Enfield.—Mr. Carnegie has written to the Enfield District Council with regard to a condition he imposed in his offer of £8,000 for public libraries, that the sites should be provided without charge to the rates. He now withdraws this condition so far as the central library is concerned, the Council having already determined to accommodate it in some new offices they intend to erect.

Limerick.—The Corporation having agreed to make a halfpenny rate for library purposes, a letter from Mr. Carnegie was received stating that he would give £7,000 for the same cause. He added that he would accept the proferred freedom of the city, as the honour was too great to be declined.

Marylebone.—With reference to the cartoon we issue with this number, it is interesting to record that Mr. Frank Debenham has been elected a member of the Marylebone Borough Council almost entirely on the Library Question. He made this a special feature in opposition to the other candidates' "anti-library" tactics, and this Borough may have its Free Library after all.

Normanton.—Mr. Carnegie has offered £2,000 for the erection of a public library at Normanton, Yorkshire, on condition that a free site is provided.

Pendlebury.—A public library has been opened here, with a stock of 2,135 volumes.

Southwark.—A Book Club and Literary Society are to be formed in connection with the St. Saviour's Public Library. We are glad to learn that the rumoured changes in connection with this Borough's Public Libraries are not likely to come into effect.

West Bromwich.—The "Surveyor" of October 17th contains a plan of the conversion of the West Bromwich Market Hall into a public library.

AMERICAN SCHEME OF BOOK DISTRIBUTION.

The latest American invasion of London intimately concerns the book-world and the circulating library. Because it promises to find new readers and provide them with up-to-date literature in an up-to-date way the scheme seems likely to win the approval of publisher and public alike.

At No. 17 Hanover Street, Hanover Square, the Book Lovers' Library has established itself. It has taken the sign of the Tabard Inn, after that old hostelry at Southwark made famous by Chaucer in "Canterbury Tales." Old-fashioned lead-lights in the windows, quaint book-cases and decorations give a setting of repose to the lively "hustle" of the American librarians.

There are two sections of the new library, both tried with much success across the Atlantic, where over forty library centres are established in the chief cities. You can join the Book Lovers' Library for an annual inclusive subscription. For that you get a monthly bulletin of new books, from which a selection of a dozen or half a dozen volumes may be made and sent to Hanover Street. The books are promptly despatched to your house in a neat case, no charge being made for carriage. They can be renewed as desired.

"The library is differentiated from those existing here," said Dr. F. W. Speirs, one of the managers, "in that we guarantee to deliver every book that is asked for if it is on our list. If there is a boom in a book we go on buying it till the demand is met or the publisher runs dry. You understand, we are a library of new books, not of standard literature. In the monthly bulletin we give a short description of each book, so that subscribers may know what they are asking for. In a word, we digest current literature for our customers, and supply them with it at the least possible trouble to themselves."

A more popular form of book distribution is the Tabard Inn Library. Briefly, the company intends to place in attractive shops all over London a revolving book-case containing about 130 volumes. At either of the shops or in Hanover Street any one may become a life member by paying a fee of half a guinea. Then he or she purchases exchange tickets at the rate of fifteen for half a crown. Books may be taken out or exchanged at any of the shops. The subscriber brings back one volume, takes another, and drops in the slot of the book-case one of his exchange tickets. There is no surveillance of this operation, no one specially in charge of the case. It is an essential part of the scheme.

" Book-readers are not thieves," was Dr. Speirs' explanation. " Our experience in America shows that the loss on books or on exchange tickets is too infinitesimal to be reckoned."

Each volume is issued boxed in a cloth case, easy to handle and helping much to keep the book clean. On the case is an imitation band of red tape. " Red tape all on the box " is the motto of the corporation, expressing in a line the fact that there are no vexatious delays between the subscriber and his service of books.—*Daily Mail*, 29th October.

APPOINTMENTS.

Heaton, Mr. Ronald, W., M.A., formerly Librarian of the Bishopsgate Institute, has been appointed Librarian of the Government Library, Pretoria, South Africa.

Thorne, W. B., St. Bride Foundation Institute Libraries, Fleet Street, E.C., to be Second Assistant at the Poplar Public Libraries, to take charge of the Bromley Branch. [63 applications].

EDITORIAL.
THE DAILY PRESS AND PUBLIC LIBRARIES.

Owing no doubt largely to the munificence of Mr. Andrew Carnegie, the Public Library has been accorded a good deal of prominence of late in the daily papers. Many and various views by all kinds of persons have appeared, and altogether the subject has received a good shaking up. As is usual when a topic of this character finds a place in the principal questions of the day, the majority of persons who give vent to their opinions are no more qualified to do so than to navigate an airship. Consequently the Public Library Movement suffers considerable opprobrium, which, if it does little harm, certainly does not do much good. When we remember the number of gentlemen there are in the Library profession who generally seem ready to take up their pen and pour forth strings of invectives against open access, indicators, catalogues, class lists, coloured labels, and other matters more or less (usually less) important, on the slightest provocation, we cannot help wondering why they do not take up the cudgels sometimes and strike a blow in defence of their profession. But we presume their minds are comfortable in the belief that it is now firmly established and proof against these outside criticisms so frequently hurled at it. This may be so, but we confess we should like to see a little spirited response occasionally.

In the *Daily Mail* of September 8th, there appeared an article entitled "Some Evils of Free Libraries," with the sub-title "The Plague of Novel Reading," by A. T. Storey. In the *Morning Leader* of September 23rd appeared "The Free Library: Some Suggestions for the Birmingham Congress," signed "Zenodotus." Judging from Mr. Storey's views, we believe that he knows absolutely nothing about the subject at all. He complains that the stock of novels in most Public Libraries is out of all proportion to other classes of literature, that there is a distinct lack of the more up-to-date serious books, especially in science, and that new Libraries are stocked on the "so much per yard" or "shilling a volume plan." Of course, the first statement is absurdly untrue, 15 to 20 per cent. being the usual stock of novels in the average Public Library, with the expenditure on the same varying from five to ten per cent. Every level-minded individual will admit that this is an extremely reasonable proportion, and in the face of this fact, that Mr. Storey must have talked without knowing. Public Librarians, who after all may be allowed some authority to speak on this subject, are not seriously dismayed at the use made of this section of their Libraries. The novels are carefully selected, and the ephemeral rubbish of the "circulating" library finds no place on their shelves.

Surely it is better for the clerk or working girl to read a good novel on the way to and from business, than its alternative in travelling literature, the "bitty" paper. Apropos of novel reading, Mr. Storey might be interested to learn that the last Report of the West Ham Libraries shows a fiction issue of only 35.4 per cent., and the population of West Ham, it should be remembered, is largely composed of the working classes.

In the *Daily News* of October 7th we notice a letter harping on the same old string—preponderance of novels, and the issue of six novels to one work on a serious subject. Our previous remarks are sufficient comment on this.

With regard to Mr. Storey's complaint that a reader is unable to keep up-to-date in the literature of the progressive sciences, we can only say that the complaint is most unreasonable. Anything less than the British Museum or a "special" library it is impossible to keep supplied with the latest books.

The average Public Library cannot aspire to more than the standard works on every subject, and if any particular section is largely developed, it is done at the expense of the other sections, which must be manifestly unfair to a certain proportion of readers, as no library has an unlimited income.

Mr. Storey said he KNEW one instance where in stocking the library the librarian was given *carte blanche* to buy so many volumes for so much, apparently without any heed to subject, and whatever saving he could effect would be regarded as his commission. This is the first time we have ever heard of such a thing being done, and if the statement is correct, feel confident that Mr. Storey must have alighted on an unfortunate and unique instance. The utmost care is usually displayed by all who have anything to do with book selection.

The gentleman who wrote the *Morning Leader* article was certainly better acquainted with his subject than Mr. Storey. The object of the article was to bring one or two suggestions before the Congress of the L.A. at Birmingham. The writer says:—

"The L.A., it must be confessed, is a somewhat feeble concern. A chartered corporation, it is the only body, unfortunately, which can suggest legislation with authority, or work for any sort of reform. But it seldom exercises this authority. The results of its labours are so small because it can never make up its mind as to the course to be taken, whether right or wrong."

We admit we have no two opinions regarding this statement, and we hope that slow-going, ponderous organization will take the hint and wake up a bit.

One suggestion is that a "combine" of librarians should compel publishers to supply books on better made paper in sheets, at the ordinary prices. Another is that a central bureau should be established, where the cataloguing for every library should be done, so that a uniform system might prevail. Both these questions, we believe, have been discussed, and no satisfactory conclusion arrived at. The first is undoubtedly desirable, but the second is well-nigh impossible. The writer advocates the institution of travelling libraries, so widely used in the United States, for providing villages, unable to support a library with books. This will probably come in time, as the movement becomes more fully-developed. He suggests the closer relationship of schools and libraries; the suppression of the worst class of cheap literature; getting books to strata of town population still untouched, and raising the standard of reading by the organization of a lecture agency, which would send out men to lecture on books, subject by subject.

The writer has touched some very good points, and in course of time, very likely, they will in the main be realized, but the L.A. will have to exert itself in the future more than it has done in the past, before this consummation can be effected.

The *Westminster Gazette* of October 1st, commenting on the Borough of Marylebone declining the gift of £30,000 from Mr. Carnegie, says:—

"It is very remarkable to find the unanimity that is displayed by some local magnates in their attitude towards works of fiction when they are discussing a requisition to establish a Free Library. They solemnly and sternly question the members of the deputation pleading for free books on this point. 'Is it not a fact that the experience of the Free Libraries everywhere is that the great proportion of books read in those places consists of works of fiction?' This is the invariable question propounded with an air that is intended to convey sorrowful indignation over the depravity of the masses in desiring such dreadful literature. The reply is quite simple. Why should people not read works of fiction? If those works are excluded, what becomes of the great standard popular literature of the country? If a man were to abstain from the public-house and devote his earnings say to the Waverley Novels, would he be any the worse morally for the change? It would be no exaggeration to say that the people who are so strongly opposed to giving facilities for free reading are often the most fiercely opposed to interfering with the facilities for getting drink."

We feel this to be stating the case to a nicety, and refrain from adding anything to it.

In conclusion we would say we have reviewed the latest efforts of the Press on the Public Library Movement, from the standpoint of one who knows something of the situation, and must express our regret that certain of the papers allow their columns to be used by irresponsible persons for the purpose of throwing mud at one of the most popular and valuable institutions of our country.

THE TECHNICAL TRAINING OF LIBRARY ASSISTANTS.
By Henry D. Roberts.

Once more I stand before you, by the invitation of your Committee, to address you on the subject of the technical education of Library Assistants. I have spoken of the subject on general lines more than once : to-night I want to refer to it more particularly in connection with the technical classes about to be commenced at this Institution.

Education is very much in the air just now. The Government has produced a Bill, which, if passed, will cause a revolution in the management of schools where elementary education is given ; a bill which is good, bad or indifferent according to the standpoint from which it is viewed, but to discuss which is not the purpose of this paper. The British Association devoted much time at its recent Belfast meeting to the question of higher and technical education, proving to its satisfaction that in this direction we are as a nation lamentably behind the times. But on this matter of technical education we do appear at last to be waking up, and even the library world has come to the conclusion that it is a necessity for it as well as for other branches of the public service. This awakening is of very recent growth as far as we are concerned. It is not six years ago since I entered a plea, at a monthly meeting of the Library Association, for means to be provided for the better education in professional matters of the assistants in our libraries. You will remember that the majority of the speakers were against me, although I am glad to recall that our Chairman of to-night (who has always been such a thorough supporter of your Association) was in the minority. The burden of the opposition was that assistants of previous generations had got along all right without lectures and classes, so why alter things now ? That was all very well, but what was good enough ten or twenty years ago is not good enough for to-day. The times are changed, and we must change with them. Libraries, thanks to the princely munificence of a few far-seeing men, hold a different position in the public mind, taking it as a whole, than they did a few years ago. In them, as Professor Dixon observed the other day at Birmingham, many men discern a hope for the world. Even if Marylebone in its wisdom looks, so to speak, a gift horse in the mouth and refuses it, that does not alter the situation in other and more progressive places. Handicapped and hampered as libraries have nearly all been in the past, yet in return for the pittance allotted to them (a pittance fixed in other circumstances and under different conditions than prevail to-day) they have done a useful and magnificent work. It will surely not be long before Parliament removes the absurd limit which has been in force for the last fifty years, and allows an intelligent community, should it be so disposed, to spend a little more of its own money than it does now on its own libraries. Many authorities would increase the rate were permission only given. And with an increased revenue better possibilities will arise for the librarian, and more will be demanded from him. No longer being obliged to get what they can for the salaries offered, Committees will, in making better remuneration to their officers, insist on getting full value for their money. The better paid posts in the profession are not now, and will be less in the future, the rightful inheritance of assistants, merely because they *are* assistants. Many lads only take to library work " until something better turns up." It doesn't, and they drag on from year to year with every hope, but not much prospect, of getting a chief's post some day. Even those who do enter libraries because the work is congenial are not always qualified for higher positions than assistants, and junior assistants at that. A considerable number of assistants to-day should not be assistants at all, but attendants. A Board School education is not enough for any one who aspires to be something better than an automatic machine for issuing and indicating books, whose only wish is for closing time to come, grumbling because he works a quarter of an hour a day longer than the staff at the Town Hall or a neighbouring library, who says with Mr. Mantalini in " Nicholas Nickleby " that his " life is one demd horrid grind." No, after leaving school he must still go on educating himself. To the ordinary assistant his school learning should be looked on only as a commencement, although to most, I am afraid, it is considered as a completion, of his education. Liberated from the discipline and duties of school routine, he so often casts aside his books and expects to succeed in life with only the rudiments of an education. Why, even the mechanic has to spend long years at practical technical work before he can, or is even qualified to, command a good position and corresponding wage. A doctor, a lawyer, an architect, a chemist, all have to do the same thing. And yet nine-tenths of the library assistants of this country do not attempt to improve their general education, to say nothing of studying technical questions. But I laboured this question of apathy in a paper I read before you in March, 1901, and will not press it now. A good foundation—that is, a good general education—is not a desirability, but an absolute necessity, before the superstructure of advanced technical work can properly be erected. We must begin right down at the bottom, and must not be content with too low a standard. I am not speaking without authority. For the preliminary examination in general subjects which used to be held by the Library Association, and which was abolished in 1894, twenty-six candidates in all presented themselves. Of these eight failed in history, eight in arithmetic, seven in geography, and six in grammar!

I find in looking back over a paper which I read to you in October, 1895, but which was never printed, as you did not possess a journal in those days, that then as now I was pressing and insisting on this same necessity for a good general education for library assistants. You may say that I am pursuing the obvious. Possibly, but the obvious is often so obvious that it is overlooked. Take Latin for example: how many assistants know even the elements of it? And yet a good knowledge of this subject is a necessity before such matters as Palæography, for example, can be touched with any hope of success. English literature, again, although as important a subject as an assistant can be acquainted with, is very little studied. Some may raise the bogey of long hours, and say that it is impossible for library assistants to find time for study. It is all nonsense, and I thought it had been exploded long since. The hours of assistants are not as long as they used to be, I think the average is about forty-four a week—not eight a day, less than those of the average City clerk. Besides, if any one wants to work he will soon make time, and hope, with Goldsmith, that "a youth of labour is an age of ease." Remember also Luther's famous reply to those who asked him how he had managed to find time to translate the Bible—" Nulla dies sine linea." To again quote the President of the Library Association, " It is one thing to love knowledge, to believe in ideas, and to be prepared to pay a high price for them; it is quite another thing reluctantly to admit their value and attempt to buy them cheap." We may pay a high price by giving up time quite as much as by spending money, for are we not told that time *is* money? We shall reap as we sow. Let us see to it that our sowing of the seed of technical education is thorough, on a soil well tilled by a good general education, and then we can confidently look forward to a good harvest, remembering Pope's saying that

> " 'Tis education forms the common mind ;
> Just as the twig is bent the tree's inclined."

It only wants an effort, and then, the attempt made for

> "The attempt and not the deed confounds us"

we can say, as did Lady Macbeth,

> "We fail!
> But screw your courage to the sticking place,
> And we'll not fail."

I hope to-night that all of us will screw our courage to the sticking place, and take up more seriously than ever this question of making ourselves fitter for the work we have to do. For I maintain that we stand now at the commencement of a new epoch, and, let us hope, of a new effort of library assistants, in the matter of our technical education. I say the commencement of a new epoch, and I think you will agree with me. The Council of the Library Association has for the past five sessions, in the face of adverse criticism from places where it might have been least expected, provided classes which have been well attended. Feeling that they could not do as much as they wished in the matter of extending and amplifying their work in this direction, and knowing also the urgent need for extension, they applied to the London Technical Education Board, and offered to allow their classes to be conducted at some approved educational institution if a grant in aid could be given. This time the negotiations, previously futile, were successful, and arrangements were made for the classes to be held on broader lines at the London School of Economics and Political Science, to my mind a very suitable home for them. The Association has an equal representation with the Governors of the School on the managing Committee, and will continue to hold professional examinations. A stipulation was made and agreed to that the classes shall be open to all comers, and that the lecturers in the purely professional classes shall be nominated by the Council of the Library Association. That the step will prove to be a wise one I am firmly convinced, although again in the pages of your Journal a note of opposition was uttered by an anonymous correspondent. The Library Association was charged with "a gross betrayal of the interests of assistants, and a dereliction of its duty of education." An appeal was made to the Hon. Secretary of the Education Committee to "once more re-commence his Sisyphean labours." The end of the letter answered itself. As I *was* in sympathy with the new movement, as well I might be, the writer might have given me credit for considering that I knew what I was about. No one has the interests of the assistants more at heart than I have, and if I approved the new scheme he might also have been sure that to my mind at least, it was a step in the right direction, for the benefit of assistants and the profession generally.

Mr. Webb, in a paper that he read before the Library Association in March last, on "The Library Service of London: its Co-ordination, Development and Education," printed in the May number of the "Library Association Record," and which you should all read, sketched what seemed rather a high ideal of the qualifications a librarian should possess. But it was only high in a relative degree ; high because our conception up to now has been too low. Although in the subsequent discussion I said Mr. Webb's ideas were Utopian, I did not any the less agree with him. The change in our conception of the qualifications of librarians will very likely be gradual, but it will be sure. And these classes, to which I want to draw your attention for a few minutes, will greatly help in this direction. Mr. Webb has been called a visionary, and worse names still. I should not term him a visionary, but a man of acute vision, who can see things coming long before the ordinary person. That this is true as far as we are concerned

I am convinced, and we may all live to see his schemes and ideas for the development of our libraries, and the better education of those serving in them, accomplished facts. One cannot forget that the very idea of this School of Economics was deemed visionary when it was first mooted, but the building in which we now are is no vision but a reality. I hope soon that no appointment will be made to any position in a library until the candidate can produce satisfactory evidences of good general education; that no promotion will be allowed to take place until the assistant in question can show that he possesses, in addition, sufficient technical qualifications to fit him for increased responsibility; and that no senior appointment will be given to any person not possessing the Association's certificate, which can easily be obtained by diligent work.

In the programme, of which you all possess copies, are no less than eighteen different classes for the earnest assistant to select from, an improvement on the two or three the Education Committee were able to offer. Of these, three of course, appeal most to you. I refer to numbers one to three. Mr. Brown's class on " Elementary Bibliography " will begin on Wednesday, 15th October, and should prove extremely useful and interesting. Number two will be spread over two terms, the lectures on the " Bibliography of Special Subjects " following directly after, on the same days, the lectures this term by Mr. Brown and those to be given in the Lent term next year by Mr. Barrett. All these classes will be held on Wednesdays, and an inclusive fee of 17/6 may be paid for the whole forty lectures, which is exactly half the amount which would be charged if the different courses were taken separately. I hope I may take it for granted that you will all join these three courses. Then with regard to the others, in the second group. Bearing in mind what I said before as to the necessity for the thorough foundation of a good education, it seems to me that these remaining classes are not likely to be of much benefit to junior assistants, although they could profit to a certain extent by attending some of them, but I would recommend them very strongly to the seniors. They are all on subjects co-related to library work, and of which a knowledge, although not indispensable, would be of material advantage to those who have control of libraries. Take the first series—Palæography and Diplomatic. Librarians of Public Libraries are not often called on to decipher ancient manuscripts, and so have as a rule very little knowledge of Palæography. But it is a subject which all ought to know at least *something* about, and I look upon Mr. Hall's courses as second to none in the syllabus. They should be well attended. The courses in History, Economics, Geography, Public Administration, and Statistics and Accountancy will also be conducted by recognised authorities in their special subjects, and deserve your careful attention. It is intended to arrange. if possible, further courses in 1903-4, and to continue them from season to season. No doubt in the course of a year or two a definite system of training will be evolved, lasting over two or three years. I should not be surprised to find the Library Association instituting, before much longer, an advanced examination for a higher professional certificate.

As far as these classes are concerned, you will notice that the fees are higher than those charged by the Library Association. That, of course, is only natural; but the Library Association has decided to pay half the fees of any assistants nominated by one of its members. This will make the fees to senior assistants about the same as those hitherto charged by the Library Association. They will be less in the case of the first three classes referred to if all are taken, for the net amount payable by nominated students will be only 8/9, whereas for three classes with the Education Committee they would have had to pay 10/-. It will mean a little more for the juniors, but

I am sure they will have nothing to grumble at, for the classes are all well worth the money, and if a thing is worth having it is worth paying for.

Fees must first be paid in full to the Director of the School, and an application then made to me, on a form provided for the purpose, for re-imbursement of half the fees paid. This applies to any or all of the classes in the programme which assistants may join. Forms for joining the School and for applying for re-imbursement are in the room now and may be had by intending students after the meeting.

In conclusion, let me say again that I consider we have arrived at an important stage in the history of the technical education of Library Assistants. The Library Association and the London School of Economics and Political Science have done their best. It only remains for you to take advantage of the exceptional opportunities offered you, and which your brethren in the provinces will envy you, join the classes in large numbers, and do *your* share also to make them—what they well deserve to be—a great success.

BOOKS, &c., RECEIVED.

NOTE.—*The Editor will be pleased to receive Library and other publications for notice on this page.*

Waterloo with Seaforth Public Library. Classified List of Books in the Library, on History, Biography, and Travel. Compiled by Edith G. Taylor. 8vo., 1902.

A compilation which should prove extremely useful to the student. To each division of the section history, is appended references to biographies of the most prominent men of those particular times, which is an interesting and serviceable feature. The classification, however, shows up some sad deficiencies, especially in the biographical section. For instance, we see a life of *Mary* Lamb, but none of her brother Charles. There is also a life of *Susanna* Wesley, but we cannot find one of Charles or John Wesley. We congratulate Miss Taylor on her production.

Manchester Public Free Library. Quarterly Guide. Vol. vi., No. 2. [Edited by Ernest Axon, Assistant Librarian].

West Ham Public Libraries. Annual Report for the year ending March 31st, 1902.

Willesden Green Public Library. Quarterly Record and Guide for Readers. September, 1902.

"Morley College Magazine." October.

"Revista delle Biblioteche." September.

NEW MEMBERS.

Seniors.—Miss Isabella I. Henderson, Aberdeen; Messrs. Horace J. Hobbs, Enfield; Ernest S. Martin, Kingston-upon-Thames; Bertram R. Moors, Portsmouth; Thomas B. Storey, Westminster; Harold Tempest, Bootle.

Juniors.—Miss Ella K. Boyd, Aberdeen; Miss Jessie B. Moon, Leyton; Miss Jessie M. Robertson, Aberdeen; Miss Lizzie P. Robertson, Aberdeen. Messrs. Daniel J. Bayley, Poplar;

Herbert M. Cashmore, Reference Library, Birmingham; Arthur M. Hamblyn, Eastbourne; Sydney E. Harrison, Reference Library, Birmingham; Lionel F. Lougheed, East Ham; Alexander C. McCombe, East Ham; Henry J. Turner, Westminster.

CORRESPONDENCE.

NOTE.—*Under this heading the Committee are prepared to answer questions or advise assistants, to the best of their ability, concerning any professional difficulties they may meet with. Questions must be put as concisely as possible, and replies will appear here to such as shall be of general interest. If a pen-name is used, the real name and address must also be enclosed. No attention will be paid to anonymous communications. All letters must be addressed to the Editor, who, however, does not hold himself responsible for any opinions that may be expressed.*

The Editor has received an anonymous letter signed " *J. L. A.*" bearing the post mark Wigan. If the writer will again read carefully the Study Circle notice he refers to, he will find he has misunderstood it, and that the use of text books is recommended, and not forbidden. In future the above rule will be rigidly adhered to, and anonymous communications ignored.—Ed.

APPOINTMENTS VACANT.

[**Notice to Library Authorities.**—*We shall be pleased to publish under this heading, free of charge, particulars of vacancies, if full details are sent to the Editor on or before the 28th of each month.*]

NOTICES.

All matter for the December number should reach the Hon. Editor on or before 20th November.

All other communications should be addressed to the *Hon. Secretary*, MR. J. RADCLIFFE, Public Library, East Ham, E.

The Library Assistant:
The Official Organ of the Library Assistants' Association.

No. 60.   DECEMBER, 1902.   Published Monthly

THE LIBRARY ASSISTANTS' ASSOCIATION.
FOUNDED 1895.   EIGHTH SESSION.   YEAR 1901-1902.

Members are requested to read carefully the announcements appearing on this and the following pages, as no further intimation of meetings and other arrangements may be expected.

DECEMBER MEETING.

This Meeting will be held at the St. Bride Institute, Bride Lane, Ludgate Circus, E.C., on Wednesday, 10th inst., at 8 p.m., when Mr. Evan G. Rees will open a discussion on "The Different Systems of Charging or Issuing Books in Public Lending Libraries." A good discussion should follow, and members are requested to come prepared.

NORTH WESTERN BRANCH.
NOVEMBER MEETING.

This meeting was held by the kind invitation of C. Madeley, Esq., the Curator, at the Museum and Library, Warrington, on Saturday, November 15th.

On arrival the members were met and conducted round the Museum by Mr. Madeley, who pointed out the chief objects of interest exhibited there. After spending a pleasant time in this department, and obtaining a passing glance at the Library, they were shown into the Lecture Room, where Mrs. and Miss Madeley entertained them to tea. After a brief interval Mr. Madeley addressed the meeting on the Warrington Museum and Library, giving a brief history of the Institution, and a description of their methods of working. Several members spoke of what they had seen and heard, and expressed themselves pleased at being privileged to visit this useful and educational Institution. After passing a vote of thanks to Mr., Mrs. and Miss Madeley for their hospitality and to Mr. Madeley for his instructive remarks, the remaining time was spent in exploring the Library and noting the several items mentioned by Mr. Madeley in his address.

ANNUAL MEETING.

The Annual Meeting will be held in the Reference Library, Manchester, on December 17th, 1902, at 7-30 p.m., when the Election of Officers of the Branch, for 1903, will take place, and general business discussed. As many members as possible are requested to attend.

FIFTH ANNUAL DINNER.

The Fifth Annual Dinner of the L.A.A. took place at Anderton's Hotel, Fleet Street, on Wednesday, November 19th, when nearly fifty members and friends gathered together. Among those present were :—

Mr. J. D. Brown (Finsbury), Mr. C. J. Courtney (Minet), Mr. W. W. Fortune (of the Library Supply Company), Mr. Hanson (of Messrs. Truslove, Hanson and Comba), Mr. L. Inkster (Battersea), Mr. L. S. Jast (Croydon), Mr. T. Johnston (Hornsey), Mr. H. W. Bull (Wimbledon), and Mr. H. E. Poole (Westminster).

Mr. E. G. Rees occupied the chair (for the third year in succession), and Mr. R. B. Wood the vice-chair. The end of the menu reached, the loyal toasts, proposed by the Chairman, were honoured with enthusiasm.

The Vice-Chairman, Mr. R. B. Wood (Saint George, Hanover Square), proposed the toast of "The Library Association," including with it the name of Mr. Stanley Jast.

Mr. Stanley Jast, in reply, spoke of the present position of the Public Library in the municipality and of its probable future. Surely an Institution which has managed to alarm the *Times*, and to draw comments from Miss Marie Corelli has a promising future. (Laughter). But the work is greatly hampered by the limits of the penny rate. He exhorted those present to endeavour by practical work to convince the ratepayer of the value of the Public Library, which result is not to be obtained by mere theoretical discussion of the question; and also to take every opportunity of forwarding the Public Library movement.

Mr. L. Inkster, Hon. Secretary of the Library Association, then proposed the toast of the L.A.A. He expressed a great interest in the Association during its seven years of active existence, and regretted his inability to follow more closely its work during that time. He remarked upon the great advantage which assistants of to-day have over those of thirty years ago, when there was no Library Assistants' Association. In those days there were no opportunities for the interchange of ideas between assistants. In conclusion he wished the L.A.A. every success.

The Chairman (Mr. E. G. Rees) responded for the Library Assistants' Association. He welcomed the Librarians present, in whose friendship he had every confidence, and who favoured the L.A.A. with their support. The L.A.A. had been looked upon by Librarians as a revolutionist society that would probably cause strikes for more money and less hours, and organise demonstrations in Trafalgar Square. But the L.A.A. was formed to give Assistants opportunities for the interchange of ideas and experiences. He had received letters from Mr. B. L. Dyer (Kimberley) and Mr. H. Ogle (Ipswich), who expressed their hearty wishes for the welfare of the L.A.A. During the dinner a telegram had been handed to him from Mr. H. T. Soper, late Editor of "The Library Assistant," expressing regret at his inability to attend, and wishing the company a pleasant evening.

Mr. W. G. Chambers asked the company to drink to the health of the Chairman (Mr. E. G. Rees). He spoke of the election of Mr. Rees as one of two representatives of the L.A.A. on the Education Committee of the Library Association, which he considered a step in the right direction. He echoed the thoughts of the Committee of the L.A.A., when he spoke of the great respect and esteem which was borne towards the Chairman by the members owing to the impartiality and kindliness which marked all his official work. The toast was enthusiastically drunk with musical honours.

The Chairman, in reply, expressed the pleasure given him by his election for the third year in succession to the office of Chairman. He wished to thank the officers and members of the Committee for the hearty manner in which they had supported him during that time, and spoke gratefully of the services of present and former officers.

The Chairman proposed the toast of the Artistes, and coupled with it the name of Mr. W. J. Harris (Hon. Secretary of the Entertainment Committee) for the admirable manner in which he had made and carried out the arrangements for such a successful evening. After singing "Auld Lang Syne" and the National Anthem, the company dispersed. During the evening a varied musical programme was contributed by the following members and friends:—

Messrs. F. C. Chidgey, C. Collins, C. J. Courtney, A. S. Crouch (at the piano), W. G. Hawkins, E. H. Parsons, F. Schofield, Dan Steed, W. B. Thorne, W. J. Vellenoweth, and W. B. Young.

E. H. P.

STUDY CIRCLE.
THE OCTOBER PAPERS.

GENERAL.—Regarded as a whole, the answers show more industry than thought. A slavish copying of the forms or practice of one's own library may produce a respectable answer, but this form of "study" will not help the assistant when he is called upon to deal with different conditions. The student who departs from the conventional, and gives a thoughtful reason for his departure, will receive a more respectful attention from the examiners than the neatest and most careful copyist.

In the answers to Question (1) the most striking feature is the extraordinary number of minor errors due to carelessness. "Whitaker's Almanack" is a favourite version. "Every man *his* own lawyer" appears several times. Three students put a '?' after "Who's Who." The mis-spellings of authors' names are too numerous to mention. The second part of the question has been generally shirked. We admit it is rather difficult. That is why it was set. It needs thought and some knowledge of the inside of the more common works of reference. Most students seem to confine themselves to an imperfect acquaintance with the outside.

Question (2) has been more difficult to mark. We cannot altogether refuse marks to students who faithfully copy the forms of their own libraries. Yet the question was not set to test the students' prowess in the use of the ruler and red ink. The ruling for a Cash Receipts Book was generally incorrect. Some students gave the form of fine receipt, others a ruling showing a day to a page. It is quite unnecessary to have a special column for every possible class of takings. As a rule the only analysis needed for the financial statement would be " Fines, Sale of Catalogues, Donations, Miscellaneous."

We would impress upon the students the fact that we are setting a somewhat high standard. Our remarks may be considered rather severe, but we have too high an opinion of the students who follow this "Circle" to fear that anyone will take offence thereat. It does not follow where no praise is given, that none is deserved; for, naturally, more attention is paid to individual fault than to general merit. But library assistants should recognise the fact that the future librarian will have to be something more than an apostle of the obvious, a timid follower in the footsteps of his predecessors; and our main purpose will be to encourage a spirit of self-reliance and independent thought even in the trivialities of daily routine.

Aedifico (1) 14.—Writes an unnecessary essay on the obvious. Writes 'Flogel,' 'concordence' (twice), 'Ascott' for 'Askew.'

(2) 15.—Binding Book shows no column for price. We disagree with his remarks on Cash Receipts Book. How is he going to show analysis at end of year?

Archibald (1) 6.—We really cannot give marks for "a gazetteer, a dictionary of quotations," etc. *What* dictionary? "'The Dictionary of National Biography' covers all that is needed in biography." Reminds us of the American boy when asked "Who was the first man? *Answer*: "George Washington." *Question*: "But what about Adam"? *Answer*: "Oh, well, if you count foreigners!"

(2) 7.—Not very good. Binding and Withdrawals rulings particularly insufficient.

Constantia (1) 16.—A very fair list.

(2) 14.—Quite mistakes Cash Receipts Book; gives ruling for ordinary single receipt.

Esca (1) 5.—We did not think it possible for this question to be misunderstood, but *Esca* has ingeniously contrived to. If we wanted a list of books for the use of the staff, we should have said so. However, even for what it professes to be, the answer is poor.

(2) 12.—A 'regulation' answer; shows no thought.

Nil Desperandum (1) 11.—Avoids the second part of the question. Includes two Commentaries and two Dictionaries of the Bible.

(2) 12.—Elementary. Makes same error as Constantia (q.v.). Stocktaking columns are of doubtful utility in a Stock Book.

Norham (1) 13.—Fair. "Liddle" should be "Liddell." Neither Classical nor Bible Dictionaries can be considered dispensable.

(2) 17.—Good.

Papyrus (1) 16. A painstaking answer, but contains several redundancies.

(2) 14.—Unusual and clumsy rulings for Stock Book and Cash Receipts Book.

Retival (1) 12.—A mere list of directories. Surely that petty monument of ineptitude "What's What" is a most dispensable work. Second part shows thought.

(2) 19.—Very good indeed.

Temporal Power (1) 9.—An erratic list. Such books as Huxley's Physiology, Pennell's Pen Drawing, etc., are not, strictly speaking, works of reference.

(2) 10.—Cash Receipts Book shows one day only. Rulings obviously copied without thought.

Tree (1) 8.—Remarkable only for its omissions. See remarks to *Esca*. Is it possible that there has been, shall we say, collaboration between these students? *See* St. Luke, VI., 39.

(2) 9.—Careless.

Vernon (1) Not answered.

(2) 14.—Withdrawals Book and Stock Book not quite satisfactory. Giving ten columns for 'class' means wasting nine.

QUESTIONS.

(5).—Draw up a reading list of books and articles on Somaliland, using all sources at your disposal. Give brief annotations.

(6).—Prepare an imaginary Routine Sheet for a small Public Library with a staff of six and the usual departments.

Answers should be sent not later than the 22nd inst., to Mr. R. B. Wood, Public Library, Buckingham Palace Road, London, S.W., signed by a pseudonym, and in the case of new students, with the real name enclosed in an envelope on which is written the pseudonym. Former students are requested to retain the same pseudonym throughout the Session.

LIBRARY ASSOCIATION.

For the benefit of our Members we reprint the programme of the Monthly Meetings in London, as arranged by this Association, and would draw particular attention to the third one, when our chairman will read a paper. As many as can should be present to support him on that occasion.

LIST OF PAPERS AND AUTHORS.

1902.

December 18.—" Library Bookbinding." By CYRIL DAVENPORT, British Museum.

This paper will open up the whole question of Library Binding, and especially the important matter of the quality and durability of leathers.

1903.

January 15.—" The Educational Needs of Library Assistants." By EVAN G. REES, Westminster Public Libraries; Chairman of the Library Assistants' Association.

Library Assistants are specially invited to attend this meeting, at which the question of professional training will be discussed.

February 19.—" Librarians' Aids." By E. WYNDHAM-HULME, Patent Office Library, London.

A discussion of the need for an intimate knowledge of professional literature, with notes on useful books and periodicals.

March 19.—" Classification in British Public Libraries." By L. STANLEY JAST, Croydon Public Libraries.

This paper will raise the question of the application of systematic classification to all departments of public libraries.

April 16.—" Disputed Points in Cataloguing." By WILLIAM C. PLANT, Shoreditch Public Libraries.

In view of the fact that the Library Association Cataloguing Rules are under revision by a Special Committee, a general discussion of difficulties and divergencies will prove useful and suggestive.

May 21.—" Public Libraries and Museums." By JOHN MINTO, M.A., Brighton Public Libraries.

A discussion of the connection between Libraries and Museums and Art Galleries, and their inter-relationships.

June 18.—" The Planning and Arrangement of Branch Libraries." By FRANKLIN T. BARRETT, Fulham Public Libraries.

A discussion of general principles, and some novel arrangements contemplated for Fulham.

Light refreshments will be served from 7.30 till 8 p.m., and Visitors will be welcomed. Library Assistants in particular are urged to attend.

JAS. DUFF BROWN.

Hon. Sec. Publications Committee, pro. tem.

October, 1902.

PROFESSIONAL EXAMINATION OF THE LIBRARY ASSOCIATION.

The next professional examination of the Library Association in Section 1—Bibliography and Literary History, and Section 3—Library Management, will be held at centres to suit the convenience of the Candidates, on Wednesday and Thursday, January 14th and 15th, 1903. Intending Candidates should send in their names, accompanied by a fee of 10s. (which may be returned at the discretion of the Education Committee), in good time. Mr. Roberts would be glad to send copies of the examination syllabus to any of our Members who do not already possess one, and has also offered to assist any member by practical advice and suggestion. We may point out that, under the new regulations, Section 1 may be taken in three parts, viz :—1, Bibliography; 2, English Literary History; 3, Literary History of another country. We hope in our next number to be able to announce the names of the Examiners. It is to be hoped there will be a good attendance of Candidates, particularly in the first part of Section 1, for which Mr. Brown's lectures are proving such an admirable preparation. The examination in Section 2 has been deferred until the end of Mr. Barrett's course of lectures next year. The date will be announced in good time.

There is a possibility of establishing a class in French or German specially for Library assistants, at very low fees. The class will be held at the Birkbeck Institute, and any of our members who care to enter for the same are requested to place themselves in communication with the Director of the School of Economics, from whom particulars can be obtained.

Stepney.—The members of the Public Library Staff of the Stepney Council were recently invited by the Warden and Residents of Toynbee Hall to a splendid reception, the purpose of which was, in the main, to create a closer connection between the work of the Public Libraries of the Borough and the educational undertakings of the Universities Statement.

The guests were received in the drawing-room, where refreshments were served, through the kindness of Canon and Mrs. Barnett.

In his address, the Warden reviewed the present standing of the two Institutions, and dwelt upon the possibilities of a closer co-operation. The Borough Librarian, Mr. A. Cawthorne, responded on behalf of the Library Staff.

After the customary votes of thanks, parties were formed for the inspection of Toynbee Hall and Baliol House, each party being conducted by one of the residents.

The Library, wherein is housed one of the finest collections of economic literature, was in turn visited.

Returning to the drawing-room, copies of Farmer's "Gaudameus" were handed to the guests, and the remainder of the evening was devoted to music and social re-union.

ANCIENT AND MODERN WRITING MATERIALS: A CHAPTER IN BIBLIOGRAPHY.

By P. Evans Lewin. Woolwich Public Libraries.

As ideas must have existed in the human mind before speech gave them expression, so speech in some form or other existed long before man was able to express his ideas by writing. The primary feelings of anger, disgust, hatred, affection, hunger, were the vehicles by which speech came into being, but it is possible that even before the sounds of words representing ideas became in any degree fixed, man was able to give expression, however feeble, to his historic and artistic senses by rude hieroglyphic drawings, representative of familiar objects around him, which in the course of time were to become the signs of abstract ideas connected with the things they represented. In this manner an arm holding a stick might denote force ; or the feathers of an ostrich represent justice, because all these feathers were supposed to be of equal length. It will be seen that these rude primitive hieroglyphics, from being the purely pictorial representations of things in the surrounding world, became also symbolic by representing some abstract idea, such as force or justice, by some conventional object. This form of writing was termed *ideography* : the writing of ideas, as distinct from the writing of sounds. From this primitive state of symbol-writing man passed by slow degrees to syllabism; that is, the symbol became identified not only with an idea, but with certain sounds representative of that idea, and, by degrees, the symbol, or part of it, became identified with the first syllable of those sounds, and was thus used not only to denote a given idea, but also to stand for a given sound. This stage being reached, it was not a long step to alphabetism, in which the syllable is no longer represented by one sign, but in which the sign becomes identified with the most important sound in the syllable. In this way, from the first rude picture writings of our ancestors on this earth, have sprung our own alphabet, and the alphabets of all other nations. Just as there never was an idea in the brain of man, nor a deed done in the world, which did not have its antecedent or result, proceeding in an endless chain into the past and future ; so the whole science and civilization of to-day, the stores of literature contained in the noble libraries of the world, are the direct outcome of that primitive symbolic writing which in itself was the result of the first rude attempt of man to portray the objects around him, of which attempt thought was the antecedent. To quite another, and not less wonderful, conclusion did the old bibliographers arrive. Adam Clarke and others assert that God first taught man the alphabet.

It is probable that all known alphabets can be traced back to but four or five individual and distinct sources ; and of these but one, the Egyptian, has received any great extension. Of the others, the cuneiform, Chinese, Aztec, and the figurative writings of Yucatan, have remained in a very primitive state. The cuneiform style of writing, unlike the Egyptian which was able to explain in some degree its own meaning, required a perfectly independent explanation before it could be understood. As it was in its oldest forms composed of straight lines arranged in different ways, so many placed in such a manner representing a house, and placed in another position a town, it had a distinctly different tendency to the writing of the ancient Egyptians, and was therefore not ideographic until a far later stage had been reached. The cuneiform writing became in course of time, probably because of the manner in which it was stamped into the clay, wedge-shaped, and thus derived the name by which it is known, from the Latin *cuneus*, a wedge.

It is probable that the earliest attempts at writing were made on stone. This may not have been so, but it is certain that the rudest and most ancient forms of writing are found graven in the rock, in the form of hieroglyphics, literally sacred sculptures. The Assyrians, Babylonians, Medians, Persians, and Egyptians, all wrote on stone. The discoveries of Sir Henry Rawlinson, and of Layard at Nineveh, have made us acquainted with these writings, whilst it is to Professor Grotefend, who, as long ago as the year 1802, took up the subject of the cuneiform inscriptions, that we are primarily indebted for a translation of the ancient writings of Nineveh. The older hieroglyphic writings of the Egyptians, with which everyone is now familiar since Cleopatra's Needle has been set up in our midst, were not deciphered until the discovery, in 1799, of the Rosetta Stone, now reposing in the British Museum. It contains an inscription recording the coronation of Ptolemy V. (Epiphanes), first in hieroglyphics, next in the later hieratic character of Egypt, and finally in Greek, and was instrumental in the hitherto almost impossible task of solving the enigma of the ancient inscriptions. Champollion the younger, Silvestre de Sacy, Dr. T. Young, Dr. Birch, and Professor Sayce have been distinguished translators of these ancient stone writings, which abound in the Nile Valley and form the most remarkable existing evidence of the progress of civilization and testimony of the truth of the historical books of the Bible. The Egyptian chronology, in spite of recent advances in the subject, is so obscure that it is almost impossible to give even an approximate date for the earliest of these writings, but it seems generally admitted that no monuments are known before the time of the last king of the third dynasty, who, according to M. Mariette, reigned about 4200 B.C., and according to Professor Lepsius 3100 B.C., a difference of more than a thousand years between these two great authorities; but it is certain that in the time of King Osymandyas, who has been identified with Ramses I., hieroglyphic writing on stone and on other substances was common, for this king founded a library having an inscription over the portals which designated the building as "the dispensary of the soul." This was in the fourteenth century before Christ, but it is generally agreed that hieroglyphic writings extend some centuries further back than 2000 B.C., and long before the time of Moses, who, it will be remembered, broke, in his anger, the tables of stone containing the Commandments. Writings on stone are also to be found in Central and South America, whither Professor Donelly informs us some of the overwhelmed inhabitants of the Lost Atlantis escaped, more particularly in Yucatan, Mexico and Brazil; Mashonaland, and Somaliland; Yemen, the abode of the Queen of Sheba of the Scriptures; in the northern portions of China, and in India.

But these stone inscriptions were not confined to rocks or walls, for books have been made out of marble. Montfaucon describes one made of marble leaves cut to a wonderful thinness, so that on turning them over one might see all the several sorts of marble. But this was of course a curiosity.

The next substance used to preserve the writings of the most ancient peoples was brick, but its use seems to have been specially confined to Babylonia and more especially to the Chaldeans and Assyrians, who carried the cuneiform writing on brick to its greatest perfection. Babylonia was essentially the land of burnt clay; it is computed that the Temple of the Sun-God at Warka was composed of over 30,000,000 bricks; and it is therefore not surprising that the Chaldeans should preserve their writings on a substance which could so easily be prepared. In some cases the inscriptions on clay are so small as to require a magnifying glass and the tablets themselves vary from a foot to an inch square. In the Library, at Nineveh, of the great king Assur-bani-pal, the Sardanapalus of the Greeks, the great patron of literature among the Assyrians, Layard found the floors of certain rooms covered to a depth of a foot or more with these ancient records, which appear not only to have been classified but also free for the use of the king's subjects. A great portion of these cuneiform-written tablets, which are generally in the shape of a cylinder, has been placed in the British Museum.

The third substance most extensively used for the purpose of inscriptions was lead, and a very ancient date can be assigned to its use. It is mentioned in the Book of Job, where the Patriarch exclaims "Oh that my words were now written! Oh, that they were inscribed in a book, that with an iron pen and lead they were engraven in the rock for ever!" meaning that he would wish his words graven in the rock and lead run therein, so that the writing might last for ever. A similar reference to a pen of iron is contained in Jeremiah. "The sin of Judah is written with a pen of iron, and with the point of a diamond." But lead was also used for incision, and Tacitus speaks of tablets of lead. Hesiod is said to have been engraved on lead, and the Greeks sometimes used small thin leaden plates, on which were engraved questions asked of the oracles or imprecations against enemies. Some few of these have come down to us, but the use of lead does not seem to have been very general, although leaden plates, on which were inscribed historical and diplomatic records, were used in the Venetian States down to the 14th or 15th century. Even small books have been made of lead, for Montfaucon relates that in the year 1699 he bought, in Rome, a volume of which the leaves, binding, and hinges were made entirely of lead. In his *Antiquité Explicée* he gives an illustration of this book, which passed into the possesion of the Cardinal de Bouillon. Its size was 4 inches by 3, and it had six leaves, written on each side and bearing figures emblematic of the twelve hours of the day. Bonnani, the Italian antiquary, in his *Museum Kirkerianum*, describes a similar book discovered in an ancient tomb.

In addition to lead other metals were used, notably brass, but also silver and gold. The use of brass, though also frequent in the East, was chiefly confined to Rome. The international transactions (*Leges foedera*), the laws (*leges* and *plebiscita*), and similar important documents were generally incised on tablets of brass. Of these, some have come down to us. Two of the most important are the *lex Acilia repetundarum* of the year 123 B.C., inscribed on a bronze tablet about six feet broad, in 90 lines of about 200 to 240 letters each, and the *tabulae Heracleenses* of 45 B.C., part of which is preserved in the British Museum. The use of this metal was general for important documents. We are told that in Vespasian's reign the fire which consumed the Capitol destroyed no less than 3000 tablets of brass.

But one of the most important substances, from a bibliographical point of view, was wood, as from its use are derived many of the most important terms used in bibliography. Wood was very commonly used among the Greeks. Plutarch tells us that Solon inscribed his laws on tablets of wood, termed *axones*, quadrangular in shape, and made to turn upon an upright axis. The axones were at first kept in the Acropolis, but were afterwards placed in the Agora (place of public assembly) for all to read, and some fragments remained to the time of Plutarch. Wood was also used for the *tabulae* or *pugillares*. Generally the word tabulae is used to signify slips of wood, usually of an oblong shape, covered with wax. The wax, which was scratched with the point of the *stylus* or *graphium*, was sometimes coloured red but usually black, so that the letters marked by the stylus were white The more expensive tablets were made of citron wood (or even ivory), but the commoner woods such as beech, fir, and box, were generally used. These tabulae or table-books were in use long before the time of Homer. They were fastened together by means of wires. Sometimes several tablets were fastened in this manner, and these were called *codex* or *codicilli*, which signifies a trunk, from their resemblance to the trunk of a tree cut into several parts. The word codex, or caudex, is a very important one, and has been considerably exemplified in its passage through the ages. In law it means a roll or volume, and is thus applied to a code of laws, as the *Codex Justinianus*, or the *Codex Theodosianus*. The term is also applied to certain early manuscripts of the Bible, as the *Codex Sinaiticus*, the *Codex Vaticanus*, and the *Codex Alexandrinus*, three of the most important manuscripts in the history of the world, and certainly the most important remaining biblical monuments. Two of these ancient tablets have been discovered in a perfect state of preservation in the Village of Abrudbanya, in Transylvania, and others have been found in Pompeii. Wooden tablets, written upon in ink, have also been found in Egypt. When two of these tabulae were fastened together at the back by means of wire they were called *diptycha*, that is double-folded tablets, and there was a raised margin round the inside of each tablet to prevent the wax of one tablet rubbing against the wax of the other. When three tablets were used they were called *triptycha*. Some fine examples of diptycha and triptycha are to be seen in the Vatican Library. The *Diptycha Consularia*, so frequently mentioned in the later Empire, were made of ivory and were presented by the Consuls to their friends, on the day they entered office, and contained the names and portraits of the consuls. Several of these Diptycha Consularia are still extant, the oldest bearing the date 406 A.D.

Sand was sometimes used for these tabulae, but this was reserved for school use in order that the Roman boys might write out their exercises and work out their problems without wasting the wax.

(*To be continued.*)

APPOINTMENTS.

VELLENOWETH, MR. W. J., of the Minet Public Library, to be Librarian of the North Camberwell Public Library.

[Our apologies are due to Mr. Vellenoweth for having neglected to record this in our last issue. We also offer him our heartiest congratulations on his advance to the "upper house." He has been a faithful member of the L.A.A. since its commencement, and we have no doubt that in his new capacity he will be a faithful friend to his old Association. We wish him all happiness and prosperity.—*Ed.*]

NOTES AND COMMENTS.

Brighton.—The New Public Library Museum and Art Galleries were opened on Wednesday, November 5th, by the Mayor. From a report kindly forwarded by our friend, Mr. Soper, we learn that "the *open access* system, which has been adopted for the section of the library not included in the comprehensive fiction department, will be sure to prove of enormous benefit to those borrowers *on whom the pressure of time* is at all heavy, and will obviate a great deal of labour on the part of the assistants." The italics are Mr. Soper's, and we seemed to hear the faint echo of a chuckle from Exeter as we perused those sentences. Perhaps they account for the strange procedure of Exeter reporting the doings of Brighton.

Plaistow.—Mr. H. H. Asquith, M.P., has laid the foundation stone of a new library, situated in the heart of the district, and provided by Mr. Passmore Edwards. Judging from the architect's drawing, the building will present a handsome appearance when completed. In connection, we understand, Mr. Edwards has also offered to provide a library for Silvertown, if it can be maintained. Unfortunately, this cannot be done without increasing the rate, but it is hoped some other means may be found for accepting the offer. Could not East Ham or Woolwich amalgamate for this purpose?

Public Libraries and the "Daily Press."—Apropos of our Editorial in last month's issue, we have received from Mr. Cotgreave a leaflet, reprinted from the "West Ham Library Notes," entitled "Public Libraries and their opponents—some misleading statements refuted," which sums the matter up and replies in a vigorous and convincing manner. We have also received from Glasgow a copy of a local paper, in which Mr. F. T. Barrett, City Librarian, and Mr. W. J. S. Paterson, of the Stirling Subscription Library, state their views on the same subject.

Steeple Claydon.—Sir Edmund Verney (an honoured member of the L.A.A.) and Lady Verney have erected here a Public Hall and Free Library, at the cost of some £1,700, which were opened to the public on November 1st. A distinguished company were present at the ceremony, including Sir Charles and Lady MacLaren, Admiral Sir Edward Seymour, Sir Isambard Owen, and Mr. and Mrs. Stanley Weyman. Several speeches were made, and Lady MacLaren performed the actual opening. The Librarian (Miss Beck) announced that over 1200 volumes had been presented; Miss Florence Nightingale having given £50 towards their purchase. A number of other presents of furniture and pictures had also been received. A short programme of vocal and instrumental music closed the proceedings.

Chester.—"The excellent work of Mr. Ernest Caddie, the Chester Librarian, was publicly acknowledged this week by a city councillor, whose allusion was in unqualified terms of praise. Speaking at Saltley, and advocating the establishment of a branch of the Free Library there, Mr. W. Vernon declared that Mr. Caddie 'had been able to bring out of chaos a library that was doing a splendid work, and was now calculated to do a vast amount of good to our young men.' Moreover, he pointed out the important fact that the number attending the reference library are continually increasing. Mr. Caddie, he added, is a thoroughly intelligent man, and well qualified to carry on the work. This is warm praise well deserved, for Mr. Caddie has shewn not only that he thoroughly understands the functions of a public library, but his anxiety to squeeze the maximum amount of good out of the institution under his management. The reading public are indebted to him for many beneficial innovations."—*Cheshire Observer.*

Glasgow.—At one o'clock on Friday, 21st November, 1902, the Mitchell Library reached a somewhat interesting point in its history. Just at that hour the number of volumes which have been issued to readers reached ten millions. The first book was issued at ten o'clock a.m. on the 5th of November, 1877, so that the issue of ten millions has occupied a fortnight more than twenty-five years, an average over the whole period of 400,000 a year. The table below gives the number of volumes and percentage of issue in each of the eight main classes in which the work is recorded.

	No. of Vols.	Percentage
Theology, Philosophy, and Ecclesiastical History ...	866,531	8·67
History, Biography, Voyages and Travels	2,088,501	20·89
Sociology (Law, Politics, Commerce, Education, etc.)	429,862	4·30
Arts and Sciences	2,160,768	21·61
Poetry and the Drama	568,354	5·68
Linguistics	230,219	2·30
Prose Fiction	891,575	8·91
Miscellaneous Literature	2,764,190	27·64
	10,000,000	100·00

It may be of interest to note the number of days required for the completion of each successive million.

Millions.	Date of Completion.	No. of Working Days
First	14th January, 1881	982
Second	1st September, 1883	808
Third	4th December, 1885	693
Fourth	8th March, 1888	693
Fifth	20th May, 1892	816
Sixth	13th June, 1894	626
Seventh	15th May, 1896	591
Eighth	2nd July, 1898	653
Ninth	26th October, 1900	712
Tenth	21st November, 1902	637

The fifth million, which occupied 816 days, included the long interval between quitting the old premises in Ingram Street and the opening of the present building in Miller Street. The later figures tell eloquently that the available accommodation does not permit further development, for since the completion of the seventh million there has been no general increase in the use of the Library.

The number of volumes reported above as issued, is independent of the large use which has from the commencement been made of the periodical publications in the Magazine Room, a use which is little less than that of the books issued over the counter.

CORRESPONDENCE.

NOTE.—*Under this heading the Committee are prepared to answer questions or advise Assistants, to the best of their ability, concerning any professional difficulties they may meet with. Questions must be put as concisely as possible, and replies will appear here to such as shall be of general interest. If a pen-name is used, the real name and address must also be enclosed. No attention will be paid to anonymous communications. All letters must be addressed to the Editor, who, however, does not hold himself responsible for any opinions that may be expressed.*

NEW MEMBERS.

Senior.—Mr. Robert J. Gourley, Belfast.
Junior.—Mr. Arthur Jenn, Tate Central, Brixton.

NEW BOOKS, ETC.,

The Enemies of Books. By WILLIAM BLADES (popular edition), pp. 155. London, 1902, 8vo.

One of the new cheap re-issues of the charming "Book Lovers' Library." This seems a good opportunity for Assistants with limited purses to obtain a selection of this series. They are only 1/6 each, and are nicely got up, and some are extremely interesting. Mr. Wheatley's "How to Form a Library," and "How to Catalogue a Library," should particularly appeal to the Assistant, not so much for the practical help they give, as for enlarging the ideas, and showing how such things are sometimes done.

Old Picture Books; with other Essays on Bookish Subjects. By ALFRED POLLARD. *Illustrated*, pp. 288. London (Methuen), 1902, 8vo.

A collection of Essays reprinted from "The Library," "Bibliographica," "The Connoisseur," etc., and forming an interesting volume. It is essentially a "booky" book, and Mr. Pollard talks pleasantly about "Books of Hours," "English books printed abroad," "the first English book sale," "printer's marks," and other analogous subjects. The reproductions of early woodcuts are excellent, and there is an appropriate dedicatory letter to Mr. John Macfarlane, late of the British Museum, now Librarian of the Imperial Library, Calcutta. It should find a place on every librarian's bookshelf, by the side of Dr. Garnett's Essays.

Organization and Administration of University Libraries. By A. H. HOPKINS, Assistant Librarian, The John Crerar Library, Chicago, Ill., p.m. 7pp. sm. 4to.

The following Reports, etc., have also been received :—
Bury (Public Library and Art Gallery Report).
Croydon (Reader's Index).
Pratt Institute Library, Brooklyn, N.Y. (Co-operative Bulletin).
Gloucester (Third Report of the Public Library).
Morley College Magazine. (November.)

NOTICES.

All matter for the January number should reach the Hon. Editor on or before 20th December.

All other communications should be addressed to the *Hon. Secretary*, MR. J. RADCLIFFE, Public Library, East Ham, E.

APPOINTMENTS VACANT.

[**Notice to Library Authorities.**—*We shall be pleased to publish under this heading, free of charge, particulars of vacancies, if full details are sent to the Editor on or before the 28th of each month.*]

The Library Assistant:
The Official Organ of the Library Assistants' Association.

No. 61. JANUARY, 1903. Published Monthly

JANUARY MEETING.
The Library Association Education Committee has arranged for a Lecture to be given on the 21st instant, at 8 p.m., at the London School of Economics, Clare Market, W.C., by Mr. C. T. Jacobi, of the Chiswick Press, on "The Technique and Types of Book-Printing Generally." It will be illustrated by lantern slides, and an instructive evening is expected. All assistants are recommended to attend.

FEBRUARY MEETING.
This Meeting will be held at the West Ham Public Library on the 18th prox., by kind invitation of Mr. A. Cotgreave, when Mr. T. W. Glazier, of the Tate Library, Streatham, will read an essay on "Anticipated Developments of Library Practice," being the Cotgreave prize essay for 1902. Further particulars will be given in our next issue.

LIBRARY ASSOCIATION.
The Professional Examination of this Association in Section I (Bibliography), and II (Library Management), will be held on Wednesday and Thursday, January 28th and 29th, instead of 14th and 15th as announced in our last issue. Further particulars can be obtained from Mr. H. D. Roberts, 44a, Southwark Bridge Road, S.E., before the 17th inst.

CATALOGUING CLASSES.
Mr. Barratt's class in cataloguing and classification will commence on 21st inst. at 3.30 p.m. Those who did not join at the time they entered for Mr. Brown's course of lectures may perhaps be glad of the opportunity now.

Intending students are requested to forward their names, together with a fee of 10s. to the Director of the School of Economics, half of which fee will be returned on the recommendation of a member of the Library Association. Forms for this purpose may be obtained from the School Director, or Mr. Roberts, as above.

NORTH WESTERN BRANCH

ANNUAL MEETING.

The Fourth Annual Meeting of the N.W. Branch was held on Wednesday, December 17th, 1902, in the Reference Library, Manchester, Mr. J. H. Swann presiding. The Annual Report was adopted, together with that of the Hon. Treasurer, which shows a balance to the credit of the Branch. The total number of members is sixty-six, being a net gain of thirteen on last year's total, only four members having resigned during the year.

The election of officers resulted in the re-election of the Chairman, Vice-Chairman, Treasurer, and Secretary, whilst the following members were chosen for the Committee :—Messrs. Berry (Oldham), Gordon (Manchester), Haworth (Manchester), Kirk (Chetham's Hospital), Montgomery (Bootle), Percival (Owens College), Shawcross (Bury), and T. Smith (Weaste, Salford). Messrs. Baker, Edwards, Hobson, and Marriott being unsuccessful nominees.

The Meetings were decided to be held monthly during the forthcoming year. The thanks of the Branch was unanimously given to the retiring officers.

JANUARY MEETING.

The first meeting for 1903 is arranged for January 14th, in the Athenæum, Manchester, (George Street entrance), at 8 p.m. Committee please assemble at 7.30 p.m. prompt.

Members are invited to introduce any practical phase of Librarianship for discussion.

SUBSCRIPTIONS.

Subscriptions to the N.W. Branch for 1903 are now due, and should be paid to the Hon. Treasurer, Mr. W. Crompton, Y.M.C.A. Library, 56 Peter Street, Manchester.

All other communications respecting the Branch should be addressed to Mr. W. Quarmby, Hon. Secretary, Central Library, Oldham.

NEW MEMBERS.

Senior.—Mr. F. Sawyer, Holbeck Branch Library, Leeds.
Junior.—Mr. F. Melloy, Mile End, E

STUDY CIRCLE.

A sentence in the report on the October papers needs correction. In calling attention to the frequent mis-spellings of the titles of well-known books, we wrote "Whittaker's Almanac is a favourite version." But it seems difficult to smuggle an error past the Editor's eagle eye, even in quotation, and, owing perhaps to the want of a danger signal in the significant little word *sic*, the corrector found himself corrected incorrectly.

We are pleased to record an increase in the number of students, 15 answers to the November papers having been received, as against 11 in October. The average number of marks obtained per question is a fraction under 12, a shade lower than last month. The remarks we then made as to lack of originality again apply to a large extent. We hope that we shall have less cause for criticism on this ground in future papers.

The principal point that calls for notice in the answers to question (3) is the scale of fines. Most students gave the "one penny per week or part of a week" scale as the fairest in their opinion, following, presumably, the practice in their own libraries. This is, we believe, the most common scale in use, but it is obviously most unfair, and, we think, most unwise to inflict the same fine for a day's over-detention as for a week's.

Some students base arguments against fines on the assumption that Municipal Libraries are "Free Libraries." We have always considered this term a misnomer, and it is now archaic—an obsolete survival of the early days of the movement. Public libraries are no more "free" than are Board Schools; the payment is indirect, but none the less real.

Question (4) was generally answered in a somewhat amateurish fashion. Although it was evident that, in many cases, much thought had been given to the answer, the results were very unpractical. There were more mistakes of omission than commission.

Aedifico (3) 15.—Good, but somewhat diffuse.
    (4) 16.—Instructions not quite full enough.
Archibald (3) 14.—Very fair.
    (4) 10.—Too brief, no columns for volumes, size, or price.
Benedict (3) 11.—Reasons illogical; last part unanswered.
    (4) 14.—Too much detail; it is unnecessary to tell a binder that the index to a volume of a magazine will be found in the last part. No columns for volumes, size. or price.
Constantia (3) 15.—Good on the whole.
    (4) 10.—Too much detail; no dates or vols. given for Annuals.
Esca (3) 7. } Shows want of pains.
    (4) 9. }
Nil Desperandum (3) 9.—Not full enough; rather careless.
    (4) 6.—Altogether unpractical.
Norham (3) 10.—Spelling and composition faulty. The suggestion of decreasing the rate of fine after the first week or two of over-detention is inequitable.
    (4) 13.—Only gives books to be bound.
Papyrus (3) 12.—Method of checking fines not good.
    (4) 13.—Too much detail; no columns for number, size, or price.
Retwal (3) 15.—Good.
    (4) 11.—A binding sheet should be ruled in columns.
Rexine (3) 12.—Too much of the "legal" aspect.
    (4) 14.—Instructions not definite enough.
Stalky (3) 17.—Very good.
    (4) 16.—No column for price. London Directory should be lettered with date.

Temporal Power (3) 6.—Poor ; composition and grammar shaky.
(4) 5.—Very poor ; author's titles and Christian names are seldom lettered on the back of Lending Library novels.
Tiny Tim (3) 15.—Method of recording fines cumbrous.
(4) 15.—Shelters behind a specification.
Tree (3) 11.—Goes quite astray in his objections. It is perfectly legal to inflict fines. Receipts should have space for number of book.
Vernon (3) 11.—Antiquated system of checking fines.
(4) 10.—No columns for volumes, size, or price. Whole tree calf for Tennyson in the Lending Library !

QUESTIONS.

(7).—Draw up a Weekly Time Sheet for a Public Library with a staff of 10, with separate Lending and Reference departments. News-room open 9 a.m. to 10 p.m. ; Lending Department, 10 a.m. to 9 p.m. ; Reference Department, 10 a.m. to 10 p.m. Lending Department closes one day at 2 p.m.

(8).—Given a top-lighted room, 50 feet by 30 feet, and 15 feet in height, draw plan of arrangement for a Lending Library worked by *(a)* indicators, *(b)* open access, giving in each case height of presses (no gallery), number of shelves to a press, total book capacity.

Answers should be sent not later than the 26th inst., to Mr. R. B. Wood, Public Library, Buckingham Palace Road, London, S.W., signed by a pseudonym, and in the case of new students, with the real name enclosed in an envelope, on which is written the pseudonym. Former students are requested to retain the same pseudonym throughout the session.

DECEMBER MEETING.

The December Meeting was held at the St. Bride Institute on Wednesday, the 10th ult. Mr. Rees, who presided, opened a discussion on the various methods of recording the issue of books in the lending department, and described the system in use at his own library. The discussion, which was carried on by most of those present, was confined to a description of the different systems in use, and all criticism was purposely avoided. A number of ingenious contrivances for facilitating either the actual issue or record were brought to light, and at the close of the proceedings all present were satisfied that they had spent a pleasant and profitable evening.

THE DAILY PRESS AND PUBLIC LIBRARIES.

Writing in the *Daily News* of December 27th, 1902, under the heading, "Our Public Libraries; the Need for Reform," Mr. Thomas Greenwood discusses the hackneyed question of the preponderating issue of Fiction, and makes some novel suggestions for suppressing it. We do not remember before to have seen it suggested that where "the junior or general member of the household" reads too much fiction "the tickets of the borrower should be suspended, *or even cancelled*." The italics are ours. We are afraid Mr. Greenwood is allowing the Fiction bogey to unduly frighten him. For our part we read the Press discussions on this matter much in the same spirit as we read of the sea-serpent or the big gooseberry. They are all hardy annuals. Mr. Greenwood admits that "little trashy or questionable fiction is bought." If this is so, and we feel quite confident it is, why trouble about the reading of standard works of British and foreign novelists? The percentage of Fiction issued in no way corresponds with the percentage of borrowers who read fiction. In fact the statistics available are perhaps the greatest bugbear libraries have to contend with. The system of issue in the different institutions varies so considerably that it would be a good thing if the issue of these figures was abolished. For instance, one library only loans volumes for seven days, another allows fourteen, whilst some of the older libraries still have a number of "three deckers" on their shelves, with the result that the issue of one of these works counts as three volumes issued, whereas in libraries that possess the modern edition it only counts as one.

We are glad to see that Mr. Greenwood protests against the modern system of log-rolling novels—good, bad or indifferent, and wish that more attention was given by the Press to the praise of standard works of literature. But, at the same time, is it not too much to expect the wives and daughters of the British ratepayers to take out volumes of Herbert Spencer or Gibbon to while away the leisure hours, or to relieve them from the monotony of domestic drudgery?

Referring to the proposed increase of the rate, Mr. Greenwood thinks "with the increase there ought to be established a system of Government inspection, and the increased grant should only be permitted where the usefulness of the Library wholly satisfied the inspector." This would, no doubt, have a very beneficial effect in some cases, but we think the advent of fully trained librarians, who are now growing ripe with experience in the larger libraries, would soon make the work of such an officer unnecessary. It must not be forgotten that, owing to the youth of the Public Library movement, quite a number of libraries are still administered by untrained officers, but there is no reason why any future post should be given to any but a fully qualified man, and if this is done, and a little more money allowed library authorities, the sphere of influence of these institutions will be very considerably widened.

"I claim for the majority of Municipal Librarians," says Mr. Greenwood, "that they are in full sympathy with their duties, and are alive to its increased possibilities. They are shockingly underpaid as a body, and in no department of our local life are the public better served."

Instead of cavilling over the issue of Fiction from Public Libraries, would it not be better to look at the other side of the picture, to consider the work done in the reference department, where all sorts and conditions of students congregate for self-improvement, or to those borrowers in the lending department, probably not less than fifty per cent of the whole, who, year in and year out, read not fiction, but History, Science, and other branches of literature which have an elevating and educating effect on the mind?

W. G. C.

CORRESPONDENCE.

To the Editor of the "LIBRARY ASSISTANT."

SIZE NOTATION.

SIR,

With regard to the new cataloguing rules now under the consideration of the Council of the Library Association, I hope the table of book sizes will be revised. According to Mr. Quinn's "Manual of Library Cataloguing," which reproduces the Library Association scale, there are frequent puzzling half-inches, for which no sizes are given, *viz.*, books up to 5 inches are 24 mo. and 32 mo., while the next size, 16 mo. and 18 mo., begin at $5\frac{1}{2}$. I know the rule is that "books on the line of height between two sizes are to be described as of the lower," still it seems to me that it would save unnecessary confusion if the 32 mo. were stated to be to $5\frac{1}{2}$, and there would then be no "between sizes." The same vacancies occur between 6 and $6\frac{1}{2}$ in., 8 and $8\frac{1}{2}$, 9 and $9\frac{1}{2}$, and 10 and $10\frac{1}{2}$, and also in the quartos—9-$9\frac{1}{2}$, 11-$11\frac{1}{2}$, 13-$13\frac{1}{2}$, etc. According to the same authority, the tallest quarto is 16 inches. Are not all books from four-fifths their height wide (but not width exceeding their height) to be described as quartos, including those over 16 inches? Where does Imperial folio finish and Atlas folio begin? I should be glad if some qualified person would take the matter up.

Yours faithfully,
MARY BERTHELET,
(Bristol).

18th December, 1902.

NOTES AND COMMENTS.

Blackburn.—It has been decided to form new branch delivery stations, and the localities to be thus served are Furthergate, Mill Hill, Nova Scotia, and Lower Darwen. These, it is confidently expected, will bring into close touch with the Central Library, the newly incorporated district about Mill Hill, and other outlying parts of the town. Already two such stations are doing good work in the Bastwell and Bank Top districts.

Neath.—We learn that all the books in the Public Library here, including many copies of first editions and other literary treasures comprised in the recently-added Rowland bequest, were destroyed by fire on the morning of the 3rd inst.

Stepney.—On Wednesday, December 17th, the staff of the St. George-in-the-East Library invited the other members of the Stepney Libraries Staff (from Limehouse, Mile End, and Whitechapel) to a Social Evening.

The Borough Librarian, Mr. A. Cawthorne, presided, and there was a full muster. Most members present contributed to the programme, and the proceedings were attended with marked success. Mr. Cawthorne, in his remarks, stated that the object of the evening, which was to bring the various staffs more in touch with each other, was good, and met with his greatest approval. It was a pleasure to him to find such unity of feeling and good fellowship amongst his staff. Mr. F. M. Roberts (Mile End) moved the toast "The St. George's Staff," which was seconded by Mr. McCall (Limehouse), and supported by Mr. Weare (Whitechapel). Mr. Roebuck, responding on behalf of his St. George's colleagues, stated the pleasure they felt at such marked appreciation of their endeavours, and hoped the evening would prove the first of a long series.

NEW BOOKS, ETC.,

Leyton Library Magazine, November 1902. (Z. Moon, Librarian).

Contains an interesting note on John Eliot, an Essex worthy, who first translated the Bible into Indian, and also a continuation of that valuable index to the biographical history of Essex.

Morley College Magazine. December.

Peterborough Public Library: Bulletin, December. (W. J. WILLCOCK, Librarian).

Contains a brief but forcible reply to the opponents of Public Libraries who air their views in the Daily Press, and an excellent "Reading List" of Books and Articles in the Library on Education.

Pratt Institute Free Library : Co-operative Bulletin, Nov. 1902.

Pratt Institute Monthly, Brooklyn, New York, December. (MARY W. PLUMMER, Librarian).

Containing the Annual Report of the Free Library, consisting of 25 pages, showing the advanced state of the Public Library Movement in America.

West Ham Library Notes. July—September, 1902. Edited by A. COTGREAVE.

Contains an article on "Public Libraries and their Opponents : Some Misleading Statements Refuted." Among the "Jottings" we observe a note on the Library Association's Annual Meeting, in which it is stated that "The meeting was opened by the President of the Association, Professor W. MacNeale." (sic) !

APPOINTMENTS.

HILL, Mr. ROLAND, Librarian, Public Library, Carlisle, to be Chief Librarian, Blackpool.

McADAM, Mr. JOHN, of the Bootle Public Library, to be Chief Assistant at the Cheltenham Public Library.

MORGAN, Mr. W. H., of Gloucester, to be Senior Assistant at the Hammersmith Public Library.

[38 Applications].

APPOINTMENTS VACANT.

[**Notice to Library Authorities.**—*We shall be pleased to publish under this heading, free of charge, particulars of vacancies if full details are sent to the Editor on or before the 28th of each month.*]

NOTICES.

All matter for the February number should reach the Hon. Editor on or before 20th January.

All other communications should be addressed to the *Hon. Secretary*, MR. J. RADCLIFFE, Public Library, East Ham, E.

The Library Assistant:
The Official Organ of the Library Assistants' Association.

No. 62.   FEBRUARY, 1903.   Published Monthly

FEBRUARY MEETING.

By kind invitation of Mr. A. Cotgreave, this meeting will be held at the West Ham Central Library on **Wednesday, February 18th,** when Mr. Glazier will read his Prize Essay on " Some anticipated Developments of Library Practice." Mr. Cotgreave, with his well-known hospitality, has promised to provide refreshments, and requests that all will endeavour to arrive at the Library by 6.30 p.m. Mr. Cotgreave has also intimated his intention of presenting to the members present copies of his "Contents—Subject Index." Members should show their appreciation of such goodwill by making every effort to attend. Ladies and friends are cordially invited, and it is hoped that the large gathering which usually occurs at West Ham, may even be surpassed on this occasion. Trains to Maryland Point Station, G.E. Railway.

L.A. MEETING FOR ASSISTANTS.

A goodly number of assistants attended the meeting on January 21st, arranged by the Library Association, when Mr. C. T. Jacobi gave a lecture on "Printing." Mr. H. R. Tedder presided, and Mr. Jacobi's remarks, which were illustrated with about fifty lantern slides, were followed with considerable interest.

NORTH WESTERN BRANCH.
JANUARY MEETING.

This meeting was held on Wednesday, January 14th, in the Athenæum, Manchester, Mr. J. H. Swann occupying the chair. After the formal business, Mr. J. D. Dickens read a short paper, in which he dealt with the publishing of the "Library Assistant." Mr. H. W. Kirk drew the attention of the meeting to an article on "Planning of some American Libraries," published in the Journal of the R. I. British Architects. It was decided that, unless there were offers of special papers from members, such articles dealing with Library Economy should be read and discussed at future meetings.

FEBRUARY MEETING.

By permission of the Feoffees, this meeting will be held in the Chetham Library, Hunt's Bank, Manchester, at 7.30 p.m., on Wednesday, February 18th. The article by Ella F. Corwin, on "Some Fads and Fallacies in Library Work," in the September number of the American Library Journal, will be read as a subject for discussion.

THE EDUCATION QUESTION.

At the January meeting of the Library Association, Mr. Evan G. Rees, Chairman of the L.A.A., read a paper on the "Educational needs of Library Assistants," in which he shewed the various ways by which the education of assistants could be improved, laying special stress on the need for the establishment of correspondence classes for Provincial assistants. A noticeable feature of the meeting was the poor attendance of librarians, not more than twelve or fourteen being present, although an hour earlier, and in the same building, a fully attended meeting of the Council took place. Apparently most of those present found they had more important engagements elsewhere. We were glad to see the good muster of assistants. It was strange that at a meeting of the Library Association there should be as many assistants as librarians present. Messrs. Wood, Harris, Chambers, Coltman, and Savage, of the L.A.A., took part in the discussion. The action of the Council in withdrawing its regulation requiring that before a candidate can sit for the professional examination he shall have served at least three years in a library was severely criticised. The Library Association has evidently forgotten the Manchester Meeting. Mr. Jast (the Chairman), who, rising towards the end of the meeting, promised to give assistants present a further opportunity of stating their views, but who closed the meeting without doing so, stated that " he was heartily sick and tired of the whole business," and other speakers hinted that assistants should accept with gratitude what was offered to them, and not, like Oliver Twist, ask for more.

W. G. C.

STUDY CIRCLE.

Several students have " dropped out " of the Circle, owing, as we are informed, to the severity of our comments. However, we still cling to the idea that the proper way to conduct our Circle is to give marks for the good and remarks for the bad. The veil of anonymity is strictly respected, and it is better for the thinnest-skinned assistant to have his feelings hurt now rather than after the Professional Examination. Some students have asked for model answers to be printed here. We cannot afford space for this, but one or two of the best answers will be sent on request to any student receiving low marks for comparison with his own answer. Anonymity could be preserved by giving the name of a fellow assistant to whom the papers might be sent. For instance, we would recommend "Temporal Power" to apply for an answer to question (5) to compare with his own.

With regard to question (10) set this month ; plans and specifications of library buildings, with their lighting, heating, and ventilation, form part of the Syllabus of the Examination. We do not ask for architects' drawings, but it is reasonable to expect an intelligent knowledge of plans, an idea of the most suitable arrangement of rooms and disposal of space. Burgoyne's "Library Construction" will be useful in answering this question, but not for copying from.

Aedifico (5) 14.—A good list, but needs arrangement. The important works are lost in the mass of magazine articles.
 (6) 11.—Two-thirds of work given to librarian and sub. ; senior assistant does junior's work.
Benedict (5) 14.—Good, what there is of it.
Constantia (5) 16.—Good ; the dates of travels might have been given.
 (6) 12.—Somewhat vague and ill-defined.
Nil Desperandum (5) 12.—Fair ; the object of annotation is to add to the information given in the title, not to repeat it in different words.
 (6) 11.—We do not wish to discourage this student, but a library assistant who mis-spells "cataloguing" and "issuing" has much to learn.
Norham (5) 16.—Good ; it would have been better to arrange first by subject and then by date of publication.
 (6) 15.—Good ; reference library assistant ought to have more work allotted.
Papyrus (5) 17.—An excellent bibliography, but not exactly a reading list. Annotations scanty.
 (6) 17.—Very good.
Retwal (5) 20.—We feel bound to give full marks to this admirable answer, although again it is more a bibliography than a reading list.
 (6) 11.—Not sufficiently detailed. No mention of reading room duties, receiving and preparing papers, &c.
Stalky (5) 10.—Not much of a help to readers. Such annotations as "An authority on Somaliland," "Another authority on the subject," are very feeble.
 (6) 7.—Apparently misunderstood. The object of the question is to apportion the various duties amongst the staff.
Temporal Power (5) 3.—A remarkably poor attempt. We should advise "Temporal Power" to take the matter more seriously if he intends to benefit by the work.
 (6) 8.—Not a routine sheet at all, but a homily upon the whole duty of library staffs. Mis-spells "catalogue" !
Vernon (5) 14.—Fair ; paucity of annotations, no dates to travels.

QUESTIONS.

(9).—Draw up a schedule of rules for guidance in the preparation of a printed catalogue, as to the use of all marks of punctuation, brackets (square and round), dashes, italics, capitals, clarendon type, &c.

(10).—Draw plans showing the main departments of a public library on two sites, (*a*) rectangular, 120 feet by 80 feet, one floor ; (*b*) triangular, 100 feet by 90 feet by 110 feet, two floors. Only a sketch is required, but it should be approximately to scale. Each plan should occupy the full size of a half sheet of foolscap. Bookcases, newspaper stands, and tables should be shown.

Answers should be sent not later than the 25th inst., to Mr. R. B. Wood, Public Library, Buckingham Palace Road, London, S.W., signed by a pseudonym, and in the case of new students, with the real name enclosed in an envelope, on which is written the pseudonym. Former students are requested to retain the same pseudonym throughout the session.

NOTES AND COMMENTS.

Resignation of the Hon. Secretary.—The Committee regret having to announce the resignation of Mr. J. Radcliffe, who has held the post of Hon. Secretary during the past 10 months, during which time much good work has been accomplished. Mr. Radcliffe has lately been unable to give the time to the multitudinous duties connected with the office that he feels should be given, and in consequence the Committee have been compelled to accept his resignation. Mr. G. E. Roebuck has kindly consented to take up the reins of office again until the Annual Meeting at least.

Greenwood's Library Year-Book.—There are still a few copies of this useful reference volume left for distribution ; new members and those who have not already received a copy can obtain one by forwarding four penny stamps (to cover postage) to the Hon. Secretary, *pro. tem.*, Mr. G. E. Roebuck, 236 Cable Street, E.

Aberdeen.—Plans and specifications for the extension of the Public Library here have been approved, and it is expected that tenders for building will be invited in the course of a week or so. The estimated cost of the extension and alterations is between £6,000 and £7,000.

Germany.—In view of the number of valuable articles which occur in the periodical press, the Konigsberg Public Library has adopted the plan of cutting them out, sorting them, and having them bound into volumes. In this country the difficulty is largely surmounted by the publication of Stead's Index and that of the "Times," but we feel that a good deal of labour for the searcher is saved by this German method.

Society of Public Librarians.—A meeting was held at the Hoxton (Shoreditch) Public Library on Wednesday evening, January 7th, 1903, when Mr. Wm. C. Plant (the Librarian) read a paper entitled "How may we increase the utility of our Reference Libraries?"

Tottenham.—We understand that in return for a small fee advertisements for situations "wanted" and "vacant" are now exhibited at the Public Libraries here.

Wakefield.—Like many other centres this city has received from Mr. Carnegie a generous offer towards the provision of a Free Library. The City Council is anxious to accept the gift, but it cannot do so because of the impossibility of obtaining a site for the building. The Corporation has no available land, and private individuals who have been approached have declined the honour of figuring as benefactors in the matter. Meanwhile Mr. Carnegie objects to the levying of a two years' rate, in order to provide the requisite money for purchasing a site. In the circumstances the scheme appears likely to fall to the ground. This is a prospect which is causing a good deal of local lamentation. But, really, if Wakefield people have not public spirit enough to raise the comparatively small amount necessary for a site, they deserve to be left in intellectual darkness a while longer.—*London Argus*, January 24th.

Woolwich.—The Committee has decided to issue a non-fictional ticket to "bonâ-fide students." They have defined a "bonâ-fide student" as one who can "produce a voucher of attendance at classes at some recognised scholastic institution!" A useful list of the "Best Bible Commentaries," compiled by the Borough Librarian of Woolwich, appears in the January and February numbers of the "Expository Times."

NEW MEMBERS.

Seniors.—Miss G. MINSHULL, Warrington. MR. T. W. E. BATTY, Fulham.

Juniors.—Miss NELLIE L. PUGSLEY, Bristol. MESSRS. G. R. BOLTON, Fulham; H. B. ILLSLEY, Smethwick; S. H. PARR, Fulham.

CORRECTION:—For MR. F. MELLOY, of Mile End, as announced last month, read Mr. W. F. LELLOW.

ANCIENT AND MODERN WRITING MATERIALS: A CHAPTER IN BIBLIOGRAPHY.

By P. Evans Lewin.

[*Continued from December, 1902.*]

The use of waxen tablets lingered in Europe till the end of the middle ages and they were not unknown in this country where they were still occasionally used so late as the 15th century. In the *Somnour's Tale* in Chaucer's *Canterbury Tales* we read " His felowe hadde a staff tipped with horn, a peyre of tables all of yvory, and a poyntel [style for writing] polisshed fetisly, and wroot the names alwey as he stood." It is refreshing to learn from Plautus that these tabulæ had other uses than those for which they were intended, for he tells of a schoolboy who, much to the joy of his fellows, broke his master's head with a table book. As a remarkable example of the lingering of old customs it is reported that until quite lately the sales of fish in the market at Rouen were noted down on waxen tablets.

Leaves were frequently used for writing upon, and Pliny asserts that man first wrote on the leaves of palm trees. It is certain that palm leaves, on account of their size and durable quality, presented an easy and suitable substance. Many peoples of the East have used and still use leaves for this purpose. The common books of the Burmese are composed of the leaves of the palmyra palm, fastened together by a string passing through holes at each end of the leaf. The Singalese generally use the leaf of the talipot tree, from which they cut strips about a foot long and about two inches broad. This leaf is thick and tough and, properly prepared, will last a considerable time. In the Sloane Museum a collection of these writing leaves is to be found. In addition to leaves, the bark of trees has been used in every age and in every country. The ancient Latins preferred the inner bark, termed *liber*. The fibrous layers of which liber is composed can at times be separated into laminæ like the leaves of a book or an ancient manuscript roll. The bark of a plant consists of four layers, of which the innermost, the liber, was generally used, and from this use has sprung the origin of the word liber, a book, and not as some suppose, from the rind, also termed liber, of the papyrus, for the pith (*medullæ*) only was used.

Linen was used from a very early period by the Romans and also by the Egyptians, and the records kept on this substance were termed *libri lintei*. Livy mentions the libri lintei. These, however, were not books, but merely public records and lists of magistrates, kept in the temple of Juno Moneta. In much later times linen was used for note-books by Aurelian.

Skins of animals have been used from the earliest times. Herodotus relates that the Ionians called their books *dipteræ* or skins, because at one time the plant *biblos* became scarce, and they had to use the skins of goats instead. The use of leather has continued among the Jews, who inscribe the law upon leathern rolls. The rolls, *volumina*, are the ancient form of a book. In the Greek Church a great number of slips of parchment were joined together, often reaching to a great length, and inscribed with the prayers and offices. These strips were fastened to and wrapped round the *kontakion*, which was a short staff. The use of parchment, which is the skin of sheep and goats carefully prepared, may be considered as a survival of the ancient use of skins, due to the circumstances of the times in which it was first prepared. It is related by Pliny that a dispute having arisen between Eumenes II., King of Pergamum, and one of the Ptolemies, the latter prohibited the export of papyrus from Egypt, so as to thwart the King of Pergamum in his attempts to establish a library in rivalry of that at Alexandria in his capital, which, with Alexandria, was destined to become the abode of Christianity and the seat of one of the seven Churches. In order to carry on his work of establishing this library, Eumenes was obliged to revert to the ancient custom of using skins, and these he caused to be prepared in such a superior manner that they could be used for writing on both sides, and could then be conveniently made up into book form. The parchment thus prepared was thenceforth called Pergamenum and Charta Pergamena. The spread of civilization caused special attention to be turned to this invention, and a much finer kind of material was prepared, made of the skin of suckling calves, and called *vellum*. The vellum was often stained purple and other rich colours, but later this art was forgotten, and the surface of the vellum was painted in imitation of the older staining, which soaked into the substance of the skin. Stained vellum books were only a luxury of the rich. St. Jerome, in his preface to the Book of Job, declaims against them. " Let those please," he says, " have books written with silver or gold letters, on purple vellum, which are rather burthens than books, so that they will but allow me and mine our poor loose papers."

Human skin has been used not only for the binding of books, but also for the leaves themselves. The Royal Library at Dresden possesses a Mexican calender traced on human skin, as well as other bibliographical curiosities, such as waxen tablets and runic calendars on boxwood.

It is to Pliny that we are indebted for a description of Papyrus, the most important of all early substances used for writing. The papyrus plant was in early times widely cultivated along the Nile, and from a very ancient date was manufactured into a writing material. Pliny describes the process at length. The head and root being cut away, the stem was slit lengthwise into two parts, and the thin scaly pellicles stripped off with the point of a knife. There seems no doubt that the outer bark, or bast, was cast away, and the pith only (the *biblos*, which name the plant itself later received, and from which our word bibliography is derived) used. The innermost pellicles were the best and were extended on a table transversely over each other, so that the fibres formed right angles. They were then covered with the water of the Nile, and having been allowed to soak for a short time, were pressed together. Finally they were covered with a paste of the finest flour mixed with vinegar, again pressed and left to dry in the sun. The manufacture was then almost completed, but the papyrus was beaten with a mallet and polished by rubbing to the smoothest surface obtainable. The manufacture seems to have been confined to Egypt, and indeed to certain provinces, and was at first a monopoly of the Government, but was probably introduced from Nubia, where the plant is found at the present time, though now extinct in lower Egypt. The widespread use of papyrus as a writing material is attested by ancient writers. The most ancient example, known as the *Prisse papyrus*, the oldest book in the world, preserved at Paris, is computed to be of the age of upwards of 2,000 years B.C., and older by several centuries than the Hebrew Exodus. Another of the most important papyrus documents is the *Book of the Dead*, the papyrus of Ani, deposited in the British Museum, which contains a description of the burial and religious rites of the Egyptians, and has been so ably dealt with by Dr. Budge.

These papyri were generally about 15 inches wide, and sometimes extended to a length of 150 feet. They were rolled up into cylindrical volumes, and when used for reading were unrolled from the ends. The rolls were placed in rectangular wooden boxes close to the scribe or reader.

The papyrus was also put to other uses, and more particularly used for the sandals worn by the priests. Even small boats were made of the plant, and it has been conjectured that the ark in which the infant Moses was placed was made of this plant.

There were several different kinds of papyrus, ranging from a superior paper used by the priests to that used by the shopkeepers for fastening parcels. The best quality, made from the broadest strips of the plant, was termed *Charta Hieratica*, sacred paper, and was appropriated solely to religious books and for the use of the priests. Afterwards, out of compliment to the Emperor Augustus, it was called *Charta Augusta*, and a slightly inferior quality was named *Charta Liviana* after his wife. Next came the *Charta Amphitheatrica*, so named from its place of manufacture in the amphitheatre of Alexandria, which was a coarse and smaller kind of paper, afterwards, having been improved by Fannius, called *Charta Fannina*. The third quality was termed *Charta Saitica*, from its place of manufacture, the city of Sais. The fourth quality, the *Charta Toeniotica*, was sold only by weight, and was of uncertain width. Finally, there was the common papyrus used only in shops, the *Charta Emporetica*, or shop-paper. Each of these papers was supposed to have a distinct size, and the measurements are given by Pliny, but there is reason to doubt the accuracy of his statements in this respect. The Augusta was held in most esteem, as it was white and smooth, and it was in later times reserved for the writing of Imperial Letters. It was improved and made thicker under Claudius, but, as a rule, papyrus did not last very long, as it was very fragile and brittle. Papyrus was in use for Papal documents down to the tenth century, but elsewhere it was little used, and by the 12th century its manufacture had entirely ceased. It is a mistake to suppose that the use of papyrus was confined to the Egyptians, for it was extensively used among the Romans and Greeks, and many rolls of papyrus have been discovered at Herculaneum and Pompeii, those at the former place partly legible, and those at the latter wholly defaced. During later periods it was no longer employed in the shape of volumina, but cut up into square pages and bound like modern books. The discovery of several classical Greek authors written on papyrus led to further searches and discoveries, and a lost, but famous, work by Aristotle, on the Constitution of Athens, has been recovered in this form, as well as lost portions of Plato and Euripides.

In the far East paper has been manufactured for centuries from the bark of the bamboo. This paper made from the bark of plants is termed *Charta Corticea*. It is, however, the general custom in China to use the interior portions of the stem of the bamboo, beaten to a pulp, for the finer varieties of paper. Such paper is thin and transparent, and the sheets are frequently doubled and glued together so that both sides may be written upon and appear as one leaf. Each province appears to have a distinct kind of paper, and different materials are used in its manufacture; the bark of the mulberry tree in one, wheat or rice straw in another, the bark of the Boehmeria, or China grass, from which rhea-fibre is produced in a third, and the cocoons of silkworms in a fourth. The finest silk paper was made at Samarkand, and at one time was very extensively used. Montfaucon mentions several volumes on silk in the Ambrosian Library at Milan, and in other Italian Libraries, but these books were probably on this silk paper, for it does not appear that silk was actually used for books until after the invention of printing, when they were produced more as curiosities than anything else. According to a celebrated Chinese author the Chinese at first wrote on bamboo-boards, but for 300 years before and after Christ the usual writing material was paper made of silk-waste, solidified in some way not described.

Another form of the Charta Corticea, or bark-paper, is the Japanese paper, now in common use in Europe for table napkins and the like, of which there are no less than sixty distinct varieties, etiquette prescribing a different use for each. Japanese paper is made from the bark and twigs of the *Broussonettia papyrifera*, or paper-mulberry, which is extensively cultivated in Japan, and the better kinds undergo a very long process of manufacture. For the coarser kinds of paper the paper-mulberry shoots after being allowed to grow five feet are cut down and soaked in water for several days. The bark is then taken off and soaked in ley, the inner and whiter bark being used for the better papers. The bark is beaten into a pulp, and a small quantity taken on to a frame and dried in the sun. The same plant is used in Hawaii for the tapa, or paper-cloth. Some very exquisite examples of Japanese paper exist, but the manufacture of the best kind seems to have been discarded. One side only of the paper is used for writing. Of the origin of paper, such as is known to Europeans, authorities differ considerably. Till quite recently it was believed that the oldest form of paper was made from the pulp of crude cotton, but the researches of Wiesner on 12,000 MSS supplied by the Archduke Rainer do not bear out this assertion, as he states that the Arabs, who are supposed to have introduced this manufacture into Europe, never at any time made their paper from cotton wool. Other authorities, however, state that paper was made from the wool of the cotton plant by the Chinese, and that the manufacture found its way as far west as Samarkand, from whence it was introduced into Europe by the Arabs when they took Samarkand in 704 A.D. Later writers, however, assert that paper was made at Samarkand from old linen cloths, and that here the Persians learned the art, establishing a manufactory at Bagdad, and that finally the art spread to Egypt, and along the North Coast of Africa into Spain, where the Arabs set up manufactories at Ceuta, Valencia, and Toledo. The paper asserted to have been made from cotton has been known as *Charta Damascena*, from Damascus, *bombycina, cuttunea, gossypina*, and *Serica*, from Seres in China. It is, however, certain that rag paper was not generally made in Europe till the 14th century, though it had been in occasional use since the 12th century, especially in Sicily, where documents on paper have been discovered bearing a date as far back as the year 1102. In England it is generally agreed that the first rag paper mill was founded at Dartford by Spielmann, in 1588, though it seems unlikely that we were dependent upon foreign paper till that date. There is ample evidence of the early use of paper in England, for the records of the Court of Hustings at Lyme Regis, commencing in the year 1309, and other early documents, were written on paper. It is very probable, however, that paper was imported into Lyme Regis from Bordeaux.

The general use of paper, coinciding with the Invention of Printing, has contributed to the advancement of the human race more than any other material employed in the arts. Without paper the invention of printing would have been comparatively useless, for only the rich would have been able to purchase books made of vellum and parchment.

CORRESPONDENCE.

[The Editor does not hold himself responsible for any opinions expressed by correspondents.]

PUBLIC LIBRARY,
BUCKINGHAM PALACE ROAD, S.W.

DEAR MR. EDITOR,

Solomon, the wise man, complained that there were three things too wonderful for him, yea, four which he knew not, but if he had been a library assistant in these present days of grace he would certainly have added a fifth, the way of the Council of the Library Association. The evil way of an eagle in the air is not more mysterious, the way of a serpent upon a rock not more tortuous, the way of a rudderless ship in the midst of the sea not more aimless, and the way of a man with a maid not more fickle than the way of the L.A. Council with the library assistant.

The technical education and professional examination of this unhappy being call forth from the Council the wildest gyrations of policy, and the most protean changes of attitude. Some time ago a regulation was made that all candidates at a Professional Examination must have been engaged in practical library work during the three years previous. It was held that the examination was a test of practical competency, and that no study of text-books was of value unless accompanied by actual experience in a library. But this sane interval was too bright, too beautiful to last, and the Council proceeded to nullify the regulation by reserving the right to suspend it at their pleasure. The principle was ostensibly still approved, but at a recent meeting the Council abandoned even the semblance of consistency and abolished the regulation altogether.

The Library Association is now offering to grant its Professional Certificate, which would be regarded by most library authorities as a guarantee of competence, after purely academic tests to persons who may never even have set foot in a library.

Assistants have for years been appealing for a much needed reform of the Professional Examination, to enable them to obtain, by the combination of experience and well-directed study, a diploma which would be a real guarantee of competence and an assurance of deserved future advancement; but they are not likely to receive enthusiastically a scheme which entirely disregards the more important half of the necessary training of a librarian. They consider that their professional association should protect them from, instead of encouraging, the unfair competition of incompetent amateurs. Since the Plymouth meeting in 1901 there has been much boast of reform by the Council, and much pharisaical self-comparison with their predecessors, but to library assistants it is evident that, so far as they are concerned, Amurath to Amurath succeeds.

I am, etc.,
REGINALD B. WOOD.

NEW BOOKS, &c.

Aberdeen Public Library: Eighteenth Annual Report. G. M. FRASER, Librarian.

An interesting pamphlet of forty pages, recording the prosperous state of affairs in this Library. It shows an increased issue by nearly 13,000 volumes, and an addition of 3,331 books during the year. The finances, too, seem very satisfactory, there being that unusual occurrence of a balance on the right side. A pleasant piece of information is that which says arrangements have been made allowing the staff certain Saturday privileges in addition to the Wednesday half-holiday.

Croydon Public Libraries : The Readers' Index, January—February. L. STANLEY JAST, Librarian.

Annotated list of additions, and a reading list of works, and articles in the Library on Motor-Cars.

Manchester Public Libraries : Fiftieth Annual Report, 1901-2. C. W. SUTTON, Chief Librarian.

Manchester Public Libraries : Quarterly Record, Vol. VI. No. 3. Edited by E. AXON.

Morley College Magazine : January.

Poplar Public Libraries : Quarterly Record, No. 1. January, 1903. H. ROWLATT, Borough Librarian.

Pratt Institute Free Library, Brooklyn, N.Y. : Co-operative Bulletin, December.

Rivista delle Biblioteche e degli archivi, Oct.—Dec., 1902.

Walthamstow Public Library : Annual Report, 1901-02. G. W. ATKINSON, Librarian.

Shows an average issue of 382 per day in the Lending Department, which, with a stock of only 8,965 volumes (including reference), seems very good work. It appears rather surprising, in view of this large demand for books, that only 171 should have been purchased during the year.

West Ham Library Notes, July—September, 1902. Edited by A. COTGREAVE, Borough Librarian.

This issue contains a continuation of that extensive " List of Books on London and the Suburbs," every one of which is possessed by the Library, an informative list of interesting articles appearing in recent Magazines and Reviews, as well as several photographs of provincial libraries.

Willesden Green Public Library : Quarterly Record and Guide for Readers. Edited by FRANK E. CHENNELL, Librarian. January, 1903.

APPOINTMENTS.

BLYTH, MISS J. H., of the Bristol Public Libraries, to be Senior Assistant at the Newcastle-on-Tyne Public Libraries.

APPOINTMENTS VACANT.

[**Notice to Library Authorities.**—*We shall be pleased to publish under this heading, free of charge, particulars of vacancies if full details are sent to the Editor on or before the 28th of each month.*]

NOTICE.

All subscriptions are now due, and should be forwarded at once to the Hon. Treasurer, Mr. W. G. Chambers, Public Library, Woolwich, S.E.

All matter for March number should be sent in on or before the 18th February.

All other communications should be addressed to the *Hon. Secretary*, Mr. G. E. Roebuck, PUBLIC LIBRARY, 236, CABLE STREET, E.

The Library Assistant:

The Official Organ of the Library Assistants' Association.

No. 63.   MARCH, 1903.   Published Monthly

MARCH MEETING.

This meeting will be held at the Public Library, Buckingham Palace Road, S.W., on **Wednesday, March 25th.** Mr. Reginald B. Wood will open a discussion on "Bookbinding for Public Libraries." Inspection of the library from 7.30 p.m.; meeting at 8. Visitors will be welcome. At this meeting Mr. Ernest A. Savage will move the following resolution :—"That a brief report on the relations of the Library Association and the Library Assistants' Association, during the past three years, with regard to the education of library assistants be read and circulated for discussion at the Annual Meeting, 1903; that a *précis* of all letters, with one exception, relating to the same subject be attached to such report, the exception, namely, a certain letter pleading for a less severe examination, and protesting against the 'open door,' to be transcribed in full."

L.A.A. CONCERT.

This year's social gathering of the L.A.A. will take the form of a Bohemian Concert, to be held at the "Haunch of Venison Hotel," Bell Yard, Temple Bar, W.C., on Wednesday, March 18th, at 8 p.m. punctually. No tickets or further announcement will be issued. Visitors are cordially invited.

Members who can aid musically, or with suggestions, will oblige by communicating, at an early date, with the Hon. Sec. Entertainment Committee, Mr. C. A. Bradley, Tate Central Library, Brixton Oval, S.W. Admission will be by programme, to be obtained on the evening of the concert.

NORTH-WESTERN BRANCH.

FEBRUARY MEETING.

A well-attended meeting of the N.W. Branch was held in the Chetham's Library, Manchester, on Wednesday, the 18th, Mr. J. D. Dickens presiding.

The paper, by Ella F. Corwen, "Some Fads and Fallacies in Library Work," was read and discussed, though not many debatable points were found.

Mr. H. W. Kirk afterwards conducted the members round the Library and surroundings, telling, briefly, the history of the Institution and its contents, as each of the various rooms were entered.

The thanks of the meeting were tendered to the Feoffees for their kind permission to meet in such an historic place as Chetham's, and to Mr. Kirk for obtaining the permission, and for the Illustrated Manual and Guide, which each one was permitted to take away as a memento of the visit.

It was decided to hold the meetings on Tuesday and Wednesday evenings alternately, these two days being at the head of the poll of members for the most convenient day on which they could attend the meetings.

MARCH MEETING—CHANGE OF DATE.

The March meeting will be held on Wednesday, 25th inst., at 7.30 p.m., in the Central Library, Oldham, when Mr. F. W. B. Haworth will read a paper on "The Educational Basis of the Free Library Movement" and, if time permits, the paper read by Mr. Rees (Chairman of the L.A.A.) at the January meeting of the Library Association. This paper, and the discussion on it, appears in the February "Library Association Record."

The Central Library, Union Street, Oldham, is only three minutes' walk from the Central Station (L. & Y. Rly.), and Clegg Street (G.C. and L. & N.W. Rly.). Trains from Victoria, Manchester, at 6.8, 6.27, and 6.50 p.m.

Any member desirous of arriving earlier, in order to visit the Annual Spring Exhibition of Pictures, in the Art Gallery, will be welcome. The secretary would be pleased to receive notification of any such intention.

Return trains: 10.12, and 10.27; arriving at Manchester 10.30, and 11.0 p.m.

Subscriptions to the N.W. Branch are due, and should be paid as early as possible to the treasurer Mr. Wm. Crompton, Y.M.C.A. Library, 56, Peter Street, Manchester.

FEBRUARY MEETING AT WEST HAM.

It is seldom our good fortune to have the pleasure of recording such a meeting as this, and we yearn for the days when they will be more frequent. A full hundred of members and friends (including a good sprinkling of ladies) presented themselves to do honour to Mr. Cotgreave's invitation. Members arrived from all parts of London by omnibus, tram, train and bicycle, and the reputation of the West Ham Annual Meeting was easily maintained. While waiting for the commencement of the proceedings the members availed themselves of the opportunity to inspect the really palatial library with its handsome fittings, artistic decorations, and unique equipment in the way of library appliances.

At about 7.15 p.m. substantial refreshments were partaken of in the Reference Library, after which, for a short time, general conversation was indulged in, the gentlemen regaling themselves with the fragrant weed thoughtfully provided by the host. At 8.30 the real business of the evening began, Mr. Z. Moon, of Leyton, presiding. The formal proceedings ended, Mr. Cotgreave rose and, regretting the absence of his chairman, who was ill, extended a cordial welcome to the members and friends of the L.A.A. He said the meeting was an annual pleasure to him, and he hoped to be able to welcome the Association every year as long as he was spared. He was grateful for such a hearty appreciation of his efforts to entertain. He had a great regard for the L.A.A., and, passing on to the Education question, expressed the opinion that he believed in practical experience, and not in persons crawling in through the back door with certificates for theoretical knowledge. To the surprise of many, Mr. Cotgreave said that in his young days he had been a sailor, and described the system adopted by the Admiralty in constituting examinations, by which a man with little practical experience, but having a store of "book learning" could pass over the heads of men with invaluable experience but deficient theoretical knowledge. Not that he wished to deprecate theoretical education, but he felt that without due practical experience a man could not succeed as he should. He recommended assistants to attend the classes provided for them, and, as the librarian of the future must be a cultured man, hard study must supplement all the work in the library, if the proper degree of success was to be attained. Mr. Moon, after commenting on the meeting as a hardy annual for edification and delectation, and expressing himself a believer in combination and association for the improvement of the individual, called on Mr. T. W. Glazier to read his Essay, entitled: "Anticipated Developments of Library Practice," which had obtained the 1902 Cotgreave Prize.

The Essay opened a number of points concerning stocktaking, fines, charges for tickets or vouchers, rates, typewriting, printing, open access, catalogues, classification, lady assistants, and other cognate matters. A vigorous discussion was maintained by Messrs. Hatcher, Hogg, McDougall, Philip, Rees, Rivers, Savage, P. H. Wood, and Thorne. A vote of thanks to Mr. Glazier, for his Essay, was proposed by Mr. Chambers, who narrated the conditions of the competition, and seconded by Mr. Harris. On the motion of Mr. Rees, supported by Mr. F. Meaden Roberts, the hearty thanks of the Association were accorded to Mr. Cotgreave for his hospitality; to the Council for their welcome and permission to meet at the Library; and to the West Ham staff for their unselfish devotion to the comforts and requirements of all present. This was carried with enthusiasm. On the motion of Mr. Savage, seconded by Mr. Bullen, the thanks of the Association were then offered to Mr. Moon for presiding. At the close of the meeting members were presented with copies of Mr. Cotgreave's valuable "Contents-Subject Index," a much appreciated souvenir of a memorable gathering. W. B. T.

STUDY CIRCLE.

A distinct improvement in quality is noticeable in the answers to the January questions. As regards Question (7) this was, perhaps, to be expected, for the weekly time-sheet is, to most assistants, the object of careful study. A rather general mistake has been to assign hours to the librarian, who can rarely be counted upon to keep them. In Question (8) the usual fault was to calculate on the assumption that no books are larger than crown 8vo., and, therefore, over-estimating the capacity of the library. At least ten inches all round should be taken as the average height for shelves. Most students appear unable, or unwilling, to look beyond the pale of their own experience. As they can deal with ideal conditions and use imagination to infuse spirit into their grasp of practical principles, this adherence to the beaten track is a little disappointing.

Aedifico (7) 8.—A carefully inequitable arrangement. Apportions hours to librarian. Keeps on seven of staff after lending department has closed. On Monday two come at 9 a.m., on Wednesday four, on Saturdays four one week and two the next. Why?
    (8) 16.—Good.

Constantia (7) 15.—Very elaborate. To the individual assistant no two days are alike. It is a better principle to alter meal times as little as possible.
    (8) 13.—Impossible to get ten shelves all round in presses 8-ft. high. Floor space wasted in open access plan.

Local Boy (7) 12.—Arrangement not good. Four assistants in reference department too many. More time off should be allowed, and there is no need for so many on duty between 9 and 10 p.m.
    (8) 15.—Indicator plan good, but open access wasteful. Number of shelves to a press should have been given.

Nil Desperandum (7) 15.—See reply to *Constantia*. It is possible to arrange a time-sheet so that each assistant should commence work and go to his meals at the same hour at least five days out of six.
    (8) 10.—Capacity over-rated. Floor space wasted.

Papyrus (7) 12.—Badly arranged. A ruled time-sheet is preferable, as it shows at a glance what assistants are on duty at any particular time. Juniors ought not to be left in sole charge of departments. With two attendants an assistant on duty in the news-room ought not to be required.
    (8) 12.—Presses of 32-ft. are far too long, and 2-ft. is an excessive width. Plan (*b*) allows only 3-ft. between presses, whereas the open access system demands at least 4-ft.

Retwal (7) 17.—Neat and accurate, but librarian should not be counted on staff.

(8) 18.—Very good, but in open access plan the supervision would not be very efficient.

Stalky (7) 15.—Much care has evidently been taken with this answer, but in his anxiety to give the same number of hours to each assistant, Stalky brings most of the staff on duty at 9 on Wednesday, when they are not required. Juniors should not be left in charge of ref. Two hours for dinner is scarcely practicable or requisite.

(8) 12.—Particulars too meagre. We wanted actual figures, number of shelves to a press, etc., not approximations.

Temporal Power (7) 5.—The staff of ten includes the librarian. The library opens at 9 and the assistants arrive at 9.30. On Thursday the only assistant in the library goes to tea from 4 to 5.15, leaving the building to look after itself.

(3) 5.—Even if this student has no books to guide him and has to rely upon his own unaided intelligence, it is difficult to excuse such answers as these. "10-ft. presses, seven shelves to a press (*sic.*), total book capacity 20,000," is the sum total of his ideas on the question. Five minutes thought and a foot rule would have prevented such an exhibition.

QUESTIONS.

(11).—Write an essay (about 500 words) explaining the Dewey classification, pointing out its peculiarities, and what you consider to be its disadvantages.

(12).—Given a lending library where the books are closely classified upon the shelves, describe its working on an indicator system, explaining the charging and how to deal with additions. The same book number should be used for cataloguing, shelving, and for the indicator.

Answers should be sent not later than the 25th inst. to Mr. R. B. Wood, Public Library, Buckingham Palace Road, London, S.W., signed by a pseudonym.

ANTICIPATED DEVELOPMENTS OF LIBRARY PRACTICE.

By T. W. GLAZIER.

With reference to library practice anticipations are to be regarded more as suggestions, and as such will probably meet with little approval from members of the profession; but, nevertheless, if probability holds a place in one's anticipations, the possibility of them becoming future actualities may be reasonably entertained. One might dilate at much length upon a vast number of appliances and contrivances peculiar to the library world which bid fair to expand and develop new phases during the next few years, but space allows only sufficient license to deal with a few prominent features.

In his recently published and most excellent paper upon South African libraries, the Librarian of Kimberley incidentally states that, "In the case of large towns each library is considered on its merits, and a fixed grant is made in aid of general revenue, while special grants may be made in aid of Building Funds, Reference Libraries, &c." Then, although the system of levying a general rate is not in vogue among our Colonial colleagues, and existing conditions are admittedly much dissimilar, if the Government of Cape Colony is able to provide a yearly grant for its libraries, surely it is not too much to anticipate a like provision being made for those of the Mother Country by our own Government in the near future?

The amount of rate levied in support of the maintenance of the Public Libraries Acts differs in many boroughs, and much comment is made upon the point. It would not, therefore, be surprising if one common levy is made throughout the United Kingdom; a very probable development of the future.

The practice of lecturing in libraries has advanced much of late years, and although there is still a strong diversity of opinion among librarians as to lecturing being within the province of their profession, yet it is not assuming too much to predict the universality of the movement and to regard the lecturing librarian as a compulsion of the future, for few places of any standing can afford to dispense with this educational effort to promote the interests of their inhabitants.

In many boroughs numbers of inhabitants reside at a considerable distance from their libraries, a drawback which no doubt deters many of them from availing themselves of the privileges and aids which such institutions confer. Obviously, then, something is needed to bring these outlying districts into closer touch, and this matter has already occupied attention in some towns; the solution being found in travelling vans. It is likely, then, that in time to come nearly every library will possess a van for distributing and collecting books among residents living outside a certain radius; in fact, miniature travelling libraries somewhat akin to Mudie's, but of a more elevated status, and with the difference of the yearly subscription.

The educational value of our libraries is becoming recognised more every year, and in a few more will attain the same recognition as in America, becoming the habitual resorts of all scholars and students. As this progresses, no doubt colleges and schools of all grades will be brought into closer contact than at present, and means be devised whereby all students above a certain age will be able to obtain access and to make use of the books, special facilities being given to those seeking special information, or pursuing some particular branch of study.

In nearly all public reading-rooms the floors are of wood, which it is well known fosters much disease, more danger of infection being liable from this source, owing to the variety of individuals using the rooms, than might generally be supposed. This leads us to look for the tiled or stone paved floor in the libraries of the future, which, although requiring a greater outlay at first, will undoubtedly prove more economical in every way than the old "wooden" method.

Most institutions close for a short period (generally a week) at "stocktaking" time, and, indeed, it is necessary if the stock is to be correctly and systematically checked. Unfortunately, however, the average borrower cannot recognise this, possessing as he does the tendency to regard the library in the light of a grocer's shop, where the tradesman simply counts his pots of jam and jots the total down in a book, and this idea reluctantly compels us to forsee the future compulsory opening of lending departments during this none too pleasant, but most necessary, function of a librarian's duties. Not a desirable anticipation.

Some institutions publish monthly or quarterly journals containing matters of general interest to the library and lists of additional works added, with detailed annotations, and, as the practice seems to be much appreciated, no doubt all librarians will gradually adopt it.

In most boroughs the libraries are empowered to make a small charge for borrowers vouchers and to exact fines for the detention of books beyond the period allowed for reading, but these methods find little popularity, being regarded by the public somewhat as impositions, and a few years hence will see them no more, the compulsory free issue of the voucher and, perhaps, the temporary suspension of tickets, or something of a similar nature, displacing them.

There is ample scope for development in the matter of shelf classification. Existing methods each, of course, find many advocates, but *the* system has yet to be found, it is not yet, and there is room for a Solomon to arise in this department of library work with a plan which will meet the requirements of the future. Let us anticipate.

The "closed," "open access," and other systems have each aroused their Goliaths in the past, and much challenging has passed between the hosts as to their respective merits, but it is likely that during years to come an amalgamation of forces will take place; for a house divided against itself cannot stand. Possibly the solution may be the joint use of the "closed" and "open" methods; the closed system being used for the irrepressible fiction readers, and the open shelves for the benefit of those who read *literature*, the indicator being retained as being the best possible record of issued books. This is the much more probable should the libraries become at any time aided by the State, for a uniformity of principles and methods will be desirable.

Many members of the profession object to the card catalogue, some to the printed catalogue, and nearly all to the class list; but in many long established libraries with an ever increasing stock, future days may see these three going hand in hand. For it is evident that the fiction-reading public *will* have its printed list or key, and the only solution (which is to prevent an impossible printing bill) will be the combination of the card catalogue and cheap class list for the non-fictional portions of the stock; thus utilising all three systems.

With the innovation of the typewriter has gone to a large extent the old method of handwriting in many branches of the profession. Committee work, office work, and cataloguing all call for the exactness and legibility of the skilful typist's work, and excepting, perhaps, the entries made at the issuing desk, practically everything will in future be typewritten. Even the smallest branch library may have its typewriter, and the typist assistant will no doubt be a compelled evolution of the days to come.

Some central institutions are connected by telephone with their branches, a very useful and expense saving mode of communication, and probability points to every central building being so connected in the future. Electric lighting will, of course, also become general, and in buildings possessing more than one floor we may see lifts being utilised in preference to stairs. We may look forward also to some improved mode of heating, for the modes now generally in use leave much to be desired, the most commom complaints being of the time which it takes to heat even a small building properly, and of the stuffy atmosphere which is produced.

Perhaps in large towns each central library may possess its own printing machines and staff, and all printing for itself and branches be carried out "upon the premises." The same may be observed with regard to the establishment of a binding department in such places; both surely economical plans after the first outlay? Juvenile reading-rooms, too, will probably be more generally established than at present.

One development of the future is sure. Hitherto the Public Library in this country has been regarded more in the light of a recreational than educational institution, but this view is rapidly changing, and the fact that it *is* an educational factor of the people's interests is fast being recognised, and in a few years its position will rival that of the American Public Library.

Now that the Library Association has adopted the welcome though somewhat belated, plan of issuing professional certificates, it is plain to see that future appointments will fall largely upon assistants holding these evidences of capability, and those possessing none of these will stand small chance of attaining the tree-top of the profession. It is not, perhaps, beyond the range of this essay to mention this, and to also anticipate a keen competition for these awards of merit.

Coming to our last item in this list of anticipations we behold a gloomy horizon, beyond which lies the question of the "Female assistant." Of late years many towns and boroughs have acquired the services of female assistants for the obvious reasons that they may be procured at a much lesser wage, and that (as a London committee-man recently expressed it) "the employment of females in the library keeps the staff constantly young and fresh." A pleasing prospect truly, but one that hardly serves the *public* interest. It smacks rather too much of the fancy shop. In places where the female assistant is employed the staff is constantly changing, and the wealth of knowledge stored in the volumes behind the counter practically lost to the people. For it is only the maintenance of a permanent staff, which can become acquainted (through a fairly long stay among the books) with the riches of the particular library in which they are employed, which can serve the interests of the information-seeking borrowers.

But whatever opinions exist on this matter of female employment in libraries, it is no use disguising the fact that, like many other professions, ours bid fair to be over-run by the irrepressible female. For the whole matter is a question of finance after all, and to committees finance is everything, even to the expense of incompetent labour.

One gleam of hope stands out for our sex, and that is, that at least committees must draw the line at employing female *porters*. There is always *that* refuge for the poor mere male. But—let us here cease to anticipate.

CORRESPONDENCE.

DEAR MR. EDITOR,

The February meeting at West Ham, at which my Essay was read and discussed, appeared to me (apart from the kind hospitality of our host, Mr. Cotgreave) to be chiefly characterised by the absence of common sense criticism, and the presence of individuals whose chief object was apparently to pose as mines of information on the library world in general, and their own sphere of action in particular.

The fact that a semi-apology was made prior to the reading, expressing regret that the Essay dealt more with retrospection than anticipation, was mostly ignored by those taking part in the discussion, and the information disbursed by one critic respecting the already established travelling vans, etc., in some libraries (of which he proudly gave the names), was bestowed with a liberality as beautiful as it was superfluous.

Among other points, umbrage was taken (owing, I presume, to the presence of some members of the fair sex), at my usage of the term *female* assistants. It appeared that only the term *lady* assistants was allowable. I admire chivalry, but it might be pointed out that as the Government uses the term *female* when announcing its official examinations for the enrolment of its *lady* employees, it could hardly have been a matter of such importance for discussion that a humble individual as myself should see fit to use it also.

For the rest of the discussion which took place, Mr. Editor, I have nothing to remark: nothing of value was brought forward which could possibly cause me to retract the opinions embodied in my Essay. One thing, however, which caught my attention when listening to the views of our members, was the total lack of unity which betrayed itself. If, instead of placing their ideas in constant combat, they were to amicably compare them, debate upon them from all points, and manfully sink individual opinions beneath the scale which shows its advantage for the *general* good, then we should have unity, and this means strength. With strength what can we *not* do? Unity among ourselves will do more to attain the objects for which our Association was founded than any amount of biased discussion.

Yours very sincerely, Mr. Editor,
T. W. GLAZIER,
Tate Central Library, Streatham.

To the Editor of *The Library Assistant*.

Dear Sir,

Every year a number of members of the Library Assistants' Association are promoted to what has been called the "Upper House," and it has occurred to me that it would be a good thing if they came together at least once a year, say, at the Annual Meeting of the Library Association, for social and professional purposes. An Association of "Old Boys of the L.A.A." would have a sphere of influence which would constantly increase, and which could render great service to the cause of professional education.

Yours truly,
AMICUS.

To the Editor of *The Library Assistant*.

Sir,

Permit me to protest against the mis-statement concerning myself, made in your report of the January meeting of the Library Association, in your last number. I did *not* state that "I was heartily sick and tired of the whole business," *i.e.*, of the Education Question, nor make any remark of a similar sort in such a connection. It is a simple fabrication, and decency would suggest an apology—for which I wait.

The other unfairly and misleading reported statement of mine I pass, leaving the reporter to reconcile it with his own idea of good faith—such as it may be.

Faithfully yours,
L. STANLEY JAST.

[We very much regret the tone of Mr. Jast's letter, as not only in our own opinion, but in the opinion of others present, the report is a perfectly correct one. We think it more than likely that Mr. Jast's recollection of what he did say is confused by his remembrance of what he perhaps intended to say. Be that as it may, we do not feel called upon to reply to charges of bad faith and want of decency.—ED.]

NEW MEMBERS.

Senior.—Messrs. E. MALE, Brighton; A. C. PIPER, Brighton; R. W. BROWN, Northampton; B. J. FROST, East Ham; F. JACKSON, Pendleton Branch Library, Salford.

Junior.—Mr. A. FIELD, Brighton.

NOTES AND COMMENTS.

Kimberley.—We have received from Mr. Dyer a copy of the *Diamond Fields Advertiser*, in which appears a paragraph on the number of women applying for posts in South Africa. One would-be emigrant applied for a billet as librarian in an important South African library, and supported her application on the sole plea of having read a great deal of fiction, and of liking such reading! The modest salary which was expected in return for a course of novel reading was to amount to from £20 to £25 a month! The writer goes on to say that few realise the cost of living out there, and the difficulties to be overcome by those who emigrate in search of a living, and the manner in which there, as elsewhere, the unfit, whether physically or mentally, go to the wall.

Exeter.—We learn that the City Librarian, Mr. H. Tapley Soper, has lately issued a list of recent additions to the library, which has been very favourably commented upon in the local Press.

Chelsea.—The Borough Council propose abolishing the necessity for a guarantor's signature, the personal guarantee of the borrower being accepted as sufficient. To guard against losses under such a system it is suggested that a common insurance fund should be established by the metropolitan boroughs.

Stepney.—The Board of Guardians have decided to approach Mr. Carnegie for a grant in aid of a school library. As there is no question of the application of the Acts in a case of this kind, the issue may be watched with interest.

Dover.—Marylebone is not the only place which is disposed to examine a little closely Mr. Carnegie's gifts. At a meeting of the Dover Corporation on Tuesday there was an animated discussion as to whether the town ought to accept the American millionaire's offer of £10,000 for a public library building under the usual conditions. There was much discussion amongst the members as to whether it was desirable that the town should allow its hands to be forced. On a vote being taken on a motion to refer the matter to a committee for favourable consideration the numbers were found to be equal. The tie was decided by the Mayor giving his vote in favour of the proposal.—*London Argus*, Feb. 14th.

Society of Public Librarians.—A meeting of this Society was held at the Bishopsgate Institute on Wednesday, February 4th, when Mr. C. W. F. Goss, the hon. secretary, read a paper entitled, "Are our Public Libraries sufficiently attractive to the working classes?" Mr. Goss reviewed the possible extension of Public Library work, and held that the secret of the success of a library lies in the essentially popular nature of its work, and that by centralizing the various activities of each borough the good work done would be enormous as compared with that accomplished in a town where such interests are widely separated.

Hammersmith.—Six firms of architects have been invited to send in designs for the proposed central library building, the outcome of Mr. Carnegie's generosity.

King's Heath and Moseley.—Although it is eight months ago since Mr. Carnegie presented this district with £3,000 for the erection of a library, we understand from the daily Press that the authorities have been unable to obtain a site yet.

NEW BOOKS, &c.

"A Guide to the Best Historical Novels and Tales." By JONATHAN NIELD. Pp. 156. 2nd Edition. 1902. 8vo. 5s. net. London: Elkin Matthews.

A very carefully selected list of Historical Novels, divided into centuries and giving the title, author, publisher, and subject. Nearly 200 are given as dealing with the 18th century. Then follows a supplementary list of notable novels, which, while not strictly "Historical," in some way represent by-gone periods. Two suggested courses of reading (juvenile) are given covering English History from the Norman Conquest for boys and girls respectively. It is equipped with a Bibliography and indexes to the titles and authors mentioned. Baker's "Handbook to Fiction" (1899) does not appear in the Bibliography. The work will be a valuable aid to librarians.

Morley College Magazine. February.

Chorley Public Library: Third Annual Report. EDWARD McKNIGHT, Librarian.

Pratt Institute Free Library, Brooklyn, New York: Co-operative Bulletin. January and February. [Contains a reading list on the Pre-Wagnerian Opera.]

NOTICES.

All subscriptions are now due, and should be forwarded at once to the Hon. Treasurer, Mr. W. G. Chambers, Public Library, Woolwich, S.E.

All matter for April Journal should be sent to the Hon. Editor before March 20th.

All other communications should be addressed to the *Hon. Secretary*, Mr. G. E. Roebuck, PUBLIC LIBRARY, 236, CABLE STREET, E.

The Library Assistant:

The Official Organ of the Library Assistants' Association.

No. 64.   APRIL, 1903.   Published Monthly

APRIL MEETING.

This meeting will be held at the Shoreditch Central Library, Pitfield Street, on Wednesday, April 22nd, at 8.0 p.m., by kind invitation of Mr. Plant, the Borough Librarian. Mr. G. E. Roebuck (Stepney) will read a paper entitled "Literature for the Blind and the Public Library Movement in connection therewith." This paper will be supplemented by a display of charts and specimens of embossed work in all its varieties; stereotyping plates; writing and arithmetic frames; embossed maps, etc. Mr. Roebuck proposes to review the origin, progress, and present standing of the several styles, and his paper should prove of interest and practical use to our members. Ladies are cordially invited. Trains to Old Street, City and South London Electric Railway.

MARCH MEETING.

This meeting was held at the St. George, Hanover Square, Public Library, Buckingham Palace Road, on the 25th ult., and was well attended. In accordance with notice given Mr. Savage moved: "That a brief report on the relations of the Library Association and the Library Assistants' Association, during the past three years, with regard to the education of library assistants, be read and circulated for discussion at the Annual Meeting, 1903; that a *précis* of all letters, with one exception, relating to the same subject be attached to such report, the exception, namely, a certain letter, unauthorised by this Association, pleading for a less severe examination, and protesting against the 'open door' to be transcribed in full."

The motion was seconded by Mr. Philip, and supported by Messrs. Harris, Lewin, Pickard, Rivers, and Stevenson; Messrs. Chambers, Hatcher, McDouall, Rees, Thorne, and Wood opposing it. After a prolonged discussion the motion was put to the meeting and declared carried by 16 votes to 9.

The Chairman then called upon Mr. R. B. Wood, who opened a discussion on "Bookbinding for Public Libraries." After some remarks on a Form of Contract, he expressed the opinion that the Library Association should draw up a model specification for library binding. He described the various methods of binding used at the St. George's Libraries, and gave the results of his experience of the different materials, etc. He thought that Persian morocco did not deserve the bad name given to it by the Society of Arts Committee, and considered it eminently suitable for lending library work. He complained of the crude and inartistic finishing of most library binders, and had felt the want of some simple, neat designs for reference library bindings. He also touched on such points as tight backs and loose backs, and the special cases under which either were preferable.

Unfortunately, owing to the time taken up in discussing the motion at the opening of the meeting, Mr. Wood was unable to deal with his subject so fully as he had intended, and in consequence much interesting and valuable information was denied his audience. In the short time that remained after he had concluded, Messrs. Chambers, Harris, Hatcher, Philip, Rivers, Roberts, Savage, and Stevenson related their ideas and experiences on several points. It was suggested that as Mr. Wood had not been able to finish his remarks, he should continue on another occasion—a suggestion which met the approval of all present.

On the motion of Mr. Rees, seconded by Mr. Philip, the thanks of the meeting were gratefully accorded to Mr. Wood for his remarks, to the Library Committee for permission to meet there, and to Mr. Pacy for his kind welcome and hospitality.

At the conclusion of the meeting copies of the Souvenir of the Library Association Conference at Wigan in 1898 were distributed, this being a gift of the Library Supply Company, per Mr. W. W. Fortune, to whom the cordial thanks of the Association are offered.

T.

NORTH WESTERN BRANCH.

MARCH MEETING.

This meeting was held in the Central Library, Oldham, on Wednesday, the 25th ult., Mr. J. H. Swann presiding.

On arrival the members were shown through the Art Gallery and inspected the Annual Spring Exhibition of Pictures, afterwards proceeding to the Assistants' Room, when Mr. Haworth read the paper, "The Educational Basis of the Free Library Movement." In the course of the paper he traced briefly the development of the Library Movement from the passing of the Public Library Act down to the present time, showing the educational benefits derived by the gathering together of the best books and pictures by Municipal Corporations.

After a vigorous discussion by Mr. Bateman, Miss Alley, Messrs. Berry, Kirk, Percival, Shawcross, Swann, Quarmby, and a brief reply from Mr. Haworth, the best thanks of the meeting were tendered to Mr. Haworth for the paper, and to Mr. Bateman and Staff for the privilege of meeting at Oldham and for their hospitality.

APRIL MEETING.

The next meeting will be held in the Reference Library, King Street, Manchester, on April 21st, at 8 o'clock, when the paper by Mr. E. G. Rees, "The Educational Needs of Library Assistants," will be read for discussion.

CORRESPONDENCE.

To THE EDITOR OF *The Library Assistant.*

DEAR SIR,

Mr. Glazier appears to object to my criticism of his use of the term "female." The word he should have used is "women" assistants. Although "lady" is in this case incorrect, "female" is not only incorrect but insulting, inasmuch as it is used by the best writers to denote physical differences in sex.

I would also point out to Mr. Glazier that "anticipated developments" are not "bygone experiments."

Yours faithfully,
A. J. PHILIP.

March 16th, 1903.

FIFTH ANNUAL SOCIAL GATHERING.

Under the auspices of the Entertainment Sub-Committee a most successful Bohemian Concert was held on the 18th March, at Temple Bar, where some 90 members and friends foregathered. Mr. Evan G. Rees, Chairman of the L.A.A., occupied the chair, and was supported by Mr. Thomas Mason, Mr. Z. Moon, Mr. F. Meaden Roberts, the Hon. Treasurer, and others. The musical programme was long and varied, and its excellent quality was testified to by all. Mr. O'Dell, of the Savage Club, who was introduced by Mr. Mason, charmed the company with a recitation entitled, "An Ode to a Goose," and as an encore he gave a humorous song which was irresistible.

The humorous songs of Messrs. A. Gamgee, W. G. Hawkins (Fulham), A. Lanham, and F. Schofield (Battersea) added greatly to the enjoyment of those present, whilst the admirably rendered songs of Miss May Marelle, Miss F. North (Battersea), and Messrs. A. Cogswell (Balham), C. Collins, C. J. Courtney (Minet), A. Howes, A. J. Moorco, W. Rees, W. J. Vellenoweth (Camberwell), and W. B. Young (Leyton), were much appreciated. Instrumental music was represented by Mr. A. M. Moslin (Stepney), Mr. A. H. Crouch, and Mr. F. C. Chidgey, who gave violin, cornet, and mandoline solos respectively. Mr. A. S. Crouch, with his customary kindness, presided at the piano.

Credit is due to Mr. C. A. Bradley, the Hon. Secretary of the Committee, for the satisfactory management of the arrangements. C.

STUDY CIRCLE.

As the questions set in the February number made perhaps a greater demand upon the time and ability of the students than any previous questions, it is gratifying to us to record that, so far from there being a diminution in the number of answers received, there has been an increase. Question (9) on the whole has not produced much noticeable work, the students confining themselves to the pound of flesh demanded, and refusing to make further inroads in a search after "etc." Question (10) on the other hand, has brought out some original ideas, and the plans generally were very creditable. The second part of the question called up several eccentricities, and one plan was distinctly reminiscent of the maze at Hampton Court. The position of the staircase caused some trouble, but only one student cut the Gordian Knot by omitting it altogether. Most of the plans were carefully drawn to scale, a very commendable feature.

Aedifico (9). 15.—Good. Might have been fuller.

(10) 15.—(*a*). Reference readers have to traverse newsroom. Librarian's office badly placed. Insufficient space between presses in lending department, 2-ft. 6ins. (*b*) Boys' Room too large. Newsroom too small. Shelves scattered. Stairs not wide enough, 4-ft. Shape of reference book store very awkward.

Benedick (9) 13.—Wants precision. "Punctuation is left to the cataloguer's discretion"!
  (10) 8.—(a) Not bad. Bookcases of 20-ft. are too long. (b) Not attempted.
Breton (9) 11.—Vague and rather careless. Three errors in grammar and spelling.
Constantia (9) 9.—Neither systematic nor complete.
  (10) 16.—(a) Good; 900 square feet of corridor is liberal. Wall cases are preferable in reference departments. (b) Supervision on first floor difficult. Boys' rooms ought to be on ground floor.
Index (9) 13.—Not sufficiently detailed or explicit. Very liberal with caps.
  (10) 13.—(a) Badly arranged. Insufficient shelving: wall space ought to be utilised for presses and news slopes. Entrances badly placed. (b) News-room too small. The only entrance is through the lending department. Most of the other rooms have no apparent entrances. On the second floor the landing appears in the centre of the reference counter.
Papyrus (9) 19.—Very good.
  (10) 9.—The reverse. (a) Lavatories take up 675 square feet, corridors 1,150, a total of 1,825 square feet out of 9,600. The news and magazine rooms are very inadequate, and it is no wonder. (b) The two floors are of entirely different shapes, and we cannot imagine any method by which they may be joined—which renders immaterial the fact that no staircase is provided. As to interior economy, the news-room is half the size of the reference, which has an eccentric fringe of bookcases jutting from the walls at every conceivable absurd angle.
Nil Desperandum (9) 8.—Reads like a bad copy of *Constantia*; we apologize if our suspicions are unfounded.
  (10) 10.—(a) Librarian poked away in a corner. Too much counter (260-ft.). Newsroom and reference too small for size of building. (b) Great waste of space throughout; one third of ground floor taken up by hall.
Retwal (9) 19.—Very good and well arranged.
  (10) 16.—(a) Has many good points; would be improved, we think, by the lending department changing places with the news-room and the reference with the magazine room. No office for Librarian. (b) Nearly three-quarters of floor taken up by hall and lending department. This should be reduced and the space thus gained thrown into news-room.

QUESTIONS.

(13).—Give the Dewey numbers for twelve of the following works:

Pearson.	"The chances of death."
Ball.	"Story of the heavens."
Ruskin.	"Eagle's nest."
————	"Queen of the air."
Lang.	"Cock Lane and common-sense."
Ribot.	"Diseases of memory."
Lavater.	"Essays on physiognomy."
Stephen.	"The English utilitarians."
Watson.	"The mind of the master."
Guest.	"Mabinogion."
Machiavelli.	"The Prince."
Bardsley.	"English surnames."
Frazer.	"The golden bough."

Bickerdyke.	"Curiosities of ale and beer."
Cox.	"Continuous-current dynamos and motors."
Crocker and Wheeler.	"Practical management of dynamos and motors."
Grimwood.	"My three years in Manipur."
Williams.	"Round London."

(14).—Name the headings under which each of the twelve books should appear in a dictionary catalogue.

Answers should be sent not later than the 30th inst. to Mr. R. B. Wood, Public Library, Buckingham Palace Road, London, S.W., signed by a pseudonym.

With these questions the Circle closes. A final report on the whole session will appear in the June number.

NOTES AND COMMENTS.

Exeter.—A porter in the employ of the Royal Albert Memorial Public Library has been sentenced to six months imprisonment for stealing books, drawings, engravings, etc., to the value of £100. The discovery of the thefts was due to an inventory being taken by the recently appointed librarian, Mr. H. Tapley Soper. As the accused showed great regret and rendered considerable assistance in the recovery of the property he was dealt with as leniently as the law would allow.

Library Association.—An examination in Cataloguing, Classification, and Shelf Arrangement (Section 2 of the Examination Syllabus) will be held on Wednesday, May 6th, 1903. Intending candidates must send in their names to Mr. H. D. Roberts, 44A, Southwark Bridge Road, S.E., by Saturday, April 25th. Centres will be arranged to suit the convenience of the candidates.

Stoke Newington.—There is a proposal afoot for the establishment of a museum in connection with the public library; the gift of a valuable collection of objects having been offered by Aske's Schools, Shoreditch. A farthing rate is suggested.

NEW BOOKS, &c.

Bootle Free Library, Museum and Technical School Journal. March. (C. H. HUNT, Librarian).

Contains eighteen pages of literary matter and four of additions to the Library—a somewhat unusual proportion. Cannot some local genius design a more artistic cover for this welcome little journal?

Croydon Public Libraries: The Reader's Index. March and April. (L. S. JAST, Librarian).

Contains the usual pithily annotated list of additions, and a really valuable annotated Reading List of books in the Libraries on Education, compiled by Mr. Robert Stevenson, of the L.A.A. We venture to think, however, that the abbreviations are somewhat overdone.

Descriptive Guide to the Best Fiction, British and American; including Translations from foreign languages; containing about 4,500 references; with copious indexes and a historical appendix. By ERNEST A. BAKER, M.A. (Lond.). (Swan, Sonnenschein & Co., Ltd. Pp. vii. + 610. 8vo. 8s. 6d. net).

Last month it was our privilege to notice a similar work by Mr. Jonathan Nield, now comes this monument of industry by the Librarian of the Midland Railway Institute. We suppose it is the outcome of his " Descriptive Handbook to Noteworthy Works of Fiction " published in 1899; be that as it may, the present volume will be a valuable aid to librarians, and we gratefully thank Mr. Baker for it. We notice that it has already been spoken well of in the daily Press, and it is fully deserving of all the praise it gets. First, there are 190 pages, giving short, succinct notes on the principal English fiction of the 19th century, then Scottish, Irish, American, Belgian, Dutch, French, German, Hungarian, Italian, Scandinavian, Finnish, Slavonic, Russian, Spanish, and Portuguese fiction is dealt with in the same way. An historical chronological appendix follows in the same order, after which is an index of authors and titles with a subject index in conclusion. We wish we had space to quote some of the annotations, or descriptions, which give a brief outline of the plot, a note on the style, and generally an estimate of the literary or historical value of the work, but under the circumstances this is impossible. We may add that to each note is also appended the best available editions; the publisher's name; the price and the date of first publication. This work must, we feel, become one of the most valued of a librarian's " tools," and we congratulate the compiler on the results of his labour. This copy will be placed in the L.A.A. Library.

Leyton Public Library Magazine. February. (Z. MOON, Librarian).

Annotated list of additions, and an interesting biographical note on an old Essex worthy, Thomas Tusser. We notice that this individual's second wife was a daughter of *Edmund Moon*, and we wonder if this was an ancestor of the genial Leyton Librarian.

Pratt Institute Free Library and Brooklyn Public Library: Co-operative Bulletin. February.

Revista delle Biblioteche e degli Archivi. February.

Revue des Bibliothèques et Archives de Belgique. No. 1, January—February. (Rédacteur, L. STAINIER).

A journal for the review of library matters and affairs connected with the preservation and registration of local historical documents in Belgium. The address "*à nos lecteurs*" runs into six pages and sets forth a rather ambitious programme, which will be instructive and useful if carried out.

We wish the venture success and hope to have the opportunity of noticing future issues. One article in this first number gives an account of the tercentenary celebrations at the Bodleian Library.

APPOINTMENTS.

*MARRIOTT, Mr. E., Assistant, Portico Library, Manchester, to be Librarian.

*McDOUGALL, Mr. D., Public Library, Canning Town, to be Assistant-in-Charge of the Passmore Edwards Public Library, Plaistow, E.

*FRETTEN, Mr. H. W., Central Library, West Ham, to be Second Assistant at the Public Library, Canning Town.

LUCY, Miss, Chief Assistant, Worcester Public Library, to be Librarian of Great Malvern.

NEWCOMBE, Mr. C. F., of Toynbee Hall, to be Assistant Librarian, Central Library, Camberwell.

*SHARP, Mr. E. T., Public Library, Canning Town, to be Second Assistant at the Passmore Edwards Library, Plaistow.

Members of the L.A.A.

NEW MEMBER.

Junior.—Mr. STEPHEN LAUGHTON, Derby.

APPOINTMENTS VACANT.

[**Notice to Library Authorities.**—*We shall be pleased to publish under this heading, free of charge, particulars of vacancies if full details are sent to the Editor on or before the 28th of each month.*]

NOTICES.

All subscriptions are now due, and should be forwarded at once to the Hon. Treasurer, Mr. W. G. Chambers, Public Library, Woolwich, S.E.

All matter for May Journal should be sent to the Hon. Editor before April 20th.

All other communications should be addressed to the *Hon. Secretary*, Mr. G. E. Roebuck, PUBLIC LIBRARY, 236, CABLE STREET, E.

The Library Assistant:

The Official Organ of the Library Assistants' Association.

No. 65.   MAY, 1903.   Published Monthly.

MAY MEETING.

By special permission of Sir E. Maunde Thompson, K.C.B., D.C.L., this Meeting will be held at the British Museum on Wednesday, May 13th, when the members will be conducted round the Libraries, by Mr. G. K. Fortescue, Keeper of Printed Books, assisted by his colleagues. Members and friends will gather on the Museum steps at 2.50 p.m., and all who intend being present should not be later, as, after the party have commenced the tour of the Libraries, it will be inconvenient for late arrivals to join. This opportunity of viewing our National Library, under such exceptional circumstances, should not be missed, and we hope to see a good gathering.

APRIL MEETING.

As announced, this Meeting took place at the Shoreditch Public Library, Pitfield Street, N., on Wednesday, 22nd ultimo, and was exceptionally well attended. Mr. W. C. Plant, Borough Librarian, occupied the chair, and expressed his pleasure at seeing the L.A.A. again in Shoreditch. Our Hon. Secretary, Mr. G. E. Roebuck (Stepney), read a thoughtful and exhaustive paper on "Literature for the Blind," which not only interested everybody present, but reflected great credit on the reader for the evident pains he had taken to make the subject as entertaining and instructive as possible. The paper, which will be printed *in extenso* in our next issue, will be invaluable to any seeking information on the subject, and will have the further advantage of being reliable in every respect, written, as it is, by one with much experience and practical observation in all its details. Mr. Plant reviewed the paper, and Messrs. Chambers, Cawthorne, Harris, Hatcher, Philip, Rees, and Savage, added their views and experiences on several points. A hearty vote of thanks to Mr. Roebuck was moved from the chair, and seconded by Mr. Rees, who also proposed a vote of thanks to Mr. Plant for his presence and chairmanship. This was seconded by

Mr. Chambers, and carried unanimously. After the meeting the members and friends examined with interest a number of examples of Moon, Braille, and other embossed types, together with embossed maps, writing appliances, and other items Mr. Roebuck had brought to illustrate his paper.

THE COMMITTEE.

In view of certain inaccuracies in the motion proposed and carried by Mr. Savage at the March meeting, the Committee decided at their last meeting to take no action in the matter. The Association year now drawing to a close, nominations must be made for the Committee and Officers for next Session. They should be made in writing, and addressed to the Hon. Secretary, who should have them in his possession by May 19th. Notices of motion for the Annual Meeting should also be sent to the Secretary by this date. At the May meeting, two Auditors will be elected to examine the accounts of the past year. Nominations may be handed to the Hon. Secretary at the commencement of the proceedings.

Difficulty having frequently been experienced in securing a convenient meeting place for Committee and sometimes ordinary meetings, the Committee have, as an experiment, engaged a room at the St. Bride Foundation Institute, Bride Lane, E.C., to be at their disposal for a certain number of evenings. If the arrangement proves satisfactory, some more definite action may be taken in the matter.

NORTH-WESTERN BRANCH.

APRIL MEETING.

This meeting was held on April 21st in the Reference Library, Manchester, Mr. J. H. Swann presiding, when Mr. E. G. Rees' paper, *"The Educational Needs of Library Assistants," was read by the Chairman. The discussion was taken up by Messrs. Haworth, Gordon, T. Smith, Swann, Quarmby and Dallimore.

The feeling of the meeting, as evinced by the brisk discussion was that the technical and business side of librarianship ought to form the principal element of any professional instruction by means of classes—correspondence or otherwise.

The literary side has a profusion of text-books, etc., by means of which private study can in some measure be undertaken ; consequently what small amount of spare time is available for

---

* See " Library Association Record," February, 1903.

attendance at classes should be occupied with subjects for which no text-books exist. Unfortunately in all Summer School schemes, classes, and the Library Association professional examination the literary and bibliographical element is always overwhelmingly large in proportion to the technical and business.

MAY MEETING.

The next meeting will be held on Wednesday, May 20th, at 7.30 p.m., in the Blackley Branch Library, Manchester. Cars from High Street, corner Market Street, to the Library door. The subject chosen for discussion is the chapter on Public Libraries in Zueblin's "American Municipal Progress."

1903 Subscriptions to the North-Western Branch are now due and should be forwarded at once to the Treasurer (Mr. W. Crompton, Y.M.C.A., 56 Peter Street, Manchester).

MANCHESTER PUBLIC LIBRARIES.
JUBILEE CELEBRATIONS, APRIL 2ND AND 3RD, 1903.

Fifty years of the Public Library movement includes the development of Free Libraries from their birth to the present day, and the Manchester Jubilee Commemoration constitutes the first great historical landmark in their progress. It was only fitting, then, that this should be celebrated in a manner worthy of its importance; and that this was the case is easily shown when we refer to the illustrious names of those who took part in the proceedings.

Arrangements made for the guests included their reception; visits to the Branch Libraries and other places of special interest; but the two most important functions were the speeches in the Whitworth Hall, Owens College, and the Manchester Free Trade Hall. The former meeting was held in the morning, April 3rd, when, after a congratulatory message from the King, significant and important utterances were made by Councillor Plummer, Chairman of the Manchester Free Libraries Committee, Professor Macneile Dixon, Mr. Tennant, M.P., Sir F. Bridge, Professor Boyd Dawkins, Dr. A. Hopkinson, Sir J. C. Browne and others, including Dr. Garnett, who emphasised the necessity for paying librarians more adequate salaries in relation to the educational importance of their work.

It was the evening meeting, however, which stirred the hearts of library enthusiasts, and its only parallel in Manchester is the Public Library Inauguration Movement in 1852, when the first Public Library was opened. A sense of continuity and connection, a link with the past, was happily given by the presence of Earl Lytton, whose speech included a flattering testimony of Manchester's loyalty to the Public Library movement.

The first speech was delivered by Lord Avebury, who dwelt on the advantages of reading and the solid work now being done by free libraries. He said we must not be too apt to judge the result of this by the apparent large issue of novels, but must remember that more serious works took much longer to read, and therefore showed badly by a mere statistical comparison. The Bishop of Manchester followed by a cheerful, homely address, carrying the audience entirely with him as he spoke on the value of reading to himself and what it could easily be to the working man. He raised the audience to a very high pitch of enthusiasm, which remained the prevailing tone for the rest of the evening. Miss Burstall spoke of the importance of libraries in educating and interesting women, giving a very impressive speech. She was followed by Sir J. C. Browne, who pointed out the value of free libraries as the natural means by which men can exercise all the faculties of their brains and thus protect themselves from the atrophy threatened by the concentration of one faculty alone on some special branch of work. Other speakers followed, and the proceedings closed after a very stirring meeting.

Many beautifully illuminated addresses of congratulation were presented to the Committee, amongst which was one from the Library Association.

F. W. B. H.

SOCIETY OF PUBLIC LIBRARIANS.

A meeting of the Society of Public Librarians was held at the Bishopsgate Institute, E.C., on Wednesday evening, April 1st, when Mr. Frank E. Chennell (Willesden Green) read a paper entitled, "Some notes on Public Library Committees." In the course of his paper Mr. Chennell spoke of the differently constituted bodies which now form the Library Committee, viz.: Library Commissioners, the Urban or Borough Council which takes entire control, and the other method whereby the Committee is composed one half of members of the local authority and one half of co-opted members. The latter, Mr. Chennell thought, formed the ideal Library Committee, inasmuch as the co-opted members in most cases had a long and intimate association with the Library. They were often concerned in the movement for the adoption of the Act; they were acquainted with the history of the building, and with the slow and steady growth of the Library as a book world; and, therefore, the better able to judge the needs of the Library, and certainly the more capable of appreciating all that is good in the Librarian. Coming to the other half of this composite committee, the Council representatives, Mr. Chennell held that these should in every respect hold briefs for the governing authority. They have to watch and to advise concerning the finances, and to see that no expenditure is incurred that cannot be sanctioned, or to which the Local Government auditor may take exception. After touching upon the various types of committee-men and the value of each in the management of the Library, Mr. Chennell dealt with the duty of the Librarian towards his committee, pointing out that the well-being, the usefulness, and the popularity of the institution depends mainly upon the relationship existing between the Library Committee and the Librarian. Mr. Chennell said that the chief aim, the chief duty, should be not so much to please as to inspire confidence, though sometimes difficult to accomplish, and requiring a vast amount of patience and tact. When once gained, however, it was not easily to be shaken.

LIBRARY BASEMENTS.

Many Library basements are the repositories of a heterogeneous mass of worn out or disused appliances and waste paper, but the authorities of the Minet Library, Camberwell, have hit upon the happy idea of putting a number of miniature forms and tables in their basement for the use of young people between the ages of seven and fourteen years. The boys are separated from the girls by means of a partition. Lining one wall are book shelves holding 1,400 vols. suitable for young intellects. A counter runs in front of these shelves, over which the books are issued by two junior members of the staff, who keep a certain amount of order. There are no "Silence" notices to depress the feelings of the readers, and it is better so, as the youngsters often draw each others notice to interesting things in their reading.

A novel feature is the Drawing Room. This is not a room for afternoon tea, but drawing books are supplied and the children are allowed to draw under the supervision of one of the juniors. Needless to say that the rooms are well patronised and the clean, happy, intelligent faces form an inspiring sight. Probably many a Library has a well-lighted basement, easy of access, which could be used in this way at little cost instead of remaining a wilderness.

W. L. C.

THE EDUCATIONAL BASIS OF THE FREE LIBRARY MOVEMENT.

By Fred W. B. Haworth.

[A Paper read at the March Meeting of the N.W. Branch.]

At practically all the meetings of this Association I have attended, and in many conversations I have had with library assistants, I have been struck with the pessimism amongst them with regard to library work, and their apparent failure to understand the fundamental basis on which the Free Library Movement stands, *i.e.*, education. I do not know that it is altogether my purpose to discuss the causes of this pessimism, &c., real as I believe them to be; but what I really do wish to bring out is that the Free Library Movement ought to be educational, progressive, and ideal, and to endeavour to show you that in the past a number of serious-minded men did not fear to speak out in decisive terms what it was they expected this movement to stand for and what should be its aims.

To understand it in its natural significance it is necessary to take a backward step, historically speaking, and clearly understand what the pioneers of Free Libraries intended, and on what lines they expected them to develop, and, further, what was their attitude of mind towards the movement generally. Going back some fifty odd years we find, even in such a dry, matter-of-fact volume as "The Report of the Select Committee on Public Libraries, 1849," quite a number of passages relative to the purpose of this paper. For instance, on page 8 of the Report it says, speaking of the development of lecturing, then much in fashion, "The lecturer himself frequently needs the assistance of books. His hearers naturally wish to pursue, by means of books, the subject on which his lectures have interested or instructed them. The power of access to standard works would tend to render the lecturer less superficial, and to promote investigation among his hearers." Again, mentioning the 'increase of classical publications, " The tendency towards popular publications in Great Britain —the result in a great degree of our superior capital and enterprise— would seem not only to facilitate, but to invite, the formation of public libraries. It is also truly observed that the establishment of such depositories of standard literature would lessen, or perhaps entirely destroy, the influence of frivolous, unsound, and dangerous works. Your Committee are glad to take this opportunity of echoing an opinion expressed by M. Van de Weyer: 'I should positively say that first-rate books ought to be put in the hands of the people instead of inferior publications. They enjoy and feel the beauties of the higher class of literature as deeply as any literary man; as in our theatres they applaud the very passages which a literary man would most admire.' This opinion is strongly confirmed by Mr. Imray, even as regards the readers in the libraries of our ragged schools. Mr. Imray is asked, 'When they (the frequenters of such libraries) read the better class of books, do they prefer them to the books you have spoken of (the inferior books)?' Answer: 'So much so that I do not think they would ever return to the lower class of books after having read the other (the better) books.' Shall we, therefore, abandon the people to the influence of a low, enfeebling, and often pestilential literature, instead of enabling them to breathe a more pure, elevated, and congenial atmosphere?"

Also, on page 11, we have the following: "By such means (the formation of village libraries) the frivolous or unprincipled books which now circulate among our rural population, may be replaced by sound, healthy, and genuinely English literature. The people may be taught many lessons which concern their material (as well as their moral and religious) welfare.

The cleanliness and ventilation of their dwellings, habits of providence, of temperance, a taste for something better than mere animal enjoyment, may be instilled into them through the instrumentality of well-chosen books."

The Minutes of Evidence, following the Report, afford much that is noteworthy in support of the educational value—or what was then supposed would be the educational value—of Public Libraries. To make a large number of extracts would be exceedingly tedious, however interesting, so I have contented myself by making only one, which is from the evidence given by Mr. Ewart and part of a letter written by Mr. John Bathgate, secretary to the Peebles Institution. It is as follows: "It is impossible to estimate the benefit which will ultimately accrue to the population from the (Peebles Public) library. There are several young men of humble parents who are educating themselves as students of divinity and teachers, to whom such a respository of historical works and general literature must be of great service in prosecuting their studies privately. The establishment of a public library in a country district affords the means of self-instruction to such as are desirous to rise from the condition in which they may be originally placed. If affords the means also of encouraging a taste for reading, and thereby weaning the young men from many of the destructive pursuits in which, if left occupied in their leisure moments, they are too apt to be engaged. Their morals are improved, and they again re-act on their families and the society of the place generally, with a salutary effect. . . . It has been said that legislation on this subject is unnecessary; that the elevation of the people ought to begin with themselves to be effectual. It is true that any efforts for the amendment of the masses will be to a great extent inoperative if not supported by them. But it is equally true that the initiative must be taken by those above them. The hand must be held out to them before they will attempt or be able to rise. It may be urged as the duty of a paternal Government to depart occasionally from the negative system pursued in this country, and render positive assistance to the people in giving them ample opportunity to enlarge their minds, improve their time, and become better members of society by gratifying the inherent desire for information which exists in every man more or less, and only requires to be called into exercise to be increased and strengthened."

Mr. Dawson, at a later date, 1866, speaking at the opening of the the Birmingham Reference Library, gave utterance to many striking thoughts descriptive of the power and use of libraries. He said, amongst other things, "Thus, whether I take it as a question of utility, of pastime, or of high discipline, I find the library—with but one or two exceptions—the most blessed place that man has fashioned or framed. The man who is fond of books is usually a man of lofty thought, of elevated opinions. A library is a strengthener of all that is great in life and the repeller of what is petty and mean; and half the gossip of society would perish if the books that are truly worth reading were but read. . . . But as we cannot dwell upon all the uses and beauties of a library let us pass on to see that this is a Corporation Library, and in that we see one of the greatest and happiest things about it, for a library supported as this is, by rates, and administered by a Corporation, is the expression of a conviction on your part that a town like this exists for moral and intellectual purposes. It is a proclamation that a great community like this is not to be looked upon as a fortuitous concourse of human atoms, or as a miserable knot of vipers struggling in a pot, each aiming to get his head above the other in the fierce struggle of competition. It is a declaration that the Corporation of a great town like this has not done all its duty when it has put in action a set of ingenious contrivances for cleaning and lighting the streets, for breaking stones, for mending ways; and has not fulfilled its highest functions even when it has given the people of the town the best system of drainage. Beyond all these the Corporation of a borough like this has every function to discharge that is discharged by the master of a household—to minister to men by every office, that of the priest excepted. And mark this; I would rather a great book or a great picture fell into the hands of a Corporation than into the hands of an individual. For the moment you put great works into the hands of a corporate body like this you secure permanence of guardianship in passionless keeping."

May I now turn your attention for a few moments to Mr. Greenwood's "Place of Public Libraries in our National Life"? In it he says, "The higher life of the citizen has received too little attention and the lower and baser life seems to have absorbed all the sympathy and care of the authorities. But we have touched the fringe of better days, and soon no municipality or local governing body will be considered complete unless it has under its administration a library and a museum, as well as a workhouse, a prison, and the preservers of law and order. It is for the provision for this higher national life that this place is made, and upon municipalities is urged the need of giving the fullest and best attention to this question. The fact should be emphasized that the municipality can do for the people in the way of libraries and museums what cannot possibly be done by private enterprise. . . . The public library movement, however, represents the determination of the community to offer special facilities for the cultivation of the mind, at the expense of the community itself. The educational welfare of the multitude has, at length, become a matter of importance to us all. There has been a revolution of public opinion as to the true functions of public libraries. For a time they may be said to have had only a slight relation to the life of the community, but the authorities are now ready to acknowledge that success or failure is to be measured by the extent to which they come in contact with, and shape for good, the mental life of the nation."

Let us consider the question in this light—"the mental life of the nation." You may urge that there are many libraries throughout the country which are simply fiction-lending institutions, and could be very questionably supposed to be adding stimulus to the national mental life. Yes, but I would remind you these are not the only ones; and it ought never to be forgotten that the utility of large municipal libraries, such as Birmingham, Liverpool, and Manchester, can be carried out to a greater or lesser degree in these smaller libraries. That is provided you have the educational nucleus in their vicinity, in the shape of a good committee and so forth, and a broad-minded, well-educated man as librarian. For here, as in any other place, the subtle individuality of a man of culture and refinement, striving for what he believes to be of vital importance, will, unless he is tied down by the exigencies of non-expansive authority, permeate library, staff, and borrowers in such a manner as shall conduce to education of the highest and deepest kind.

It is a mistake, I think, to consider education as only of one order. Indeed, it were a poor look out for some of us if this were so. But it consists neither in commercial acumen nor stereotyped professionalism; nay, rather such ideal educational reformers as Froebel, Pestalozzi, and Ruskin have placed it in very different, and what would now be regarded as very homely objects; and yet, it is by cultivation of these very objects that a man is most likely to be of service, to the many people he will come in contact with, as librarian.

I would make the call to us library assistants of the very highest order, and lay the deepest stress on the value of our work; for in us, if we do our work well, lies the safeguard of the Free Library movement in the future. Even now, as I write, a controversy is silently waging in the *Manchester Guardian*, and, perhaps, even more powerfully in the mind of many a humble citizen, calling attention to the fact that the movement, so far as it affects the working classes, is falling away from the high aspirations of its founders. It would be idle of me to suggest for one moment that the cause of this lay in the hands of its present administrators; because I believe the root of the evil to be far deeper seated, and vested in the complex machinery of our social life, which, despite its complexity, is quite inadequate to carry out the schemes of social reformers, either past or present. But the question becomes a vital one if we wish to remain in the library world, and needs our whole-heartedness and broadest sympathies if we are to help to re-establish the fundamental value of our work.

I know, only too well, that to many of us the outlook has often appeared gloomy, but—and the whole weight of the question bears on this—are you interested in your work? Does it tend to bring out the best within you? Old-fashioned notions these, you may think, but, nevertheless, the soundest you can apply to judge yourself and your work by. If I put the question to myself, I reply immediately in the affirmative, when I am permitted to come in contact with the higher branches of the work; for then my interest and sympathies being fully aroused, I feel the pride one has a right to feel, and can look forward with hope. But, if I am always to be regarded as a mere mechanical appliance, with no opportunity to lift up my eyes to the hills, then I say "No," and so ought every library assistant who respects himself and wishes to respect his occupation.

You will see that I have made this paper very personal. What else could I do to bring the matter out in its proper light, believing the vocation of the library assistant to be very vital to the welfare of the Library Movement? Let us remember that we stand measured by a very high standard, if we are to aid and contribute to the development of "the mental life of the nation." Let us search and know ourselves from every point of view, seeking by organisation, education, and frankness, to mould public opinion, library committees, and library associations, to that great and high ideal, the education of the people, prophesied and looked forward to by the pioneers of Public Free Libraries. And, if at any time we falter, let us remember it is not the nobleness of our calling which is at fault, but the controlling power of some outside force that has not yet learnt, or been allowed to learn, the fulness of the larger life. We, who are yet young and unaffected by the pessimism of stagnation, ought to carry on the work to the best of our ability, and leave its position clear and well defined for those who follow after us.

Do not misunderstand me by thinking I expect these attributes of library assistants are easy to acquire. I do not. I know too well the difficulties in the way, such as long hours, small pay, and limited opportunity for self-improvement. Yet, in spite of all these obstacles, if we really make up our minds to succeed, I think we can influence far more than at first sight one would imagine. The great key, admitting us to a deeper interest in our work, is association, companionship. Very often it seems a large sacrifice to attend such meetings as these; but those who do attend them, and those of the Summer School, know their worth and their influence for good in many directions. We know the value of this association, and cherish the comradeship it also brings. It is to such organisations as these one is compelled to look for the moving spirit which is to teach the library assistant his part in the

Library movement and enable him to voice those ambitions and aspirations which are so often liable to be hidden under the lethargy which creeps on through lack of healthy stimulation, and which are far too little helped by the bodies at present controlling public libraries, which bodies in many cases have only insufficiently realised the educational power for which these libraries stand. The uses of this stimulation, or, to be more correct, natural development through association, have been very graphically described by Sir E. M. Thompson, when speaking at the Library Association Meeting, Reading, in 1890. He said: "Upon the practical advantage which is gained by these meetings I need not enlarge. The fact that they are held and are so well attended is sufficient indication of your estimation of their utility. It is not the mere discussion of points of library management, the hearing of papers and the other solemn parts of the business of our meetings which recommend them to your attendance and your attention. It is still more the fact that here you stand face to face, that you interchange ideas, that you see what manner of men you individually are, and that when you part company and separate to your homes you carry back with you a personal knowledge of your fellows, and, I trust, a higher view of your duties and an encouragement to still more strenuous exertions. 'Iron sharpeneth iron ; so a man sharpeneth the countenance of his friends.'"

In closing let me read these words of Sydney Smith (quoted in Greenwood's "Public Libraries"), which are inscribed upon the walls of more than one Public Library in the United States:—

"Therefore when I say, in conducting your understanding, love knowledge with a great love, with a vehement love, with a love co-eval with life, what do I say but love innocence, love purity—love that which, if you are rich, will sanctify the blind fortune which made you so, and teach men to call it justice—love that which, if you are poor, will make poverty respectable, and forbid the proudest to mock the meanness of your fortune—love that which will comfort and adorn you, and open to you the kingdom of thought and all the boundless regions of conception. Therefore if any young man has embarked his life in the pursuit of knowledge let him go on without doubting the result. Let him not be daunted by her cheerless beginnings, or by the difficulties hovering round her. Let him rather follow her as the angel that guards him, and the genius of his life. She will bring him out at last into the light of day."

STOKE NEWINGTON.

The Borough Council at its meeting on April 21st decided by 17 votes to 3 not to adopt the Museums Act. Our contemporary, the *Library World*, announced in its March issue that the Act *had* been adopted, but its prophecy has not turned out to be very accurate!

STUDY CIRCLE.

The Report on the March questions is held over until next month, when the final Report on the work of the Session will appear.

COTGREAVE PRIZE ESSAYS (1903).

The subjects chosen for this year's competition are as follows :—

Senior:—"The Planning and Arranging of a Public Library." Not to exceed 2,000 words. Prize, one guinea.

Junior :—" A Description of the various Charging Methods." Not to exceed 1,000 words, and must not be critical. Prize, one guinea.

All essays, signed with a pseudonym, accompanied by the real name and address in a sealed envelope, should reach the Hon. Secretary by August 18th. The results will be announced at the inaugural meeting in October.

NEW BOOKS, ETC.

Hampstead Public Libraries : Descriptive Catalogue of the Books......at the Kilburn Branch Library. 8vo., 165 pp. 1902. (W. E. DOUBLEDAY, Librarian).

We have just received this Catalogue for the L.A.A. Library, it being the first produced on the Monotype Composing Machine. Of course, there is no visible difference in its appearance from any other, but it is distinctly interesting as an example of this machine's capabilities. There are five faces of type used.

Kimberley Public Library : Twentieth Annual Report, 1902. (BERTRAM L. DYER, Librarian).

Shows a very prosperous state of affairs; from one table we observe that the Library has grown from 3,000 volumes in 1883, to 26,551 in 1902, with an annual circulation of 2,388 in the former year, and 40,129 in the latter. There is also a long interesting article on the Library, written by the Librarian, and reprinted from the " Diamond Fields Advertiser."

Morley College Magazine. April.

Revue des Bibliothequès et Archives de Belgique. No. 2. March—April. Mont-St.-Guilbert (Belgium).

This second number is, if anything, an improvement on No. 1. There are several articles of great bibliographical interest; the first, a study of the *Hortus Musarum* of Pierre Phalèse (Louvain, 1552), containing facsimiles, is followed by one on the Archives in the priories of Val-Saint-Martin in Louvain. There is also a sketch of the life and work of Pierre Caron, a bookbinder in Ghent in the 16th century, and an article on the early paintings and engravings of the Tournaisienne School, together with reviews of some recent bibliographical and kindred works, among which is one of Mr. Greenwood's " Edward Edwards." The number concludes with a list of the latest bibliographies in all languages.

Revue Générale de Bibliographie Francaise. (Schleicher Fréres et Cie, 15 Rue des Saints-Peres, Paris. Published every other month ; 7 francs p.a.)

We have received Nos. 1 and 2 (January and March) of this new Review of French Bibliography, and find it interesting and likely to be useful. The Editors complain that it has been difficult to obtain an honest, reliable, unbiassed review of modern publications, and they hope now to supply the reading world with notices of the most important books, which may be accepted with safety. Each review is signed, and is allotted space consistent with the importance of the book under notice. There is also a classified list with all particulars of the latest French literature.

Revista delle Biblioteche e degli archivi. Marzo—Aprile. Firenze.

Contains an illustrated article on book illustrations in Venice in the 17th and 18th centuries, and a continuation of the life of Amerigo Vespucci, of Florence, amongst other interesting matter.

Wigan Free Public Library : Catalogue of Books in the Lending Department. 8vo., 246 pp. 1903. (H. T. FOLKARD, Librarian).

A new edition, containing upwards of 26,000 entries, representing nearly 15,000 vols. The matter is arranged in double columns, and the charge made of sixpence, must be considerably below cost price. It is compiled on the dictionary plan, and makes a sensible, serviceable, informative guide to the Library.

APPOINTMENTS VACANT.

[**Notice to Library Authorities.**—*We shall be pleased to publish under this heading, free of charge, particulars of vacancies if full details are sent to the Editor on or before the 28th of each month.*]

St. Bride Foundation, Bride Lane, Fleet Street, E.C. A Junior Assistant required, with previous experience preferred. Wages to commence, 10s. per week. Apply by letter to the Librarian.

NOTICES.

All subscriptions are now due, and should be forwarded at once to the Hon. Treasurer, Mr. W. G. Chambers, Public Library, Woolwich, S.E.

All matter for June Journal should be sent to the Hon. Editor before May 20th.

All other communications should be addressed to the *Hon. Secretary*, Mr. G. E. Roebuck, PUBLIC LIBRARY, 236, CABLE STREET, E.

The Library Assistant:

The Official Organ of the Library Assistants' Association.

No. 66.   JUNE, 1903.   Published Monthly.

ANNUAL MEETING.

The Eighth Annual Meeting will be held, by kind permission of Mr. J. Y. W. MacAlister, F.S.A., in the North Room, 20, Hanover Square, W., on **Wednesday, June 3rd**, at 8 p.m., and it is hoped that delegates from the N.W. Branch will be present.

The Report of the Committee and Balance Sheet will be submitted; the Officers and Committee for the ensuing year will be elected; and any business, of which notice has been given, will be considered.

All nominations received will be found on the Ballot Paper (enclosed herewith to all members qualified to vote), and these papers will be opened and counted on the evening of the meeting, at 7 p.m.

Members are earnestly requested to be present, and subscribers to the Journal are cordially invited to attend.

THE VISIT TO THE BRITISH MUSEUM.

The May Meeting took the form of a visit to our great National Library, on the 13th ult., and was an unqualified success, about seventy members and friends being present. Our party gathered punctually on the steps at 3 p.m., and was met by Mr. W. R. Wilson, who conducted us through the Grenville Library, pointing out notable manuscripts on the way, to the King's Library, where we were met by Mr. G. K. Fortescue, Keeper of Printed Books. He extended to us a few words of cordial welcome, and then proceeded to remark upon the books exhibited in the cases, which illustrated the development of printing from the magnificent 42-line Gutenburg Bible, of 1455, down to some latter-day productions. Here, too, was pointed out the new method of storing postage stamps, and also Mr. Cyril Davenport gave some information concerning the historical bookbindings shewn at the far end of the Library. The Cataloguing Room was next visited, and the mysteries of the "B.M." system were explained to the curious, who learned, incidentally, that the printed catalogue contained upwards of four and a half million entries! The Music and old Reading Rooms were then traversed, until the Binding Room was reached. Mr. Davenport explained the various methods employed, and, in response to an enquiry, said that morocco, buckram and cloth were the principal stuffs used for their bindings. He recommended morocco beyond all other leathers for durability and service. Leaving this department, the main Reading Room was reached, with its dome, second in diameter only to the Pantheon at Rome, which is two feet wider! The immensity of the place can be felt better than described. At the tables accommodation is provided for 460 readers, and at times, especially on Saturday afternoons, every one of these is occupied, and there are numbers of people waiting. The Iron Library was next inspected, and its sliding book stacks explained, and the Newspaper Room, where thousands of defunct and living journals are filed, was visited.

This brief survey of the wonders of the Libraries occupied nearly two hours, and as we had been on the move almost all the time, our friends who were absent will gain some idea of the extent of the place. Here our worthy guide, Mr. Fortescue, took leave of us, after mentioning several items in the other parts of the Museum which were of more than ordinary interest. Mr. Rees voiced the thanks of the Association for Mr. Fortescue's kindness, and the pains he had taken to explain things, as well as for his permission in allowing the visit. He also included his colleagues who had done much towards the success of the occasion. Mr. Fortescue having briefly replied, the gathering broke up.

At this meeting Messrs. Lewin (Woolwich) and Poulter (Stepney) were elected to audit the year's accounts.

NOTES AND COMMENTS.

Kingston-on-Thames.—The new Public Library, towards which Mr. Carnegie contributed £2,000, was opened by that gentleman on May 11th. Part of the proceedings consisted of presenting Mr. Carnegie with the Freedom of the Borough. Some interesting speeches were made, amongst which was one by Professor McNeile Dixon, in reply to the toast of "The Library Association." Under the superintendence of Mr. Benjamin Carter (Librarian), the library books, which number about 10,000 in the lending department, and between 2,000 and 3,000 in the reference department, have been transferred from Clattern House to the new premises, which opened to the public on Monday, May 18th. The open access system will be employed as heretofore.

Since writing the preceding note, news has reached us that Mr. Carnegie has increased his gift by £6,400, so that the new building was opened free from debt.

Plaistow.—On the afternoon of May 9th, Mr. Andrew Carnegie visited South West Ham to open a new Free Library, presented to Plaistow by Mr. Passmore Edwards. Mr. Carnegie, in the course of his speech, remarked that he found himself in the delightful position of opening a public library, to which he had not contributed a penny. He was persuaded that the pursuit of wealth, and the estimate in which wealth was held, were to occupy men's thoughts less and less as they became more advanced. Mr. Passmore Edwards was the leading and true disciple of the Gospel of Wealth, which holds the duty of the rich to be to live simply, to scorn delights, and give for the service of their fellow-men. Mr. Carnegie said it was an additional pleasure to him to open a library in this district, because it was a district not of the rich and noble, but of the workers and the poor, and this was where a library was most needed. The republic of letters knew nothing of heredity or of wealth. Votes of thanks were accorded to Mr. Carnegie and Mr. Passmore Edwards. An interesting souvenir of the opening was issued.

STUDY CIRCLE.

With the reports upon the answers to the March and April questions, our work for the session comes to an end. Although the extent of this Circle has been for some months a diminishing quantity, and although it never at any time attained the proportions we wished for, or even expected, we do not feel disappointed with the results achieved. Owing to the many demands upon the space of our little journal, we cannot even attempt to give a critical report upon the session as a whole.

Benedick. (13). 18. Good. Ruskin is better at 292. Crocker should be 621·3 ; Cox is 537·8, but perhaps the confusion is a clerical error.
    (14). 16. Ribot is wrong under Medicine. Ruskin should appear under Mythology.

Breton. (13). 13. Confuses the two dynamo books. Stephen wrong. Rall, Ribot, and Bardsley not carried far enough.
    (14). 12. Travel is no proper heading for Grimwood, neither is a title entry required. Bardsley should appear under " Names," not " English."

Constantia. (11). 15. Presents no especial point for criticism save in the undue length of sentences and awkwardness of the idiom.
    (12). 14. Nibbles at the subject ; gives neither description nor explanation.
    (13). 17. Confuses the dynamo books. Ribot should be carried to ·8.
    (14). 19. Very good.

Index. (11). 16. This " is divided into ten classes numbered one to nine." A painstaking attempt.
    (13). 9. Has attempted too much, seven books quite wrong, and two others insufficient,

(14). 4. Question misunderstood. We wanted the headings under which each book should be found in a dictionary catalogue ; you give the main divisions for a classified catalogue.

Nil Desperandum. (11). 10. Fair, but does not strictly answer the question. Spelling should be closely watched.

(12). 8. Information given upon several subjects, but nothing of consequence upon the subject set.

(13). 13. Fairly good. Confuses the dynamo books. Ribot can be carried further. Watson not good.

(14). 9. Subjects should seldom be indexed under descriptive adjectives. Title entries are only necessary when the subject is not clearly conveyed.

Papyrus. (11). 15. Only the ordinary obvious features given. We would prefer criticism to quotation from text-books.

(12). 14. Insufficient. That book No. 201 should be placed next to book No. 200 was hardly worth the saying; we wanted a method of dealing with additions when the space originally allotted to any one class became filled.

(13). 17. Good, but would have been better without so many alternative answers and signs of doubt.

(14). 17. Good.

Retwal. (11). 17. A very fair answer, but might have been fuller with advantage.

(12). 15. Too theoretical. Fb 69fe, etc., is more likely to confuse than to simplify a system.

(13). 17. Good. Ball is better at 523. Stephen should be 171·5.

(14). 19. Very good.

The total number of marks obtainable was 280. *Retwal* is to be congratulated upon his very creditable score of 226. *Papyrus* comes second with 204, and *Constantia* is a very good third with 201. A prize value twenty shillings has been awarded to *Retwal*, and prizes value ten shillings each to *Papyrus* and *Constantia*.

A student writes:—"I feel I cannot allow the opportunity to go by without expressing to you and your colleagues my sincere thanks for the kindness and trouble you have taken during the session in the correction and adjudication of the papers. Although some of the questions have demanded a sacrifice of time and a fair amount of care and thought, and your criticism has been rather severe, the experience gained and knowledge acquired in the preparation of the answers, does, in my opinion, more than compensate for the time expended. I may also say that, while studying for the Professional Examination in Library Management held last January, the Study Circle was of great assistance to me, and contributed to my success at that Examination."

APPOINTMENTS.

*ROBERTSON, Mr. R., Assistant at the Mitchell Library, Glasgow, to be Librarian of the Elder Library, Govan.

HATCHER, Mr. A., Junior Assistant at the Leyton Public Library, to be Junior Assistant at the Central Library, West Ham.

* *Member of the Library Assistants' Association.*

NEW MEMBERS.

Junior.—Messrs. EDWARD HIGGINSON and F. FIELD HINDLE, Preston.

LITERATURE FOR THE BLIND AND THE PUBLIC LIBRARY MOVEMENT IN CONNECTION THEREWITH.

By George E. Roebuck.

Whatever measures other Associations may have taken it is a fact that the L.A.A. has not until this evening devoted its monthly discussion to this topic, and I am honoured by the permission to lay before your notice a few items of interest regarding the movement, which is slowly, but surely, worming its way within the radius of our professional labours. That it is doing so is, one knows, liable to a challenge, but I hope to prove that my assertion is not a bald one, and also that more of the said movement may be expected in the near future. In order to deal systematically with the subject, I will divide it into three main sections, viz. :—
 (1) The Blind themselves.
 (2) Literature for the Blind and its production.
 (3) The work of Public Libraries in connection with the Blind.

The first section suggested may be considered somewhat out of place in this paper, but I think it necessary because no one can be expected to have any interest in a subject which they do not understand, and we know that enthusiasm, which alone makes a success of any movement, is but born of excessive interest.

Only those who come in contact with the blind realize their nature and circumstances, therefore I ask your kind attention to the introductory section.

The Blind Themselves.

One interesting feature concerning the blind is that there are few sources from which one can obtain any idea of their numerical strength. The Census of 1891 gave a return of 31,605 blind as resident in the United Kingdom, of whom some 7,000 were in institutions founded for various purposes. Many persons give approximate figures, of which the most generally accepted is that there is one blind person per thousand head of the total population. Few blind are seen in our streets, but they are the bolder spirits (generally blind from birth) who tread the pavements, judging the proximity of danger by the location of sounds, and their whereabouts through a process of numerical counts. But a far greater number of the blind are confined to their homes unable thus to venture without sighted guidance. For the better understanding of my remarks I would suggest the division of the blind into two groups, viz. :—Those persons who have been blind from birth ; and the previously-sighted blind, who become afflicted after years of sight and understanding. The latter section have a distinct advantage over the persons blind from birth ; they have read and have seen things, and can in their later affliction call back to memory much which they read or saw. One of our borrowers at Stepney (who became blind at the age of 21) can repeat almost any act, scene or play of Shakespeare without the least preparation ; and this he remembers at 60 years of age, ever since the onset of his affliction. The early blind, or persons blind from birth, have not had these opportunities, understanding only from reading or conversation, and sometimes, even then, but imperfectly. As regards the reading and writing of the blind, this depends upon, and is entirely regulated by the sense of touch. This faculty is most acute in the early blind, but it is difficult to acquire it after years. Nevertheless, it comes in a sense of compensation as soon as blindness claims its victim. One person writes to another by means of the board and frame, but a good number of blind persons use an ordinary typewriter with great exactitude. Arithmetic and mathematical calculations are worked out by means of the multi-arrangement of leads in a zinc tray.

The literature available for the use of the blind is very limited at most, but more opportunities are given to these readers at a Public Library, because in the majority of other cases the blind obtain their books at the discretion of a Superintendent of an Instruction Centre or some other Institution, the objects of which are not the same as those of our Public Libraries. By this means a good deal of genuine reading matter is lost sight of, being considered secular.

Here are a few headings from the catalogue of an embossing agency which has lately learned a little more broad-mindedness; instances of the matter, which, until quite recently, was considered suitable to console, enlighten, and amuse our afflicted brothers and sisters :—*Poetry.*—Bull's Hymns, 3 vols. (Vol. 1 from the Olney Hymns, vols. 2 and 3 from various collections); Hymns on Resignation, &c.; Keble's Christian Year (selections from); Starless Crown, &c.; The Old, Old Story. *Religious Works.*—Grace and Truth under Twelve Aspects, in 5 vols.; Texts of Consolation; Sunbeams for Human Hearts; The Lowest Place; Prayers and Promises; Remarkable Answers to Prayer, in 24 parts or 6 vols.; *Tales and Anecdotes.*—Praying Willys; Highland Kitchenmaid; Dying Robber; The Patchwork Quilt; Sam, the Converted Sailor; There is Room for You; Pious Teacher; Blind Irishman; The Publican's Joint. *Scientific and General Works.*—Wonders of Light; Wonders of Coal; Wonders of the Magnet; Wonders of Digestion, (1 vol.). *Music.*—A Church Service; Hold the Fort; Longing; The Parting Hour.

This sort of thing is the natural outcome of the direction of the embossing presses by charity organisations, unopposed by an outer demand. These societies have issued very little from their presses, but we must not forget that the objects of such bodies are to ameliorate the condition of the blind, and as the provision of literature is but one (and perhaps the most costly) branch of their work, we must give full measure of credit for the little. Each of the several societies establish Centres in various parts of London and the larger provincial towns, where the blind meet (say) twice a week for social intercourse, and here receive slight pecuniary assistance, and instruction in constructive fine art.

Within the last 20 years the School Boards have established, at such schools as it is necessary, a special class for blind children, who are taught by a blind instructor. The compulsion clause of the Act applies to blind children the same as to the sighted. Scholarships are also instituted by means of which a clever blind student may proceed to the Royal Normal Colleges for the Blind, where a practical education is received, and the students eventually find themselves earning their livings, or partially so, by pianoforte tuning, music, mat, brush or shoe making, or one of the other branches of handiwork, by means of which the blind are taught to maintain themselves. How the blind managed prior to 1784, when the first school of instruction was founded, in Paris, I cannot imagine, but, perhaps they lived their days in hospitals or asylums founded for them, the first of which was established in the year 1260, by Louis IX, for the reception of soldiers who lost their sight during the Crusades. This short introduction brings us to the more practical portion of this paper.

LITERATURE FOR THE BLIND, AND ITS PRODUCTION.

As I have shown, the literature embossed is but scant in quantity, and mostly of an exceedingly religious or moral quality. Such as has been embossed is set up mainly in accordance with the four most prominent styles which are known as the "Moon," "Braille," "Alston," and "Lucas" types, but several other systems have been introduced from time to time. In 1873, Dr. Moon published a book entitled "Light for the Blind," from which we learn that the earliest authentic record of an attempt to provide reading for the blind is that of the invention of a

Spaniard, Francesco Lucas, who, in the 16th century, engraved characters on wooden blocks. Rampezzetto made a similar attempt in 1575, but engraved upon a s ngle board the size of a page, instead of using moveable letters. Both of these attempts failed, owing to the letters being sunk below the surface of the wood, instead of appearing in relief. Pierre Moreau, well known to the student of typography, in the first place tried his hand at relief printing, and in 1640 cast moveable leaden type for the use of the blind. He had the practical idea, but financial difficulties compelled him to relinquish his schemes, and to apply his genius to the broader field of typography, wherein he gained no mean prominence. For some time after Moreau's discontinuance, little was done to advance the movement, and not until we arrive at the experiments of the blind man, Du Puiseaux, do we find any further mechanical attempt recorded. Du Puiseaux used wooden letters at first, but later called in the services of a friendly pewterer, who cast the letters in metal. This proved a failure, as the castings were rough to the touch, and almost, if not entirely, useless. One marked distinction of this latest attempt was the decided reduction in the size of the letters used. In 1783 the Philanthropic Society of Paris ordered punches and matrices for a new type for the use of the blind, all expenses being defrayed by Mons. De l'Etang. These letters, though smaller than those of Du Puiseaux, were still too large for the touch, so smaller types were produced. This later set of types was cast at the foundry of Mons. Vaflard, and consisted of large and small italics. In 1817 the large and small Roman character succeeded the Italic form. Concurrently with these experiments, attempts were being made in Germany. Weissembourg, a resident in Mannheim, who lost his sight at the age of 7 years, was accustomed to cut letters from pieces of cardboard, and, accidentally, so to speak, the idea of pricking outline maps in cardboard appealed to him. He found his idea a good one, so successful indeed, that, by means of these maps, he succeeded in teaching geography to Mddle. Paradis. This lady in time visited Paris, and conveyed the idea to Professor Valentine Hüay, who used it to great advantage. Professor Hüay founded the first *school* for the education of the blind at Paris in 1784, and it was whilst acting as its Director that he had the good fortune to become acquainted with Weissembourg's cardboard method, from which the idea of embossing paper sheets was easily taken.

In 1786 Professor Hüay brought forward his system of printing *on paper*, letters recognisable to the touch from flat movable types. Hüay's alphabet was of the italic form. The Academy of Sciences reported in favour of the invention, and exhibitions of embossed work took place before Louis XVI.

No further movement seems to have been made until 1826, when Dr. William Gall, of Edinburgh, improved upon Hüay's system by employing one alphabet instead of the two capitals and smalls—used by the Professor, and, further, by excluding curves and circles and substituting straight lines and angles. Dr. Gall must be regarded as the principal promoter of the art in Britain. He altered his original type to a modified Roman character, which in the course of subsequent simplification attained resemblance to some of the older characters, such as Punic and Greek. Dr. Gall published in 1827 the first book embossed in Great Britain, followed by several further outputs, amongst others being "The Gospel according to Saint John," which was the first book of the Bible printed for the Blind. Later on Dr. Gall again modified his alphabet and embossed most of the New Testament. Thus far had the movement proceeded when, in 1832, the Society of Arts in Scotland offered their Gold Medal for the best suggestion as to an alphabet and printing system for the use of the Blind. Dr. Fry had the honour to receive the reward, but Dr. Fry's system cannot have been in much favour, for we find in 1837, only five years later, that Mr. Alston, of Glasgow, improved upon Fry's types, making the letters sharper and more tangible. In 1848 the whole Bible was embossed at Glasgow, but in the year previous Dr. Moon introduced *his* famous system. Dr. Moon's alphabet consists of a simplification of common capital forms, six of the Roman characters remain unaltered, two others have parts left out (as the cross-piece in the " A " and the side-piece in the " D "), and the remainder are simple stroke or circle forms, words being embossed at full length.

So far we have considered the progress of types which have been based upon the forms of Roman and Italic characters, but a series of more complicated systems came to be used about the same period.

Mr. M. T. Lucas, a shorthand writer, of Bristol, in 1858 introduced a system which professed to be to a blind person what stenography was to the sighted. He based his suggestion upon Byrom's system of shorthand, the alphabet consisting of 36 characters, 12 of which were used for double letters. Not only were all letters omitted which were not necessary to sound, but also in many cases single characters stood for words, as " B " for " by " and " M " for " me." The advantages claimed were the saving of type, paper, and labour in printing. Results, however, proved to the reverse, for more space was required than as if the words had been written at full length in Roman capitals, whilst the system was difficult and lent itself to complication. Frere introduced types for a system which, like the Lucas, was stenographic, being based upon Gurney's shorthand system, but it differed from the latter, being phonetic. Characters here represented *sounds* instead of letters, and each word was made up according to its pronounciation. There were 32 characters, and vowel sounds (five long and five short) were represented by single dots placed in ten different positions.

We have now dealt with the stenographic systems, and before passing to the final representation it is only fair to mention the most ingenious arrangement of Messrs. David Macbeath and Robert Milne, two blind inmates of the Edinburgh Asylum for the Blind, who concocted a system of representing letters by a variety of forms of knots tied upon a piece of cord. But this, of course, was not embossing.

One system, the Braille, and a modification thereof, the Carton, remain to be described. Professor Louis Braille, a pupil at the Institute founded by Hüay, introduced in 1832 the scheme which is now most universally in practice.

It is quite a relief to consider Braille's idea, because it came clean and clear from the mind of its inventor, no common character or system of shorthand leading to its conception. Braille's alphabet consists of a combination of six or less dots, severally arranged, and further combinations represent the prefixes, affixes, and generally accepted contractions.

Carton altered Braille's scheme, using the general idea, but arranging the dots more in conformity with the shapes of the Roman letters.

I have now described the evolution of the Blind Man's A B C, but it must be clearly understood that few of the systems mentioned are in active use to-day. Carton's is used in the States, but finds little favour amongst the British Blind; the systems of Gall, Alston, Lucas, and Frere find support from isolated enthusiasts, but the Moon and Braille systems are the only styles which seem to have come to stay. As a proof of this I should mention that I have tested the utility of the "actual character" systems (as Gall and Alston) by asking several of our Blind to read the raised word on a Bovril bottle, and find that they have much difficulty in doing so.

As for the stenographics, a lady asked me to provide her with the names and addresses of the Lucas readers amongst the East London Blind in order that she might send presentation copies of her books in that type. I was only able to discover four after diligent search. No! It lies between the Braille and Moon systems. The rising generation are being accustomed to the Braille, but Moon will always be required for the aged readers; the bold characters being more tangible to the decaying sense of touch than the Braille system of closely arranged dots. Braille claims advantages over the Moon inasmuch as by its use one person can write to another without the assistance of machinery, and, further, each blind person can transcribe into Braille for future reference such items as a sighted person makes a pencil-note of. Moon's work must be embossed by plates with machine power, and therefore it cannot be used for ordinary purposes other than machine production. Another great factor in favour of the Braille system is the question of space taken up in embossing. The economy of the Braille system is best illustrated by comparison between works from the two presses; and a further economy is now made possible by the use of the "interpointed" Braille, whereby only 75 per cent. of the paper is used that would be necessary for "interlined" Braille.

The third and most interesting section of this paper deals with the

PUBLIC LIBRARY WORK IN CONNECTION WITH THE BLIND,
and, as I openly admit my advocacy of the movement, it is expected that some reasons should be presented in support of my standing.

Libraries for the Blind have for some years been established at Ashton-under-Lyne, Birmingham, Liverpool, Manchester, Middlesborough, Norwich, Nottingham, Penzance, Plymouth, Swansea, Wick, and other towns, and the continuance of these special sections is proof that they are appreciated. But our Metropolitan Library Authorities have not until recently taken the matter up, and it is interesting to note that London's pioneer movements emanate from the East End. The Borough of Poplar has a small collection of books in Braille, and the Council of the sister-borough of Stepney have taken great interest and an active part in furthering the movement.

But the provision of embossed literature is to receive much more attention in the future; there is a great difference between buying what is to be purchased, and demanding works as yet not published. So far such libraries as are established have purchased, or received donations of such embossed literature as was available, the best, but poor compared with what it might be. But why cannot we purchase the late productions, the up-to-date matter which is the privelege of the sighted; the standard works which our libraries include in their stocks? The reason is as follows:—To procure a book in Braille (which we will assume to be the type mostly in demand) you must either employ a blind person to write it at a cost of 2d. per sheet or purchase a stereotyped copy. An ordinary 6s. novel if hand-written would cost about £4 to set up, whereas if it were stereotyped the same might be obtainable for 10s. or 12s. Now the stereotyping is a costly undertaking for the embossing societies, and one which they will not readily commence without some prospects of return. Therefore they wait a demand and stereotype accordingly. What is the consequence? The average channels through which demands are largely advanced are likely to urge for the stereotyping of some works which, beyond a doubt, are good, but perhaps too much so to form the recreation of a class who already have affliction sufficient to make them serious and contemplative. The further establishment of Public Libraries for the Blind will create a demand of a more general nature, and I have it from the most eminent authority that such demands would be met. Further, the objects of a Public Library are to distribute learning—to circulate good, wholesome reading amongst *all* classes of the local community; so far, however, but few districts have been entirely fair in this respect. Boys and girls, men and women, all are catered for so long as they have their sight, but what of the residents who are not thus blessed? For that class nothing is provided, and apparently it is assumed that nothing should be provided. Leave blind people to their charities, let them continue the grooved reading they have " palmed off " on to them! We go to great ends to study and cater for the tastes of school children, we throw our stocks open to any chance employee, we spend enormous sums annually in perfecting or amassing collections of specific literature—all of which is good and proper—but I think we should do something for our blind, who, in most cases, are old established residents, and often ratepayers. The argument carries its own support. We claim that the work of free book distribution should be entirely in our hands, and I know that when Public Library work with the Blind becomes a generally accepted item of extension work, then the various charity organisations will discontinue their supplies of books to their Instruction Centres, and the borrowers will be compelled to attend their Public Libraries for reading matter. Here they will find a selection of literature more to their liking, and both parties to the contract will receive satisfaction. Our work and aims will in this way be furthered, and we shall be in a position to regulate, or to largely assist in the regulation, of the markets of production.

But what of the cost entailed by the innovation? This question is the first to be brought forward at Committee Meetings. Even now the cost of a nucleus stock of embossed books need not be enormous, and in a few years there need be little difference in the cost of embossed and the ordinary printed book. To form a thoroughly representative stock of embossed books will take years of the future, and all that can be done, as yet, is to collect what there is to be purchased, and to make further demands.

When the Stepney Council undertook to specialize in embossed literature, it was found easier to provide a sum for expenditure on this section, than it was to spend it. You can get blind people to emboss whatever you like for 2d. per sheet, and thus afford employment to the local people,—but —this is a far too costly method of procedure. The books which you include in stock must be stereotyped (at an average cost of 4s. 6d. per volume), because books will need replacing in time, and the expense of replacing works at from £5 to £8 would soon tend to check the progress of the movement.

It is, perhaps, advisable that I should clearly explain the terms " handwritten " and " stereo-typed." By the first term we understand matter that is set up by hand on a writing frame, which means that only one copy of the work is embossed at a time. The second term applies, as in printing, to work printed, or rather embossed, from a series of metal plates, each plate representing one page, from which the matter can be duplicated hundreds of times over, by machine power.

Agreed, then, that stereotyped books are to be purchased, it is astonishing how little there is to buy, and I can safely assert that, at the present state of affairs, £30 will purchase all the stereotyped matter (excluding music) which the average Librarian would care to offer to his readers. But the Librarian need not stop here if he is enterprising. Throughout the kingdom there are numbers of ladies and gentlemen of independent means, who make a hobby of Braille work, and, having time at their disposal, are diligent workers on behalf of the Blind. These generous persons, having embossed a work, are confronted by a (to them) great difficulty—How is the work embossed to reach the needy Blind? Truly, there are the Societies to present work to, but a

Public Library in a necessary locality is just the institution they look for! An appeal through a popular Press medium will bring voluntary offers by the score. At least, so we find it, for our Library at Stepney is constantly being enriched by many such kindnesses. For us the unembossed works of Dickens are being set up in Shropshire; the works of W. W. Jacobs are being embossed in Hampshire; the Arthurian legends arrive (in parts) weekly from Essex and Norfolk; children's literature is occasionally to hand from the wives of regimental officers at Simla; whilst these are but a few of many instances.

In three different parts of the Home Counties, Braille Clubs have been formed amongst the wealthier ladies, and we receive their work.

It is true that these donations are not stereotyped, but they cost nothing to acquire, and they are most useful so long as they are readable. Many donors would swamp the libraries with gifts of the "goody-goody" kind, but we need not circulate all we receive, although it is good policy to receive it most thankfully. These remarks should make it plain that the barriers in the way of the formation of a library of embossed literature are not so numerous as appear upon first consideration. Having agreed to provide the local blind with books the question of methods of circulation has to be considered, and the difficulty of this phase of the subject varies according to the ages of the blind residents and the present existing arrangements made for them. My suggestions on this point will be those upon which you may make some contrary remarks, but I simply propose to speak of our methods which experience has proved to be practical. In dealing with the blind it is well to forget their affliction, so to speak, and to treat them on the same lines as sighted borrowers. A blind person likes less than anything to be constantly reminded of the affliction. As for membership, the persons you wish to enrol being blind, it is useless to insert direct notices to them through the newspaper columns, but appeals for co-operation in making the movement known to all the local blind might be inserted to the usual news readers. Two sources of assistance are to hand—the clergy and the superintendent of a class of instruction. These persons can generally supply the names and addresses of all the blind in their areas, and do good work in carrying news to the blind of the library which is being formed for them. As the readers cannot endorse the form of application such must be dispensed with entirely. At Stepney we enrol a borrower who brings a note from a ratepayer, or one of the afore-mentioned sources, stating the name and address of the applicant. This is all that is needed, because a moment's consideration will shew that there is little risk entailed in thus freely circulating books to blind persons, the books meet with careful treatment, are returned well within time, and the necessity of guarantee for payment incurred at any time, which exists when considering ordinary sighted applications, is in these instances much lessened. Having become enrolled, the borrower now wishes to know what embossed books the library possesses, and this is a lengthy matter to attend to unless the Librarian is a Braille operator, and has set up a catalogue in Braille for his readers. A catalogue thus embossed must be a mere list under catchword and author, as the blind reader will soon lose all grasp of the meaning of a page indented or otherwise technically treated.

With such a list at hand the choice is soon made, and the issue can be recorded in the usual manner. But that section of the blind who cannot get about—the aged and the nervous blind—has to be considered, and it is quite out of the question to expect assistants to take books to these persons' homes, the willing co-operation of district visitors and the clergy should be cultivated. The Home Teaching Society's blind instructors distribute a good deal of our literature (principally the Moon works) among the aged and invalid. By such means as these much difficulty is overcome.

Before proceeding further permit me to emphasize the desirability of the Librarian and his deputy becoming acquainted with Braille. It is quite simple to learn, and indispensable where embossed communications come through the post and must be read and answered as sent. Should anyone care to learn the system they can procure a supply of paper and all implements, together with a complete book of instructions, from the British and Foreign Blind Association, 206, Great Portland Street, W., for 7s. 6d.

But to resume, one cross theory to that which I have advocated has been advanced, viz.:—that it is better to pay so much a year for periodical loan of books from the Societies, so as to be constantly replacing your stock by new batches. This is an excellent idea in provincial towns where the blind population is not numerous enough to justify the establishment of a permanent library section, but so far as London is concerned it is good only so far as the Societies' books go. I have pointed out that the books stereotyped are few, and therefore in a short time your new batch of borrowed books will be the same as you have had some time before, and should you continue re-using in this manner you will be more out of pocket than by buying outright, in which case you possess the books and can do what you like with them. Of course the same argument applies to a collection of books permanently acquired, for they will some time become read perhaps. Let us hope so. Then what will follow? Although the purpose of this paper is not to point anticipations, I think it likely that in a few years, when all the libraries of embossed books necessary for the London areas are established, that some arrangement will be made for interchange between localities, or, maybe, the blind readers will be permitted a freer borrowing limit by which to obtain books from other collections than the local one through the medium of their public librarian. Then our stocks will never be stale, and our possibilities will be almost without limit.

Nearing the end of my paper, I wish to conclude with a few words of caution, from which others may benefit by the experiences of pioneer workers. In starting the movement, the greatest care should be taken to discover the possible means of success, for it is plainly evident that *too many* libraries for the blind can be established. In the provinces the wisdom of the departure must be decided by the number of local blind, but in London the *only* guide to success is the existence or non-existence of a Centre of Instruction in the particular locality. With such a Centre in his area, the Librarian may proceed with confidence, but also with energy— without such a Centre it is fatal to take any steps to develop the movement, resulting, as it must, in damaging the reputation of the officer responsible for its inception, and also checking the movement which he has endeavoured to further.

Finally, I wish to remark that there may be several libraries where, unknown to me, work is being done in connection with the blind, and which I have not mentioned. This is owing to the fact that I have not circularised our institutions for the purpose of gleaning statistical and other returns, with which to fatten my humble paper, preferring, rather, that comment should be freely given through the medium of our Journal.

What I have said, I know to be perfectly correct, and it pleases me to think that the revival of this movement lies within the province of the public librarian; it will enable him, whilst doing his duty and furthering the institution under his direction, to create or restore a feeling of citizenship amongst, and lead to municipal attention to, a most deserving section of the community. *April 22nd, 1903.*

LIBRARY ASSISTANTS' ASSOCIATION.

EIGHTH ANNUAL REPORT.

To be presented at the Eighth Annual Meeting in the North Room, 20 Hanover Square, W., on Wednesday, June 3rd, 1903.

The Committee begs to submit the Eighth Annual Report on the work of the L.A.A., and has pleasure in reporting another year of steady progress.

The Seventh Annual Meeting was held on Wednesday, June 18th, 1902, at 20, Hanover Square, by kind invitation of Mr. MacAlister. For the third year, Mr. Evan G. Rees was thereat elected Chairman of the Association; Mr. W. G. Chambers was re-elected Hon. Treasurer, and Mr. J. Radcliffe was elected Hon. Secretary. The result of the ballot for seats upon the Committee for the ensuing session was declared. The resolution of a Special Meeting held on December 11th, 1902, altering the Annual Meeting from the summer to the winter session was rescinded upon the motion of Mr. Chambers, seconded by Mr. R. B. Wood.

A motion standing to the name of Mr. Pocock, that reports of Committee proceedings be published in the journal, was defeated.

The opening meeting of the Session was held at the London School of Economics, Clare Market, on Wednesday, October 8th, 1902, Mr. L. Inkster presiding. Mr. Henry D. Roberts addressed a large gathering on "The Technical Education of Library Assistants." This address had special bearing upon the course of classes in Library Administration which the Library Association subsequently held. At this meeting the election took place to fill a vacancy upon the Committee caused by Mr. Soper's resignation, and Mr. W. B. Thorne was duly elected.

The ordinary meetings have been held from October until May, and the Committee is extremely grateful to the various gentlemen who have addressed, or presided at the meetings. Special mention should be made of the kindness of Sir E. Maunde Thompson, K.C.B., D.C.L., for permission to visit the Libraries of the British Museum, and of the able manner in which our party was conducted by Mr. G. K. Fortescue, Keeper of the Printed Books, and his staff.

The Committee is most pleased to note another year of good work by the N.W. Branch, whose sessional programme appears on page 266. The papers read have been of a practical character, and the Committee heartily congratulates the Branch upon the outcome of its year's endeavour.

It is the desire of the Committee to extend the system of Branches, and proposals to that end will be gladly received. It is to be regretted that the movement to establish a Midlands Branch in the Birmingham district fell through, but the Committee intends to make a further effort later and hopes for better support.

In November the Fifth Annual Dinner was held at Anderton's Hotel, Fleet Street, and was a decided success. In February a Bohemian Concert was arranged, the results of which left nothing to be desired. It is pleasing to note that both social gatherings were financially successful.

The Study Circle, started in 1900 by the efforts of Mr. J. Wilson Brown, has been continued during the winter months upon a slightly different basis. Instead of setting courses of study from text books, questions of a miscellaneous character, upon the subject of "Library Management" in general have been set month by month, and comments upon the answers received have been printed in the Journal. The object was to test the knowledge gathered from the practical experience of the students, and to stimulate thought upon, and preparation of, this subject, with a view to the Professional Examination of the Library Association. A report upon the work of the session appears on page 261. The Committee is more than ever convinced that a comprehensive scheme of correspondence classes is a necessity to the proper technical education of library assistants and realize that any effort of the L.A.A. must be altogether inadequate, and hopes that the work will be taken in hand by the Library Association.

The Hon. Librarian reports that during the year ended 30th April, 1903, twelve volumes and a number of library reports and bulletins were added to the library. The number of volumes now stands at 300. No ordinary member of the Association has presented a volume, other than reports and catalogues, for several years, and the committee would like to remind members that no funds are available for the purchase of books, and that if each member presented one volume, it would materially benefit the library. Those who are not able to give, might, with little trouble, use their influence to obtain books which have been put aside upon the completion of studies, but which are eagerly desired by our less fortunate members. Donations will be acknowledged in the Journal, and may be sent to Mr. A. H. Carter, 115, St. Martin's Lane, W.C. The catalogue issued with the October and November (1901) "Library Assistant" contains nearly all the books in the library, and additions since that date have been regularly recorded in the Journal. Cutter's Expansive Classification has been added, as issued, through the kindness of Miss M. S. R. James. The number of volumes issued was 34.

In October, owing to his appointment as City Librarian of Exeter, the Committee lost the able services of Mr. H. Tapley Soper, whose editing of the "Library Assistant" did much to increase the usefulness of our medium. Mr. W. B. Thorne undertook to carry on the office, and his services speak for themselves.

In February, with regret, we accepted the resignation of Mr. J. Radcliffe, whose opportunities for carrying on the office of Hon. Secretary were curtailed, and Mr. G. E. Roebuck again agreed to undertake the office.

The Association now numbers 245 members, of whom 136 are Senior, 98 Junior, and 11 Honorary Members, being a net increase of 15 compared with last year. Sixty-three of these members are accredited to the North-Western Branch. A complete list is appended.

The Financial condition is satisfactory and the Committee desire to offer its thanks to the following gentlemen who have given donations during the year, viz.:—Mr. A. Cotgreave, £2; Mr. B. L. Dyer, £3 3s.; Mr. Hy. Ogle, 10s. 6d.; "M.B.R.," £3; Mr. F. Meaden Roberts, 5s. The donation of Mr. Cotgreave was for the Prize Essay, which bears his name, that of Mr. Dyer was for the Prize Essay Fund, or such other purpose as the Committee may decide to put it, whilst that of "M.B.R." was also for the Prize Essay Fund.

The "Library Assistant" has been published regularly each month, all the papers read before the Association during the past Session have appeared for the most part *in extenso*, and in the May number a paper read before the N.W. Branch was printed.

A scheme is under consideration for increasing the size of the Journal, whereby further space can be allowed for Branch affairs. As this will entail an increased outlay, the Committee looks for support from members, whom they trust will do a little missionary work in making known the benefits of the Association amongst their fellows who have not already joined. With a larger income a larger Journal can be produced, which undoubtedly, would prove of advantage to every assistant interested in his profession.

In September Mr. E. G. Rees and Mr. R. B. Wood were elected by the Council of the Library Association upon its Education Committee, as representing the L.A.A. Your Committee desires to express its thanks to the Library Association for this appreciation. We have every reason to hope that the Education Committee, through its open-minded consideration and energetic treatment of the difficult question of the professional examination and technical education of Library Assistants, will evolve a scheme that will give general satisfaction.

The Committee has to acknowledge with many thanks the receipt of copies of "Contents-Subjects Index" from Mr. Cotgreave, and "L.A. Souvenirs" (1898) from Mr. Fortune.

Owing to the difficulty in finding a meeting place which has been experienced lately, the Committee have engaged a room for Ordinary and Committee Meetings at the St. Bride Institute, Bride Lane, E.C.

The Committee begs to acknowledge the kindness of members and others who have from time to time given assistance.

Signed on behalf of the Committee,

EVAN G. REES, *Chairman.*

G. E. ROEBUCK, *Hon. Secretary.*

20th May, 1903.

ATTENDANCES OF COMMITTEE.

NAME.	GENERAL COMMITTEE.		SUB-COMMITTEES.		TOTAL.	
	Conv'd	Atten.	Conv'd	Atten.	Conv'd	Atten.
Bradley, C. A.	12	6	7	4	19	10
Bullen, R. F.	12	9	3	2	15	11
Burt, A. G.	12	5	8	4	20	9
Chambers, W. G.	12	9	19	11	31	20
Green, T.	12	6	—	—	12	6
Harris, W. J.	12	9	7	7	19	16
Hatcher, S. A.	12	9	3	2	15	11
Hogg, J. F.	12	8	3	3	15	11
McDouall, W. B.	12	6	7	3	19	9
Parsons, E. H. (resigned Feb. 1903)	8	5	3	3	11	8
Radcliffe, J. (resigned Feb. 1903)	8	8	14	11	22	19
Rees, E. G.	12	9	19	15	31	24
Roebuck, G. E. (elected Feb. 1903)	4	4	4	4	8	8
Soper, H. T. (resigned Oct. 1902)	3	2	1	1	4	3
Stevenson, R.	12	8	8	5	20	13
Thorne, W. B. (elected Oct. 1902)	10	9	10	9	20	18
Wood, P. H. (resigned Apl. 1903)	10	2	7	1	17	3
Wood, R. B.	12	10	19	17	31	27

STATEMENT OF RECEIPTS AND EXPENDITURE, 1902-3.

RECEIPTS.	£	s.	d.	EXPENDITURE.	£	s.	d.
Balance	24	9	4	Printing and Stationery	59	0	7
Members' Subscriptions	32	5	0	Prize Essays	3	0	0
" N.W. Branch	8	18	0	Postages	17	1	3
Advertisement " in, and Sale of " Library Assistant "	33	0	5	Hire of Room	1	0	0
Donations	8	18	6	Clerical Work	1	0	0
				Grant to Entertainment Committee	1	1	0
				Balance	25	8	5
	£107	11	3		£107	11	3

ENTERTAINMENT SUB-COMMITTEE, 1902-3.

RECEIPTS.	£	s.	d.	EXPENDITURE.	£	s.	d.
By Sale of 46 Dinner Tickets at 3s. 6d.	8	1	0	To 43 Dinners at 3s.	6	9	0
Grant from Committee	1	1	0	„ Printing	1	8	0
Sale of 65 Programmes, at 3d.	0	16	3	„ Postages, &c.	1	4	0
				„ Hire of Hall (Bohemian Concert)	0	10	6
				„ Balance	0	6	9
	£9	18	3		£9	18	3

W. GEO. CHAMBERS, *Treasurer.*

Audited and found correct,

P. EVANS LEWIN, } *Auditors.*
H. W. POULTER,

May 25th, 1903.

PROGRAMME OF MEETINGS.

Eighth Session, 1902-3.

LONDON.

Date.	Lecturer.	Paper or Business.	Where Held.
1902			
June 18		Seventh Annual Meeting	20 Hanover Square
Oct. 8	Mr. H. D. Roberts	"Technical Training of Library Assistants"	London School of Economics
Nov. 19		Fifth Annual Dinner	Anderton's Hotel,
Dec. 10	Mr. E. G. Rees	Discussion on "Issuing Methods"	St. Bride Institute
1903			
Feb. 18	Mr. T. W. Glazier	"Anticipated Developments in Library Practice"	West Ham Central
Mar. 25	Mr. R. B. Wood	"Bookbinding"	S. George, Hanover Square.
Apl. 22	Mr. G. E. Roebuck	"Literature for the Blind"	Shoreditch Central
May 13		Visit to British Museum	

N.W. BRANCH.

Date	Lecturer	Paper or Business	Where Held
1902			
Sep. 17	Mr. B. H. Mullen, M.A.	"Sight indices for a Classified Catalogue"	Peel Park, Salford
Nov. 15	Mr. C. Madeley	"History and Development of Warrington Museum & Library"	Museum & Library, Warrington
Dec. 17		Annual Meeting	Reference Library, Manchester
1903			
Jan. 14	Mr. J. D. Dickens / Mr. H. N. Kirk	"The Library Assistant" / "Planning of some American Libraries"	Athenæum, Manchester
Feb. 18	Miss E. F. Coxwen	"Some Fads and Fallacies in Library Work"	Chetham's Library, Manchester
Mar. 25	Mr. F. W. B. Haworth	"Educational Basis of the Free Library Movement"	Cent. Lib., Oldham
Apl. 21	Mr. E. G. Rees	Discussion upon "The Educational Needs of Library Assistants"	Reference Library, Manchester
May 20		Zueblin's "American Municipal Progress"	Blackley Branch, Manchester

OFFICERS AND COMMITTEE, 1902-1903.

CHAIRMAN:

[b][d] EVAN G. REES, City of Westminster.

COMMITTEE:

Baker, A., Chester.
[c] Bradley, C. A., Lambeth.
[a] Bullen, R. F., Poplar.
[b] Burt, A. G., Fulham.
Cunningham, W., Liverpool.
Gordon, P. D., Mudie's, Manchester.
Green, T., Shoreditch.
[c] Harris, W. J., Hornsey.
[a] Hatcher, S. A., West Ham.
[a] Hogg, J. F., Battersea.
[c] Macdouall, W. B., Hammersmith.
MacKenzie, W. M., Aberdeen.
Montgomery, W. T., Bootle.
Parsons, E. H., Stepney. (Resigned, February, 1903).
Quarmby, W., Oldham.
[d] Soper, H. T., Stoke Newington.
[b] Stevenson, R., Croydon.
Swann, J. H., Manchester.
[d] Thorne, W. B., Poplar.
[c] Wood, P. H., Southwark. (Resigned, April, 1903).
[b][d] R. B. Wood, Westminster (*Vice-Chairman*).

HON. SECRETARY:

J. Radcliffe, East Ham. (Resigned February, 1903).
G. E. Roebuck, Stepney. (Elected February, 1903).

HON. TREASURER:

[b][d] W. Geo. Chambers, Woolwich.

HON. EDITOR:

H. T. Soper, Stoke Newington. (Resigned October, 1902.)
W. B. Thorne, Poplar. (Elected October, 1902).

HON. LIBRARIAN:

A. H. Carter, City of Westminster.

[a] Branches Sub-Committee. [b] Education Sub-Committee.
[c] Entertainment Sub-Committee. [d] Journal Sub-Committee.

LIST OF MEMBERS.

HONORARY MEMBERS.

SAMUEL J. CLARKE.
BERTRAM L. DYER.
RICHARD GARNETT, C.B., LL.D.
THOMAS GREENWOOD.
Miss M. S. R. JAMES.

J. Y. W. MACALISTER, F.S.A.
HENRY OGLE.
R. A. PEDDIE.
F. MEADEN ROBERTS.
H. TAPLEY SOPER.

CHARLES WELCH, F.S.A.

ORDINARY MEMBERS.

*Anderson, A. A. R., Stepney.
Anderson, G. C., West Ham.
*Ayton, J. G., Poplar.
Bacon, S., Stepney.
Bain, R., Glasgow.
*Batty, T. W. E., Fulham.
*Baxter, W. D., *Library of Wynne Baxter*.
Bayley, D. J., Poplar.
Beer, F. A. R., West Ham.
Blackmore, C. F., Stoke Newington.
Blakely, A. A., Bermondsey.
Bolton, G. R., Fulham.
*Bonner, F. H., Croydon.
Boyd, Miss E. K., Aberdeen.
*Brace, W., Shoreditch.
*Bradley, C. A., Lambeth.
*Brown, J. W., Kimberley.
*Brown, R. W., Northampton.
*Buddery, E. E., West Ham.
*Bullen, R. F., Poplar.
*Burgoyne, F. J. P., Battersea.
*Bursill, P. C., Westminster.
*Burt, A. G., Fulham.
*Bushnell, F. C., Fulham.
Cameron, A. E., Croydon.
Camplin, P. W., Shoreditch.
*Carter, S. A. H., Westminster.
*Carter, W. A., Cripplegate Inst.
Cashmore, H. M., Birmingham.
*Chambers, W. G., Woolwich.
Chivers, P. W., Croydon.
*Clayton, C. E. A., Roy. Med. and Chir. Soc.
Clinch, C. H., Ealing.
*Cogswell, A., Wandsworth.
*Coltman, W. L., Woolwich.
Cook, W., Croydon.
*Coutts, H. T., Croydon.
*Crockford, A. W., Richmond.

Davis, J., Penge.
Davison, C. E., Bermondsey.
*Denne, G. E., Richmond.
*Dinelli, H. P., Hammersmith.
Dixon, Miss, Leyton.
Earl, F., Wandsworth.
*Eidmans, F., Bermondsey.
Ellison, J. B., Leeds (Institute of Science, Art and Literature).
*Ewing, J. C., Glasgow.
*Faraday, J. G., Hornsey.
Farnell, W. J. C., Walsall.
Fermage, P., Kimberley.
Field, A., Brighton.
*Frost, B. J., East Ham.
Gabbatt, C. W., Barrow.
Garner, E. W., Southwark.
*Gentry, E. J., Lincoln.
Gillespie, D. A., Westminster.
*Gillespie, N. L., Westminster.
*Glazier, T. W., Wandsworth.
*Gourley, R. J., Belfast.
*Green, T., Shoreditch.
*Hall, S. B., Lambeth.
Hamblyn, A. M., Eastbourne.
*Harper, B. J., Stoke Newington.
Harradine, F. C., Poplar.
*Harris, W. J., Hornsey.
Harrison, S. E., Birmingham.
*Hatcher, S. A., West Ham.
*Hatton, A. E., Leyton.
*Hawkins, W. G., Fulham.
*Henderson, Miss B. I., Aberdeen.
Henderson, W. G., Aberdeen.
Henley, C., Poplar.
Henn, F., Imperial Institute.
Hirst, L., Kensington.
*Hobbs, H. J., Enfield.
*Hogg, J. F., Battersea.
Illesley, H. B., Smethwick.
*Ineson, R., Leeds.

Jackson, C. P., Woolwich.
Jenn, A., Lambeth.
Jones, G. P., Stepney.
*Kettle, B., Guildhall.
King, H. J., Poplar.
Laughton, S., Derby.
*Law, W., Brighton.
*Lawler, E. A., Westminster.
Leighton, T., West Ham.
Lellow, W. F., Stepney.
*Lewin, P. E., Woolwich.
Loney, R., Stepney.
Lougheed, L. F., East Ham.
Lumsden, H. S., Aberdeen.
McCombe, A. C., East Ham.
*McDouall, W. B., Hammersmith.
*McDougall, D., West Ham.
McDougall, O., West Ham.
*McGill, W., Glasgow.
*Mackenzie, W. M., Aberdeen.
McLaren, F. W., Walthamstow.
*Male, E., Brighton.
*Martin, E. S., Kingston.
*Mash, M. H. B., Croydon.
Maule, A. C. S., Hornsey.
Moon, Miss J. B., Leyton.
*Moors, B. R., Portsmouth.
Morgan, Miss G. M., Shoreditch.
*Moslin, A. M., Stepney.
*Nash, A., Wandsworth.
*Neesham, E. W., Kendal.
*Norrie, J., Walthamstow.
Packington, L. J., Lambeth.
Parr, S. H., Fulham.
*Parsons, E. H., Stepney.
Payne, E., Poplar.
*Peplow, W. A., Croydon.
*Philip, A. J., Hampstead.
*Pickard, W., Bermondsey.
*Piper, A. C., Brighton.
Pocock, F., Holborn.
Polley, G. E., Westminster.
*Poulter, H. W., Stepney.
*Procter, W., Leeds.
Pugsley, Miss N. L., Bristol.
*Radcliffe, J., East Ham.
*Rees, E. G., Westminster.

*Rivers, J., Hampstead.
Rix, H. J., West Ham.
*Roach, Miss, Kimberley.
Robarts, H. M., Walthamstow.
Robertson, Miss J. M., Aberdeen.
Robertson, Miss L. P., Aberdeen.
Robertson, R., Glasgow.
*Robinson, F., Ipswich.
Robinson, S. C., Poplar.
*Roebuck, G. E., Stepney.
*Savage, E. A., Croydon.
Sawyer, F., Leeds.
*Seidel, F. L., Willesden Green.
*Seward, F., Bromley, Kent.
*Sharp, E., West Ham.
*Sharphouse, D., Leeds.
Sheppard, R. W., Day's Library.
*Simnett, W. E., Institute of Civil Engineers.
*Smith, Miss A., Paddington.
*Smith, H., Bishopsgate Institute.
Smith, J., Glasgow.
*Stevenson, R., Croydon.
Stewart, J. D., Croydon.
Stone, O. W., East Ham.
*Story, T. B., Westminster.
*Strother, G. W., Leeds.
Sunley, W. H., Leyton.
*Sureties, H. G., Hornsey.
Terry, E., Woolwich.
*Thorne, W. B., Poplar.
*Tumath, A. J., Holborn.
Turner, H. J., Westminster.
Usherwood, V. B., Woolwich.
*Verney, Sir E., Middle Claydon.
*Waite, C. H., Kensington.
*Ward, A. T., Cripplegate Inst.
*Warman, A. J., Newport, Mon.
Warner, J., Croydon.
*Welch, H. C., Guildhall.
Welham, H. G., West Ham.
*Whitwell, C., West Ham.
*Wood, P. H., Southwark.
*Wood, R. B., Westminster.
*Yates, A. H., Hornsey.
*Young, W. B., Leyton.

* *Senior Members.*

NORTH-WESTERN BRANCH.

President:
MR. C. W. SUTTON, M.A.

Vice-Presidents:

Mr. R. BATEMAN.	Mr. H. GUPPY, M.A.
,, P. COWELL.	,, C. MADELEY.
,, W. R. CREDLAND.	,, B. H. MULLEN, M.A.

Mr. G. T. SHAW.

Chairman: J. H. SWANN.   *Vice-Chairman:* J. D. DICKENS.

Hon. Sec.: W. QUARMBY.   *Hon. Treasurer:* W. CROMPTON.

ORDINARY MEMBERS.

*Alley, Miss J. T. F., Manchester.
Ashton, J. C., Wigan.
*Baker, A., Chester.
Barnfield, T., Salford.
*Berry, W. H., Oldham.
Burgess, J., Salford.
*Clare, A., Oldham.
*Crompton, W., Y.M.C.A., Manchester.
Crook, B., Chorley.
*Cunningham, W., Liverpool.
Dallimore, F., Wigan.
*Dickens, J. D., Athenæum, Manchester.
*Dockray, C. F., Salford.
Eastwood, T. R., Oldham.
*Edwards, A. H., Liverpool.
*Evans, E., Northwich.
*Fletcher, G., Ashton.
France, Miss E., Blackpool.
*Furey, J. H., Salford.
*Galloway, H., Mudie's, Manchester.
*Goodier, S., Lyceum, Oldham.
*Gordon, P. D., Mudie's, Manchester.
Harrison, Miss M., Blackpool.
Harwood, W., Stalybridge.
*Haworth, F. W. B., Manchester.
Haworth, H., Accrington.
Hesketh, A., Accrington.
*Hobson, A., Salford.
Ingall, Miss, Salford.
*Irwin, R., Manchester.
*Jackson, F., Salford.
Kershaw, J., Salford.

*Kirk, H. W., Chetham's College, Manchester.
*Knight, Miss L. E., Blackpool.
*Lamb, S., St. Helen's.
*Lea, Miss E., Wigan.
*Luke, E., Manchester.
McKnight, J., Wigan.
*Marriott, E., Portico Library, Manchester.
Marsden, J. R., Burnley.
Marsden, Miss O., Darwen.
Mee, F. H., Wigan.
*Mellor, C., Ashton.
*Minshall, Miss G., Warrington.
*Montgomery, W. T., Bootle.
*Moorhouse, T., Stalybridge.
*Peel, T., Salford.
*Percival, H., Owen's College, Manchester.
Phillips, P. H., Chester.
*Pomfret, J., Blackburn.
*Pyne, O. M., John Ryland's, Manchester.
*Quarmby, W., Oldham.
Shaw, J. H., Bury.
*Shawcross, H. W., Bury.
Smith, A., Salford.
*Smith, J. H., Salford.
*Smith, T., Salford.
*Sutton, O. J., John Rylands, Manchester.
*Swann, J. H., Manchester.
Tempest, H., Bootle.
Wadsworth, A., Salford.
Williams, W., Bootle.
*Young, E., Athenæum, Liverpool.

* *Senior Members.*

RULES.

1. NAME.—The Association shall be called "THE LIBRARY ASSISTANTS' ASSOCIATION."

2. OBJECTS.—Its objects shall be to promote the social, intellectual, and professional interests of its members, by meetings of a social character, by discussions, and in such other ways as may be suggested from time to time.

3. MEMBERS.—(A) All persons engaged in library administration, other than chief librarians, shall be eligible for election. Applications shall be made in writing to the Hon. Secretary, and shall be considered at the next meeting of the Committee. (B) When a member is raised to the status of chief librarian, or leaves the profession, such person shall cease to be a member six months afterwards. (c) The Committee shall have power to elect honorary members, such members not having the right of voting. (D) The Association shall have power to expel, at an ordinary meeting, after one month's official notice of expulsion shall have been given, any member by a vote of 20% (twenty per cent.) of the total number of members of the L.A.A. (or the affiliated branch to which he belongs), in favour of that course.

4. SUBSCRIPTION.—(A) The Annual Subscription shall be 5s. for Senior, and 2s. 6d. for Junior Assistants, payable in advance on October 1st. (B) Members being 6 months in arrear with their subscriptions shall cease to belong to the Association.

5. OFFICERS.—(A) The Officers of the Association shall consist of a Chairman, Treasurer, Secretary, and a Committee of ten London and ten non-London members, who shall be elected at the Annual Meeting. (B) In the event of any of these offices falling vacant, the vacancy shall be filled at the next Ordinary Meeting of the Association.

6. MEETINGS.—(A) There shall be an Annual General Meeting of the Association fixed to take place some time during the Summer session. (B) Ordinary meetings shall be held monthly from October to May at such times and places as shall be decided by the Committee. (c) Special General Meetings shall be called on the requisition of twenty members of the Association, such meeting to be held within six weeks from the date of receipt of such requisition by the Hon. Secretary.

7. BRANCHES.—Application for the formation of a branch shall be made in writing to the L.A.A. Committee, by not less than 10 members in the proposed district.

Each branch shall be bound by the Rules of the Association, but may formulate special rules for its local government, providing the same are confirmed by the Committee of the L.A.A. All proposed local rules must be deposited with the Hon. Secretary, of the Branches' Sub-Committee for approval. Members of a branch shall pay their subscriptions to the treasurer of the branch, who shall remit to the treasurer of the L.A.A. for every Senior Member 3/6, and for every Junior Member 2/-, to cover the cost of the official publications.

8. PROCEDURE.—(A) Amendments to these rules shall only be considered at the Annual General Meeting, or at a Special General Meeting convened for that purpose.

NORTH-WESTERN BRANCH.

MAY MEETING.

This meeting was held in the Blackley Library and Institute on Wednesday, the 21st inst., when Mr. Swann occupied the chair.

The Blackley Library is the latest addition to the Manchester Branch Libraries, and is worthy of a better attendance than Wednesday's. Mr. H. Bradbury (Librarian in charge) conducted the members, on arrival, round the Book-store, Boys' Reading Room, and the Gymnasium, Boys' and Girls' Recreation Rooms, Public Hall and Committee Room of the Institute adjoining the Library. In the latter room the meeting was held, when the chapter on Public Libraries in Zueblin's " American Municipal Progress " was read and discussed.

The author in his chapter points out the many sides of Library Economy as practised in the States, dividing it into five headings:—(1) Reference Libraries; (2) Circulating and Branch Libraries; (3) Children's and School Libraries; (4) Periodicals; (5) Students, each of which he treats separately, dwelling very fully on Open Access; the connection of the Schools with the Libraries; and the Students using the Libraries, including the Training of Assistant Librarians.

JUNE AND JULY ARRANGEMENTS.

It has been decided not to hold an ordinary meeting during June, but the Committee hope to be at liberty to announce arrangements for a Picnic during the month of July, and will be pleased to receive suggestions from members as to suitable places and dates.

NOTICES.

All subscriptions are now due, and should be forwarded at once to the Hon. Treasurer, Mr. W. G. Chambers, Public Library, Woolwich, S.E.

All matter for July Journal should be sent to the Hon. Editor before June 20th.

All other communications should be addressed to the *Hon. Secretary*, Mr. G. E. Roebuck, PUBLIC LIBRARY, 236, CABLE STREET, E.

The Library Assistant:

The Official Organ of the Library Assistants' Association.

No. 67.   JULY, 1903.   Published Monthly

EIGHTH ANNUAL MEETING.

About forty members and friends were present at this meeting held at 20 Hanover Square, on the 3rd ult. Unfortunately no representative of the N.W. Branch was able to be present. Mr. E. G. Rees, who occupied the chair, called upon the Secretary to read the minutes of the last Annual Meeting, on the conclusion of which Mr. W. Pickard (Bermondsey) protested that in face of a motion passed at a meeting held at West Ham in December, 1901, the Meeting held in June, 1902, was not an Annual Meeting, and wished to have his protest recorded. The minutes were then confirmed and signed.

The Chairman next proceeded with the Eighth Annual Report, which, having been issued with the June Journal, was taken as read. In moving its adoption, he remarked on the steady progress made by the Association, and was of the opinion that much good work had been accomplished. He also expressed the gratitude of the Committee to those gentlemen who had helped by reading papers, promoting meetings, &c. The motion was seconded by Mr. R. B. Wood, supported by Mr. W. G. Chambers, and carried unanimously.

The result of the ballot for Officers and Committee was then announced as follows:—

Chairman: Mr. E. G. REES (City of Westminster).
Hon. Treasurer: Mr. W. G. CHAMBERS (Woolwich).
Hon. Secretary: Mr. G. E. ROEBUCK (Stepney).

LONDON MEMBERS.

Lewin (P. E.)	 90	Philip (A. J.)	... ...	73
Thorne (W. B.)	 80	Bullen (R. F.)	... ...	70
Burt (A. G.)	 76	Bradley (C. A.)	... ...	68
Hogg (J. F.)	 75			
Rivers (J.)	 74	*Not Elected.*		
Wood (P. H.)	 74	Green (T.)	... ...	65
Wood (R. B.)	 73	McDouall (W. B.)	... ...	65

Non-London Members.

Elected.			Not Elected.		
Harris (W. J.)	...	69	Baker (A.)	...	49
Gordon (P. D.)	...	66	Cunningham (W.)	...	48
Swann (J. H.)	...	66	Montgomery (W. T.)	...	48
Savage (E. A.)	...	65	Percival (H.)	...	47
Stevenson (R.)	...	65	Berry (W. H.)	...	39
Quarmby (W.)	...	63	Mackenzie (W.)	...	36
Faraday (J. G.)	...	61	Smith (J. H.)	...	33
Hatcher (S. A.)	...	60	Brown (J. W.)	...	31
McGill (W.)	...	50	Ewing (J. C.)	...	29
Young (W. B.)	...	50	Pomfret (J.)	...	26

Before this announcement was made, Mr. Stevenson asked whether every nominee for the election had given his consent for his name to appear in the list of candidates, and quoted a letter from a candidate to the effect that he had received no intimation of his nomination, and, further, that he did not desire to go on the Committee. The Chairman replied that the usual procedure had been followed in the matter, and it was further pointed out that the gentleman in question should have lodged his complaint with the Hon. Secretary.

In accordance with notice given, Mr Harris, after referring to the difference between his motion as forwarded to the Hon. Sec., and as printed in the Agenda—a difference, the Chairman explained, caused by a misunderstanding, moved that the following addition be made to the Rules:—

> Provincial Members and Provincial Committeemen may vote, by proxy or by letter, on any matter of which due notice has been given in the "Library Assistant," or on Committee Agenda.

Considerable discussion followed, and eventually Mr. Philip moved the following amendment, which, seconded by Mr. Chambers, was carried:—

> Provincial members of the Committee may vote by letter on any matter of which due notice has been given in the "Library Assistant," or on Committee Agenda.

Mr. Philip then proceeded to move:—

> That the Association do something for the good of bibliography or to promote the cause of the profession; and that the most useful and suitable method would be publishing a list of modern pen-names or pseudonyms.

In giving his reasons for the motion he stated that he thought the Association had now secured a position which gave it the authority to do something of the sort. He was not particular that this actual work should be done, but at the same time thought that this would be the easiest and most useful to accomplish.

He also produced figures as to cost in support of the motion. Mr. Rivers seconded, and the various points were discussed at length. As the hour was getting late and no decision had been arrived at, Mr. Savage moved and Mr. Coutts seconded that the next business be proceeded with. The motion was carried. Mr. Philip then moved the adjournment of the meeting, this was not seconded, and the Chairman moved a vote of thanks to Mr. MacAlister for the use of the room and his hospitality, which was seconded by Mr. Chambers. The Chairman, properly ignoring a motion by Mr. Lewin, seconded by Mr. Stevenson, that Mr. MacAlister be asked for an extension of time, then declared the meeting closed.

NORTH-WESTERN BRANCH.
ANNUAL PICNIC.

On the kind invitation of Mr. Edward McKnight, the Committee have arranged to visit the Chorley Library on July 11th.

Train from Manchester Victoria (No. 6), 1.35 p.m., arriving at 2.51. Excursion Fare, 2s. 3d.

On arrival at Chorley, members and friends will please assemble at the Library, when, after inspecting same, Mr. McKnight will give a short account of the Institution and the methods of working. Afterwards all proceed to Rivington for tea, and spend the rest of the time in rambling round this beautiful district.

LIBRARY ASSOCIATION PROFESSIONAL EXAMINATION.

The examination in Section 2, Cataloguing and Classification, was held at centres in Belfast, London, Newcastle-on-Tyne, and Wigan, on May 6th, 1903. Twelve candidates entered and presented themselves, namely two at Belfast, eight in London, and one each at Wigan and Newcastle. Of the twelve candidates nine only entered for Classification, but all twelve presented themselves in Cataloguing.

PASS LIST.
Cataloguing.

The following candidates have satisfied the examiners in the subject of Cataloguing, theoretical and practical, the names being arranged in order of merit:—

*William J. Harris, Hornsey Public Libraries (*with merit*).
*Frank Dallimore, Free Public Library, Wigan (*with merit*).
*A. Nash, Public Library, Clapham.
T. E. Turnbull, Public Libraries, Newcastle-on-Tyne.
William F. Rapple, Queen's College Library, Belfast.
Miss Winifred Smith, Clerkenwell Public Library.
*F. C. Bushnell, Fulham Public Libraries.

Miss Mabel E. Morton, Linen Hall Library, Belfast.
*W. G. Hawkins, Public Libraries, Fulham.
*Walter Cook, Public Libraries, Croydon.

FRANKLIN T. BARRETT, } *Examiners.*
JAMES DUFF BROWN.

Classification.

The following candidates have satisfied the examiners in the subject of Classification, theoretical and practical, the names being arranged in order of merit:—

T. E. Turnbull, Public Libraries, Newcastle-on-Tyne *(with merit).*
*William J. Harris, Hornsey Public Libraries.

E. WYNDHAM HULME, } *Examiners.*
L. STANLEY JAST,

* Members of the L.A.A.

CORRESPONDENCE.

To THE EDITOR, *Library Assistant.*

DEAR SIR,—

I shall be glad to know the names of any of our members who would care to join a party of library assistants and friends for a *cycle outing* to Stoke Pogis, late in August.

The local features are interesting and the scenery *en route* very fine. Should a sufficient number signify their intention to be present arrangements may be made for our reception at Stoke Pogis, and also for an interesting introduction to such matters of note as are associated with this pleasant old-time spot.

Will members requiring further information kindly communicate before the end of this month with

G. E. ROEBUCK,
236 Cable Street, E.

SIR,—

I desire to inform the members of the L.A.A. in general, and those who were present at the Annual Meeting in particular, that Mr. Chambers subsequently admitted to me that the statement he made at the Annual Meeting that "*all* the representatives of the North-Western Branch had been thrown out" of the Committee by those who issued the election circular, was incorrect. No less than three members of the North-Western Branch were elected, which represents about one-third of the Non-London Committee.

Faithfully yours,
ROBERT STEVENSON,
June 4th, 1903. Central Library, Croydon.

PETRARCH.
By H. G. Sureties.

Francesco Petrarca, or Petrarch, as the great Italian poet and scholar is more familiarly known, was born at Arezzo on July 20th, 1304. His parents were citizens of Florence, and, he tells us, "of humble circumstances." From that city they were banished in the month of January, 1302—a like fate which was shared by Petrarch's illustrious contemporary, Dante, even to the same date—a strange coincidence. Petrarch has been styled the first of the Italian humanists, and there is no doubt he did much for the cause of education. He foresaw the revival of classical learning, and advocated the establishment of public libraries, a fact in itself sufficient to give him some claim to our remembrance. By all accounts he was handsome in appearance, fond of rich clothing, and of Court life. The darker side of his character revealed a somewhat irritable temperament, easily susceptible to offence, and an inclination to be jealous of his reputation. Perhaps, however, the greatest blot in his character was that which allowed him, in his early youth, to form an illicit connection with a woman below him in station, by whom he had two children. With regard to his great abilities, Petrarch the scholar must not be forgotten in Petrarch the poet; although, perhaps, it is as a poet that he is best remembered in modern times. In his time Petrarch's influence was far wider than that of Dante's—a strange fact when we compare the position of the two great poets in the public estimation of to-day.

Petrarca *père* was a notary of Florence, and a great friend of Dante. Before his enforced banishment he had held a responsible position in the Florentine Republic. He intended that his son should follow in his footsteps, and, with this object, Petrarch tells us he was sent to study law at Montpellier, where he spent four years, and from thence to Bologna for a further period of three years. Late in life he speaks of these seven years, "Not so much spent as totally wasted." Of the law itself he was conscious of its dignity; but he rebelled against what he considered the degradation of the manner of its practice, considering it dishonest and against the dictates of his conscience; and on the death of his father, in April, 1326, Petrarch relinquished all intention of following the law as a profession. He had little or no knowledge of the Greek language, and this was, perhaps, the great gap in his education, as he was in a measure precluded from reading and studying the great Greek writers. Petrarch's connection with Boccaccio was a lengthy one, extending right up to the time of Petrarch's death, and the two were always fast friends, and in constant correspondence. Boccaccio repeatedly refused Petrarch's earnest invitation to live with him. The two great epochs in the poet's life were his meeting with Laura and his crowning as poet laureate. It was on his return from Bologna that the poet's company began to be sought for by prominent men. "Wherefore," he says, "I cannot say." Amongst these ardent admirers was King Robert of Naples, and after paying the King a visit at Naples, where he underwent a three days' examination, he journeyed to Rome and there received the laurel crown on Easter Sunday, April 8th, 1341. It is worthy of note that at this time Petrarch had done little to merit the honour. However, about this time he finished his great epic poem, "Africa," a work on which he based his claim to fame, although afterwards he disliked hearing the work mentioned.

It was at Avignon, on the 6th day of April, 1327, in the Church of Santa Clara, that Petrarch first met Laura. This has been rightly said to have been the great event of his life. His passion was unrequited, yet it influenced his whole life and the trend of his thoughts. Of the lady herself little is known. It is probable that she was married in 1325 to

Hugo de Sade, and bore him eleven children. Her character was without reproach, a circumstance the more to be wondered at, considering that the Court at Avignon was at that time shamefully corrupt. Of the purity of Petrarch's love for Laura there can be no question—neither time nor death quenched his passion. Laura died of the plague that swept over Italy, on 6th April, 1348, exactly 21 years after her meeting with the poet whose passion she inflamed. This year was one of trouble and tribulation to Petrarch. Long after he says, "This year I now perceive to have been the beginning of sorrow." Not only did he lose his beloved Laura, but some of his friends in this ill-fated year. Yet his brain did not remain dormant or his pen idle. Sixteen hours a day were devoted to reading and study. All his life Petrarch had been an enthusiastic collector of MSS. His favourite authors were Cicero and Virgil. At school it is recorded that he was eagerly devouring Cicero when his fellow-students were struggling with the simpler classics. Within a few years of the end of his life he formed the resolution of presenting his collection of MSS. to Venice for the public use, on condition that the collection should not be broken up, and should be well housed. The gift was accepted; but the spirit in which Petrarch intended his library to be used was not respected. Years after those books which he had loved and cherished were found by the antiquary, Tomasini, cast aside in a dark room. Some had crumbled into powder, and others were irretrievably spoilt. The few that had escaped destruction are now in the Ducal Palace at Venice. The last four years of his life Petrarch spent at his retreat in the Euganean Hills, whither he had retired for quietness from the noise and bustle of the city. He had been in failing health for some time, and on July 18th, 1374, with his face bowed on the book before him, his spirit passed away. So ended the life of one of Italy's greatest sons, a true man, earnest patriot and great scholar.

LIBRARY ASSOCIATION SUMMER SCHOOL.
N.W. BRANCH.

The sixth meeting of the Summer School was held in the John Rylands Library, Manchester, on June 17th, 18th and 19th, at which the following series of lectures were delivered :—" The Evolution of Books," by Mr. H. Guppy; " Questions for consideration in Cataloguing," by Mr. Guthrie Vine; " Books of Reference, and how to use them," by Mr. Julian Peacock; " Selection of Books for Public Lending Libraries," by Mr. C. W. Sutton; and a practical demonstration of bookbinding by Mr. John Fazackerley. In connection with these lectures a capital synopsis was issued, citing most of the principal points and giving excellent lists of books on the subjects where possible. A copy will be placed in the L.A.A. Library by courtesy of Mr. Guppy. Prizes will be awarded for the best reports of the lectures.

APPOINTMENTS.

DALLIMORE, F., of Wigan, to be Assistant at the Mitchell Library, Glasgow.

SEED, W. H., Sub-Librarian, Accrington, to be Senior in Charge of the Seacombe Branch of the Wallasey Libraries.

WILLIS, J., of Carlisle, to be Senior Assistant at Stoke-upon-Trent.

NOTES AND COMMENTS.

Brierley Hill.—Mr. Carnegie has forwarded to the town clerk the sum of £2,000 towards the cost of erecting a public library.

Honours.—Our congratulations to Mr. W. R. Wilson, of the British Museum, upon whom was conferred the Imperial Service Order among the King's Birthday Honours.

We understand that Mr. J. Passmore Edwards has again had a knighthood offered him, but has respectfully declined the honour.

Hull.—At a meeting of the Hull Public Library Committee on the 23rd ult., the Chairman announced that Mr. Carnegie had promised £3,000 towards a branch library on Anlaby Road. It was decided to accept the offer with thanks.

Manchester.—At the Town Council last month, Mr. Plummer, in moving the adoption of the Free Library Committee's minutes, referred to the offer of Mr. Greenwood to provide a library, and said that gentleman was sparing no expense to make it as perfect and as useful as possible. The library would consist of books in many languages relating to bibliography, the history and administration of libraries, the annals of printing and bookbinding in various countries, with practical treatises on those arts; works on palæography, and similar subjects. Mr. Greenwood's aim was to gather together all the books that might be called a librarian's bibliographical or professional "tools." That description did not, however, indicate fully the comprehensive nature of the collection, which would include literary aids and bibliographies of value to workers in various regions of knowledge —theological, historical, economic, scientific and technical. The books would be available for use under the ordinary conditions at the Reference Library, but it was Mr. Greenwood's desire that they should also be at the service of librarians and others engaged in library administration throughout the country, and to this end certain regulations would be framed, under which the volumes may be lent to librarians. The Committee, Mr. Plummer added, was glad to announce that, together with this library, Mr. Greenwood will give a sum of money for investment, the interest of which will be sufficient for the general upkeep of the collection and for all incidental expenses. For some time past we had entertained the hope that this collection would be added eventually to the "William Blades," "Talbot Baines Reed" and "John Southward" collections at the St. Bride Foundation Institute. Had this been done the most complete library of Bibliography and Typography would then have been established in a centre, which, we venture to think, would have been more convenient than Manchester. At the same time, we expect there is little in Mr. Greenwood's collection which St. Bride's do not already possess, but we feel it would have been better to have had one complete whole rather than two imperfect halves.

St. Anne's-on-Sea (Lancs.).—Mr. Carnegie has forwarded to the Urban Council the sum of £3,500 for a public library upon the usual conditions. A committee has been appointed to secure a site, about which it is anticipated there will be no difficulty.

Stoke Newington.—Mr. Carnegie has promised to provide £4,000 for the extension of the Library and the erection of a Lecture Hall.

Sunderland.—Mr. Carnegie has intimated that he is prepared to give £10,000 to Sunderland for the erection of two branch libraries in the town. The condition attached to the gift is that all of the penny rate be devoted to the maintenance of the libraries, and that the sites for the branches be given without charging the library rate.

Taunton.—The local authorities are advertising for designs for a Public Library.

Tilbury.—Mr. Carnegie has replied to a communication from the Parish Council on the subject of a public library in terms which suggest that if he is satisfied as regards certain points, he will present a library to the Parish.

NEW BOOKS, &c.

Bootle Free Library and Museum Committee: Sixteenth General Report, 1902-3. (C. H. HUNT, Librarian).

Bootle is one of those favoured places whose fiction issue is very low, viz.:—1901-2, 68·2 per cent.; 1902-3, 66·7 per cent.; and has perceptibly declined during the past six years. An interesting fact is that the whole of the Bootle Board Schools are now associated with the Lending Library Department.

Bootle Free Library, Museum, and Technical School Journal. No. 22. June.

Contains the usual notes on books, local items, list of additions, &c., and the first portion of an article by Mr. J. J. Ogle, "An Educational Tour in North Germany."

Bootle Free Libraries: A Chronological List of Historical Novels and Tales contained in the Central Library. Compiled by CHAS. H. HUNT and W. T. MONTGOMERY.

A useful annotated pamphlet which should do much to stimulate the study of history.

Croydon Public Libraries: Reader's Index, May-June, 1903. (L. STANLEY JAST, Librarian).

Contains the usual list of additions, a special catalogue of a circulating collection of photographs in the fine arts, and an annotated reading list of books in the Libraries on " Out-of-Door " subjects, compiled by Mr. H. T. Coutts of the Libraries staff. A special " Illustration Ticket " is issued for those wishing to make use of the art photographs in their own homes.

Croydon Public Libraries: The Reader's Index. July-August. (Edited by L. STANLEY JAST, Chief Librarian).

Contains the usual annotated list of additions, with selections from the Annual Report. There are also two topical Reading Lists on " Mountaineering " and " Free Trade and Protection," compiled by Messrs. E. C. Grigsby and E. A. Savage respectively.

Croydon Public Libraries: Fourteenth Annual Report. (L. S. JAST, Chief Librarian).

An admirable report, which would convince the most incredulous that the Public Library Movement in Croydon is a very " live " affair. The work done is excellent, and the methods employed most up-to-date and original.

Eastbourne Public Libraries: Seventh Annual Report, 1902-3. (J. H. HARDCASTLE, Librarian).

Reports an increase in the issue at the Central Library, the opening of a Branch, and a gift of £10,000 from Mr. Carnegie to defray the cost of a new building for the Central Library, which is not a bad year's work. We do not think the presence of such publications as " Answers," " Tit-bits " and " Scraps " in a Public Library reading room adds to the intellectual dignity of the place.

Fulham Public Libraries: Fifteenth Annual Report, 1902. (FRANKLIN T. BARRETT, Librarian).

Shows an increase in the year's issues of nearly 43,000 vols. The Open Access System has proved both successful and popular at the South Branch Library, and the Committee regret that lack of suitable accommodation at the Central Library prevents the adoption of the same methods. Among the lectures given we notice that Mr. Cecil T. Davis re-delivered his address on Captain Marryat, which some of our readers will remember with interest.

Hereford Public Library and Museum: Thirty-first Annual Report, 1902-3. (J. COCKROFT, Librarian and Secretary).

Hornsey Public Libraries: Fourth Annual Report, 1902-3. (THOS. JOHNSTON, Librarian).

The opening of the Highgate Branch in June, 1902, appears to have somewhat crippled the work of the other two Libraries—at least for the time being—both the Central and Stroud Green Branch show a decrease in issues, and the new books added to these Libraries are practically *nil*. However, everything cannot be done at once, and that much good is being done is evinced by the single fact that "one in every seven of the inhabitants of Hornsey at present hold tickets entitling them to borrow books from the Libraries."

Jahr (Torstein) and Adam Julius Strohm: Bibliography of Co-operative Cataloguing and the printing of Catalogue Cards. 4to. Washington, 1903.

This is a monograph of 116 pages reprinted from the Report of the Librarian of Congress for 1902 and "aims to present a chronological conspectus of the growth of the literature about plans and enterprises in co-operative cataloguing and international bibliography." That is to say it consists of an annotated list of a number of articles and books which have dealt with the possibility of producing a complete catalogue of all the books published in every country from the invention of printing to the present date. The list seems to be very, very American in its composition, and we think we have seen other British efforts in this direction which are not recorded here. Our Bibliographical Society is not even mentioned so far as we can discover, and surely it has done some things worthy of recognition in such a monograph? The compilation, by the way, shows what a large amount of "gassing" can be done without a tittle of the real work being accomplished! Nevertheless, such productions have their value, and so far as it goes, this little work has been well carried out.

Kendal Public Library: Eleventh Annual Report, 1902-3. (C. J. MELLOR, Librarian).

Leyton Public Library Magazine, May, 1903. (Edited by Z. MOON, Librarian).

Leyton Public Libraries: Annual Report, 1902-3. (Z. MOON, Librarian).

An encouraging report, although limited means has prevented the established branches from being a success. It is pleasing to note that the fiction issue is only 52 per cent. Without prejudice, we must confess we regret to see the following statement made by the Librarian:—"The introduction of lady assistants has been exceedingly satisfactory; they have displayed a diligence and ability which will, I believe, encourage the Committee to appoint lady assistants to fill future vacancies." We wonder whether Mr. Moon would really like to see a lady appointed to succeed him. It is curious to learn, too, that to the first vacancy that occurred after this was published a male assistant was appointed!

Library Assistants' Association, North-Western Branch: Fourth Annual Report, 1903.

The Committee report an encouraging increase in membership during the year, but properly point out that considering the number of assistants employed in the district, their numerical strength is not what it might and ought to be. A good year's work has been accomplished and some instructive and interesting papers have been read. With pardonable pride the Committee call attention to the fact that the members of the Branch have secured the majority of the prizes offered in connection with the Study Circle. Altogether the Executive are to be congratulated on what has been done, and distinctly deserve the support of the three hundred odd assistants engaged within the North-Western Boundary.

Manchester Public Free Libraries: Record of the Jubilee Celebrations. (Edited by CHARLES W. SUTTON, M.A., Chief Librarian). 1903.

A brochure of 104 pages, containing verbatim reports of the proceedings at the Jubilee Celebrations. All the speeches are included, and they embody much which should prove inspiring and encouraging to the younger members of the profession. Dr. Richard Garnett made a bold appeal for the librarian, urging that "nothing could be more conducive to the attainment of the objects for which free libraries were founded, than to bring about during the next half-century as great an elevation of status of the librarian as the last half-century has seen in the position of the library." A poem specially written for the occasion by Sir Lewis Morris appears on the first page of the brochure.

Morley College Magazine: May and June.

Revista delle Biblioteche e degli archivi. May-June. (Florence).

Includes a paper by A. D'Ancona and G. Fumagalli, entitled: "Proposals for the compilation of an Italian bibliography," as well as other papers of a bibliographical nature.

Revue des Bibliothèques et Archives de Belgique. No. 3. May-June.

Opens with "Some words on the early days of the printing press in Russia," and contains several other equally instructive and interesting articles, besides a record of all the principal library and bibliographical publications.

Richmond Public Library: Twenty-second Annual Report. 1902-3. (A. A. BARKAS, Librarian).

Waterloo-with-Seaforth Public Library: Fifth Annual Report, 1902-3. (Miss KATE FEARNSIDE, Librarian).

West Ham Library Notes: (Edited by ALFRED COTGREAVE, Borough Librarian.) No. 31, Jan.-March, 1903.

Opens with an article on the Progress of the Public Library Movement in West Ham, incorporated with which is a list of Mr. Passmore Edwards' benefactions to libraries and charitable institutions to date, which makes a formidable array. There is also a supplementary list of books on London and the suburbs added to the Libraries while the other list has been in preparation, together with the usual lists of recent additions annotated.

West Ham Public Libraries: A Souvenir of the Opening of the Passmore Edwards Public Library at Plaistow. (Prepared by ALFRED COTGREAVE, Borough Librarian). 8vo. pp. 100, 1903.

Gives a resumé of the history of the West Ham Municipal Libraries, together with descriptions, photographs, plans, etc., as well as several local views and portraits of councillors. A capital portrait of Andrew Carnegie forms the frontispiece.

OBITUARY.

The death of Miss M. S. R. James on June 5th, in Boston, Mass., leaves the library world of Great Britain the poorer by one of its most active and intelligent workers. Miss James had been ailing all the spring, and finally succumbed to typhoid fever following on a severe attack of measles. Up to the time of her death her energy in keeping up with library affairs was unceasing, and it manifested itself in the various papers she read and speeches she made on both sides of the Atlantic—her name is down for a paper to be read at Leeds this year.

It is hardly necessary to do more than recall to mind the various steps in her career. She joined the People's Palace in the early days of its existence, and quickly came to the front by reason of her enthusiastic zeal for everything that helped to increase the usefulness of the library, and when her chief, Miss Constance Black, left to marry Mr. Edward Garnet, Miss James was offered the vacant post. On May 12th, 1890, she read a most interesting paper on the People's Palace Library before the Library Association.

In 1903 she went to the International Exposition of Chicago as one of the British Library delegates, and early in 1894 she left the People's Palace to accept a position in the Library Bureau. After six months preparatory work at the head office in Boston she came back to help start a London branch.

Her interest in any scheme that seemed likely to promote the advance of the Library movement never flagged, and when the Library Assistants' Association was started she was one of the first honorary members.

In 1897 she gave up her London work to take up another position in the Library department of the same firm in America, and there she was working at the time of her death, although at different times she had had tempting offers made to her by the Library of Congress, the Pratt Institute, and other large libraries in the United States. Her thoughts, however, turned to England, and she looked forward to the day when suitable work should offer itself to come back and settle once more among us.

M. Petherbridge.

NOTICES.

All matter for August Journal should be sent to the Hon. Editor before July 20th.

All other communications should be addressed to the *Hon. Secretary*, Mr. G. E. Roebuck, Public Library, 236, Cable Street, E.

The Library Assistant:
The Official Organ of the Library Assistants' Association.

No. 68.   AUGUST, 1903.   Published Monthly

COTGREAVE PRIZE (1903).
Members are finally reminded that Tuesday, August 18th, is the last day for receipt of essays. It is hoped that a good number will be forthcoming.

PROPOSED L.A.A. PICNIC.
The Committee have considered the suggestion that a picnic be organized, and have decided that such an outing shall be arranged for Wednesday, September 16th, at Burnham Beeches, providing that sufficient support is evidenced.

All members who propose to avail themselves of this suggestion are asked to communicate with Mr. W. B. Young, Public Library, Leyton, on or before August 18th, stating the number of friends they propose bringing with them.

NORTH-WESTERN BRANCH—SUMMER MEETING.
The Summer Meeting of the N.W. Branch was held at Chorley on July 11th, by the kind invitation of Mr. E. McKnight.

On reaching Chorley the small party from Manchester proceeded to the Library under the direction of Mr. McKnight, and there met a few more who had availed themselves of the opportunity to visit Chorley. After spending a short time in inspecting the library, newsrooms, etc., with Mr. McKnight as guide, a hurried departure was made in order to catch the train for Adlington. From there, after a ramble of about $1\frac{1}{2}$ miles, Rivington was reached, and the Rev. S. Thompson was waiting to conduct the party round the old Unitarian Chapel, built early in 1700, and standing to-day as then, not having had any structural or interior alterations.

An adjournment was next made to a neighbouring hostelry, where tea had been prepared by the kind hospitality of Mr. McKnight, after partaking of which, a hearty vote of thanks was passed to both the Rev. S. Thompson, for so kindly showing the members over the Chapel and his gardens, and to Mr. McKnight for his kind hospitality and the splendid arrangements made.

The rest of the time was devoted to rambling through Dean Woods, and making the return to Adlington and Chorley, when the rain which had long been threatening began to fall in earnest.

LIBRARIES AND MUSEUMS.

By P. Evans Lewin.

In spite of the recent development of libraries, it is surprising to find that, with a few brilliant exceptions, there has been no corresponding advance in the movement for forming local museums. It is so obvious and so generally admitted that a museum is the natural adjunct of every public library that it would be thought that no library would be so poor in spirit, as I shall presently demonstrate, as to be without one. Yet the fact remains that very few of our rate-supported libraries contain any collection of antiquities or natural objects worthy of the name of museum ; and the majority of our local collections are so full of objects of the curiosity type, such as the shoe-horn used by (say) Lord Nelson's grandfather, or a lock of hair of some long-forgotten murderer, objects interesting from the sentimental point of view only, that their educational influence is practically *nil*. The public spirit which was aroused in many of our country towns in the early forties and fifties, when the Literary and Scientific Institutions and Working Men's Institutes were in full swing, has been allowed to become dormant, and the valuable collections then formed have in many cases been dispersed, or are hidden away in lumber rooms. I have in mind one most flagrant example—a unique collection being sold for an old song, for " want of space " ! It is only of comparatively recent date that a feeling has been abroad that whilst libraries are a luxury, museums are a necessity. From the time of the libraries at Alexandria and Pergamos to the present day, the museum has been an adjunct of the library—and rightly so. The mind of man is not first awakened by a perusal of Aristotle, or the metaphysical subtleties of Plato, but by a personal observation of his natural surroundings ; and what can be better than to turn from our own investigation of nature to the thoughts and opinions of those who have observed before us—the right course being from the natural object to the book. In the country the observation of nature is comparatively easy—the fields are the student's observatory—though even here museums are desiderata ; but in our larger towns the case is entirely different. It is here that our busy workers feel the real need of a museum, and it is in too many cases the apathy, to a great extent, of the local bodies, accompanied by a lack of enthusiasm on the part of the librarian, which have deprived them of what should be their natural heritage. Almost invariably one meets with two excuses : lack of funds and want of space. The former is no excuse at all, and the latter is generally due to a deficiency in foresight on the part of the committee responsible for the building of the library.

A good local antiquarian and natural collection can be formed almost entirely by the efforts of the librarian, helped by those enthusiasts of whom there are many in any town only too ready to lend their aid, who are members of the local field and antiquarian societies. Save perhaps for the cost of the cases and some few other initial expenses, such a museum as I shall outline can be formed practically without recourse to the public rates. The first essential of such a collection is, then, that it shall be thoroughly representative, not only of the history, the geology, botany, and fauna, but of the industries and social life of the district. Such a collection itself would be an invaluable help to the student. But it should aim to be something more. From the district to the world at large may appear to be a long step, but in reality a collection representative of the social and political history, geography, and natural life of the many different countries can be gathered together, perhaps with considerable trouble, but with very little expense. Such a collection need include no expensive works of art—these will come, no doubt in time—for expense is not a criterion of usefulness or merit, and many of the objects which it should contain can be had as a rule for the asking.

Firstly, then, the museum is to be of a local character, and its nature will, of course, largely depend upon the features of the surrounding district. If we start from natural history in its popular sense, we shall at once find that three broad principles must be laid down for our guidance. The leading principle is that objects should be displayed so as to convey as full an idea as possible of the haunts and habits of the creatures shown and of the circumstances under which they pass their lives. This naturally applies mainly to quadrupeds, birds and higher organisms. It is painful sometimes to go into a museum and find a stuffed bird perched upon a wooden stick in a glass case labelled "Sparrow," or possibly only "Pyrgita Domestica." If he be a sparrow where is his partner? what is she like? where are her eggs? and what is his home like? These and similar questions should be answered by the exhibit itself, if it is to be of any real educational value. It is not enough to set up a stuffed bird or beast. The second principle is that specimens should be displayed with others of the same family or genus, and this will apply more especially to the shells and lower organisms. And here there should be no break between the past and the present, the natural principle of evolution shows that; and therefore I conceive it to be essential that specimens of the same genus, whether now living or extinct, should be exhibited together. Then we shall find abundant exercise for our minds in attempting to discover why one family perished so soon whilst another, apparently weaker, lasts so long. The third great principle, and a duty which is too often overlooked or perfunctorily performed, is that full and adequate descriptions should accompany every exhibit, not only demonstrating class and habits, but referring the student to all passages in books in the library dealing with the object displayed. Failing this the exhibit is often meaningless to the average visitor. Here is an opportunity for the librarian and his assistants to become personally acquainted with the contents of the books under their charge. It is too much to expect every librarian to be a scientist, but he can at least point the way. With the botanical collections the same principles, to a great extent, can be observed. The aid of the expert will always be a necessity, but the librarian often reaps where others have sown, and much of the praise becomes his inheritance.

After the local natural section comes the historical department, showing, of course, in an orderly progression, the social and political life of the district. Here the librarian will perhaps be more at home, for one of his first duties will have been to enter somewhat fully into the past history of his town. This section will be mainly devoted to maps, plans, prints, election squibs and addresses, and photographs of the district, and I would even plead for the ubiquitous pictorial postcard. Many of these are in a short time out of print, and the scenes they have represented no longer exist. Pedigrees of important families can also be displayed with advantage. Lastly, on the local side, comes the industrial section. This should perhaps be made the *pièce de resistance*. Every district has some industry more prominently represented than the others, and all the numerous processes carried on in that industry should not only be fully demonstrated, but—and this is a thing seldom or never attempted—the social surroundings and life, both business and home, of the workers should be shown in the best way possible, by photographs, newspaper cuttings and tabulated statements. The social side of the museum would be invaluable to the local politician, and such an exhibit could be made, I believe, intensely interesting.

Thus far the local museum. The other is far more difficult to deal with. What to include and what to reject will be of paramount importance. It would never do to accept everything that comes along, simply because it is given. I believe that the main principle to be followed is not so much to form a systematic museum representative of the whole world, but a museum suitable for the instruction of the young. The real student would not wander into our small typical museums for his mental pabulum; he would rather attend some of our national treasure houses. How rare a bird he is can be ascertained by a visit to any of the large London Museums, the Soane, the Royal Architectural Museum, the United Service Institution, the half-dozen subsidiary collections at South Kensington, or even—but this is treason—the British Museum itself. In most of these the solitary curator regards a visitor as a find. In our wider collection we do not seek the student, then. This museum should be for the man-in-the-street. There is one section which can be available for everyone—and that is the art section. There is no excuse for the library which does not purchase liberally all the reproductions of the great pictures of the world. These are now so cheap and plentiful, and withal so good that it is a shameful neglect not to buy them. Want of space is here no excuse, for a fresh show could be made every day. And under the heading "Art" I would include, not only these reproductions, but also postage stamps, coins which are invaluable in long series, especially those at present current, which could easily be obtained, for every tourist returns with some; photographs of foreign places and peoples, and especially the many series of costume postcards; and photographs or prints of the sovereigns and leading men of all nations, authors, scientists, politicians, warriors and what not, accompanied by a short written biography in each case. *This* would be no dry-as-dust collection, but a living embodiment of the present world. A veritable mine of information is here ready to hand, and at little cost. It is almost incredible that these things should be allowed to remain in shop windows only. If anything happen in a particular country, then our collection of postcards should be to the fore. If a celebrated man die our portrait and biography are available. If there be a political crisis we have our collection of photographs of cabinet ministers. The thing may appear trivial, but I am convinced that its educational importance is immense.

If the library be rich in typographical curiosities or books of bibliographical interest, as sometimes happens even in the rate-supported library, a very interesting exhibit can be formed, showing the progress of printing—and this section can always be supplemented by tne many fac-similes which are now available.

Then finally our small museum should have Roman and Greek remains or replicas, typical curiosities of all countries, especially adapted for the instruction of the young, and, in fact, anything which can throw any light upon the manners and customs of other peoples. All this can surely be done without any addition to the rates. If the Museums Act be adopted so much the better, but until this be done, much can be accomplished with the help of experts and students. If the library is to be, as it often claims to be, the intellectual centre of the district, it must do something more than it is now doing. It must be awake to the changing ideas of the times, and from its present condition of intellectual somnolence, become the meeting place, not only of reading circles, University Extension Classes, and Browning Societies, but of the natural history and antiquarian clubs of the district. The library is no longer a place for the storage of books only, and it never has been. That was only the mistaken mediæval unlovely idea of its functions. Nor is it a school or university. It should be a centre of information and mental recreation, open to all who care to enter. This is easy of achievement. The one thing lacking is enthusiasm.

THE COMMITTEE.

The inaugural meeting of the Committee was held at Headquarters on July 22nd. Present: Mr. Rees (in chair), Messrs. Bullen, Chambers, Faraday, Hatcher, Lewin, Philip, Rivers, Savage, Stevenson, Young and Roebuck. Mr. Hatcher was elected Vice-Chairman. The constitution of the Sub-Committees was discussed and the following elections made:

Publications Sub-Committee—
The Chairman, Hon. Treasurer, Hon. Secretary, Hon. Editor (Mr. Thorne), Hon. Sec. N.W. Branch, Messrs. Hatcher, Lewin, Philip and Rivers.

Education Sub-Committee—
The Chairman, Hon. Treasurer, Hon. Secretary, Messrs. Bullen, Savage and Thorne.

Branches Sub-Committee—
Hon. Sec. (General and N.W. Branch), Messrs. Harris, Hatcher and Hogg.

Entertainments Sub-Committee—
Hon. Treasurer, Hon. Secretary, Messrs. Bradley, P. H. Wood and Young.

The programme of meetings, etc., for the Ninth Session will appear in our next issue.

APPOINTMENTS.

BRIARS, Mr. G. C., of Stockport, to be an Assistant at the York Public Library.

*BUDDERY, Mr. E. E., of West Ham, to be Librarian of the new Public Library, Chatham.

*BURT, Mr. A. G., of Fulham, to be Chief Librarian of the Public Libraries, Handsworth.

*NORRIE, Mr. J., of Walthamstow, to be District Librarian of the Kingston Public Library, Glasgow.

*POULTER, Mr. H. W., of Stepney, to be Assistant Librarian of the Walthamstow Public Library.

TAYLOR, Mr. P., of York, to be Librarian of the Public Library, Barnsley.   *Members of the L.A.A.

NOTES AND COMMENTS.

Carnegie Gifts.—The following are such of the donations Mr. Carnegie has distributed during the past month as we have been able to discover from various sources, viz.:

Brighton	£10,000	Leyton	£8,000
Calne	£1,200	Ramsey, Isle of Man	
Hackney	£25,000	Southend-on-Sea	£8,000
Hemel Hempstead	£3,000	Torquay	£7,500
Hove	£10,000	Whitehaven	£5,000

We do not know what amount has been offered to Ramsey, but understand it runs into four figures. The offer was made through Mr. Hall Caine, and one of the conditions is that Mr. Caine shall present a site. The claims of other communities in the Island Mr. Carnegie has also promised to consider. The Town Council of Torquay has decided to adopt the Acts in order to avail itself of the offer. The gift to Leyton is for the establishment of branches.

Westminster.—The Westminster City Council have accepted the offer of Mr. J. Passmore Edwards to place a marble bust of the late William Ewart, M.P., in the Great Smith Street Public Library.

The United parishes of St. Margaret and St. John (Old Westminster) were foremost in adopting the Libraries Act of 1855. The Library for this district, in Great Smith Street, was opened in 1857 (the new building in 1893), and was the only public Library in London under the Act until the Wandsworth Library was opened in 1885.

NEW BOOKS, ETC.

Manual of Library Economy. By JAMES DUFF BROWN. Demy 8vo. xii., & 475 pp. Illus. (Scott, Greenwood & Co.—7s. 6d. net). Contents :—Foundations and Committees. Staff. Buildings. Fittings and Furniture. Book Selection and Accession. Classification and Shelf Arrangement. Cataloguing, Indexing, Filing. Maintenance and Routine Work, Public Service. Index.

Since we first saw this book announced we have looked forward with no little interest to its perusal, and with the names of Mr. J. D. Brown as author and Messrs. Scott, Greenwood & Co. as publishers, we naturally anticipated a volume which would be at once valuable and authoritative. Without more ado, we may say that we have not been disappointed; it is an admirable book, and author and publishers alike deserve all praise for its production. The idea of the author is to provide " a text-book of advanced library practice," and with the possible exception of Mr. Macfarlane's " Library Administration," his claim to have brought out the first work in English to treat of modern library economy in a comprehensive manner is justified. In the preface, and all through the book, Mr. Brown bewails the limitation of the rate. He says that while the public libraries of France and the United States are hampered by conservatism and uniformity, those of Great Britain are paralysed by the fixed rate. Of course in the brief space at our disposal it is impossible to deal with every subject the book treats on, and equally, of course, it would have been impossible for Mr. Brown to have written such a book as this and at the same time to have written it to the liking of every librarian. Doubtless he will find many ready to rise up and dispute or argue almost every statement he makes, but nevertheless, we contend that Mr. Brown has treated most things he writes about with a commendable impartiality, although here and there, where experience has taught him that such and such methods are the best, he has expressed himself in bold and vigorous language.

In the section dealing with the Staff a table of librarians' salaries, graduated according to the library income, is given, which, while they *may* cause some mouths to water, are remarkably fair and carefully worked out. Mr. Brown deals very fairly and liberally with assistants. He advocates an examination in general knowledge before appointing juniors, saying, "Nothing is more exasperating to intending readers than to be served by some youth who is ignorant of the most elementary subjects in general knowledge." Passing on to the appointment of seniors, the author says, " Examinations are held by the Library Association, . . . but they are not suitable for the purpose of aiding selection for first appointments. But any candidate . . . . who possesses one of the L.A. Certificates should be selected for interview as a matter of course." Attendance at the classes to prepare for these exams is urged, and librarians are advised to encourage their assistants in this. Payment of their fees is also recommended. Mr. Brown puts in a good word for the L.A.A., which, he says, all assistants would do well in supporting. A useful list of books for the librarian's library is given, while at the end of each chapter a list of authorities is appended, which is of service to those who would wish to study the matter further. As might be expected, the book holds a brief for "Open access," but little or nothing new is said upon the subject. All that appears is quoted from a well-remembered pamphlet issued in 1899 "by the librarians in charge of open-access libraries." Even in this, however, Mr. Brown is not unfair, for he quotes freely from a paper, which he says is the best he has seen, written by Mr. W. E. Doubleday for the "Library" (New Series), opposing the system and bringing to light its weak points.

A good index is provided, and there is hardly an item of ordinary public library work on which the book may not be profitably consulted. It must at once become the standard text-book on the subject of British Public Library Economy, not because it is the *only* book as yet, but because of its value and practicability. We trust that every librarian will add one or two copies to his shelves, as the price makes it difficult for the average junior assistant to acquire, but at the same time we recommend every assistant to procure a copy for his own individual use if he can. We venture to give expression to our feeling, however, that there is still room for an elementary manual of British library methods, suitable for placing in the hands of juniors, to be published at about eighteen-pence.

Two notes in the book rather interest us, one—that any profits arising from its sale will be handed over to the Library Association, and two—Mr. Jast, of Croydon, has in preparation a work on the whole theory, practice and philosophy of public access to the shelves.

Battersea Public Libraries: Sixteenth Annual Report, 1902-1903. (Lawrence Inkster, Chief Librarian).

Shows a good year's work in increased issues and books added to the stock. Unfortunately the £15,000 presented by Mr. Carnegie in 1902 cannot at present be made use of, as the rate limit will not allow it. When an increased income is possible, three new branches, a reading room and books for the blind, free lectures, additional reading rooms for children and an improved scale of salaries for the staff are needed. We hope the rate limit will soon be removed!

Kimberley Public Library: Rules and Bye-Laws. (B. L. DYER, Librarian).

We notice sixpence is charged for this leaflet of eight pages! How many borrowers would pay that amount for a copy of the rules over here?

Kimberley Public Library: The Library Record, May, 1903.

Newcastle-upon-Tyne Public Libraries: Catalogue of books on the useful arts in the Central Library. Compiled by BASIL ANDERTON, B.A., Librarian. Royal 8vo. pp. 287. 1903.

An elaborate catalogue of the books in Class 600 of Dewey's Decimal Classification, divided into three parts, viz.:—Author List, Anonymous Works and Periodicals, Subject List. We cannot help but feel this to be a very useful piece of work, useful not only to the borrowers from the library, but also as a guide to future compilers of catalogues or lists on the Dewey system. As it is said in the Preface, it is not essential that readers should trouble to master the classification, a free use of the index will obviate that, and they will reap the unquestionable advantage of having books they knew not of being brought under their immediate notice. We do not venture any criticism, but congratulate the compilers on their handiwork.

Stoke Newington Public Libraries: Thirteenth Annual Report, 1902-3. (GEORGE PREECE, Chief Librarian).

Reports an increase of over 8,000 in the year's issues and an addition of 1,920 vols. to the stock. Ten books have been stolen from among the works which are placed in the Reference Library for unrestricted use by readers, which fact will doubtless delight the hearts of the "anti-open-access party."

Westminster Public Libraries: Report of the Public Libraries Committee, 1902-3.

This is a composite report, prefaced by a few remarks by the Chairman of the Committee. Each Librarian—Mr. Pacy, Mr. Poole and Mr. Mason—then give independently an account of what has been done in their respective libraries during the year. Progress in each library is reported, and the figures—both in finance and attendance—are larger than one usually meets in annual reports.

NOTICES.

All matter for September Journal should be sent to the Hon. Editor before August 19th.

All other communications should be addressed to the *Hon. Secretary*, Mr. G. E. Roebuck, PUBLIC LIBRARY, 236, CABLE STREET, E.

The Library Assistant:

The Official Organ of the Library Assistants' Association.

No. 69.   SEPTEMBER, 1903.   Published Monthly

ANNOUNCEMENTS.

Through lack of support the projected visit to Burnham Beeches has had to be abandoned.

Very few essays for the Prize Competition were received.

On another page the Programme for the 1903-4 Session will be found. Unless otherwise stated, all meetings will be held at the St. Bride Foundation Institute, Bride Lane, Ludgate Circus, E.C., and invitation is extended to all assistants whether members of the Association or not. It will be observed that the papers to be read are without exception on practical and important subjects, so that assistants who wish to increase their knowledge of library matters will do well to attend whenever possible. Further particulars will be printed each month.

DONATION TO THE L.A.A. LIBRARY.

We have pleasure in acknowledging from Mr. Guppy, of the John Rylands Library, a series of useful and interesting papers for the L.A.A. Library. The first is the initial issue of the Quarterly Bulletin of the Rylands Library, which is designed " to record the titles of works acquired for the library during the quarter preceding the date of each issue, in order that students, not only in Manchester, but also in other and distant parts of the world, may be kept informed of the growth of its collections." It is also hoped that reading lists on specific subjects and articles on special collections or famous books, may from time to time be included. This first number is an elaborate affair, quarto in size, on special paper with deckle edges, and containing 57 pages.

There is a pamphlet by Mr. J. P. Edmond, Librarian to the Earl of Crawford, entitled : " Suggestions for the description of books printed between 1501 and 1640," with examples. This is a very helpful paper as we know from experience. Somewhat similar is Augustus de Morgan " On the difficulty of correct description of books." This has an introduction by Mr. Guppy, which tells how this paper was written for the " Companion to the Almanac " for 1853. It is none the less interesting and instructive in spite of the 50 years which have passed since it was first printed.

A fine specimen of printing is the brochure entitled: "The John Rylands Library, Manchester: a brief description of the building and its contents, with a descriptive list of the works exhibited in the main library." Printed for private circulation in July, 1902. There are also two papers by Mr. Guppy—"The Cataloguing of anonymous literature," and "French fiction and French juvenile literature for the Public Library," both reprinted from the "L.A. Record." These, together with the "Synopsis of Lectures," delivered before the Sixth Meeting of the Summer School of the L.A. N.W. Branch, form one of the most acceptable gifts made to the Library for a long time, and the thanks of the Association are due to the donor for his kindly thought in forwarding them.

SESSIONAL PROGRAMME.
1903-1904.

The attention of members is drawn to the following arrangements for next Session, which it is hoped will be fully carried out. Further notice of meetings will be given in our columns from time to time. *Unless otherwise stated, they will be held at the Headquarters of the Association, St. Bride Institute, Bride Lane, E.C.*, at 7.30 for 8 p.m. All library assistants, whether members or not, are cordially invited to attend.

AUTUMN HALF-SESSION.

1903.

Oct. 7. **Inaugural Meeting.**

> To be held at the St. George Public Library, Stepney, by kind invitation of the Stepney Library Authority. Visitors will assemble in the afternoon to view the Royal Mint and Tower of London, and an address will be delivered in the evening by Mr. A. Cawthorne, the Borough Librarian. Further details later.

Nov. 11. **Classification in the Patent Office Library**; by E. WYNDHAM HULME, Librarian.

> Local meeting to be held at the Patent Office at 7.30 *sharp*. Members will be taken round the Library after the paper.

Dec. 16. **Committee Work**; by L. STANLEY JAST, Croydon Public Libraries. Discussion to be opened by R. F. Bullen.

SPRING HALF-SESSION.

1904.

Jan. 13. **Books in Relation to National Efficiency**; by SIDNEY LEE.

Feb. 10. **Lending Library Bookbinding;** by A. J. PHILIP, Hampstead Public Libraries. Discussion to be opened by S. A. Hatcher.

<small>Will describe new cloth binding recently adopted at Hampstead, and exhibit specimens.</small>

Mar. 2. **Prize Essay Reading.** Local meeting at West Ham.

Mar. 16. **Records and Research Work;** by P. EVANS LEWIN, Port Elizabeth Public Library. Discussion to be opened by W. B. Thorne.

<small>Deals with the part of the Public Library in our national and local records. [Will be read by a member of Committee.]</small>

April 20. **The Newspaper of To-Day and the Importance of Our Public Newsrooms;** by G. E. ROEBUCK, Stepney Public Libraries. Discussion to be opened by W. J. Harris.

May 11. **The Principles of Annotation;** by JAS. DUFF BROWN, Finsbury Public Libraries. Discussion to be opened by A. J. Philip.

June 8. **Annual Meeting.**

TWO RECENT ADVERTISEMENTS.

We print the following, which are the duties required of the Librarian to be appointed at the Aylesbury Literary Institution:

<small>To live upon the premises, keep the building and contents in a clean and proper condition, and attend to the lighting and warming thereof; to act as Librarian and be in attendance for the issue and return of books on such days as the Committee shall determine; to see that the Magazines and Newspapers are properly supplied, stamped and arranged on the tables, to collect all monies and subscriptions and pay the same to the Secretaries each week; to act as Billiard Marker, and, if required, undertake catering for the members; to devote his whole time to the duties, and generally carry out the instructions and requirements of the Committee.</small>

Variety is charming, and no doubt it would be a welcome relief to the monotony of cataloguing, to spend an alternate hour at the refreshment bar, serving ginger beer and sandwiches, to say nothing of the excitement of an occasional " hundred up " in the billiard room!

In a recent issue of the " Surrey Comet " the Kingston-on-Thames Public Library advertised for a junior, who was not to be under 16, and preferably one who had passed the Junior Oxford or Cambridge local examinations. For this they were prepared to pay £18 10s. per annum, increasing at the rate of £3 5s. per annum to a maximum of £45 15s.; salary to be paid weekly. As a correspondent points out, the lad would start the job drawing 7s. 1¼d. per week, and when he was 25 years of age, having reached the maximum, he would be in receipt of the princely salary of 17s. 7²/₁₃d. per week!

NOTES, NEWS, AND COMMENTS.

Abuse of Reading Rooms.—In the *Standard, Daily News, Cardiff News*, and other papers, there have been sundry comments and suggestions for restricting Reading Rooms to bona-fide readers, and repressing the ubiquitous somnolent individual. This is a new phase of the "big gooseberry" and "sea serpent" business so familiar at this time of year.

Annfield Plain.—The Public Libraries Acts have been adopted by the Annfield Plain Urban District Council (near Newcastle).

Bishop's Stortford.—A public library is proposed as part of the memorial to Cecil Rhodes in his native town of Bishop's Stortford. Mr. Carnegie is to be applied to for financial help.

British Museum.—A correspondence was carried on in the *Daily Chronicle*, August 7th to 13th, concerning the behaviour of attendants and other small grievances in the Reading Room. The complaining letters were apparently from one or two chronic grumblers.

Carnegie Donations:—

Birkdale (nr. Southport)	£5,000.
Bournemouth	£10,000 for four branches.
Dublin	£28,000.
Erith (Kent)	£7,000.
Exmouth	£3,000.
Ilford	£10,000.
Ince (Lancs.)	£5,000 (declined).
Kensal Rise	£3,000 for extension.
Peterborough	£6,000.
St. Helens (Sutton & Newtown districts)	£6,000.
Teddington	£4,000 for a new building.
Walsall	£8,000.
Yarmouth	£5,000 for extension.
Yarmouth	£2,000 for branches.

Chatham.—The "Cotgreave" Indicator has been adopted at the new library here.

Dunfermline.—When Mr. Carnegie's father began housekeeping in Moodie Street, Dunfermline, a number of young men met and resolved to bring all their books into one place, and thus form a library. When collected they only numbered twenty volumes, and the members of this early library—of which Mr. Carnegie's father was one of the first officials—agreed to tax themselves to the extent of a few pence a month. From this fund they purchased Watt's "Logic," "Improvement of the mind," Beattie on "Truth," Campbell on "Miracles," and "The Gospel its own witness." This was the beginning of the Tradesmen's Library of Dunfermline, and it is interesting to note that the Institute was merged in the Carnegie Free Library founded by the distinguished Scots-American twenty years ago. Visitors to Dunfermline seldom leave the town without seeing Moodie Street and the humble cottage in which the millionaire first saw the light.—*Westminster Gazette*.

Hackney.—In the *Daily News* of August 31st is a letter from a prominent ratepayer, appealing for the establishment of a public library in this large Borough, which would complete the circle of educational institutes provided.

Harwich.—The question of adopting the Public Libraries Acts has been referred to the Corporation School Committee with power to take a poll of the borough if they think desirable.

Lewisham.—The design of Mr. Albert L. Guy, A.R.I.B.A., has been accepted by the Borough Council for the public library at Lower Sydenham. The building will be of red brick with sandstone dressings.

Librarians' Salaries.—In the *Globe* of August 5th and 6th attention was called to the inadequate remuneration of librarians and their assistants, especially in small localities. The wish was expressed that Mr. Carnegie's enthusiasm might extend itself in this direction.

Lord Goschen and Mr. H. G. Wells on Public Libraries.— In the *Times* of August 13th a speech by the former at Oxford is reported. It was delivered at the opening of the proceedings of the University Extension Conference, and dealt with the relationship which ought to exist between that body and the public library. Mr. Wells writes in the August number of the *Fortnightly Review*, in the ninth chapter of his "Mankind in the making," which treats particularly of the organization of higher education. As is usual nowadays, he complains that the public library is not fulfilling its purpose, and suggests the formation of an association which shall publish periodical guides to the best literature in all classes, and to work in conjunction with the library authorities.

New York Public Library.—There is at present on view a collection of dinner menu cards gathered together by a lady member of the staff of the Astor Library. Over 11,000 specimens have been collected in the course of about three years. They have come from all parts of the world, and are written in every language of civilised man. Some are of great historical interest.

Northfleet.—The following advertisement has been published by the District Council, viz.:

"Notice is hereby given that at a Special Meeting of the Northfleet Urban District Council, duly convened and holden at the Council Chamber on Tuesday, the 18th day of August, 1903, at seven p.m., the following resolution was passed unanimously, namely:

"'That the Public Libraries Acts, 1892 to 1901, be adopted for the District of Northfleet, and that such adoption come into operation on the first day of October, 1903.'

"Dated this 19th day of August, 1903.

"CHAS. E. HATTEN, Clerk."

Scunthorpe, Lincs.—The foundation stone of the new public library has been laid, for the building of which Mr. Carnegie has given the sum of £1500.

Shakespeare Memorial Library.—This Library, which was begun exactly forty years ago in Birmingham with little over 1,000 volumes, now contains 11,489. Amongst its treasures are a copy of the first folio (1623), in excellent condition; copies of the second folio (1632); third folio, first issue (1663); third folio, second issue (1664); and fourth folio (1685); and a set of reprints of the early quartos, forty-eight volumes. The Library, we learn, may be said to contain practically every edition and every translation of Shakespeare; all the commentators—good bad and indifferent; in short, every known book connected with the life or the works of our great poet. An index to the library, consisting of 265 pages, has just been issued, from which it appears that there are editions of Shakespeare in the collection in the following languages, in addition to English, French, and German:— Bohemian, Croatian, Danish, Dutch, Finnish, Flemish, Frisian, Greek, Hebrew, Hungarian, Icelandic, Indian, Italian, Latin, Norwegian, Polish, Portuguese, Roumanian, Russian, Ruthenian, Serbian, Spanish, Swedish, and Welsh,

Southend.—By ten votes to eight the Town Council have decided to accept Mr. Carnegie's offer of £8,000, and to adopt the Acts, which will come into force in December next.

The Heywood, Rawtenstall, and Wakefield Councils are advertising for competitive designs for new libraries.

We are informed that a cheap elementary book, on original lines, dealing with British library practice, is in course of preparation, and that publication may be expected shortly.

LIBRARY PUBLICATIONS RECEIVED.

Bournemouth Public Library: Tenth Annual Report, 1902-3. (CHARLES RIDDLE, Librarian).

Croydon Public Libraries: The Readers' Index, Sept.—Oct. Edited by L. STANLEY JAST, Chief Librarian.

> Opens with some running remarks on the notable books of the year, with references to several of the more authoritative reviews. We believe this to be a new idea, and certainly it seems to be a wise move to bring the best books prominently under the notice of readers. There is a useful classified and annotated Reading List on Astronomy, compiled by H. T. Coutts, which is got out in connection with a course of 25 lectures to be given on the subject.

Leyton Library Magazine: August. Edited by Z. MOON.

> Contains a reproduction from a curious old picture of the Dunmow Procession in connection with the famous Dunmow Flitch; a continuation of the biographical index to Essex, and the usual annotated list of recent additions.

Manchester. Public Libraries Quarterly Record. Vol. VII., No. 1. Edited by E. AXON.

> List of recent additions, and list of Parliamentary papers published between January and March, 1903.

Stepney Public Libraries: List of Embossed Books Provided for the Blind.

> A brief author and title list, running into ten pages. All kinds of books are represented—from Euclid down to Doyle's "Adventures of Sherlock Holmes"—including a dictionary. The style of embossing employed in each case is placed in parenthesis after the title. In view of the labour expended upon it this Library for the Blind deserves the success it has attained.

Tottenham Public Libraries: Report for the year ending March, 1903. (F. J. WEST, Librarian.)

West Ham Library Notes, April—June. Edited by A. COTGREAVE, Chief Librarian.

Includes an interesting article entitled "The Mutability of Literature: A colloquy in Westminster Abbey," together with the usual annotated lists of additions. There are also three illustrations, one of which is a very nice photograph of Andrew Marvell's cottage at Highgate, in existence so late as 1868. Altogether this is an interesting and useful number, and will doubtless be appreciated by readers in West Ham.

Willesden Green Public Library: Ninth Annual Report, 1902-3. (F. E. CHENNELL, Librarian).

An interesting report telling of much good work done. Open access has been experimented in by placing about 400 books on open shelves. These are changed every day, so the report says, and a better non-fiction percentage is supposed to have resulted.

APPOINTMENTS.

*BATTY, Mr. T. W. E., First Assistant at the South Branch, to be First Assistant at the Central Library.

BELL, Mr. E. J., of Shepherd's Bush, to be Junior Assistant at the South Branch Library.

*HAWKINS, Mr. W. G., Senior Assistant at the Central Library, to be Sub-Librarian.

*LEWIN, Mr. P. Evans, of Woolwich, to the Public Library, Port Elizabeth, S.A.

We very much regret losing Mr. Lewin so soon after his election on Committee as well as for other reasons, nevertheless we wish him every happiness in his new sphere, and trust that prosperity may attend him. Mr. Charles Welch, of the Guildhall, made the appointment.

*WARMAN, Mr. A. J., of Newport (Mon.), to be Librarian of the Evesham Public Library.

* Members of L.A.A.

NEW MEMBERS.

Senior.—Miss EMILY P. BIBBY, Blackley Branch Library Manchester.

Miss MARGARET J. HOYLE, Widnes.

Junior.—H. HENDERSON, Liverpool Lyceum.

G. PHILPOT, Whitechapel.

NOTICES.

All matter for October Journal should be sent to the Hon. Editor before September 19th.

All other communications should be addressed to the *Hon. Secretary*, Mr. G. E. Roebuck, PUBLIC LIBRARY, 236, CABLE STREET, E.

LIBRARY ASSISTANTS' ASSOCIATION LIBRARY.

CATALOGUE.

Compiled by A. H. CARTER, Hon. Librarian.

LIBRARY MOVEMENT—HISTORY, STATISTICS.

ADMINISTRATION AND APPLIANCES.

DESCRIPTIONS OF LIBRARIES.

LIBRARY ASSOCIATIONS—TRANSACTIONS AND PROCEEDINGS.

LIBRARY SCHOOLS, STUDY CLUBS, &c.

LIBRARY PRIMERS AND HANDBOOKS.

CLASSIFICATIONS.

BOOKBINDING.

PRINTING AND PRINTERS.

BIBLIOGRAPHY.

ANNOTATED LISTS, SPECIAL BIBLIOGRAPHIES.

LITERATURES—ENGLISH, FRENCH, RUSSIAN.

PERIODICAL PUBLICATIONS (OTHER THAN THOSE OF LIBRARY ASSOCIATIONS).

GENERAL.

The Library is located at the St. Martin's Public Library, Charing Cross. Books are loaned to members of the L.A.A. upon paying cost of postage.

LIBRARY MOVEMENT—HISTORY AND STATISTICS.

Greenwood (T.) Free Public Libraries, 1887
    Public Libraries, 3rd Ed., 1890
         ,,   4th Ed., 1894. (3 copies)
    Library Year Book, 1897
        ,,   ,,   1900-01.

Ogle (J. J.) The Free Library: its History and Present Condition, 1897 (Library Ser. 1)

Fovargue and Ogle. Library Legislation, 1855-1890. (Public Lib. Manual, pt. 1) 1892
Public Library Legislation, 1893. (L.A., Ser. 2)

Fovargue (H. W.) Adoption of the Public Libraries Acts in England and Wales, 1896. (L·A. Ser. 7)

Free Libraries Acts, Further Return relating to, 1877

A Bill to amend the Acts relating to Public Libraries, &c., and to regulate the Liability of Managers of Libraries to Proceedings for Libel, 1898

L.C.C. Return relating to Public Libraries in County of London, 1899

Proposals for a Publick Library at Aberdeen, 1764. (Reprinted 1893)

Hales (S.) Working Men and Free Public Libraries, 1889

Spivak (Dr.) How every town may secure a Medical Library, 1897

Why do we need a Public Library? (A.L.A. Library, Tract 1) 1900

Wire (Dr. G. E.) How to Start a Public Library. (A.L.A. Library Tract, 2) 1900

Reyer (Prof.) Entwicklung und Organisation der Volksbibliotheken, 1893

Schwenke (Dr. P.) Adressbuch der Deutschen Bibliotheken, 1893

United States. List of Institutions, Libraries, Colleges, etc. (Smithsonian Inst.) 1872

Public Libraries in the United States. Part 1, 1876

Statistics of Public Libraries, by Weston Flint, 1893

LIBRARY ADMINISTRATION AND APPLIANCES.

Burgoyne (F. J.) Library Construction Architecture, Fittings and Furniture, 1897. (Library Ser. 2)

Macfarlane (John). Library Administration 1898. (Library Ser. 3)

Wheatley (H. B.) Prices of Books, 1898. (Library Ser. 4)

Brown (J. D.) Library Appliances, 1892. (L.A. Ser. 1)

Cowell (P.) Public Library Staffs, 1893. (L.A. Ser. 3)

Biggs (Miss) Women as Public Librarians, 1898. (3 pp.)

Three Papers on Library Trustees read before the American Library Association, 1890

New York Public Library. Preliminary Competition for the building to be erected. 1897

Paris. Instructions pour le Classement et le Fonctionnement des Bibliothèques Municipales, 1892

Swan (R. T.) Paper and Ink. (A.L.A. Pub. Section 2). 1895

DESCRIPTIONS OF LIBRARIES.

Credland (W. R.) The Manchester Public Free Libraries, 1899

The Cambridge (Mass., U.S.A.) Public Library, 1891

Kershaw (S. W.) Lambeth Palace Library and its Kentish Memoranda

Glasgow. Brief Notices of Glasgow and its Libraries, 1897

Milman (Rev. W. H.) Brief Account of the Library of Sion College, 1897

Southward (J.) St. Bride Foundation Institute. A Brief Outline of the Contents of the William Blades and Passmore Edwards Libraries, 1895

Whitney (J. L.) An Index to the Pictures and Plans of Library Buildings to be found in the Boston Public Library, 1899

West Ham. A Souvenir of the Opening of the Technical Institute and Central Public Library, 1898

LIBRARY ASSOCIATIONS—TRANSACTIONS, PROCEEDINGS, ETC.

Library Association, Transactions & Proceedings, Edinburgh, 1880
„   „   „   „   Liverpool, 1883
„   „   „   „   Dublin,   1884
„   „   „   „   Plymouth, 1885
„   „   „   „   Aberdeen, 1893
„   „   „   „   Belfast,   1894
„   „   „   „   London,   1897
  Monthly Notes, V. 3-4. (V. 4 imperfect)
  The Library Chronicle, V. 1-5, 1884-88
  The Library, V. 1-5, 1889-1893
  Year Book for 1892 and 1895.
  L.A. Record, Vol. 1, 1899, to date

Library Assistants' Association. The Library Assistant, vol. 1, 1898-99 to date

Library Association of Australasia :—
  Proceedings of First Conference, Melbourne, 1896 (2 copies)
  Proceedings of Sydney Meeting, 1898

American Library Association. Eighteenth Annual Conference, 1896. Preliminary Papers.
  General Index to the Library Journal, vols. 1-22. (1876-1897)
  See also Periodical Publications

LIBRARY SCHOOLS, STUDY CLUBS, ETC.

Dewey (M.) Simplified Library School Rules, 1898

A.L.A. Report on Library Schools, 1896-97 (8 pp.)

University of the State of New York :—
  Regents' Bulletin, No. 6. Books and Apparatus, 1891
  Extension   „   4. Libraries and University Extension, 1892
     „   „   5. Development of University Extension, 1893
     „   „   7. Extension Teaching, 1894
     „   „   9. Summer Schools, 1895 (3 copies)
     „   „   11. Study Clubs, 1895
     „   „   12. Report of Extension Department, 1894. 1895

v.

LIBRARY PRIMERS AND HANDBOOKS.
Dana (J. C.) A Library Primer, 1899 (2 copies)

Denver Public Library Handbook, 1895

Plummer (M. W.) Hints to small Libraries, 2nd ed., 1898

CLASSIFICATIONS.
Brown, (J. D.) Adjustable Classification for Libraries, 1898. Manual of Library Classification and Shelf Arrangement, 1898

Cutter (C. A.) Expansive Classification, 1891 (added as published).

Dewey (Melvil) Decimal Classification and Relativ Index, 5th Ed. 1894

CATALOGUING.
Quinn (J. H.) Manual of Library Cataloguing, 1899

Wheatley (H. B.) How to Catalogue a Library, 2nd Ed. 1889

Perkins (F. B.) San Francisco Cataloguing, 1884

Library Association Series, No. 5, Cataloguing Rules, 1893

Linderfelt (K. A.) Eclectic Card Catalogue Rules, 1890

U.S. Bureau of Education, Catalogue of " A.L.A." Library, 1893

A.L.A. List of Subject Headings for use in Dictionary Catalogues, 2nd, Ed. 1898

Cutter (C. A.) Rules for a Dictionary Catalogue. Alfabetic-order Table. Two-figures Tables, 1896. Do. Altered and fitted with three figures, by Miss Sanborn

Sacconi-Ricci (G.) Un Nuovo Sistema di Legatura Meccanica per Cataloghi, 1891 (11 pp.)

Cotgreave (A.) Selection of Pseudonyms, or Fictitious Names, 1891

The Cole Cataloguer's Size Card

BOOKBINDING.
Zaehnsdorf (J. W.) The Art of Bookbinding, 1890
Rogers, (F.) The Art of Bookbinding, : A Lecture, 1894 (2 copies)

PRINTING AND PRINTERS.

Southward (John) Practical Printing, 4th Ed. 1892
    Progress in Printing during the Victorian Era, 1897

Duff (E. Gordon) Early Printed Books, 1893.
    Hand-lists of English Printers, 1501-1556, Part 1 (Biblio. Soc.)

Encyclopædia Britannica, 9th Ed. Article "Typography." 1888

BIBLIOGRAPHY.

Bibliographical Society, Transactions, Vol 1, 2, 3 pt. 1. 1893-5

Hyett (F. A.) County Bibliographies, 1896. (24 pp.)

Encyclopædia Britannica, 9th Ed. Article " Bibliography." 1875

Brunet (J.-C.) Manuel du Libraire, 5v. 1844

Lowndes (W. T.) The Bibliographer's Manual, 6v. 1864

Campbell (Frank) The Theory of National and International Bibliography, 1896
    A Plea for Annual Lists of State Papers, 1892
    The Bibliography of the Future, 1895
    Theory of State-Paper Catalogue, 1891
    The Battle of Bibliography, 1893
    Catalogue of Official Reports relating to India, 1893

Delisle (L.) Sir Kenelm Digby et les Anciens Rapports des Bibliothèques Françaises avec la Grande-Bretagne, 1892

Bulletin de l'Institut International de Bibliographie.
    Do. 1895-6. 1e. Année. Fasc. 6.
    Do. 1897. 2e.   „   „ 1-2.
    Do. 1899. 4e.   „   „ 1-2.

ANNOTATED LISTS, SPECIAL BIBLIOGRAPHIES.

Acland (A. H. D.) Guide to the Choice of Books, 1891

Baker (E. A.) Handbook to Fiction. 1899

Burgoyne (F. J.) and Ballinger (John) Books for Village Libraries, 1895 (L.A. Series 6)

Brown (J. D.) Guide to the Formation of a Music Library, 1893 (L. A. Ser. 4).

Cornu (S.) and Beer (W.) List of French Fiction, 1898 (A.L.A. Annotated Lists).

Cotgreave (A.) Analytical or Subject Index to English Prose Fiction, 1891

Chicago Circulating Library, Reference Catalogue for Readers

Hewins (C. M.) A.L.A. Annotated Lists. Books for Boys and Girls, 1897

Leypoldt (A. H.) and Iles (G.) Books for Girls and Women, 1895

Ripley (W. Z.) Selected Bibliography of the Anthropology and Ethnology of Europe, 1899

Sargent (J. F.) Reading for the Young, 1890-96

Sturgis (R.) and Krehbiel (H. E.) Annotated Bibliography of Fine Art, 1897

New York State Library Bulletins, Bibliography:—
 No. 9. The Netherlands, 1898.
  10. Renaissance Art of the 15th and 16th Centuries, 1898
  11. History of the Latter Half of the 15th Century, 1898
  12. Best Books of 1897. 1898
  13. Fairy Tales for Children, 1898
  14. Index to Subject Bibliographies, 1898
  21. Best Books of 1899. 1900.

LITERATURE, ENGLISH.

Arnold (T.) Chaucer to Wordsworth

Brooke (Rev. S.) English Literature (Lit. Primers) 1887

Gosse (E.) A History of 18th Century Literature, 1891

Morley (H.) A First Sketch of English Literature, 1894

Saintsbury (G. A.) History of 19th Century Literature, 1896. A History of Elizabethan Literature, 1894

LITERATURE, FRENCH.

Keene (H. G.) The Literature of France, 1892

Saintsbury, (G.) A Short History of French Literature, 1892

LITERATURE, RUSSIAN.

Panin (I.) Lectures on Russian Literature, 1889

PERIODICALS.

Library Notes, Edited by Melvil Dewey, V. 1-4. 1886-1898

Library World, Vol. 1, 1898, to date (2 copies)

Public Libraries (Chicago) Vol. 2, 1897 to Vol. 5, 1900 (imperfect)

Rivista delle Biblioteche e degli Archivi. v. 9 (Nos. 6-12.)
  Do. v. 10. complete
  Do. v. 11. Nos. 2-3, 7-9, 10-11
  Do. v. 12. Nos. 1, 6-7

Centralblatt für Bibliothekswesen, XIII Jahr. 7 Heft. Juli 1896,
  Do. XIV Jahr. 1-7 Heft. Jan-Jun. 1897

Medical Libraries, Vol. 1. 1898 (Nos. 1, 4-9).
  Do. Vol. 2. 1899 (Jan., May, June)

The Coöperative Index to Periodicals, 1891

The Annual Literary Index, 1892, 1893, 1894

Union List of Periodicals currently received by the New York Libraries, 1887

GENERAL.

Cotgreave, A. Contents-subject index to general and periodical literature, 1900

Dunning (A. E.) The Sunday-School Library, 1884

Hutchins (F. A.) Travelling Libraries (A.L.A. Library Tract, No. 3) 1900

Humphreys (A.L.) The Private Library, 1897

Encyclopædia Britannica, 9th Ed. Article " Libraries "

School Libraries, Reprinted from the " Schoolmaster," 1893

New York State Library, 80th and 81st Reports, 1897-98

Labour Annual, 1895-1899, 5v.

Thomas (E. C.) editor. The Philobiblon of Richard de Bury, 1888

Royal Geographical Society, Year-Book 1898-1899, 2v.

Technical Education Board, Report on Commercial Education, 1899. Annual Report, 1898-9

FIRST PART OF A NEW VOLUME.

VOL. 3.　　OCTOBER, 1901.　　No. 1.

THE OFFICIAL ORGAN OF THE
Library Assistants' Association.

Edited by
H. TAPLEY SOPER,
Public Library, Stoke Newington, N.

Contents.

Ourselves.
Inaugural Meeting *(Seventh Session)*.
Study Circle.
August River Trip.
Mr. J. P. Anderson *(Portrait)*.
L.A. Annual Meeting.
N.W. Branch.
Correspondence.
Notes and News.
Appointments Vacant.

INAUGURAL MEETING (Seventh Session), See Page 3.

Entered at Stationers' Hall.　　No. 46.

ANNUAL SUBSCRIPTION, INCLUDING POSTAGE TO ANY ADDRESS, EITHER AT HOME OR ABROAD

... SOME COTGREAVE LIBRARY AIDS ...
A FEW TESTIMONIALS.

The Indicator.

"**Library Construction, Architecture, Fittings, and Furniture.**"
By F. J. BURGOYNE.

"The Cotgreave Indicator is that in use in the majority of the British Free Libraries."

"**The Free Library: Its History and Present Condition.**"
By J. J. OGLE.

"The Recording Indicator is almost certainly the invention of Mr. A. Cotgreave (Public Libraries, West Ham, London, E.), and is that most largely used."†

"THE SCOTSMAN."

"All the London Free Public Libraries which use indicators, except one, have adopted the Cotgreave System, which has been found to work well."‡

N.B. See also "Greater London," by E. Walford, M.A., F.S.A. (page 360); Methods of Social Reform," by Prof. W. Stanley Jevons, M.A., F.R.S., LL.D.; "Public Libraries," by T. Greenwood, F.R.G.S.; &c., &c.

† As a matter of fact it will be found in about nine-tenths of the Libraries using Indicators. Over 350 Institutions are now using it.

‡ *Sixty-two Public Libraries in London and the Metropolitan area are using it.*

The Simplex Shelf Supports

The Shelves can be raised or lowered by one person without moving or disarranging a single book, and in half the time required by any other system. No space is lost; no mechanism to get jammed, or otherwise out of order, or nip the fingers; no danger to Bindings by projecting metal or wooden fittings; no tilting of shelves. The Fittings are entirely out of sight when the Books are in position, unless more space is allowed between the shelves than is generally required. While No. 1 is perhaps best for very heavy books, No. 2 is quite safe for ordinary books, and is cheaper and more readily fitted. Two-thirds of the woodwork required with other designs is saved, while the cost of joinery is greatly reduced. It can be fitted to iron stacks.

The Contents=Subject Index,
TO GENERAL AND PERIODICAL LITERATURE.

Large Post 8vo., Cloth, Gilt (750 pp.), 10s. 6d. (Reduced to 7s. 6d. for Library Assistants.)

ACADEMY. —" We consider that the author has done a great service to literary workers and students."
WESTMINSTER REVIEW.—" It has been left to Mr. Cotgreave to compile a work which supplies precisely the information required by the general reader."
SATURDAY REVIEW. —" It represents a vast amount of work, and will be prized by students of current literature."
PUBLIC OPINION. —" We have nothing but praise for this work."
BOOKMAN. —" Such a work as this is of inestimable value to librarians."
SCHOOL GUARDIAN.—" This is a very valuable book of reference."

NEARLY READY. Views and Memoranda of Public Libraries (several hundred illustrations). Subscription price 7/6, when published 10/6 net

Full particulars of the above and also of other Library Aids sent upon application to the

LIBRARY AIDS CO.,
166a, Romford Road, Stratford, London, E.

...The British Library Year Book, 1900-1901. ...
A Record of Library Progress and Work.
54 Illustrations, crown 8 vo., 345 pp.
Price 3s. net, post free.

RECENT TECHNICAL WORKS.

Re-Issue of Chemical Essays of C. W. Scheele, 5s.
Colour Matching on Textiles, 7s. 6d.
The Prevention of Smoke, 7s. 6d.
Analysis of Resins, 7s. 6d.
Workshop Wrinkles for Decorators, etc., 2s. 6d.
Dyeing of Cotton Fabrics, 7s. 6d.
Manufacture of Paint, 7s. 6d.
Notes on Lead Ores, 2s. 6d.
Manufacture of Lake Pigments from Artificial Colours, 7s. 6d.
Practical Treatise on the Manufacture of Leather, 21s.
Glue and Glue Testing, 10s. 6d.
Practical Compounding of Oils and Grease for lubrication, 7s. 6d.
Soaps, the manufacture of domestic, toilet and other soaps, 12s. 6d.
Iron Corrosion, Anti-fouling, and Anti-corrosive Paints, 10s. 6d.
Lubricating Oils, Fats and Greases, 10s. 6d.
Chemistry and Essential Oils and Artificial Perfumes, 12s. 6d.
Hops in their Botanical and Technical aspect, 12s. 6d.
History of Decorative Art, 2s. 6d.
House Decorating and Painting, 3s. 6d.
Dyeing of Paper Pulp, with 157 dyed patterns, 15s.
Practical Treatise on the Bleaching of Linen and Cotton Yarn and Fabrics, 12s. 6d.
Risks and Dangers of Various Occupations and their Prevention, 7/6
Gas and Coal Dust Firing, 7s. 6d.
Recovery Work after Pit Fires, 10s. 6d.
Pure Air, Ozone and Water, in the manufacture of oil, glue, etc., 5s.
Leather Worker's Manual, 7s. 6d.
Architectural Pottery, 15s.
Painting on Glass and Porcelain, 10s. 6d.
Colour : A handbook of the theory of colour, 7s. 6d.
Colour Printing of Carpet Yarns, 7s. 6d.
Science of Colour Mixing, 7s. 6d.
Hints to Plumbers, 7s. 6d.
Principles of Hot Water Supply, 7s. 6d.
External Plumbing Work, 7s. 6d.
The Manufacture of Alum and the Sulphates and other Salts of Alumina and Iron, 12s. 6d.
Drying Oils, Boiled Oil and Solid and Liquid Driers, 12/6.
Technology of Petroleum, 21s.
Dictionary of Chemicals and Raw Materials used in the Manufacture of Paints, Colours, Varnishes and Allied Preparations, 7/6.
Bone Products and Manures, 7/6.
Practical X Ray Work, 10s. 6d.
Drying by means of Air and Steam, 5s.

Catalogues on application.

SCOTT, GREENWOOD & Co., Publishers,
19 Ludgate Hill, London, E.C.

SPECIAL—TO LIBRARIANS.

Books Supplied and Bound from the Quire, in flexible Pigskin, Morocco, or a Sanitary Washable Cloth specially manufactured for us.

GUARANTEE:
We guarantee that our Binding will outlast the Book,

BOOKS RE-BOUND.   READERS' TICKETS IN LEATHER OR CLOTH.

Solid Leather Reading Covers, made in one piece, without Lining or Stitches; practically indestructible.

AN INEXPENSIVE READING COVER IN OUR SANITARY WASHABLE CLOTH.

One of the many Testimonials received by us:—

"CHELSEA PUBLIC LIBRARIES,"
December 3rd, 1896.

Messrs. Banting & Son have been the bookbinders to these Libraries from the commencement, in 1888, and have given every satisfaction.

Their work is lasting, reasonable in price, and carefully carried out.

The fact that they are binders under contract to a large number of Public Libraries is sufficient proof that in this particular line they are difficult to beat.

J. HENRY QUINN,
Chief Librarian and Clerk to the Commissioners.

PARTICULARS, PRICES, AND SAMPLES ON APPLICATION.

J. BANTING & SON

Bookbinders and Booksellers,

KING'S ROAD, CHELSEA, LONDON.

Printed by R. TOMSETT & CO., at 21 Station Road, Kensal Rise, W., and Published for the Library Assistants' Association, October 1st, 1901.

Vol. 3. NOVEMBER, 1901. No. 2.

THE OFFICIAL ORGAN OF THE
Library Assistants' Association.

Edited by
H. TAPLEY SOPER,
Public Library, Stoke Newington, N.

Contents.

	PAGE.
London Meetings ...	13
Vacancy on Committee ...	14
Fourth Annual Dinner ...	14
N.W. Branch Meetings ...	14-16
The Inaugural Meeting ...	16
Study Circle ...	18
The Young Librarian, by C. WELCH, F.S.A.	19
New Members ...	23
Edward Foskett, F.R.S.L. An appreciation, by C. F. Newcombe ...	24
Notes and News ...	23, 26
Appointments and Changes ...	27, 28
Notices ...	28

Entered at Stationers' Hall.   No. 47.

ANNUAL SUBSCRIPTION, INCLUDING POSTAGE TO ANY ADDRESS, EITHER AT HOME OR ABROAD, 3s.

... SOME COTGREAVE LIBRARY AIDS ...
A FEW TESTIMONIALS.

The Indicator.

"**LIBRARY CONSTRUCTION, ARCHITECTURE, FITTINGS, AND FURNITURE.**"
BY F. J. BURGOYNE.

"The Cotgreave Indicator is that in use in the majority of the British Free Libraries.

"**THE FREE LIBRARY: ITS HISTORY AND PRESENT CONDITION.**"
BY J. J. OGLE.

"The Recording Indicator is almost certainly the invention of Mr. A. Cotgreave (Public Libraries, West Ham, London, E.), and is that most largely used."†

"THE SCOTSMAN."

"All the London Free Public Libraries which use indicators, except one, have adopted the Cotgreave System, which has been found to work well."†

N.B. See also "Greater London," by E. Walford, M.A., F.S.A. (page 360); Methods of Social Reform," by Prof. W. Stanley Jevons, M.A., F.R.S., LL.D.; "Public Libraries," by T. Greenwood, F.R.G.S.; &c., &c.

† As a matter of fact it will be found in about nine-tenths of the Libraries using Indicators. Over 350 Institutions are now using it.

† *Sixty-two Public Libraries in London and the Metropolitan area are using it.*

The Simplex Shelf Supports

The Shelves can be raised or lowered by one person without moving or disarranging a single book, and in half the time required by any other system. No space is lost; no mechanism to get jammed, or otherwise out of order, or nip the fingers; no danger to Bindings by projecting metal or wooden fittings; no tilting of shelves. The Fittings are entirely out of sight when the Books are in position, unless more space is allowed between the shelves than is generally required. While No. 1 is perhaps best for very heavy books, No. 2 is quite safe for ordinary books, and is cheaper and more readily fitted. Two-thirds of the woodwork required with other designs is saved, while the cost of joinery is greatly reduced. It can be fitted to iron stacks.

The Contents=Subject Index,
TO GENERAL AND PERIODICAL LITERATURE.

Large Post 8vo., Cloth, Gilt (75 pp.), 10s. 6d. Reduced to 7s. 6d. for Library Assistants.)

ACADEMY. —" We consider that the author has done a great service to literary workers and students."
WESTMINSTER REVIEW. —" It has been left to Mr. Cotgreave to compile a work which supplies precisely the information required by the general reader."
SATURDAY REVIEW. —" It represents a vast amount of work, and will be prized by students of current literature."
PUBLIC OPINION. —" We have nothing but praise for this work."
BOOKMAN. —" Such a work as this is of inestimable value to librarians."
SCHOOL GUARDIAN. —" This is a very valuable book of reference."

NEARLY READY. Views and Memoranda of Public Libraries (several hundred illustrations). Subscription price 7/6, when published 10/6 net

Full particulars of the above and also of other Library Aids sent upon application to the

LIBRARY AIDS CO.,
166a, Romford Road, Stratford, London, E.

Vol. 3.   DECEMBER, 1901,   No. 3.

THE OFFICIAL ORGAN OF THE
Library Assistants' Association.

Edited by
H. TAPLEY SOPER,
Public Library, Stoke Newington, N.

Contents.

	PAGE
December Meetings	29
Account of November Meetings	29-33
N.W. Branch, January Meeting	33
Opening of the Woolwich Library	33
The President of the Library Association on 'Salaries'	34
Society of Public Librarians—Annual Meeting	35
Study Circle	35
Notes and News	36
New Members	40
Appointments	40
Appointments Vacant	40
Errata	40
Notices	40

Entered at Stationers' Hall.   **No. 48.**

ANNUAL SUBSCRIPTION, INCLUDING POSTAGE TO ANY ADDRESS, EITHER AT HOME OR ABROAD, **3s.**

SOME COTGREAVE LIBRARY AIDS.
A FEW TESTIMONIALS.

The Indicator.

"**LIBRARY CONSTRUCTION, ARCHITECTURE, FITTINGS, AND FURNITURE.**"
BY F. J. BURGOYNE.
"The Cotgreave Indicator is that in use in the majority of the British Free Libraries."

"**THE FREE LIBRARY: ITS HISTORY AND PRESENT CONDITION.**"
BY J. J. OGLE.
"The Recording Indicator is almost certainly the invention of Mr. A. Cotgreave (Public Libraries, West Ham, London, E.), and is that most largely used. '†

"THE SCOTSMAN."
"All the London Free Public Libraries which use indicators, except one, have adopted the Cotgreave System, which has been found to work well."†

N.B.—See also "Greater London," by E. Walford, M.A., F.S.A. (page 360); "Methods of Social Reform," by Prof. W. Stanley Jevons, M.A., F.R.S., LL.D.; "Public Libraries," by T. Greenwood, F.R.G.S.; &c., &c.

† As a matter of fact it will be found in about nine-tenths of the Libraries using Indicators. Over 350 Institutions are now using it.

† Sixty-two Public Libraries in London and the Metropolitan area are using it.

The Simplex Shelf Supports

The Shelves can be raised or lowered by one person without moving or disarranging a single book, and in half the time required by any other system. No space is lost; no mechanism to get jammed, or otherwise out of order, or nip the fingers; no danger to Bindings by projecting metal or wooden fittings; no tilting of shelves. The Fittings are entirely out of sight when the Books are in position, unless more space is allowed between the shelves than is generally required. While No. 1 is perhaps best for very heavy books, No. 2 is quite safe for ordinary books, and is cheaper and more readily fitted. Two-thirds of the woodwork required with other designs is saved, while the cost of joinery is greatly reduced. It can be fitted to iron stacks.

The Contents=Subject Index
TO GENERAL AND PERIODICAL LITERATURE.
Large Post 8vo., Cloth, Gilt (750 pp.), 10s. 6d. Reduced to 7s. 6d. for Library Assistants.

ACADEMY.—"We consider that the author has done a great service to literary workers and students,"
WESTMINSTER REVIEW.—"It has been left to Mr. Cotgreave to compile a work which supplies precisely the information required by the general reader."
SATURDAY REVIEW.—"It represents a vast amount of work, and will be prized by students of current literature."
PUBLIC OPINION.—"We nave nothing but praise for this work."
BOOKMAN.—"Such a work as this is of inestimable value to librarians."
SCHOOL GUARDIAN.—"This is a very valuable book of reference."

NEARLY READY. Views and Memoranda of Public Libraries (several hundred illustrations). Subscription price 7/6, when published 10/6 net

Full particulars of the above and also of other Library Aids sent upon application to the

LIBRARY AIDS CO.,
166a, Romford Road, Stratford, London, E.

Vol. 3. JANUARY, 1902. No. 4.

THE OFFICIAL ORGAN OF THE
Library Assistants' Association.

Edited by
H. TAPLEY SOPER,
Public Library, Stoke Newington, N.

Contents.

	PAGE
A. Cotgreave, Esq., F.R.Hist.S. (*port.*)	41
January Meeting	41
December Meeting	41
N.W. Branch Annual Meeting	42
N.W. Branch January Meeting	43
N.W. Branch Subscriptions	43
Fourth Annual Dinner	43
Librarianship in South Africa	46
L.A., N.W. Summer School	47
Study Circle	47
How to popularise a Public Library. By W. J. Harris	49
Notes and News	51
New Members	51
Appointments and Changes	52
Appointments Vacant	52
Notices	52

Entered at Stationers' Hall.
No. 49.

ANNUAL SUBSCRIPTION,
INCLUDING POSTAGE TO
ANY ADDRESS, EITHER
AT HOME OR ABROAD, **3s.**

SOME COTGREAVE LIBRARY AIDS.
A FEW TESTIMONIALS.

The Indicator.

"LIBRARY CONSTRUCTION, ARCHITECTURE, FITTINGS, AND FURNITURE."
BY F. J. BURGOYNE.

"The Cotgreave Indicator is that in use in the majority of the British Free Libraries."

"THE FREE LIBRARY: ITS HISTORY AND PRESENT CONDITION."
BY J. J. OGLE.

"The Recording Indicator is almost certainly the invention of Mr. A. Cotgreave (Public Libraries, West Ham, London, E.), and is that most largely used."†

"THE SCOTSMAN."

"All the London Free Public Libraries, which use indicators, except one, have adopted the Cotgreave System, which has been found to work well."†

N.B.—See also "Greater London," by E. Walford, M.A., F.S.A. (page 360); "Methods of Social Reform," by Prof. W. Stanley Jevons, M.A., F.R.S., LL.D.; "Public Libraries," by T. Greenwood, F.R.G.S.; &c., &c.

† As a matter of fact it will be found in about nine-tenths of the Libraries using Indicators Over 350 Institutions are now using it.

† *Sixty-two Public Libraries in London and the Metropolitan area are using it.*

The Simplex Shelf Supports

The Shelves can be raised or lowered by one person without moving or disarranging a single book, and in half the time required by any other system. No space is lost; no mechanism to get jammed, or otherwise out of order, or nip the fingers; no danger to Bindings by projecting metal or wooden fittings; no tilting of shelves. The Fittings are entirely out of sight when the Books are in position, unless more space is allowed between the shelves than is generally required. While No. 1 is perhaps best for very heavy books, No. 2 is quite safe for ordinary books, and is cheaper and more readily fitted. Two-thirds of the woodwork required with other designs is saved, while the cost of joinery is greatly reduced. It can be fitted to iron stacks.

The Contents=Subject Index

TO GENERAL AND PERIODICAL LITERATURE.

Large Post 8vo., Cloth, Gilt (750 pp.), 10s. 6d. Reduced to 7s. 6d. for Library Assistants.

ACADEMY.—"We consider that the author has done a great service to literary workers and students."
WESTMINSTER REVIEW.—"It has been left to Mr. Cotgreave to compile a work which supplies precisely the information required by the general reader."
SATURDAY REVIEW.—"It represents a vast amount of work, and will be prized by students of current literature."
PUBLIC OPINION.—"We have nothing but praise for this work."
BOOKMAN.—"Such a work as this is of inestimable value to librarians."
SCHOOL GUARDIAN.—"This is a very valuable book of reference."

NEARLY READY. Views and Memoranda of Public Libraries (several hundred illustrations). Subscription price 7/6, when published 10/6 net

Full particulars of the above and also of other Library Aids sent upon application to the

LIBRARY AIDS CO.,
166a, Romford Road, Stratford, London, E.

Vol. 3.   FEBRUARY, 1902.   No. 5.

THE OFFICIAL ORGAN OF THE
Library Assistants' Association.

Edited by
H. TAPLEY SOPER,
Public Library, Stoke Newington, N.

Contents.

	PAGE
February Meeting	53
Social Gathering	53
January Meeting	53
N.W. Branch January Meeting...	54
N.W. Branch March Meeting	55
Opening of the Mile End Library	55
,, ,, Rankin Reading Room, Glasgow	56
The Woes of a Librarian, by F. E. Chennell ...	56
Study Circle ... ..., ...	61
Notes and News	62
Mr. Macalister's Annual Prizes	62
Appointments and Changes	63
New Members	64
Books, &c., Received	64
Appointments Vacant	64
Notices...	64

Entered at Stationers' Hall.   No. 50.   ANNUAL SUBSCRIPTION, INCLUDING POSTAGE TO ANY ADDRESS, EITHER AT HOME OR ABROAD, **3s.**

SOME COTGREAVE LIBRARY AIDS.
A FEW TESTIMONIALS.

The Indicator.

"**LIBRARY CONSTRUCTION, ARCHITECTURE, FITTINGS, AND FURNITURE.**"
BY F. J. BURGOYNE.

"The Cotgreave Indicator is that in use in the majority of the British Free Libraries."

"**THE FREE LIBRARY: ITS HISTORY AND PRESENT CONDITION.**"
BY J. J. OGLE.

"The Recording Indicator is almost certainly the invention of Mr. A. Cotgreave (Public Libraries, West Ham, London, E.), and is that most largely used."†

"**THE SCOTSMAN.**"

"All the 'London Free Public Libraries which use indicators, except one, have adopted the Cotgreave System, which has been found to work well."†

N.B.—See also "Greater London," by E. Walford, M.A., F.S.A. (page 360); "Methods of Social Reform," by Prof. W. Stanley Jevons, M.A., F.R.S., LL.D.; "Public Libraries," by T. Greenwood, F.R.G.S.; &c., &c.

† As a matter of fact it will be found in about nine-tenths of the Libraries using Indicators Over 350 Institutions are now using it.

† Sixty-two Public Libraries in London and the Metropolitan area are using it.

The Simplex Shelf Supports

The Shelves can be raised or lowered by one person without moving or disarranging a single book, and in half the time required by any other system. No space is lost; no mechanism to get jammed, or otherwise out of order, or nip the fingers: no danger to Bindings by projecting metal or wooden fittings; no tilting of shelves. The Fittings are entirely out of sight when the Books are in position, unless more space is allowed between the shelves than is generally required. While No. 1 is perhaps best for very heavy books. No. 2 is quite safe for ordinary books, and is cheaper and more readily fitted. Two-thirds of the woodwork required with other designs is saved, while the cost of joinery is greatly reduced. It can be fitted to iron stacks.

The Contents=Subject Index

TO GENERAL AND PERIODICAL LITERATURE.
Large Post 8vo., Cloth, Gilt (750 pp.), 10s. 6d. Reduced to 7s. 6d. for Library Assistants.

ACADEMY.—"We consider that the author has done a great service to literary workers and students."
WESTMINSTER REVIEW.—"It has been left to Mr. Cotgreave to compile a work which supplies precisely the information required by the general reader."
SATURDAY REVIEW.—"It represents a vast amount of work, and will be prized by students of current literature."
PUBLIC OPINION.—"We have nothing but praise for this work."
BOOKMAN.—"Such a work as this is of inestimable value to librarians."
SCHOOL GUARDIAN.—"This is a very valuable book of reference."

NEARLY READY. Views and Memoranda of Public Libraries (several hundred illustrations). Subscription price 7/6, when published 10/6 net

Full particulars of the above and also of other Library Aids sent upon application to the

LIBRARY AIDS CO.,
166a, Romford Road, Stratford, London, E.

Vol. 3.   MARCH, 1902.   No. 6.

SOCIAL GATHERING (see page 65).

THE OFFICIAL ORGAN OF THE

Library Assistants' Association.

Edited by
H. TAPLEY SOPER,
Public Library, Stoke Newington, N.

Contents.

	PAGE
Editorial: The Library Association Classes	68
Titles of Honour in Catalogues, by P. EVANS LEWIN	69
March Meeting	65
N.W. Branch March Meeting	67
February Meeting	66
Study Circle	72
Notes and News	72
Appointments and Changes...	76

Entered at Stationers' Hall.
No. 51.

ANNUAL SUBSCRIPTION, INCLUDING POSTAGE TO ANY ADDRESS, EITHER AT HOME OR ABROAD, **3s.**

SOME COTGREAVE LIBRARY AIDS.
A FEW TESTIMONIALS.

The Indicator.

"**LIBRARY CONSTRUCTION, ARCHITECTURE, FITTINGS, AND FURNITURE.**"
BY F. J. BURGOYNE.

"The Cotgreave Indicator is that in use in the majority of the British Free Libraries."

"**THE FREE LIBRARY: ITS HISTORY AND PRESENT CONDITION.**"
BY J. J. OGLE.

"The Recording Indicator is almost certainly the invention of Mr. A. Cotgreave (Public Libraries, West Ham, London, E.), and is that most largely used."†

"**THE SCOTSMAN.**"

"All the London Free Public Libraries which use indicators, except one, have adopted the Cotgreave System, which has been found to work well."‡

N.B.—See also "Greater London," by E. Walford, M.A., F.S.A. (page 360); "Methods of Social Reform," by Prof. W. Stanley Jevons, M.A., F.R.S., LL.D.; "Public Libraries," by T. Greenwood, F.R.G.S.; &c., &c.

† As a matter of fact it will be found in about nine-tenths of the Libraries using Indicators. Over 350 Institutions are now using it.

‡ *Sixty-two Public Libraries in London and the Metropolitan area are using it.*

The Simplex Shelf Supports

The Shelves can be raised or lowered by one person without moving or disarranging a single book, and in half the time required by any other system. No space is lost; no mechanism to get jammed, or otherwise out of order, or nip the fingers; no danger to Bindings by projecting metal or wooden fittings; no tilting of shelves. The Fittings are entirely out of sight when the Books are in position, unless more space is allowed between the shelves than is generally required. While No. 1 is perhaps best for very heavy books, No. 2 is quite safe for ordinary books, and is cheaper and more readily fitted. Two-thirds of the woodwork required with other designs is saved, while the cost of joinery is greatly reduced. It can be fitted to iron stacks.

The Contents=Subject Index
TO GENERAL AND PERIODICAL LITERATURE.

Large Post 8vo., Cloth, Gilt (750 pp.), 10s. 6d. Reduced to 7s. 6d. for Library Assistants.

ACADEMY.—"We consider that the author has done a great service to literary workers and students."
WESTMINSTER REVIEW.—"It has been left to Mr. Cotgreave to compile a work which supplies precisely the information required by the general reader."
SATURDAY REVIEW.—"It represents a vast amount of work, and will be prized by students of current literature."
PUBLIC OPINION.—"We have nothing but praise for this work."
BOOKMAN.—"Such a work as this is of inestimable value to librarians."
SCHOOL GUARDIAN.—"This is a very valuable book of reference."

NEARLY READY. Views and Memoranda of Public Libraries (several hundred illustrations). Subscription price 7/6, when published 10/6 net

Full particulars of the above and also of other Library Aids sent upon application to the

LIBRARY AIDS CO.,
166a, Romford Road, Stratford, London, E.

Vol. 3. APRIL, 1902. No. 7.

THE OFFICIAL ORGAN OF THE

Library Assistants' Association.

Edited by
H. TAPLEY SOPER,
Public Library, Stoke Newington, N.

Contents.

	PAGE
April Meeting	77
March Meeting	77
N.W. Branch March Meeting	80
N.W. Branch April Meeting	80
OUR WORK, by R. W. MOULD, F.S.A., SCOT.	80
Notes and News	87
Study Circle	89
"Cotgreave" & "L.A.A." Prizes	90
Correspondence	90
Appointments Vacant	92

Entered at Stationers' Hall.   No. 52.

ANNUAL SUBSCRIPTION, INCLUDING POSTAGE TO ANY ADDRESS, EITHER AT HOME OR ABROAD, 3s.

SOME COTGREAVE LIBRARY AIDS.
A FEW TESTIMONIALS.

The Indicator.

"LIBRARY CONSTRUCTION, ARCHITECTURE, FITTINGS, AND FURNITURE."
BY F. J. BURGOYNE.

"The Cotgreave Indicator is that in use in the majority of the British Free Libraries."

"THE SCOTSMAN."

"All the London Free Public Libraries which use indicators, except one, have adopted the Cotgreave System, which has been found to work well."†

N.B. See also "Greater London," by E. Walford, M.A., F.S.A. (page 360); "Methods of Social Reform," by Prof. W. Stanley Jevons, M.A., F.R.S., LL.D.; "Public Libraries," by T. Greenwood, F.R.G.S.; &c., &c.

As a matter of fact it will be found in about nine-tenths of the Libraries using Indicators. Over 350 Institutions are now using it.

Recently adopted at the Birmingham, Cologne, and many other Libraries.

† *Sixty-two Public Libraries in London and the Metropolitan area are using it.*

The Simplex Shelf Supports

The Shelves can be raised or lowered by one person without moving or disarranging a single book, and in half the time required by any other system. No space is lost; no mechanism to get jammed, or otherwise out of order, or nip the fingers; no danger to Bindings by projecting metal or wooden fittings; no tilting of shelves. The Fittings are entirely out of sight when the Books are in position, unless more space is allowed between the shelves than is generally required. While No. 1 is perhaps best for very heavy books, No. 2 is quite safe for ordinary books, and is cheaper and more readily fitted. Two-thirds of the woodwork required with other designs is saved, while the cost of joinery is greatly reduced. It can be fitted to iron stacks.

The Contents=Subject Index

TO GENERAL AND PERIODICAL LITERATURE.

Large Post 8vo., Cloth, Gilt (750 pp.), 10s. 6d.

A limited number will be supplied to Library Assistants at 3s. 6d.

ACADEMY.—"We consider that the author has done a great service to literary workers and students."

WESTMINSTER REVIEW.—"It has been left to Mr. Cotgreave to compile a work which supplies precisely the information required by the general reader."

SATURDAY REVIEW.—"It represents a vast amount of work, and will be prized by students of current literature."

PUBLIC OPINION.—"We have nothing but praise for this work."

BOOKMAN.—"Such a work as this is of inestimable value to librarians."

SCHOOL GUARDIAN.—"This is a very valuable book of reference."

Views and Memoranda of Public Libraries (several hundred illustrations). Subscription price 7/6, when published 10/6 net.

Full particulars of the above and also of other Library Aids sent upon application to the

LIBRARY AIDS CO.,
166a, Romford Road, Stratford, London, E.

Vol. 3.   MAY, 1902.   No. 8.

ANNUAL MEETING (see page 93).

THE OFFICIAL ORGAN OF THE

Library Assistants' Association.

Edited by
H. TAPLEY SOPER,
Public Library, Stoke Newington, N.

Contents.

	PAGE
Editorial: The L.A. Revised Examination Syllabus ...	95
War and the Library—Stray Notes. By BERTRAM L. DYER	97
May Meeting ...	93
April Meeting ...	94
N.W. Branch May Meeting	94
Library Association Examination ...	95
Study Circle ...	101
Notes and Comments	102
Books received	103

Entered at Stationers' Hall.   **No. 53.**

ANNUAL SUBSCRIPTION, INCLUDING POSTAGE TO ANY ADDRESS, EITHER AT HOME OR ABROAD, **3s.**

SOME COTGREAVE LIBRARY AIDS.
A FEW TESTIMONIALS.

The Indicator.

"LIBRARY CONSTRUCTION, ARCHITECTURE, FITTINGS, AND FURNITURE."
BY F. J. BURGOYNE.

"The Cotgreave Indicator is that in use in the majority of the British Free Libraries."

"THE SCOTSMAN."

" All the London Free Public Libraries which use indicators, except one, have adopted the Cotgreave System, which has been found to work well."†

N.B.—See also "Greater London," by E. Walford, M.A., F.S.A. (page 360); "Methods of Social Reform," by Prof. W. Stanley Jevons, M.A., F.R.S., LL.D.; "Public Libraries," by T. Greenwood, F.R.G.S.; &c., &c.

As a matter of fact it will be found in about nine-tenths of the Libraries using Indicators. Over 350 Institutions are now using it.

Recently adopted at the Birmingham, Cologne, and many other Libraries.

† *Sixty-two Public Libraries in London and the Metropolitan area are using it.*

The Simplex Shelf Supports

The Shelves can be raised or lowered by one person without moving or disarranging a single book, and in half the time required by any other system. No space is lost; no mechanism to get jammed, or otherwise out of order, or nip the fingers; no danger to Bindings by projecting metal or wooden fittings; no tilting of shelves. The Fittings are entirely out of sight when the Books are in position, unless more space is allowed between the shelves than is generally required. While No. 1 is perhaps best for very heavy books, No. 2 is quite safe for ordinary books, and is cheaper and more readily fitted. Two-thirds of the woodwork required with other designs is saved, while the cost of joinery is greatly reduced. It can be fitted to iron stacks.

The Contents-Subject Index

TO GENERAL AND PERIODICAL LITERATURE.

Large Post 8vo., Cloth, Gilt (750 pp.), 10s. 6d.

A limited number will be supplied to Library Assistants at 3s. 6d.

ACADEMY.—"We consider that the author has done a great service to literary workers and students."

WESTMINSTER REVIEW.—"It has been left to Mr. Cotgreave to compile a work which supplies precisely the information required by the general reader."

SATURDAY REVIEW.—"It represents a vast amount of work, and will be prized by students of current literature."

PUBLIC OPINION. "We have nothing but praise for this work."

BOOKMAN.—"Such a work as this is of inestimable value to librarians."

SCHOOL GUARDIAN. "This is a very valuable book of reference."

Views and Memoranda of Public Libraries (several hundred illustrations). Subscription price 7/6, when published 10/6 net.

Full particulars of the above and also of other Library Aids sent upon application to the

LIBRARY AIDS CO.,
166a, Romford Road, Stratford, London, E.

ANNUAL REPORT NUMBER.

VOL. 3.   JUNE, 1902.   No. 9.

PROPOSED CONFERENCE—See Page 106.

THE OFFICIAL ORGAN OF THE

Library Assistants' Association.

Edited by
H. TAPLEY SOPER,
Public Library, Stoke Newington, N.

Contents.

	PAGE
Annual Meeting	105
Prize Essays—Special Notice	106
Summer Programme	106
May Meeting	107
Study Circle	109
Correspondence	110
Notes and Comments	113 & 125
Appointments	128

Entered at Stationers' Hall.   **No. 54.**

ANNUAL SUBSCRIPTION,
INCLUDING POSTAGE TO
ANY ADDRESS, EITHER
AT HOME OR ABROAD, **3s.**

SOME COTGREAVE LIBRARY AIDS.
A FEW TESTIMONIALS.

The Indicator.

"LIBRARY CONSTRUCTION, ARCHITECTURE, FITTINGS, AND FURNITURE."
BY F. J. BURGOYNE.

"The Cotgreave Indicator is that in use in the majority of the British Free Libraries."

"THE SCOTSMAN."

"All the London Free Public Libraries which use indicators, except one, have adopted the Cotgreave System, which has been found to work well."†

N.B.—See also "Greater London," by E. Walford, M.A., F.S.A. (page 360); "Methods of Social Reform," by Prof. W. Stanley Jevons, M.A., F.R.S., LL.D.; "Public Libraries," by T. Greenwood, F.R.G.S.; &c., &c.

As a matter of fact it will be found in about nine-tenths of the Libraries using Indicators. Over 350 Institutions are now using it.

Recently adopted at the Birmingham, Cologne, and many other Libraries.

† *Sixty-two Public Libraries in London and the Metropolitan area are using it.*

The Simplex Shelf Supports

The Shelves can be raised or lowered by one person without moving or disarranging a single book, and in half the time required by any other system. No space is lost; no mechanism to get jammed, or otherwise out of order, or nip the fingers: no danger to Bindings by projecting metal or wooden fittings: no tilting of shelves. The Fittings are entirely out of sight when the Books are in position, unless more space is allowed between the shelves than is generally required. While No. 1 is perhaps best for very heavy books, No. 2 is quite safe for ordinary books, and is cheaper and more readily fitted. Two-thirds of the woodwork required with other designs is saved, while the cost of joinery is greatly reduced. It can be fitted to iron stacks.

The Contents=Subject Index

TO GENERAL AND PERIODICAL LITERATURE.

Large Post 8vo., Cloth, Gilt (750 pp.), 10s. 6d.

A limited number will be supplied to Library Assistants at 3s. 6d.

ACADEMY.—"We consider that the author has done a great service to literary workers and students."

WESTMINSTER REVIEW.—"It has been left to Mr. Cotgreave to compile a work which supplies precisely the information required by the general reader."

SATURDAY REVIEW.—"It represents a vast amount of work, and will be prized by students of current literature."

PUBLIC OPINION.—"We have nothing but praise for this work."

BOOKMAN.—"Such a work as this is of inestimable value to librarians."

SCHOOL GUARDIAN.—"This is a very valuable book of reference."

Views and Memoranda of Public Libraries (**several hundred illustrations**). Subscription price **7/6**, when published **10/6 net**.

Full particulars of the above and also of other Library Aids sent upon application to the

LIBRARY AIDS CO.,
166a, Romford Road, Stratford, London, E.

Vol. 3.   JULY, 1902.   No. 10.

BRIGHTON EXCURSION.—*Page 133.*

THE OFFICIAL ORGAN OF THE

Library Assistants' Association.

Edited by

H. TAPLEY SOPER,

Public Library, Stoke Newington, N.

Contents.

	PAGE
Report of Annual Meeting ...	129
Correspondence ...	133
Study Circle Report ...	135
New Members ...	136
Wolverhampton Conference ...	136
Notes and Comments ...	135
Appointments ...	136

Entered at Stationers' Hall.

No. 55.

ANNUAL SUBSCRIPTION, INCLUDING POSTAGE TO ANY ADDRESS, EITHER AT HOME OR ABROAD, **3s**

SOME COTGREAVE LIBRARY AIDS.
A FEW TESTIMONIALS.

The Indicator.

"LIBRARY CONSTRUCTION, ARCHITECTURE, FITTINGS, AND FURNITURE."
BY F. J. BURGOYNE.

"The Cotgreave Indicator is that in use in the majority of the British Free Libraries."

"THE SCOTSMAN."

"All the London Free Public Libraries which use indicators, except one, have adopted he Cotgreave System, which has been found to work well."

N.B. See also "Greater London," by E. Walford, M.A., F.S.A. (page 360); "Methods of Social Reform," by Prof. W. Stanley Jevons, M.A., F.R.S., LL.D.; "Public Libraries," by T. Greenwood, F.R.G.S.; &c., &c.

As a matter of fact it will be found in about nine-tenths of the Libraries using Indicators. Over 350 Institutions are now using it.

Recently adopted at the Birmingham, Cologne, and many other Libraries.

† *Sixty-two Public Libraries in London and the Metropolitan area are using it.*

The Simplex Shelf Supports

The Shelves can be raised or lowered by one person without moving or disarranging a single book, and in half the time required by any other system. No space is lost; no mechanism to get jammed, or otherwise out of order, or nip the fingers; no danger to Bindings by projecting metal or wooden fittings; no tilting of shelves. The Fittings are entirely out of sight when the Books are in position, unless more space is allowed between the shelves than is generally required. While No. 1 is perhaps best for very heavy books, No. 2 is quite safe for ordinary books, and is cheaper and more readily fitted. Two-thirds of the woodwork required with other designs is saved, while the cost of joinery is greatly reduced. It can be fitted to iron stacks.

The Contents=Subject Index

TO GENERAL AND PERIODICAL LITERATURE.
Large Post 8vo., Cloth, Gilt (750 pp.), 10s. 6d.

A limited number will be supplied to Library Assistants at 3s. 6d.

ACADEMY.—"We consider that the author has done a great service to literary workers an students."

WESTMINSTER REVIEW.—"It has been left to Mr. Cotgreave to compile a work which supplies precisely the information required by the general reader."

SATURDAY REVIEW.—"It represents a vast amount of work, and will be prized by students of current literature."

PUBLIC OPINION.—"We have nothing but praise for this work."

BOOKMAN.—"Such a work as this is of inestimable value to librarians."

SCHOOL GUARDIAN.—"This is a very valuable book of reference."

Views and Memoranda of Public Libraries (several hundred illustrations). Subscription price 7/6, when published 10/6 net.

Full particulars of the above and also of other Library Aids sent upon application to the

LIBRARY AIDS CO.,
166a, Romford Road, Stratford, London, E.

Vol. 3. AUGUST, 1902. No. 11.

THE OFFICIAL ORGAN OF THE

Library Assistants' Association.

Edited by
H. TAPLEY SOPER,
Public Library, Stoke Newington, N.

Contents.

	PAGE
Excursion to Epping Forest	137
N.W. Branch: September Meeting	138
L.A.A. Junior (1902) Prize	138
Notes and Comments	138-139
Some Systems of Classification, by P. Evans Lewin	140-146
Appointments	146
Obituary—John Southward	147
Appointments Vacant	148

Entered at Stationers' Hall.   **No. 56.**

ANNUAL SUBSCRIPTION, INCLUDING POSTAGE TO ANY ADDRESS, EITHER AT HOME OR ABROAD, **3s**

SOME COTGREAVE LIBRARY AIDS.
A FEW TESTIMONIALS.

The Indicator.

"LIBRARY CONSTRUCTION, ARCHITECTURE, FITTINGS, AND FURNITURE."
BY F. J. BURGOYNE.
"The Cotgreave Indicator is that in use in the majority of the British Free Libraries."

"THE SCOTSMAN."

" All the London Free Public Libraries which use indicators, except one, have adopted the Cotgreave System, which has been found to work well."†

N.B. See also "Greater London," by E. Walford, M.A., F.S.A. (page 360): "Methods of Social Reform," by Prof. W. Stanley Jevons, M.A., F.R.S., LL.D.: "Public Libraries," by T. Greenwood, F.R.G.S.; &c., &c.

As a matter of fact it will be found in about nine-tenths of the Libraries using Indicators. Over 350 Institutions are now using it.

Recently adopted at the Birmingham, Cologne, and many other Libraries.

† *Sixty-two Public Libraries in London and the Metropolitan area are using it.*

The Simplex Shelf Supports

The Shelves can be raised or lowered by one person without moving or disarranging a single book, and in half the time required by any other system. No space is lost; no mechanism to get jammed, or otherwise out of order, or nip the fingers; no danger to Bindings by projecting metal or wooden fittings; no tilting of shelves. The Fittings are entirely out of sight when the Books are in position, unless more space is allowed between the shelves than is generally required. While No. 1 is perhaps best for very heavy books, No. 2 is quite safe for ordinary books, and is cheaper and more readily fitted. Two-thirds of the woodwork required with other designs is saved, while the cost of joinery is greatly reduced. It can be fitted to iron stacks.

The Contents=Subject Index

TO GENERAL AND PERIODICAL LITERATURE.
Large Post 8vo., Cloth, Gilt (750 pp.), 10s. 6d.
A limited number will be supplied to Library Assistants at 3s. 6d.

ACADEMY.—" We consider that the author has done a great service to literary workers an students."

WESTMINSTER REVIEW.—" It has been left to Mr. Cotgreave to compile a work which supplies precisely the information required by the general reader."

SATURDAY REVIEW.—" It represents a vast amount of work, and will be prized by students of current literature."

PUBLIC OPINION.—" We have nothing but praise for this work."

BOOKMAN.—" Such a work as this is of inestimable value to librarians."

SCHOOL GUARDIAN.—" This is a very valuable book of reference."

Views and Memoranda of Public Libraries (several hundred Illustrations). Subscription price 7/6, when published 10/6 net.

Full particulars of the above and also of other Library Aids sent upon application to the

LIBRARY AIDS CO.,
166a, Romford Road, Stratford, London, E.

Vol. 3. SEPTEMBER, 1902. No. 41.

THE OFFICIAL ORGAN OF THE

Library Assistants' Association.

Edited by
W. BENSON THORNE,
St. Bride Institute,
Bride Lane, Fleet Street, E.C.

Contents.

	PAGE
Announcements	149
N.W. Branch: September Meeting	149
Study Circle	150
New Hon Member: H. Tapley Soper	154
John Durie, by P. Evans Lewin	150
Notes and Comments	154
Books Received	156
Appointments	156
New Members	156

Entered at Stationers' Hall. No. 57.

ANNUAL SUBSCRIPTION, INCLUDING POSTAGE TO ANY ADDRESS EITHER AT HOME OR ABROAD, **3s**

SOME COTGREAVE LIBRARY AIDS.
A FEW TESTIMONIALS.

The Indicator.

"LIBRARY CONSTRUCTION, ARCHITECTURE, FITTINGS, AND FURNITURE."
BY F. J. BURGOYNE.

"The Cotgreave Indicator is that in use in the majority of the British Free Libraries."

"THE SCOTSMAN."

"All the London Free Public Libraries which use indicators, except one, have adopted the Cotgreave System, which has been found to work well."†

N.B.—See also "Greater London," by E. Walford, M.A., F.S.A. (page 360); "Methods of Social Reform," by Prof. W. Stanley Jevons, M.A., F.R.S., LL.D.; "Public Libraries," by T. Greenwood, F.R.G.S.; &c., &c.

As a matter of fact it will be found in about nine-tenths of the Libraries using Indicators. Over 350 Institutions are now using it.

Recently adopted at the Birmingham, Cologne, and many other Libraries.

† *Sixty-two Public Libraries in London and the Metropolitan area are using it.*

The Simplex Shelf Supports

The Shelves can be raised or lowered by one person without moving or disarranging a single book, and in half the time required by any other system. No space is lost; no mechanism to get jammed, or otherwise out of order, or nip the fingers; no danger to Bindings by projecting metal or wooden fittings; no tilting of shelves. The Fittings are entirely out of sight when the Books are in position, unless more space is allowed between the shelves than is generally required. While No. 1 is perhaps best for very heavy books, No. 2 is quite safe for ordinary books, and is cheaper and more readily fitted. Two-thirds of the woodwork required with other designs is saved, while the cost of joinery is greatly reduced. It can be fitted to iron stacks.

The Contents=Subject Index

TO GENERAL AND PERIODICAL LITERATURE.

Large Post 8vo., Cloth, Gilt (750 pp.), 10s. 6d.

A limited number will be supplied to Library Assistants at 3s. 6d.

ACADEMY.—"We consider that the author has done a great service to literary workers an students."

WESTMINSTER REVIEW.—"It has been left to Mr. Cotgreave to compile a work which supplies precisely the information required by the general reader."

SATURDAY REVIEW.—"It represents a vast amount of work, and will be prized by students of current literature."

PUBLIC OPINION.—"We have nothing but praise for this work."

BOOKMAN.—"Such a work as this is of inestimable value to librarians."

SCHOOL GUARDIAN.—"This is a very valuable book of reference."

Views and Memoranda of Public Libraries (several hundred illustrations). Subscription price 7/6, when published 10/6 net.

Full particulars of the above and also of other Library Aids sent upon application to the

LIBRARY AIDS CO.,
166a, Romford Road, Stratford, London, E.

THE OFFICIAL ORGAN OF THE

Library Assistants' Association.

Edited by
W. BENSON THORNE,
St. Bride Institute, Bride Lane, E.C.

OCTOBER, 1902.
VOL. III. No. 13.

... Contents. ...

Announcements	157
N.W. Branch	158
Study Circle	158
Enemies of Books	159
Public Libraries and Children	159
Printing for Librarians	160
Notes and Comments	163
Vacancies, etc.	164

Annual Subscription, including postage to any address, either at Home or Abroad, 3s.

ENTERED AT STATIONERS' HALL.   No. 57.

SOME COTGREAVE LIBRARY AIDS.
A FEW TESTIMONIALS.

The Indicator.

"LIBRARY CONSTRUCTION, ARCHITECTURE, FITTINGS, AND FURNITURE."
BY F. J. BURGOYNE.

"The Cotgreave Indicator is that in use in the majority of the British Free Libraries."

"THE SCOTSMAN."

"All the London Free Public Libraries which use indicators, except one, have adopted the Cotgreave System, which has been found to work well."†

N.B.—See also "Greater London," by E. Walford, M.A., F.S.A. (page 360); "Methods of Social Reform," by Prof. W. Stanley Jevons, M.A., F.R.S., LL.D.; "Public Libraries," by T. Greenwood, F.R.G.S.; &c., &c.

As a matter of fact it will be found in about nine-tenths of the Libraries using Indicators. Over 350 Institutions are now using it.

Recently adopted at the Birmingham, Cologne, and many other Libraries.

† *Sixty-two Public Libraries in London and the Metropolitan area are using it.*

The Simplex Shelf Supports

The Shelves can be raised or lowered by one person without moving or disarranging a single book, and in half the time required by any other system. No space is lost; no mechanism to get jammed, or otherwise out of order, or nip the fingers; no danger to Bindings by projecting metal or wooden fittings; no tilting of shelves. The Fittings are entirely out of sight when the Books are in position, unless more space is allowed between the shelves than is generally required. While No. 1 is perhaps best for very heavy books, No. 2 is quite safe for ordinary books, and is cheaper and more readily fitted. Two-thirds of the woodwork required with other designs is saved, while the cost of joinery is greatly reduced. It can be fitted to iron stacks.

The Contents=Subject Index

TO GENERAL AND PERIODICAL LITERATURE.
Large Post 8vo., Cloth, Gilt (750 pp.), 10s. 6d.

A limited number will be supplied to Library Assistants at 3s. 6d.

ACADEMY.—"We consider that the author has done a great service to literary workers an students."

WESTMINSTER REVIEW.—"It has been left to Mr. Cotgreave to compile a work which supplies precisely the information required by the general reader."

SATURDAY REVIEW.—"It represents a vast amount of work, and will be prized by students of current literature."

PUBLIC OPINION.—"We have nothing but praise for this work."

BOOKMAN.—"Such a work as this is of inestimable value to librarians."

SCHOOL GUARDIAN.—"This is a very valuable book of reference."

Views and Memoranda of Public Libraries (several hundred illustrations). Subscription price 7/6, when published 10/6 net.

Full particulars of the above and also of other Library Aids sent upon application to the

LIBRARY AIDS CO.,
166a, Romford Road, Stratford, London, E.

SPECIAL SUPPLEMENT.

The Library Assistant

THE OFFICIAL ORGAN OF THE

Library Assistants' Association.

Edited by
W. BENSON THORNE,
St. Bride Institute, Bride Lane, E.C.

NOVEMBER, 1902.
VOL. III. No. 14.

... Contents. ...

Announcements	165
N.W. Branch	165
Study Circle	166
Inaugural Meeting	167
Notes and Comments	170
The Daily Press and Public Libraries	172
Technical Training of Library Assistants	175
Correspondence	180

Annual Subscription, including postage to any address, either at Home or Abroad, **3s.**

ENTERED AT STATIONERS' HALL.   No. 59.

SOME COTGREAVE LIBRARY AIDS.
A FEW TESTIMONIALS.

The Indicator.
"Library Construction, Architecture, Fittings, and Furniture."
By F. J. BURGOYNE.

"The Cotgreave Indicator is that in use in the majority of the British Free Libraries."

"THE SCOTSMAN."

"All the London Free Public Libraries which use indicators, except one, have adopted the Cotgreave System, which has been found to work well."†

N.B.—See also "Greater London," by E. Walford, M.A., F.S.A. (page 360); "Methods of Social Reform," by Prof. W. Stanley Jevons, M.A., F.R.S., LL.D.; "Public Libraries," by T. Greenwood, F.R.G.S.; &c., &c.

As a matter of fact it will be found in about nine-tenths of the Libraries using Indicators Over 350 Institutions are now using it.

Recently adopted at the Birmingham, Cologne, and many other Libraries.

† *Sixty-two Public Libraries in London and the Metropolitan area are using it.*

The Simplex Shelf Supports

The Shelves can be raised or lowered by one person without moving or disarranging a single book, and in half the time required by any other system. No space is lost; no mechanism to get jammed, or otherwise out of order, or nip the fingers; no danger to Bindings by projecting metal or wooden fittings; no tilting of shelves. The Fittings are entirely out of sight when the Books are in position, unless more space is allowed between the shelves than is generally required. While No. 1 is perhaps best for very heavy books, No. 2 is quite safe for ordinary books, and is cheaper and more readily fitted. Two-thirds of the woodwork required with other designs is saved, while the cost of joinery is greatly reduced. It can be fitted to iron stacks.

The Contents=Subject Index
TO GENERAL AND PERIODICAL LITERATURE.
Large Post 8vo., Cloth, Gilt (750 pp.), 10s. 6d.

A limited number will be supplied to Library Assistants at 3s. 6d.

ACADEMY.—"We consider that the author has done a great service to literary workers an students."

WESTMINSTER REVIEW.—"It has been left to Mr. Cotgreave to compile a work which supplies precisely the information required by the general reader."

SATURDAY REVIEW.—"It represents a vast amount of work, and will be prized by students of current literature."

PUBLIC OPINION.—"We have nothing but praise for this work."

BOOKMAN.—"Such a work as this is of inestimable value to librarians."

SCHOOL GUARDIAN.—"This is a very valuable book of reference."

Views and Memoranda of Public Libraries (several hundred illustrations). Subscription price 7/6, when published 10/6 net.

Full particulars of the above and also of other Library Aids sent upon application to the

LIBRARY AIDS CO.,
166a, Romford Road, Stratford, London, E.

THE LIBRARY ASSISTANT

THE OFFICIAL ORGAN OF THE

Library Assistants' Association.

Edited by
W. BENSON THORNE,
Bromley Library, 126 Brunswick Road, E.

DECEMBER, 1902.

VOL. III. No. 15.

... Contents. ...

December Meeting	181
N.W. Branch	181
Fifth Annual Dinner	182
Study Circle	184
Library Association	186
Ancient and Modern Writing Materials. (By P. E. LEWIN)	189
Notes and Comments	192
New Books, etc.	195

Annual Subscription, including postage to any address, either at Home or Abroad, **3s.**

ENTERED AT STATIONERS' HALL. No. 60.

SOME COTGREAVE LIBRARY AIDS.
A FEW TESTIMONIALS.

The Indicator.

"LIBRARY CONSTRUCTION, ARCHITECTURE, FITTINGS, AND FURNITURE."
BY F. J. BURGOYNE.

"The Cotgreave Indicator is that in use in the majority of the British Free Libraries."

"THE SCOTSMAN."

"All the London Free Public Libraries which use indicators, except one, have adopted he Cotgreave System, which has been found to work well."†

N.B.—See also "Greater London," by E. Walford, M.A., F.S.A. (page 360); "Methods of Social Reform," by Prof. W. Stanley Jevons, M.A., F.R.S., LL.D.; "Public Libraries," by T. Greenwood, F.R.G.S.; &c., &c.

As a matter of fact it will be found in about nine-tenths of the Libraries using Indicators Over 350 Institutions are now using it.

Recently adopted at the Birmingham, Cologne, and many other Libraries.

† *Sixty-two Public Libraries in London and the Metropolitan area are using it.*

The Simplex Shelf Supports

The Shelves can be raised or lowered by one person without moving or disarranging a single book, and in half the time required by any other system. No space is lost; no mechanism to get jammed, or otherwise out of order, or nip the fingers; no danger to Bindings by projecting metal or wooden fittings; no tilting of shelves. The Fittings are entirely out of sight when the Books are in position, unless more space is allowed between the shelves than is generally required. While No. 1 is perhaps best for very heavy books, No. 2 is quite safe for ordinary books, and is cheaper and more readily fitted. Two-thirds of the woodwork required with other designs is saved, while the cost of joinery is greatly reduced. It can be fitted to iron stacks.

The Contents=Subject Index

TO GENERAL AND PERIODICAL LITERATURE.

Large Post 8vo., Cloth, Gilt (750 pp.), 10s. 6d.

A limited number will be supplied to Library Assistants at 3s. 6d.

ACADEMY.—" We consider that the author has done a great service to literary workers an students."

WESTMINSTER REVIEW.—" It has been left to Mr. Cotgreave to compile a work which supplies precisely the information required by the general reader."

SATURDAY REVIEW.—" It represents a vast amount of work, and will be prized by students of current literature."

PUBLIC OPINION.—" We nave nothing but praise for this work."

BOOKMAN.—" Such a work as this is of inestimable value to librarians."

SCHOOL GUARDIAN.—" This is a very valuable book of reference."

Views and Memoranda of Public Libraries (several hundred illustrations). Subscription price 7/6, when published 10/6 net.

Full particulars of the above and also of other Library Aids sent upon application to the

LIBRARY AIDS CO.,
166a, Romford Road, Stratford, London, E.

THE LIBRARY ASSISTANT

THE OFFICIAL ORGAN OF THE
Library Assistants' Association.

Edited by
W. BENSON THORNE,
Bromley Library, 126 Brunswick Road, E.

JANUARY, 1903.
VOL. III. No. 16.

... Contents. ...

Notices	197
N.W. Branch	198
Study Circle	199
Daily Press and Public Libraries	200
Notes and Comments	203
New Books, etc.	203

Annual Subscription, including postage to any address, either at Home or Abroad, **3s.**

ENTERED AT STATIONERS' HALL.   No. 61.

SOME COTGREAVE LIBRARY AIDS.
A FEW TESTIMONIALS.

The Indicator.

"LIBRARY CONSTRUCTION, ARCHITECTURE, FITTINGS, AND FURNITURE."
BY F. J. BURGOYNE.
"The Cotgreave Indicator is that in use in the majority of the British Free Libraries."

"THE SCOTSMAN."

"All the London Free Public Libraries which use indicators, except one, have adopted he Cotgreave System, which has been found to work well."†

N.B.—See also "Greater London," by E. Walford, M.A., F.S.A. (page 360); "Methods of Social Reform," by Prof. W. Stanley Jevons, M.A., F.R.S., LL.D.; "Public Libraries," by T. Greenwood, F.R.G.S.; &c., &c.

As a matter of fact it will be found in about nine-tenths of the Libraries using Indicators. Over 350 Institutions are now using it.

Recently adopted at the Birmingham, Cologne, and many other Libraries.

† *Sixty-two Public Libraries in London and the Metropolitan area are using it.*

The Simplex Shelf Supports

The Shelves can be raised or lowered by one person without moving or disarranging a single book, and in half the time required by any other system. No space is lost; no mechanism to get jammed, or otherwise out of order, or nip the fingers; no danger to Bindings by projecting metal or wooden fittings; no tilting of shelves. The Fittings are entirely out of sight when the Books are in position, unless more space is allowed between the shelves than is generally required. While No. 1 is perhaps best for very heavy books, No. 2 is quite safe for ordinary books, and is cheaper and more readily fitted. Two-thirds of the woodwork required with other designs is saved, while the cost of joinery is greatly reduced. It can be fitted to iron stacks.

The Contents=Subject Index

TO GENERAL AND PERIODICAL LITERATURE.
Large Post 8vo., Cloth, Gilt (750 pp.), 10s. 6d.
A limited number will be supplied to Library Assistants at 3s. 6d.

ACADEMY.—"We consider that the author has done a great service to literary workers an students."

WESTMINSTER REVIEW.—"It has been left to Mr. Cotgreave to compile a work which supplies precisely the information required by the general reader."

SATURDAY REVIEW.—"It represents a vast amount of work, and will be prized by students of current literature."

PUBLIC OPINION.—"We have nothing but praise for this work."

BOOKMAN.—"Such a work as this is of inestimable value to librarians."

SCHOOL GUARDIAN.—"This is a very valuable book of reference."

Views and Memoranda of Public Libraries (several hundred illustrations). Subscription price 7/6, when published 10/6 net.

Full particulars of the above and also of other Library Aids sent upon application to the

LIBRARY AIDS CO.,
166a, Romford Road, Stratford, London, E.

THE OFFICIAL ORGAN OF THE
Library Assistants' Association.

Edited by
W. BENSON THORNE,
Bromley Library, 126 Brunswick Road, E.

FEBRUARY, 1903.
VOL. III. No. 17.

... Contents. ...

February Meeting at West Ham	205
N.W. Branch	205
Study Circle	207
Notes and Comments	208
Ancient and Modern Writing Materials, II., By P. Evans Lewin	210
Correspondence	214

Annual Subscription, including postage to any address, either at Home or Abroad, **3s.**

ENTERED AT STATIONERS' HALL.   No. 62.

SOME COTGREAVE LIBRARY AIDS.
A FEW TESTIMONIALS.

The Indicator.
"LIBRARY CONSTRUCTION, ARCHITECTURE FITTINGS AND FURNITURE."
BY F. J. BURGOYNE.

'The Cotgreave Indicator is that in use in the majority of the British Free Libraries.'

"THE SCOTSMAN."

"All the London Free Public Libraries which use indicators, except one, have adopted the Cotgreave System, which has been found to work well."†

N.B.--See also "Greater London," by E. Walford, M.A., F.S.A. (page 360); "Methods of Social Reform," by Prof. W. Stanley Jevons, M.A., F.R.S., LL.D.; "Public Libraries," by T. Greenwood, F.R.G.S.; &c., &c.

As a matter of fact it will be found in about nine-tenths of the Libraries using Indicators Over 350 Institutions are now using it.

Recently adopted at the Birmingham, Cologne, and many other Libraries.

† *Sixty-two Public Libraries in London and the Metropolitan area are using it.*

The Simplex Shelf Supports

The Shelves can be raised or lowered by one person without moving or disarranging a single book, and in half the time required by any other system. No space is lost; no mechanism to get jammed, or otherwise out of order, or nip the fingers; no danger to Bindings by projecting metal or wooden fittings; no tilting of shelves. The Fittings are entirely out of sight when the Books are in position, unless more space is allowed between the shelves than is generally required. While No. 1 is perhaps best for very heavy books, No. 2 is quite safe for ordinary books, and is cheaper and more readily fitted. Two-thirds of the woodwork required with other designs is saved, while the cost of joinery is greatly reduced. It can be fitted to iron stacks.

The Contents=Subject Index
TO GENERAL AND PERIODICAL LITERATURE.
Large Post 8vo., Cloth, Gilt (750 pp.), 10s. 6d.

A limited number will be supplied to Library Assistants at 3s. 6d.

ACADEMY.—" We consider that the author has done a great service to literary workers an students."

WESTMINSTER REVIEW.—" It has been left to Mr. Cotgreave to compile a work which supplies precisely the information required by the general reader."

SATURDAY REVIEW.—" It represents a vast amount of work, and will be prized by students of current literature."

PUBLIC OPINION.—" We have nothing but praise for this work."

BOOKMAN.—" Such a work as this is of inestimable value to librarians."

SCHOOL GUARDIAN.—" This is a very valuable book of reference."

Views and Memoranda of Public Libraries (several hundred illustrations). Subscription price 7/6, when published 10/6 net.

Full particulars of the above and also of other Library Aids sent upon application to the

LIBRARY AIDS CO.,
166a, Romford Road, Stratford, London, E.

THE OFFICIAL ORGAN OF THE

Library Assistants' Association.

Edited by
W. BENSON THORNE,
Bromley Library, 126 Brunswick Road, E.

MARCH, 1903.
VOL. III. No. 18.

... Contents. ...

Notices	217
N.W. Branch	217
West Ham Meeting	218
Study Circle	220
Anticipated Developments of Library Practice. By T. W. GLAZIER	221
Correspondence	225
New Books, etc.	228

Annual Subscription, including postage to any address, either at Home or Abroad, 3s.

ENTERED AT STATIONERS' HALL.   No. 63.

SOME COTGREAVE LIBRARY AIDS.

A FEW TESTIMONIALS.

The Indicator.

"LIBRARY CONSTRUCTION, ARCHITECTURE, FITTINGS AND FURNITURE."
BY F. J. BURGOYNE.

"The Cotgreave Indicator is that in use in the majority of the British Free Libraries."

"THE SCOTSMAN."

"All the London Free Public Libraries which use indicators, except one, have adopted the Cotgreave System, which has been found to work well."

N.B.—See also "Greater London," by E. Walford, M.A., F.S.A. (page 360); "Methods of Social Reform," by Prof. W. Stanley Jevons, M.A., F.R.S., LL.D.; "Public Libraries," by T. Greenwood, F.R.G.S.; &c., &c.

As a matter of fact it will be found in about nine-tenths of the Libraries using Indicators Over 350 Institutions are now using it.

Recently adopted at the Birmingham, Cologne, and many other Libraries.

Sixty-two Public Libraries in London and the Metropolitan area are using it.

The Simplex Shelf Supports

The Shelves can be raised or lowered by one person without moving or disarranging a single book, and in half the time required by any other system. No space is lost; no mechanism to get jammed, or otherwise out of order, or nip the fingers; no danger to Bindings by projecting metal or wooden fittings; no tilting of shelves. The Fittings are entirely out of sight when the Books are in position, unless more space is allowed between the shelves than is generally required. While No. 1 is perhaps best for very heavy books, No. 2 is quite safe for ordinary books, and is cheaper and more readily fitted. Two-thirds of the woodwork required with other designs is saved, while the cost of joinery is greatly reduced. It can be fitted to iron stacks.

The Contents=Subject Index

TO GENERAL AND PERIODICAL LITERATURE.

Large Post 8vo., Cloth, Gilt (780 pp.); 10s. 6d.

A limited number will be supplied to Library Assistants at 3s. 6d.

ACADEMY.—"We consider that the author has done a great service to literary workers and students."

WESTMINSTER REVIEW.—"It has been left to Mr. Cotgreave to compile a work which supplies precisely the information required by the general reader."

SATURDAY REVIEW.—"It represents a vast amount of work, and will be prized by students of current literature."

PUBLIC OPINION.—"We have nothing but praise for this work."

BOOKMAN.—"Such a work as this is of inestimable value to librarians."

SCHOOL GUARDIAN.—"This is a very valuable book of reference."

Views and Memoranda of Public Libraries (several hundred illustrations). Subscription price 7/6, when published 10/6 net.

Full particulars of the above and also of other Library Aids sent upon application to the

LIBRARY AIDS CO.,

166a, Romford Road, Stratford, London, E.

PUBLISHED MONTHLY.

THE OFFICIAL ORGAN OF THE
Library Assistants' Association.

Edited by
W. BENSON THORNE,
Bromley Library, 126 Brunswick Road, E.

APRIL, 1903.
VOL. III. No. 19.

... Contents. ...

Notices	229
March Meeting	229
N.W. Branch	231
Study Circle	232
Notes and Comments	234
New Books, etc.	235
Appointments	236

Annual Subscription, including postage to any address, either at Home or Abroad, **3s.**

Entered at Stationers' Hall.   No. 64

SOME COTGREAVE LIBRARY AIDS.
A FEW TESTIMONIALS.

The Indicator.

"LIBRARY CONSTRUCTION, ARCHITECTURE. FITTINGS AND FURNITURE.
BY F. J. BURGOYNE.

'The Cotgreave Indicator is that in use in the majority of the British Free Libraries.'

"THE SCOTSMAN."

"All the London Free Public Libraries which use indicators, except one, have adopted the Cotgreave System, which has been found to work well."†

N.B.—See also "Greater London," by E. Walford, M.A., F.S.A. (page 360); "Methods of Social Reform," by Prof. W. Stanley Jevons, M.A., F.R.S., LL.D.; "Public Libraries," by T. Greenwood, F.R.G.S.; &c., &c.

As a matter of fact it will be found in about nine-tenths of the Libraries using Indicators Over 350 Institutions are now using it.

Recently adopted at the Birmingham, Cologne, and many other Libraries.

† *Sixty-two Public Libraries in London and the Metropolitan area are using it.*

The Simplex Shelf Supports

The Shelves can be raised or lowered by one person without moving or disarranging a single book, and in half the time required by any other system. No space is lost; no mechanism to get jammed, or otherwise out of order, or nip the fingers; no danger to Bindings by projecting metal or wooden fittings; no tilting of shelves. The Fittings are entirely out of sight when the Books are in position, unless more space is allowed between the shelves than is generally required. While No. 1 is perhaps best for very heavy books, No. 2 is quite safe for ordinary books, and is cheaper and more readily fitted. Two-thirds of the woodwork required with other designs is saved, while the cost of joinery is greatly reduced. It can be fitted to iron stacks.

The Contents=Subject Index

TO GENERAL AND PERIODICAL LITERATURE.

Large Post 8vo., Cloth, Gilt (750 pp.), 10s. 6d.

A limited number will be supplied to Library Assistants at 3s. 6d.

ACADEMY.—"We consider that the author has done a great service to literary workers an students."

WESTMINSTER REVIEW.—"It has been left to Mr. Cotgreave to compile a work which supplies precisely the in ormation required by the general reader."

SATURDAY REVIEW.—"It represents a vast amount of work, and will be prized by students of current literature."

PUBLIC OPINION.—"We have nothing but praise for this work."

BOOKMAN.—"Such a work as this is of inestimable value to librarians."

SCHOOL GUARDIAN.—"This is a very valuable book of reference."

Views and Memoranda of Public Libraries (several hundred illustrations). Subscription price 7/6, when published 10/6 net.

Full particulars of the above and also of other Library Aids sent upon application to the

LIBRARY AIDS CO.,
166a, Romford Road, Stratford, London, E.

PUBLISHED MONTHLY.

THE OFFICIAL ORGAN OF THE
Library Assistants' Association.

Edited by
W. BENSON THORNE,
Bromley Library, 126 Brunswick Road, E.

MAY, 1903.
VOL. III. No. 20.

... Contents. ...

Notices	237
The Committee	238
N.W. Branch	238
Manchester Free Libraries : Jubilee ...	239
Library Basements	241
The Educational Basis of the Free Library Movement. By F. W. B. HAWORTH. ...	242
Cotgreave Prize Essays (1903)	247
New Books, etc.	247

Annual Subscription, including postage to any address, either at Home or Abroad, **3s**.

Entered at Stationers' Hall, and at New York Post Office as Second Class Matter. **No. 65.**

SOME COTGREAVE LIBRARY AIDS.
A FEW TESTIMONIALS.

The Indicator.

"LIBRARY CONSTRUCTION, ARCHITECTURE, FITTINGS AND FURNITURE.
BY F. J. BURGOYNE.

'The Cotgreave Indicator is that in use in the majority of the British Free Libraries.'

"THE SCOTSMAN."

"All the London Free Public Libraries which use indicators, except one, have adopted the Cotgreave System, which has been found to work well."†

N.B. See also "Greater London," by E. Walford, M.A., F.S.A. (page 360); "Methods of Social Reform," by Prof. W. Stanley Jevons, M.A., F.R.S., LL.D.; "Public Libraries," by T. Greenwood, F.R.G.S.; &c., &c.

As a matter of fact it will be found in about nine-tenths of the Libraries using Indicators Over 350 Institutions are now using it.

Recently adopted at the Birmingham, Cologne, and many other Libraries.

† *Sixty-two Public Libraries in London and the Metropolitan area are using it.*

The Simplex Shelf Supports

The Shelves can be raised or lowered by one person without moving or disarranging a single book, and in half the time required by any other system. No space is lost; no mechanism to get jammed, or otherwise out of order, or nip the fingers; no danger to Bindings by projecting metal or wooden fittings; no tilting of shelves. The Fittings are entirely out of sight when the Books are in position, unless more space is allowed between the shelves than is generally required. While No. 1 is perhaps best for very heavy books, No. 2 is quite safe for ordinary books, and is cheaper and more readily fitted. Two-thirds of the woodwork required with other designs is saved, while the cost of joinery is greatly reduced. It can be fitted to iron stacks.

The Contents=Subject Index

TO GENERAL AND PERIODICAL LITERATURE.

Large Post 8vo., Cloth, Gilt (750 pp.), 10s. 6d.

A limited number will be supplied to Library Assistants at 3s. 6d.

ACADEMY.—" We consider that the author has done a great service to literary workers an students."

WESTMINSTER REVIEW.—" It has been left to Mr. Cotgreave to compile a work which supplies precisely the in ormation required by the general reader."

SATURDAY REVIEW.—" It represents a vast amount of work, and will be prized by students of current literature."

PUBLIC OPINION.—" We have nothing but praise for this work."

BOOKMAN.—" Such a work as this is of inestimable value to librarians."

SCHOOL GUARDIAN.—" This is a very valuable book of reference."

Views and Memoranda of Public Libraries (several hundred illustrations). Subscription price 7/6, when published 10/6 net.

Full particulars of the above and also of other Library Aids sent upon application to the

LIBRARY AIDS CO.,
166a, Romford Road, Stratford, London, E.

PUBLISHED MONTHLY.

\ THE OFFICIAL ORGAN OF THE

Library Assistants' Association.

Edited by
W. BENSON THORNE,
Bromley Library, 126 Brunswick Road, E.

JUNE, 1903.
VOL. III. No. 21.

... Contents. ...

Annual Meeting...	249
Visit to British Museum	249
Study Circle	251
Appointments	252
Literature for the Blind. By G. E. ROEBUCK	253
Eighth Annual Report	261
List of Members	268
N.W₁ Branch	272
Notices	272

Annual Subscription, including postage to any address, either at Home or Abroad. **3s.**

Entered at Stationers' Hall, and at New York Post Office as Second Class Matter.   **No. 66.**

SOME COTGREAVE LIBRARY AIDS.
A FEW TESTIMONIALS.

The Indicator.

"LIBRARY CONSTRUCTION, ARCHITECTURE, FITTINGS AND FURNITURE.
BY F. J. BURGOYNE.
The Cotgreave Indicator is that in use in the majority of the British Free Libraries."

"THE SCOTSMAN."
"All the London Free Public Libraries which use indicators, except one, have adopted the Cotgreave System, which has been found to work well."

N.B.—See also "Greater London," by E. Walford, M.A., F.S.A. (page 380); "Methods of Social Reform," by Prof. W. Stanley Jevons, M.A., F.R.S., LL.D.; "Public Libraries," by T. Greenwood, F.R.G.S.; &c., &c.

As a matter of fact it will be found in about nine-tenths of the Libraries using Indicators. Over 350 Institutions are now using it.

Recently adopted at the Birmingham, Cologne, and many other Libraries.

Sixty-two Public Libraries in London and the Metropolitan area are using it.

The Simplex Shelf Supports

The Shelves can be raised or lowered by one person without moving or disarranging a single book, and in half the time required by any other system. No space is lost; no mechanism to get jammed, or otherwise out of order, or nip the fingers; no danger to Bindings by projecting metal or wooden fittings; no tilting of shelves. The Fittings are entirely out of sight when the Books are in position, unless more space is allowed between the shelves than is generally required. While No. 1 is perhaps best for very heavy books, No. 2 is quite safe for ordinary books, and is cheaper and more readily fitted. Two-thirds of the woodwork required with other designs is saved, while the cost of joinery is greatly reduced. It can be fitted to iron stacks.

The Contents=Subject Index

TO GENERAL AND PERIODICAL LITERATURE.
Large Post 8vo., Cloth, Gilt (750 pp.), 10s. 6d.
A limited number will be supplied to Library Assistants at 3s. 6d.

ACADEMY.—"We consider that the author has done a great service to literary workers and students."

WESTMINSTER REVIEW.—"It has been left to Mr. Cotgreave to compile a work which supplies precisely the information required by the general reader."

SATURDAY REVIEW.—"It represents a vast amount of work, and will be prized by students of current literature."

PUBLIC OPINION.—"We have nothing but praise for this work."

BOOKMAN.—"Such a work as this is of inestimable value to librarians."

SCHOOL GUARDIAN.—"This is a very valuable book of reference."

Views and Memoranda of Public Libraries (several hundred Illustrations). Subscription price 7/6, when published 10/6 net.

Full particulars of the above and also of other Library Aids sent upon application to the

LIBRARY AIDS CO.,
166a, Romford Road, Stratford, London, E.

PUBLISHED MONTHLY.

THE OFFICIAL ORGAN OF THE

Library Assistants' Association.

Edited by
W. BENSON THORNE,
Bromley Library, 126 Brunswick Road, E.

JULY, 1903.
VOL. III. No. 22.

... Contents. ...

Eighth Annual Meeting	273
N.W. Branch	275
L.A. Professional Examination	275
Correspondence	276
Petrarch. By H. G. SURETIES	277
Notes and Comments	279
New Books	280
Obituary	284

Annual Subscription, including postage to any address, either at Home or Abroad, 3s.

Entered at Stationers' Hall, and at
New York Post Office as Second Class Matter.   No. 67.

SOME COTGREAVE LIBRARY AIDS.
A FEW TESTIMONIALS.

The Indicator.

"**Library Construction, Architecture, Fittings and Furniture.**
By F. J. BURGOYNE.
'The Cotgreave Indicator is that in use in the majority of the British Free Libraries.'

"THE SCOTSMAN."

" All the London Free Public Libraries which use indicators, except one, have adopted the Cotgreave System, which has been found to work well."†

N.B.—See also "Greater London," by E. Walford, M.A., F.S.A. (page 360); "Methods of Social Reform," by Prof. W. Stanley Jevons, M.A., F.R.S., LL.D.; "Public Libraries," by T. Greenwood, F.R.G.S.; &c., &c.

As a matter of fact it will be found in about nine-tenths of the Libraries using Indicators. Over 350 Institutions are now using it.

Recently adopted at the Birmingham, Cologne, and many other Libraries.

† *Sixty-two Public Libraries in London and the Metropolitan area are using it.*

The Simplex Shelf Supports

The Shelves can be raised or lowered by one person without moving or disarranging a single book, and in half the time required by any other system. No space is lost; no mechanism to get jammed, or otherwise out of order, or nip the fingers; no danger to Bindings by projecting metal or wooden fittings; no tilting of shelves. The Fittings are entirely out of sight when the Books are in position, unless more space is allowed between the shelves than is generally required. While No. 1 is perhaps best for very heavy books, No. 2 is quite safe for ordinary books, and is cheaper and more readily fitted. Two-thirds of the woodwork required with other designs is saved, while the cost of joinery is greatly reduced. It can be fitted to iron stacks.

The Contents=Subject Index

TO GENERAL AND PERIODICAL LITERATURE.
Large Post 8vo., Cloth, Gilt (750 pp.), 10s. 6d.
A limited number will be supplied to Library Assistants at 3s. 6d.

ACADEMY.—" We consider that the author has done a great service to literary workers an students."

WESTMINSTER REVIEW.—" It has been left to Mr. Cotgreave to compile a work which supplies precisely the information required by the general reader."

SATURDAY REVIEW.—" It represents a vast amount of work, and will be prized by students of current literature."

PUBLIC OPINION.—" We have nothing but praise for this work."

BOOKMAN.—" Such a work as this is of inestimable value to librarians."

SCHOOL GUARDIAN.—" This is a very valuable book of reference."

Views and Memoranda of Public Libraries (several hundred illustrations). Subscription price 7/6, when published 10/6 net.

Full particulars of the above and also of other Library Aids sent upon application to the

LIBRARY AIDS CO.,
166a, Romford Road, Stratford, London, E.

PUBLISHED MONTHLY.

THE OFFICIAL ORGAN OF THE

Library Assistants' Association.

Edited by
W. BENSON THORNE,
Bromley Library, 126 Brunswick Road, E.

AUGUST, 1903.
VOL. III. No. 23.

... Contents. ...

Notices	285
N.W. Branch	285
Libraries and Museums, By P. EVANS LEWIN	286
The Committee	289
Appointments	289
New Books	290

Annual Subscription, including postage to any address, either at Home or Abroad, 3s.

Entered at Stationers' Hall, and at
New York Post Office as Second Class Matter.   No. 68.

SOME COTGREAVE LIBRARY AIDS.
A FEW TESTIMONIALS.

The Indicator.

"LIBRARY CONSTRUCTION, ARCHITECTURE FITTINGS AND FURNITURE.
BY F. J. BURGOYNE.

The Cotgreave Indicator is that in use in the majority of the British Free Libraries."

"THE SCOTSMAN."

"All the London Free Public Libraries which use indicators, except one, have adopted the Cotgreave System, which has been found to work well."†

N.B. See also "Greater London," by E. Walford, M.A., F.S.A. (page 360): "Methods of Social Reform," by Prof. W. Stanley Jevons, M.A., F.R.S., LL.D.; "Public Libraries," by T. Greenwood, F.R.G.S.; &c., &c.

As a matter of fact it will be found in about nine-tenths of the Libraries using Indicators. Over 350 Institutions are now using it.

Recently adopted at the Birmingham, Cologne, and many other Libraries.

† *Sixty-two Public Libraries in London and the Metropolitan area are using it.*

The Simplex Shelf Supports

The Shelves can be raised or lowered by one person without moving or disarranging a single book, and in half the time required by any other system. No space is lost; no mechanism to get jammed, or otherwise out of order, or nip the fingers; no danger to Bindings by projecting metal or wooden fittings; no tilting of shelves. The Fittings are entirely out of sight when the Books are in position, unless more space is allowed between the shelves than is generally required. While No. 1 is perhaps best for very heavy books, No. 2 is quite safe for ordinary books, and is cheaper and more readily fitted. Two-thirds of the woodwork required with other designs is saved, while the cost of joinery is greatly reduced. It can be fitted to iron stacks.

The Contents=Subject Index

TO GENERAL AND PERIODICAL LITERATURE.

Large Post 8vo., Cloth, Gilt (750 pp.), 10s. 6d.

A limited number will be supplied to Library Assistants at 3s. 6d.

ACADEMY.—" We consider that the author has done a great service to literary workers and students."

WESTMINSTER REVIEW.—" It has been left to Mr. Cotgreave to compile a work which supplies precisely the information required by the general reader."

SATURDAY REVIEW.—" It represents a vast amount of work, and will be prized by students of current literature."

PUBLIC OPINION. " We have nothing but praise for this work."

BOOKMAN.—" Such a work as this is of inestimable value to librarians."

SCHOOL GUARDIAN. "This is a very valuable book of reference."

Views and Memoranda of Public Libraries (**several hundred illustrations**). Subscription price 7/6, when published 10/6 net.

Full particulars of the above and also of other Library Aids sent upon application to the

LIBRARY AIDS CO.,
166a, Romford Road, Stratford, London, E.

PUBLISHED MONTHLY.

THE OFFICIAL ORGAN OF THE
Library Assistants' Association.

Edited by
W. BENSON THORNE,
Bromley Library, 126 Brunswick Road, E.

SEPTEMBER, 1903.
VOL. III. No. 24.

... Contents. ...

Notices	293
Donations to Library	293
Sessional Programme	294
Notes and Comments	296
Library Publications Received	299
Appointments	300

Annual Subscription, including postage to any address, either at Home or Abroad, 3s.

Entered at Stationers' Hall, and at
New-York Post Office as Second Class Matter.   No. 89.

SOME COTGREAVE LIBRARY AIDS.
A FEW TESTIMONIALS.

The Indicator.
"LIBRARY CONSTRUCTION, ARCHITECTURE, FITTINGS AND FURNITURE.
BY F. J. BURGOYNE.
'The Cotgreave Indicator is that in use in the majority of the British Free Libraries.'

"THE SCOTSMAN."
"All the London Free Public Libraries which use indicators, except one, have adopted the Cotgreave System, which has been found to work well."

N.B.—See also "Greater London," by E. Walford, M.A., F.S.A. (page 360); "Methods of Social Reform," by Prof. W. Stanley Jevons, M.A., F.R.S., LL.D.; "Public Libraries," by T. Greenwood, F.R.G.S.; &c., &c.

As a matter of fact it will be found in about nine-tenths of the Libraries using Indicators. Over 350 Institutions are now using it.

Recently adopted at the Birmingham, Cologne, and many other Libraries.

+ *Sixty-two Public Libraries in London and the Metropolitan area are using it.*

The Simplex Shelf Supports

The Shelves can be raised or lowered by one person without moving or disarranging a single book, and in half the time required by any other system. No space is lost; no mechanism to get jammed, or otherwise out of order, or nip the fingers; no danger to Bindings by projecting metal or wooden fittings; no tilting of shelves. The Fittings are entirely out of sight when the Books are in position, unless more space is allowed between the shelves than is generally required. While No. 1 is perhaps best for very heavy books, No. 2 is quite safe for ordinary books, and is cheaper and more readily fitted. Two-thirds of the woodwork required with other designs is saved, while the cost of joinery is greatly reduced. It can be fitted to iron stacks.

The Contents=Subject Index
TO GENERAL AND PERIODICAL LITERATURE.
Large Post 8vo., Cloth, Gilt (750 pp.), 10s. 6d.
A limited number will be supplied to Library Assistants at 3s. 6d.

ACADEMY.—"We consider that the author has done a great service to literary workers and students."
WESTMINSTER REVIEW.—"It has been left to Mr. Cotgreave to compile a work which supplies precisely the information required by the general reader."
SATURDAY REVIEW.—"It represents a vast amount of work, and will be prized by students of current literature."
PUBLIC OPINION.—"We have nothing but praise for this work."
BOOKMAN.—"Such a work as this is of inestimable value to librarians."
SCHOOL GUARDIAN.—"This is a very valuable book of reference."

Views and Memoranda of Public Libraries (several hundred illustrations). Subscription price **7/6**, when published **10/6 net**.

Full particulars of the above and also of other Library Aids sent upon application to the

LIBRARY AIDS CO.,
166a, Romford Road, Stratford, London, E.

The North of England School Furnishing Co., Ltd.
DARLINGTON.

Manufacturers of Library Fittings, etc.

| Reading Stands, Reading Tables, etc. | Bookcases, Library Chairs, etc. |

Libraries supplied recently.
Hull, Central Library; Woolwich Library;
Gladstone Memorial Library, Hawarden;
Royal Leamington Spa Library;
Willesden Library, etc., etc.

Our long experience in this line enables us to guarantee satisfaction.

ESTIMATES FREE.

DISCOUNT BOOKSELLERS & STATIONERS

Addresses—   *Telegrams* "SCHOLASTIC."

DARLINGTON, NEWCASTLE, SUNDERLAND, MIDDLESBROUGH, NORWICH.

Catalogues on application.   Enquiries Solicited.
A New Booklet of Library Fittings just Published.

... BOOKBINDING. ...

H. J. HARDY,

(Bookbinder to Croydon and other Libraries.)

Offers SPECIAL TERMS to Booksellers, Public Libraries, etc.

... ESTIMATES GIVEN. ...

Machine Ruling and Account Book Manufacturing.

Printers' Pamphlet Work quickly made up.

H. J. HARDY,
68, London Road, West Croydon.

... Catalogues ...
"Ye Mitre Press"
(W. D. BAXTER, Manager).

30 Fetter Lane, Fleet Street, E.C.
Phone Number 2996 Central.

Special attention given to the Printing of Catalogues.
General and other Printing executed for PUBLIC LIBRARIES.

JOHN & EDWARD BUMPUS, LTD
Booksellers to H. M the Queen and the Royal Family,

350 Oxford Street, London, W.
(And 5 and 6 Holborn Bars, E.C.)

One of the largest and best selected stocks in the kingdom, displayed in Three Departments, viz:—
1.—**NEW BOOKS** (ground floor). All the standard and current literature.
2.—**LEATHER BOUND BOOKS** (first floor). A very great variety.
3.—**SECOND-HAND BOOKS** (second and third floors). Many thousands of volumes

The supply of Public Libraries is specially catered for, the discount allowed off the prices of New Books being unequalled. (Terms on application.)

Also a liberal discount is allowed from the marked prices of Second-hand Books.

Messrs. BUMPUS have the supply, in addition to others, of the following Free Libraries—

West Ham, Hampstead, Shoreditch, Streatham, Hertford, Leyton, St. Bride's, Cripplegate, Richmond.

New Methods of Library Binding.
A TRIAL INVITED.

Please send us a dozen of THE WORST BOOKS IN YOUR LIBRARY, ALTOGETHER UNFIT FOR REBINDING BY ANY OTHER METHOD. After being rebound put them into circulation, and judge the result. Real goat morocco backs of any colour required Carriage paid each way. Prices no higher than ordinary.

IF NOT APPROVED MONEY RETURNED.

C. R. HEYNER & Co., 28 Canonbury Villas, Islington, London, N.

Library Bookbinding

B. RILEY & CO.,
... **Library Binders and Specialists,** ...

SUPPLY TO PUBLIC LIBRARIES

THE BEST VALUE OBTAINABLE IN LIBRARY BINDING.

New Books and Re-placements supplied, bound direct from the Publishers' Sheets, in Pigskin, Pegamoid, or Washable Cloth, 33⅓ per cent. allowed off Published price of New Books.

Our flexible Pigskin Binding is in use in upwards of 100 Public Libraries in the Country.

New Catalogue of Standard Fiction: Price Lists for Re-binding and samples to be had free on application to

B. RILEY & CO., Bookbinders,
Westgate, Huddersfield.

Telephone :   *Telegrams :*
"9228, LONDON WALL."   "WILLEKEUR, LONDON."

We Solicit Enquiries ...

FOR

... Catalogue Printing,

AND CAN GUARANTEE THAT

Our type is excellent, and most of it new.
    Our work is exceptionally free from error.
        Our printing is good, and
           Our prices are moderate.

Librarians are invited to send copies of Tender Forms for printing Catalogues.

WILLIS & CO.,   22 & 24 Lamb's Buildings, Bunhill Row, E.C.

The North of England School Furnishing Co., Ltd.
DARLINGTON.

Manufacturers of Library Fittings, etc.

| Reading Stands, Reading Tables etc. | Bookcases, Library Chairs, etc. |

Libraries supplied recently.
LONDON : Buckingham Palace Road, Brixton, Lower Marsh, Streatham, Whitechapel, Woolwich, etc., also Beaney Institute, Canterbury, and Hull Public Library, etc.

Our long experience in this line enables us to guarantee satisfaction.

ESTIMATES FREE.

DISCOUNT BOOKSELLERS & STATIONERS

Addresses—   *Telegrams* "*SCHOLASTIC.*"

DARLINGTON, NEWCASTLE, SUNDERLAND, MIDDLESBROUGH, NORWICH.

Catalogues on application.   Enquiries Solicited.

WANTED.

Odd numbers or sets of the "Library Assistant" in good condition. Good prices given. Apply to "Alpha," 49 Vernham Road, Shooters Hill.

Price One Shilling. Post Free. ...

The Public Library Systems
... OF ...
GREAT BRITAIN, AMERICA ...
AND SOUTH AFRICA,

By BERTRAM L. DYER,
(Librarian of Kimberley, Hon. Member of the L.A.A., Member of the S.A.A.A.S., S.A.P.S., S.A., &c., &c.)

Being a reprint (with addenda) of a paper read at the first Congress of the South African Association for the Advancement of Science, held at Cape Town, April-May, 1903.

Copies may be had from the **Author**, or from **Mr. W. G. Chambers**, Public Library, Woolwich, S.E.

SPECIAL—TO LIBRARIANS.

Books Supplied and Bound from the Quire, in flexible Pigskin, Morocco, or a Sanitary Washable Cloth specially manufactured for us.

GUARANTEE:
We guarantee that our Binding will outlast the Book.

BOOKS RE-BOUND.   READERS' TICKETS
IN LEATHER OR CLOTH.

Solid Leather Reading Covers, made in one piece, without Lining or Stitches; practically indestructible.

An Inexpensive Reading Cover in our Sanitary Washable Cloth.

One of the many Testimonials received by us:—

"CHELSEA PUBLIC LIBRARIES,"
December 3rd, 1896.

Messrs. Banting & Son have been the bookbinders to these Libraries from the commencement, in 1888, and have given every satisfaction.

Their work is lasting, reasonable in price, and carefully carried out.

The fact that they are binders under contract to a large number of Public Libraries is sufficient proof that in this particular line they are difficult to beat.

J. HENRY QUINN,
Chief Librarian and Clerk to the Commissioners.

PARTICULARS, PRICES, AND SAMPLES ON APPLICATION.

J. BANTING & SON

Bookbinders and Booksellers,

KING'S ROAD, CHELSEA, LONDON.

Printed by R. TOMSETT & CO., at the "Electric Press," Kensal Rise, London, N.W., **and** Published for the Library Assistants Association. August 6th, 1903.

CPSIA information can be obtained
at www.ICGtesting.com
Printed in the USA
LVHW080218290720
661750LV00053B/865